Advances in Historical Orthography, c. 1500–1800

The early modern period is a key historical era for the standardisation of languages in Europe, in which orthographies played an important role. This book traces the development of European spelling systems in the early modern era, and is unique in bringing together several strands of historical research, across a diverse range of Germanic, Romance and Balto-Slavic languages, including Polish, German, French, Spanish, Lithuanian, Czech, Croatian and English. Whilst each chapter includes a case study on a particular language or script, the volume in general follows a broad thread of discussion based on models and methods relevant to many languages, showing how empirical approaches can be applied across languages to enrich the field of historical orthography as a whole. As one of the first volumes to diachronically explore the standardisation of spelling systems from a cross-linguistic perspective, this is an invaluable resource for specialists and those interested in European historical studies more broadly.

Edited by
MARCO CONDORELLI, University of Central Lancashire, Preston

Advances in Historical Orthography, c. 1500–1800

Edited by

Marco Condorelli

University of Central Lancashire

CAMBRIDGE
UNIVERSITY PRESS

CAMBRIDGE
UNIVERSITY PRESS

University Printing House, Cambridge CB2 8BS, United Kingdom

One Liberty Plaza, 20th Floor, New York, NY 10006, USA

477 Williamstown Road, Port Melbourne, VIC 3207, Australia

314–321, 3rd Floor, Plot 3, Splendor Forum, Jasola District Centre, New Delhi – 110025, India

79 Anson Road, #06–04/06, Singapore 079906

Cambridge University Press is part of the University of Cambridge.

It furthers the University's mission by disseminating knowledge in the pursuit of education, learning, and research at the highest international levels of excellence.

www.cambridge.org
Information on this title: www.cambridge.org/9781108471800
DOI: 10.1017/9781108674171

First published 2020

A catalogue record for this publication is available from the British Library.

Library of Congress Cataloging-in-Publication Data
Names: Condorelli, Marco, 1990– editor.
Title: Advances in historical orthography, c. 1500–1800 / edited by Marco Condorelli.
Description: Cambridge, UK ; New York : Cambridge University Press, 2020. | Includes bibliographical references and index.
Identifiers: LCCN 2020022958 (print) | LCCN 2020022959 (ebook) | ISBN 9781108471800 (hardback) | ISBN 9781108674171 (ebook)
Subjects: LCSH: Writing – Europe – History – To 1800. | Language and languages – Orthography and spelling.
Classification: LCC P211.3.E85 A38 2020 (print) | LCC P211.3.E85 (ebook) | DDC 411.094–dc23
LC record available at https://lccn.loc.gov/2020022958
LC ebook record available at https://lccn.loc.gov/2020022959

ISBN 978-1-108-47180-0 Hardback

Contents

Figures

Tables

Contributors

PER AMBROSIANI Umeå University, Sweden

MARCO CONDORELLI University of Central Lancashire, United Kingdom

LISA DÜCKER University of Bamberg, Germany

MEL EVANS University of Leicester, United Kingdom

ALENA A. FIDLEROVÁ Charles University, Czech Republic

STEFAN HARTMANN University of Bamberg, Germany

TOMASZ LISOWSKI Adam Mickiewicz University in Poznań, Poland

ELENA LLAMAS-POMBO IEMYRhd, University of Salamanca, Spain

GIEDRIUS SUBAČIUS University of Illinois at Chicago, USA

RENATA SZCZEPANIAK University of Bamberg, Germany

CAROLINE TAGG Open University, United Kingdom

ANJA VOESTE Justus Liebig University Giessen, Germany

MATEO ŽAGAR University of Zagreb, Croatia

Assisting Contributors

MARIJA LAZAR Sächsische Akademie der Wissenschaften zu Leipzig, Germany

HANNA RUTKOWSKA Adam Mickiewicz University in Poznań, Poland

1   From the Early Modern Era to an International Research Area

Marco Condorelli

The study of orthography in the early modern era has followed different strands, according to various geographical areas and periods of time. Areas of discussion and investigation have ranged from the question of biscriptality, the topics of codification and nation-building to spelling reform and to the role of the introduction of printing technology in orthographic developments and standardisation. The variation related to the study of historical orthography across Europe should not surprise us, if we consider the obvious differences across languages in Europe on different linguistic levels (including orthographic, phonetic, syntactic and so on), the different political decisions made in the administration of educational curricula (especially at university level) and the natural divergence of interests related to profound historical, cultural and political differences in every corner of Europe – all of which undoubtedly represent an element of richness and diversity which should be valued and fostered in the future for the sake of progress in the field. Despite the profound differences in interests and goals, however, some common threads are identifiable in the investigation of orthography across early modern languages, and especially with regard to some of the most recent research trends and advances. The end of the twentieth century and the beginning of the twenty-first have marked the beginning of a change in the field of historical orthography, especially for the early modern period. For approximately two decades now, and in connection with the development of historical sociolinguistics as a separate sub-discipline, the focus of several studies in historical orthography has shifted to exploring the sociolinguistic aspects of writing systems, without necessarily taking a position in the

While I fully authored this introductory chapter and I have edited this volume alone, I am indebted to Marija Lazar, Elena Llamas-Pombo, Hanna Rutkowska and Anja Voeste for enriching this chapter with some valuable subject-specific reference material. Many thanks are also owed to Gijsbert Rutten, for his bibliographical suggestions for Dutch.

relational–autonomist debate.[1] The first studies to have investigated ortho-graphic variation from a diachronic sociolinguistic standpoint appeared in the late 1990s and early 2000s.[2] The main focus of these studies has been on the diffusion of early standard spelling practices in late-fifteenth-century correspondence, and the correlation of selected spelling innov-ations with the authors' age, gender, style, social status and social networks. A few other studies have covered a variety of both orthographic and extra-linguistic variables, with a sociolinguistic framework that has allowed scholars to investigate patterns from the perspective of the author profiles and the socio-historical and cultural factors as drivers which have contributed to the regularisation of spelling.[3]

In addition to a slight change in perspective, research in historical ortho-graphy has been subject to a complex interplay between technological development, the implementation of new analytical approaches, and theor-etical and methodological innovations and discussions. Much as in historical linguistics more generally, the traditional approach used to investigate his-torical orthography has been predominantly qualitative. Examples of

[1] Sgall, 'Towards a theory', 2–3, labelled as 'relational' and 'autonomistic' the two main points of view concerning the connection between the notions of speech and language on the one hand, and writing and language, on the other. From the relational perspective, represented mainly by structuralists (e.g. de Saussure, Bloomfield, Sapir, Hockett), speech equated language, and writing had only a subsidiary role. This concept was expressed by de Saussure as follows: '[l]anguage and writing are two distinct systems of signs; the second exists for the sole purpose of representing the first' (de Saussure, *Troisième cours de linguistique générale*, 41a). In contrast, autonomists (e.g. Vachek, Bolinger, Stetson, McIntosh, Venezky) claimed that '[m]uch is written that is not pronounced' (Stetson, 'The phoneme and the grapheme', 35) and that '[w]riting is any manifestation of language in visible signs; a written language is a code that may not need preliminary decipherment into speech to be understood' (Vachek, 'English orthography', 38). See Rutkowska, 'Linguistic levels', for a more detailed discussion of both approaches, as well as of their implications for the definition of a grapheme.

[2] Aquino-Weber et al., *Sociolinguistique historique*; Blas Arroyo, 'Tras las huellas'; Branca-Rosoff, 'Sociolinguistique historique'; Branca-Rosoff and Schneider, *L'Écriture des citoyens*; Bravo García, 'Indicadores sociolingüísticos'; Conde-Silvestre and Hernández-Campoy, 'A sociolinguistic approach'; Gadet, *La Variation sociale*; Hernández-Campoy and Conde-Silvestre, 'Sociolinguistic and geolinguistic approaches'; 'The social diffusion'; Kristol, 'Sociolinguistique historique'; Martineau, 'Pratiques d'écriture'; Martinez, *La Variation graphique*; Medina Morales, 'Problemas metodológicos'; Oesterreicher, 'Aproximación'; Stockmann-Hovekamp, *Untersuchungen*; Tyne et al., *La Variation en question(s)*; Wandt, *Die Schreibsprache*.

[3] Cf. Rutkowska and Rössler, 'Orthographic variables' for an overview of early sociolinguistic research in diachronic orthographic variation; other relevant references are Aquino-Weber et al., *Sociolinguistique historique*; Biedermann-Pasques, *Les Grands Courants orthographiques*; Blas Arroyo, 'Tras las huellas'; Branca-Rosoff, 'Sociolinguistique historique'; Cerquiglini, *Le Roman de l'orthographe*; Gadet, *La Variation sociale*; García Santos, 'La ortografía nebrisense'; Golubović, 'Nauka o pismu u srpskoj lingvistici'; Kristol, 'Sociolinguistique historique'; Maquieira, 'Teoría y práctica ortográficas'; Martinez, *La Variation graphique*; Tyne et al., *La Variation en question(s)*; Zhivov, 'Deadaptatsiia v orfografii'; 'Norma i variativnost''; 'Sozdanie grazhdanskogo shrifta'.

variation have been selected and discussed in context, sometimes leading to limited understanding of orthographies in historical languages. Most studies, at least to some extent, have discussed the extra-linguistic conditioning of the orthographic variation in this period, with particular attention paid to orthographic regularisation and various stages of vernacular standardisation (i.e. a vernacular variety being adopted as a socially accepted norm, with a consequential adoption of specific orthographic norms). Many have employed a purely qualitative approach to the data, focusing mainly on extra-linguistic factors like the role of nation-building policies, the prestige of certain varieties, the Reformation movements, the introduction of printing technology, and debates over spelling reform in the process of orthographic standardisation.[4] A smaller number of studies have combined both qualitative and quantitative approaches, and have used corpora of various sizes, yet some of the current limitations in digitisation technologies sometimes provide an incomplete perspective into topics and issues that are relevant to historical orthography.[5] The limited accessibility of primary sources, often not available in digitised format, let alone transcribed, has prompted the development of research programmes geared towards enlarging the quantity of available digitised data. From this point of view, researchers investigating the history of orthographic variation in many languages across Europe are in a relatively good position, owing to the dynamic growth of corpora and databases with texts previously available only in paper form, in selected libraries. Similar sources have appeared and are beginning to grow

---

[4] Baddeley, *L'Orthographe française*; Bataillon, 'Diego de Enzinas en Amberes'; Berger, 'Religion and diacritics'; Biedermann-Pasques, *Les Grands Courants orthographiques*; Bunčić, 'The standardization'; Bustos Tovar, 'Las propuestas ortográficas'; Cerquiglini, *Le Roman de l'orthographe*; Demonet, 'Tentatives de modernisation'; García Santos, 'La ortografía nebrisense'; Giesecke, 'Orthotypographia'; Gutiérrez Cabero, 'La enseñanza'; Johnston, 'Mateo Alemán's problem with spelling'; Kaverina, *Stanovlenie russkoĭ orfografii*; Klimaŭ, *Rèfarmatsyia ŭ historyi litaraturnykh moŭ slavian*; Korompay, '16th-century Hungarian orthography'; Llamas-Pombo, 'Variation and standardization'; Maquieira, 'Teoría y práctica ortográficas'; Marcos Marín, *Reforma y modernización*; Marti, 'On the creation of Croatian'; Michel, 'Italian orthography'; Nordlund, 'Standardization of Finnish orthography'; Porák, *Humanistická čeština*; Ramírez Santacruz, 'Ruptura y renovación'; Sourkova, '*Azbuka* and/or *Abeceda*'; Urbańczyk and Olesch, *Die altpolnischen Orthographien*; Zhivov, 'Deadaptatsiia v orfografii'; 'Sozdanie grazhdanskogo shrifta'.

[5] Baddeley, 'French orthography'; Cazal and Parussa, *Introduction*; Elmentaler, *Struktur und Wandel*; Fidlerová et al., 'Užívání velkých písmen'; Hernández-Campoy, 'Authorship and gender'; Markus, 'Abbreviations'; Martínez Marín, 'La estandarización'; Nevalainen, 'Variable focusing'; Osiewicz, *Wariantywność leksemów*; Ruge, *Aufkommen*; Rutkowska, 'Late medieval dialectal and obsolescent spellings'; 'Orthographical regularization'; *Orthographical Systems*; 'Selected orthographic features'; 'Typographical and graphomorphemic features'; Sönmez, 'Perceived and real differences'; Voeste, *Orthographie*; 'The emergence of suprasegmental spellings'; Zheltukhin, 'Variable norms'.

considerably in languages like English,[6] Dutch,[7] German,[8] French[9] and Spanish.[10] Pan-linguistic digitisation initiatives are also worth mentioning, and especially the Early European Books project, which aims to comprise all books printed in Europe from the 1550s to 1701.[11] Recent advances have afforded scholars the ability to undertake systematic research to investigate the process of orthographic standardisation and have prompted a fundamental reconsideration of the approaches to the study of historical orthography. This statement is especially true for some of the most widely studied language groups across Europe, including Germanic,[12] Latinate[13] and Slavic.[14]

Aside from a rising interest in digitisation activities, other patterns are identifiable in research in historical orthography across Europe, within the remits of the historical era of interest in this volume. These patterns reveal an interest of the scholarly community in broadening the perspective on spelling to include a variety of factors. Some of the recent publications have investigated correlations between orthographic features and various combinations of extra-linguistic variables, including, for example, gender and text type,[15] gender, register and genre;[16] gender and authorship,[17] text type and register,[18] register

[6] Culpeper and Kytö, *A Corpus of English Dialogues*; Early English Books Online: Text Creation Partnership (EEBO-TCP); Taavitsainen et al., *Early Modern English Medical Texts*.

[7] Nobels and Rutten, 'Language norms'; van der Wal et al., The *Letters as Loot/Brieven als Buit Corpus*.

[8] Schröder et al., *Das Bonner Frühneuhochdeutschkorpus*; Wegera et al., *Referenzkorpus Frühneuhochdeutsch*.

[9] Frantext.

[10] CHARTA; CICA; CODEA+ 2015; CORDE; Corpus del español; Miguel Franco and Sánchez-Prieto Borja, 'CODEA'; Sánchez-Martínez et al., 'An Open Diachronic Corpus of Historical Spanish'.

[11] Early European Books.

[12] E.g. Baron et al., 'Word frequency'; Schneider, 'Computer assisted spelling normalization'.

[13] E.g. Díez del Corral Areta, 'Encrucijada de ediciones'; 'La problemática'; 'Utilidad y límites'; Díez del Corral Areta and Martín Aizpuru, 'Sin corpus no hay historia'; Lavrentiev, 'Linguistique de corpus'; Marchello-Nizia, 'Écrire'; Moyna, *Compound Words in Spanish*; Torrens Álvarez and Sánchez Prieto Borja, *Nuevas perspectivas*.

[14] E.g. Kučera, 'Vývoj účinnosti'; Scherrer and Erjavec, 'Modernising historical Slovene words'.

[15] Baranda, 'Mujeres'; Cerquiglini, 'L'Orthographe des *Précieuses*'; Demaizière, *L'Écriture*; García Macho and Pascual, 'Sobre la lengua'; Mancho Duque, *Teresa de Jesús*; Oldireva-Gustafsson, *Preterite and Past Participle Forms*; Sairio, *Language and Letters*, 226–61; Schutzeichel and Szczepaniak, 'Die Durchsetzung'; Sönmez, 'Perceived and real differences'.

[16] Cerquiglini, 'L'Orthographe des *Précieuses*'; García Macho and Pascual, 'Sobre la lengua'; Mancho Duque, *Teresa de Jesús*; Markus, 'Abbreviations'.

[17] Capdevila et al., *Le Genre face aux mutations*; Cattan, 'Cuestiones'; Hernández-Campoy, 'Authorship and gender'.

[18] Branca-Rosoff and Schneider, *L'Écriture des citoyens*; Bravo García, 'Indicadores sociolingüísticos'; Martineau, 'Pratiques d'écriture'; Osiewicz, *Wariantywność graficzna*; Taavitsainen, 'Scientific language and spelling standardisation'; Voeste, 'Die Norm'; Zhivov, 'Norma i variativnost'.

and level of formality;[19] typographical considerations (spacing, line justification, word division)[20] and palaeographic factors.[21] Orthographic variation has also been viewed from the perspective of discourse communities,[22] community norms,[23] ideology,[24] social networks[25] and communities of practice.[26] A few researchers have compared the orthographic practice of printers across several editions of the same book.[27] With regard to orthographic variables, studies on early modern orthographies have often highlighted correspondences between graphemes and phonemes.[28] Several studies have also considered various

[19] Branca-Rosoff and Schneider, *L'Écriture des citoyens*; Bravo García, 'Indicadores sociolingüísticos'; Martineau, 'Pratiques d'écriture'; Osiewicz, *Wariantywność leksemów*; Porák, *Humanistická čeština*; Tieken-Boon van Ostade, 'Disrespectful and too familiar?'; 'Lowth's language'.

[20] Agata, 'Improvements'; Andrieux-Reix and Monsonégo, *Segments graphiques*; Arabyan, *Le Paragraphe narratif*, 'La Notion de paragraphe', 'Histoire et emplois de l'alinéa ouvrant'; Branca-Rosoff, 'Deux points'; Demonet, 'Rhétorique'; Egido, 'Los manuales'; Güthert, *Herausbildung*; Howard-Hill, 'Early modern printers'; Juda, *Pismo drukowane w Polsce*; Llamas-Pombo, 'Variación gráfica'; Marti, 'Ein "Kulturkampf" in der *Slavia romana*'; McConchie, 'Compounds and code-switching'; Nikitina, 'Istoriiā perenosa slov'; Rutkowska, 'Typographical and graphomorphemic features'; Shute, 'Pressed for space'; Voeste, 'Proficiency'; 'The emergence of suprasegmental spellings'; Zhivov, 'Sozdanie grazhdanskogo shrifta'.

[21] Llamas-Pombo, 'Variation and standardization'; Nikitina, 'Istoriiā perenosa slov'; Osipov, 'Istoriiā slitnych i razdel'nykh napisaniĭ'; Sánchez Prieto Borja, 'Para una historia'.

[22] Cerquiglini, *Le Roman de l'orthographe*; Maquieira, 'Teoría y práctica ortográficas'; Taavitsainen, 'Scriptorial "house-styles"'.

[23] Bunčić, 'In-group spelling'; Cerquiglini, 'L'Orthographe des *Précieuses*'; Černá, 'Specifika pravopisného'; García Macho and Pascual, 'Sobre la lengua'; Koupil, 'Psáti neb tisknouti?'; Macha, *Der konfessionalle Faktor*; Rössler, *Schreibvariation*; Rütter, *Konstruktion*; Zheltukhin, 'Variable norms'.

[24] Vosters, 'Dutch, Flemish or Hollandic?'; Vosters et al., 'Spelling and identity'.

[25] Castillo Gómez, 'Del tratado'; Kozhinova, 'Rannie vostochnoslavianskie kriptograficheskie sistemy'; Maître, *Les Précieuses*; Sairio, *Language and Letters*; Tieken-Boon van Ostade, 'Social network theory'.

[26] Gutiérrez Cabero, 'La Enseñanza'; Koupil, 'Psáti neb tisknouti?'; Mediavilla, *Histoire*; Rutkowska, 'Typographical and graphomorphemic features'; Sairio, 'Elizabeth Montagu's *Shakespeare essay*'; Tyrkkö, 'Printing houses'.

[27] Aronoff, 'The orthographical system'; Badiou-Monferran, 'Ponctuation noire'; Behr, *Buchdruck*; Blake, 'English versions'; Chartier, *La Main de l'auteur*; Colombo Timelli, 'Les Dialogues'; Fidlerová et al., 'Užívání velkých písmen'; Horobin, 'The language'; Lisowski, *Grafia*; Rezetko and Young, *Historical Linguistics*; Rieke, *Studien*; Rutkowska, 'Late medieval dialectal and obsolescent spellings'; 'Orthographical regularization'; *Orthographic Systems*; 'Selected orthographical features'; 'Typographical and graphomorphemic features'; Sebastián Mediavilla, 'A propósito del *Persiles*'; Voeste, 'Den Leser im Blick'.

[28] Almeida Cabrejas, 'Escuchar los textos'; Amirova, *K istorii i teorii grafemiki*; Berger, 'Religion and diacritics'; Bunčić, 'The standardization'; Carrasco Santos, 'Análisis'; Carrasco Santos and Carrasco Santos, 'Las ordenanzas'; Elmentaler, 'Der Erkenntniswert'; Fournier, 'La Généralité'; 'La Notion'; Kuźmicki and Osiewicz, *Dokument pisany*; Mihm, 'Druckersprachen'; 'Graphematische Systemanalyse'; 'Zur Deutung'; Morin, 'The phonological status'; Nordlund, 'Standardization of Finnish orthography'; Osipov, *Fonetika i pis'mo na raznykh etapakh ikh istoricheskogo razvitiiā*; *Fonetika i pis'mo v ikh razvitii*; Parussa, 'La *Vertu*'; Porák, *Humanistická čeština*; Rospond, *Dawność mazurzenia*; Rutten and van der Wal, *Letters as Loot*; 'Local dialects'; Tejera and Silva Nones, 'El seseo'; Urbańczyk and Olesch, *Die altpolnischen Orthographien*.

orthographic realisations of lexical items and morphological categories (e.g. inflectional endings and derivational suffixes), and have discussed the competition between phonological and etymological principles in the orthographies, resulting in different levels of phonography and morphography in particular languages.[29] In other studies, specific diatopic and non-standard orthographic instances of variation (and its levelling) have been examined.[30] Likewise, abbreviations and contractions have received some attention,[31] together with the systematisation of punctuation and capitalisation.[32]

Alongside some of the detailed work conducted on fine-grained aspects of historical orthography largely from a single-language perspective, a few contributions have revealed an interest in a comparative, cross-linguistic approach to orthography in the early modern period and beyond. Some of the most recent publications, and in particular the edited collection by Susan Baddeley and Anja Voeste and the special journal issue edited by Laura Villa and

[29] E.g. Abad Nebot, 'Juan de Valdés'; Baddeley, 'French orthography'; Cerquiglini, *L'Accent du souvenir*; *Le Roman de l'orthographe*; Conde-Silvestre and Hernández-Campoy, 'A sociolinguistic approach'; Esteve Serrano, *Estudios*; Hernández-Campoy and Conde-Silvestre, 'Sociolinguistic and geolinguistic approaches'; Korompay, '16th-century Hungarian orthography'; Llamas-Pombo, 'Variation and standardization'; Martínez de Sousa, *Reforma*; Michel, 'Italian orthography'; Nejedlý, 'Humanistický a barokní pravopis'; Oldireva-Gustafsson, *Preterite and Past Participle Forms*; Osiewicz, *Wariantywność leksemów*; Rivarola, 'Ortografía'; Ruge, *Aufkommen*; 'Die Graphematik-Morphologie-Schnittstelle'; Sairio, *Language and Letters*, 226–61; Sönmez, 'Perceived and real differences'; Taavitsainen, 'Scriptorial "house-styles"'; Voeste, 'The emergence of suprasegmental spellings'; Zhivov, 'Norma i variativnost'.
[30] Arias Álvarez, 'Problemas'; Auer, 'Europe's sociolinguistic unity'; Borecki, *Kształtowanie*; Bunčić, 'The standardization'; Holtus et al., *Lexicon*; Isasi, 'Peculiaridades'; Kaverina, 'Ustranenie omofonii'; Kozhinova, 'Rannie vostochnoslavianskie kriptograficheskie sistemy'; Llamas-Pombo, 'Variation and standardization'; Mihm, 'Regionalsprachen'; Nevalainen, 'Variable focusing'; Osiewicz, *Wariantywność leksemów*; Polanco Martínez, 'Análisis'; Reynaud Oudot, 'Aspectos ortográficos'; Rospond, *Dawność mazurzenia*; Rutkowska, 'Late medieval dialectal and obsolescent spellings'; Sönmez, 'Perceived and real differences'; Tarelka, 'Adaptacyia arabskaga pis'ma'; Vosters and Rutten, 'Three Southern shibboleths'; Vosters et al., 'Norms and usage'; Wiesinger, 'Zur oberdeutschen Schriftsprache'.
[31] Audisio and Bonnot-Rambaud, *Lire le français d'hier*; *Diccionario*; Markus, 'Abbreviations'; Ruge, *Aufkommen*; Rutkowska, 'Typographical and graphomorphemic features'; Tieken-Boon van Ostade, 'Disrespectful and too familiar?'; 'Lowth's language'; Voeste, *Orthographie*.
[32] Bikialo and Rault, *Imaginaires de la ponctuation*; Branca-Rosoff, 'Deux points'; Bunčić, 'The standardization'; Dauvois and Dürrenmatt, *La Ponctuation*; Favriaud, 'Ponctuation(s)'; Fidlerová et al., 'Užívání velkých písmen'; Gautier et al., *La Ponctuation*; Kirchhoff and Primus, 'The architecture'; Korompay, '16th-century Hungarian orthography'; Kosek, 'Interpunkce'; Llamas-Pombo, 'Ponctuer, éditer, lire'; Michel, 'Italian orthography'; Moulin, *Der Majuskelgebrauch*; Osipov, *Istoriia russkoĭ orfografii i punktuatsii*; Rutkowska, *Orthographic Systems*, 88–96; Sebastián Mediavilla, 'A propósito del *Persiles*'; *Fray Luis y Santa Teresa*; *La puntuación del* Quijote; *La puntuación en los siglos XVI y XVII*; *Puntuación, humanismo*; Šlosar, 'Poznámky'; 'Průřez vývojem staročeské interpunkce'; Voeste, 'Interpunktion'; Wegera, 'Zur Geschichte'.

Rik Vosters,[33] suggest useful higher-level, cross-linguistic empirical general-isations as well as more widely applicable theoretical concepts. The former contribution has provided an overview of the development of spelling practices in Europe over the early modern period highlighting some interesting similar-ities and differences, while the special issue of *Written Language and Literacy* has collected several studies on the social and ideological context in which spelling developments and standardisations took place across languages. More generally, the field of historical sociolinguistics has recently received increas-ing attention from the international scholarly community with an interest in historical orthography, with two new book series devoted entirely to historical sociolinguistic perspectives (published by Peter Lang and John Benjamins) and academic journals such as *Written Language and Literacy*, the *Journal of Historical Sociolinguistics* and the *Journal of Historical Pragmatics*. Another convincing indication of the subject's growing maturity is the increas-ing number of monographs devoted entirely to the study of orthographic variation.[34] There are also volumes which focus on the interrelation between orthography and cognate areas of investigation like palaeography, typography and transmission from manuscript to print.[35]

While the work leading towards a broader, comparative perspective has been encouraging, however, there are still problems related to the organ-isational and institutional side of historical orthography, as well as issues related to the progress of knowledge in the field more broadly. One of the most outstanding organisational and institutional problems seems to be the tendency of scholars to work in relative isolation, largely following an individual philology-oriented approach due to disciplinary boundaries in the academy.[36] This isolated approach may have been caused by the fact that most scholars of European languages have touched upon a range of individual research areas, which have resulted in a diversification of goals

---

[33] Baddeley and Voeste, *Orthographies*; Villa and Vosters, *The Historical Sociolinguistics of Spelling*. See also Bunčić et al., *Biscriptality*; see further Salmon, 'Orthography and punctu-ation', for a comprehensive overview of the practice of and developments concerning ortho-graphy, capitalisation and punctuation in manuscripts and printed documents in Early Modern English, correlated with the views of contemporary (i.e. early modern) spelling reformers, grammarians, orthoepists and phoneticians.

[34] Baddeley, *L'Orthographe française*; Baddeley and Voeste, *Orthographies*; Borecki, *Kształtowanie*; Bunčić et al., *Biscriptality*; Elmentaler, *Struktur und Wandel*; Güthert, *Herausbildung*; Lisowski, *Grafia*; Osipov, *Istoriiā russkoĭ orfografii i punktuatsii*; Rieke, *Studien*; Rössler, *Schreibvariation*; Ruge, *Aufkommen*; Rutkowska, *Orthographic Systems*; Solling, *Zur Getrennt-, Zusammen- und Bindestrichschreibung*; Voeste, *Orthographie*; Zheltukhin, *Orthographic Codes*.

[35] E.g. Dumville, *English Caroline Script*; Hellinga, *Texts in Transit*; Janečková, *K jazyku českého baroka*; Kaverina, *Stanovlenie russkoĭ orfografii*; Shute, 'Pressed for space'; Thaisen and Rutkowska, *Scribes*; Traxel, *Language Change*; Zhivov, 'Sozdanie grazh-danskogo shrifta'.

[36] Cf. Amirova, *K istorii i teorii grafemiki*, 6–7; Baddeley and Voeste, *Orthographies*, 1.

and interests for each individual language. Additionally, orthography still remains one of the most under-investigated areas in historical linguistics, with theoretical and methodological aspects which have remained relatively unexplored and await comprehensive discussion. Examples include the role of printing houses and normative writings in the process of orthographic standardisation; enhanced terminological precision,[37] as well as some clarification and uniformity with a view to facilitating comparisons of findings across various studies. One of the possible reasons for the relative immaturity of historical orthography as a branch of historical linguistics could be the fact that scholars have mistakenly considered the study of writing, and consequently the study of orthography, as a subject that largely falls outside the remits of linguistics, unless it is treated as a source of evidence for phonological developments.

At the time when this introduction is being written, several issues and questions remain unresolved in studies on historical orthographic variation and in historical orthography more broadly. Some of the problems at stake include the limited understanding of the interrelation between linguistic and extra-linguistic factors in the shaping of orthographic systems; the relative incompatibility of the current theoretical approaches to orthography and writing both from a universal point of view and from a language-specific perspective; and the understanding of patterns of convergence and regularisation of writing practices as a complex process of change on multiple linguistic and non-linguistic levels. The intriguing yet problematic relationship between sound and spelling and the extent to which orthographic variation can reveal insights into phonological change, writers' or printers' linguistic characteristics, and geographical and dialectal variation are also still at the heart of research, and will have to remain so for the foreseeable future. Some areas in historical orthography have been explored less consistently and thoroughly than others, leaving holes in the understanding of patterns of regularisation, though recent years have seen a growing interest in some of the less developed areas of investigation like capitalisation and punctuation. Last but not least, the connection of new advances in historical and socio-historical linguistics with 'old' issues such as that of 'standardisation', and the effectiveness of language policy are still topics that remain largely or wholly unexplored. With the use of new tools to approach and understand orthography, some of these questions can now be explored empirically for the first time in history and can be investigated in a much more systematic way than before and discussed within the framework of a much broader dataset and innovative theories than in traditional scholarship. While most of the

---

[37] Cf., however, Catach, *L'Orthographe française*.

problems above cannot be addressed straightforwardly in any one small period of time or project, this edited collection aims to take a first, bold step forward towards covering some of the areas of investigation mentioned above.

The increasing interest in topics related to orthographic variation both from a language-specific and from a pan-linguistic perspective, as well as the increasing speed at which steps forward in historical orthography are being made, call for a volume that showcases the latest advances in the field and that brings together some of the main, most recent lines of research across different languages in Europe. The chapters collected in this book document an upsurging interest in advancing approaches to the study of historical orthographic variation common to various languages on different levels. Concurrently, the collection introduces readers to a comparative perspective on some of the most outstanding similarities and differences in research interests and goals across languages and different geographical areas. The majority of the chapters included in the book are the result of an intensive process of editorial selection which has taken into account the relevance and quality of research ideas in combination with the contributors' expertise. Additionally, the languages covered in the present collection represent the three largest language groups in Europe, namely the Germanic (English, German), Romance (Spanish, French), and Balto-Slavic (Croatian, Czech, Polish, Church Slavonic and Lithuanian). The focus of the book lies mainly in the early modern period, and especially from c. 1500 to the first few decades of 1800, a juncture of particular interest with respect to patterns in orthography across Europe.[38] While the dating of the early and late modern periods is a matter of debate,[39] a flexible chronological delimitation of the early modern era constitutes an agreed framework for the present collection, in order to guarantee comparability across the chapters and across languages, especially in light of the fact that not all orthographies in Europe standardised uniformly at the same time.[40] The time period indicated as an approximation in the title to this book, therefore, enables an overview of the development of patterns in orthography from a time of relatively unfamiliar systems to the beginning of an era of greater stability and predictability.[41] Of course, the specific focus of each chapter means that not

---

[38] The geographical boundaries of early modern Europe are those defined in previous scholarship on the matter, and especially Baddeley and Voeste, *Orthographies*.

[39] Cf. Baugh and Cable, *A History of the English Language*; Blake, 'Early Modern English'; Čornejová et al., *Dějiny českého pravopisu*; Dobson, *English Pronunciation 1500–1700*; Görlach, *Introduction to Early Modern English*; Graband, *Die Entwicklung*; Hartweg and Wegera, *Frühneuhochdeutsch*, 21–8; Partridge, *Tudor to Augustan English*; Zhivov, *Istoriia iazyka russkoĭ pis'mennosti*.

[40] Subačius, 'Two types'.

[41] Brengelman, 'Orthoepists'; Görlach, *Introduction to Early Modern English*; Jodłowski, *Losy polskiej ortografii*; Kaverina, *Stanovlenie russkoĭ orfografii*; Nevalainen, *An Introduction to*

every contribution covers the full time period indicated above, but each of the chapters included in this collection contributes to covering part of the four centuries in question. A natural limitation in the present edited volume can be seen in the range of topics discussed, which cannot be addressed exhaustively by any one collection of chapters on the matter. Nevertheless, the book touches upon a broad range of aspects and includes a variety of different perspectives, with a view to seeking relevance to audiences beyond single languages and geographical sites. The following section will explain in more detail the content of each chapter and will provide a rationale for the structure of the book.

1.1   Contents of the Book

The chapters collected in this book have been ordered in a way that enables a unified narrative throughout: the goal is to showcase some of the latest advances in historical orthography, with specific interest in early modern languages across Europe. The case studies included in the book are of different extents, which naturally reflect different individual, cultural and topic-based approaches to exploring orthography. The rules concerning notation in the volume are used in a way that purposefully reflects the flexibility and nuances intended by the individual authors, i.e. angle brackets enclose graphemes, vertical lines graphs, slashes phonemes and square brackets allophones, and italics are occasionally used to indicate words or spellings as more general entities, free from the assumptions intertwined with the concepts of graphemes and phonemes. The book takes as its starting point a discussion of relatively traditional, phonological insights into the study of orthography, as a foundation for an understanding of progression in the field that also encompasses more traditional approaches. The book then goes on to follow the thread of empirical innovation, exploring case studies which use a range of new empirical methods and models or simply reflect on new applications of more traditional approaches, with the potential of reassessing the traditional view of historical orthography and defining benchmarks for the most promising methods of orthographic enquiry. Some of the chapters included in the book drive towards establishing or rethinking one or more models for the understanding of orthography; others are more practical and implementation-focused, and use empirical methods more implicitly as a means to improve our openness to new knowledge from a language specific, as well as from a more synergic point of view. The concluding chapter

---

Early Modern English; Osipov, *Istoriiā russkoĭ orfografii i punktuat͡sii*; Porák, *Humanistická čeština*; Roelcke, 'Die Periodisierung'; Takada, *Grammatik und Sprachwirklichkeit*; Vallins and Scragg, *Spelling*; Zhivov, *Istoriiā iāzyka russkoĭ pis'mennosti*.

provides a reflection on the contents of the book and a discussion of future directions in the field.

In Chapter 2, Tomasz Lisowski works with structuralist oppositions and systemic representations of the language (graph–allograph representations of language) and refers to the theoretical paradigm proposed in the structuralist framework to compare different editions of a text. The author analyses the spelling systems of two editions of Baltazar Opec's *Żywot Pana Jezu Krysta* (*Life of Our Lord Jesus Christ*)[42] and provides a discussion of socio-historical factors,[43] in order to contextualise insights into the functionality[44] of two spelling systems in Early Modern Polish. In Chapter 3, Per Ambrosiani engages with the typological model of biscriptality recently developed by Daniel Bunčić et al.,[45] in order to offer an innovative approach to the analysis of graphematic features in Church Slavonic orthography. By introducing a clear distinction between scripts, glyphic variants of scripts and orthographies, Bunčić et al.'s model offers a much needed framework for biscriptality situations on a macro level. Per Ambrosiani argues that there are areas of the model that could be further explored, particularly when it comes to the analysis of graphemes and graphematic features from a micro-level point of view. In the chapter, the biscriptality model is applied to two South Slavic *New Testament* texts[46] printed in Glagolitic and Cyrillic letters in 1562/3 and 1563, respectively, in Urach near Tübingen. Through a detailed analysis of some important features of the printed texts of the *New Testament*, concepts such as *letters*, *graphemes* and *allographs* are used to characterise both the internal script contexts within the two texts and their external biscriptal relations. The chapter outlines a model for biscriptal isomorphism that is applied to six grapheme classes: the segmental graphemes *letters* and *numerals*, and the supragraphemes *capitalisation*, *superposition*, *abbreviation* and *ligature*.

Chapter 4 proposes to establish a multifactorial model for the development of capitalisation in Early New High German in handwritten texts, accounting for a range of linguistic dimensions of analysis, including the semantic, syntactic and pragmatic domains. Diachronic patterns of capitalisation are discussed in view of a range of contextualising factors which are judged to have an impact on the trends, including animacy, frequency, semantic roles, syntactic functions and socio-pragmatic factors. In their chapter, Lisa Dücker, Stefan Hartmann

---

[42] Opec, *Żywot Pana Jezu Krysta*; *Żywot Wszechmocnego Syna Bożego*.
[43] Cf. Coulmas, *The Writing Systems of the World*, 223–41, further discussed in Bunčić et al., *Biscriptality*.
[44] Lisowski, *Grafia*, 101; also cf. Mathesius, *Jazyk, kultura a slovesnost*; Vachek, 'English orthography'; *Selected Writings*; *Written Language*.
[45] Bunčić et al., *Biscriptality*.
[46] Jembrih, *Novi testament* (1562/3), *Novi testament* (1563).

and Renata Szczepaniak move beyond previous work by developing a systematic and empirical approach to understanding diachronic capitalisation in German, a feature which appears increasingly more complex and precise during the course of its development. The authors' analytical paradigm may provide a starting point to discuss its applicability to handwritten and printed texts from different languages in the early modern period. Chapter 5, in turn, proposes a model for the study of diachronic variation in punctuation from a comparative perspective. Elena Llamas-Pombo approaches the study of punctuation from a cross-linguistic perspective, focusing on Early Modern French and Spanish. This type of contrastive, diachronic avenue of research remains virtually unexplored and is achieved by introducing a model inspired from variational linguistics with a view to reveal differences and similarities in punctuation patterns across French and Spanish. The author extends recent theoretical attempts to define and further advance the emerging sub-field of comparative graphematics.[47] The cross-linguistic approach to diachronic punctuation is an important element of originality, as most of the existing work in this field focuses on individual languages. The model of analysis followed in the chapter sheds new light on developments and variation in the history of punctuation from a cross-linguistic point of view.

In Chapter 6, Giedrius Subačius addresses orthographic variation and change in Simonas Daukantas's Lithuanian manuscript 'Istoryje Žemaytyszka' ('History of the Lithuanian Lowlands', 1831–4)[48] from diachronic, diaphasic, diaprecise and aesthetic perspectives, and discusses the impact of the author's agency and text materiality on the orthographic features of the book. The study demonstrates how manuscripts may serve as spaces for linguistic experimentation, which may result in higher (sometimes even purposefully intended) linguistic heterogeneity. Furthermore, the author shows that the palpability – materiality – of the manuscript may accrue its own symbolic ideological value, and diminishes the importance of the purely linguistic content of the manuscript. New evidence is provided from non-dominant European language contexts on how the writing medium constrains orthographic preferences (heterogeneity versus uniformity) of the text and how the political and ideological message of the text could suppress the importance of linguistic uniformity. The author suggests that Daukantas may have considered the orthographic materials within which his text would appear to be of primary importance, and that the use of an accurate, almost calligraphic longhand, and the luxurious leather binding may have been part and parcel of a wider political strategy behind the volume.

[47] Cf. Weingarten, 'Comparative graphematics'; see also Houston, *Shady Characters*; Watson, 'Points of contention'.
[48] Daukantas, 'Istoryje Žemaytyszka'.

In Chapter 7, Anja Voeste presents an overview of different methods of data collection (intra-textual, inter-textual and cross-textual variable analyses) and explains and discusses in detail their advantages and disadvantages. All three approaches are well known and established, but they have never been discussed in comparative terms with regard to how they are handled empirically or with respect to any methodological problems resulting from using each of the three methods. The chapter approaches the methods in question in two ways: firstly, some fundamental problems for each method are addressed on an abstract level, then these problems are illustrated using concrete examples from the German-speaking territories of the fifteenth and sixteenth centuries, a period of significant spelling variation. The chapter concludes that each method of description favours certain types of explanatory hypotheses, and makes readers more aware of the presuppositions that may affect the outcome of an investigation, even before data analysis. In Chapter 8, Alena Fidlerová sets out to investigate selected orthographic variables perceived as characteristic of Czech printers' and scribal spelling systems between the late sixteenth and early eighteenth centuries and documents them with examples from selected printed and handwritten texts. The author aims to re-evaluate the character and mutual relations of the two orthographic systems and discusses them with reference to selected material characteristics of extant handwritten and printed books and the social context of their creation and circulation. The chapter assesses several possible explanations for the long-time coexistence of the two systems, assessing a range of new and older ideas. In doing so, the author combines traditional philological and (socio-)linguistic approaches with methods commonly used to study the history of the book, focused on the materiality and the social role of texts. The chapter further encourages an exploration of text materiality in the context of experimental methodological frameworks in historical orthography, and proposes its own, complex explanation for the shared characteristics detected between the systems, based on the sociolinguistic approach to orthography as a dynamic interaction between extra- and intra-linguistic processes and pressures.

Chapter 9 also follows the comparative, inter-textual approach thread set out in the previous chapters in order to analyse the orthography used in the Glagolitic *New Testament* of 1562/3. The analysis is conducted making occasional reference, for comparison, to earlier Glagolitic texts and the parallel Cyrillic and Latin versions of the *New Testament*, which were published concurrently.[49] In this chapter, Mateo Žagar showcases a grapholinguistic method for analysing and comparing historical orthographic variation. The chapter proposes to employ an already developed methodology and analytical framework on newly transliterated, digitised material, an approach which promises to give innovative results

---

[49] Jembrih, *Novi testament* (1562/3), *Novi testament* (1563).

on a theoretical, methodological and practical level. The author attempts to identify, analyse and evaluate the characteristics and the purposes of the graphetic and the graphemic strands of analysis, thus furthering the understanding of the grapholinguistic method. The results presented in the chapter suggest that the proposed graphetic/graphemic distinction is useful and provides a more systematic framework for a multi-layered, empirical analysis of orthography. Chapter 10 aims to demonstrate the importance of spelling analysis at the micro-level, examining the spelling practices of early modern women letter-writers through the lens of new media research. Mel Evans and Caroline Tagg's chapter offers an innovative perspective on English spelling practices that considers historical variation using concepts initially developed for new media writing. The examination of spelling in terms of micro-level and macro-level practices is not in itself novel,[50] but the decision to conduct the analysis across the lifespan of four individuals, combined with corpus linguistic methods, offers new insights into the development of English spelling, especially in respect to finding thematic and functional correlations, as well as potential continuities between sixteenth-century and twenty-first-century orthographic practices. Importantly, the new media framework articulates the potentially indexical nature of individuals' distinctive spelling profiles in the early modern period. The chapter draws on the combined expertise of its authors in the language of new media and Early Modern English to provide a novel reading of historical spelling variation at the micro-level.

The diachronic focus on spelling is extended in Chapter 11 with a discussion of innovative interpretations of Early Modern English spelling change. In this chapter, I introduce a rationale for a new approach to studying spelling variation from a diachronic perspective, giving insights into some of the wholesale semantic processes underlying spelling developments in Early Modern English. The discussion takes as its starting point an assessment of some of the conceptual flaws existing in traditional approaches to studying spelling variation quantitatively, and illustrates how these limitations may have a profound effect on our perception of the process of change and development in spelling. The chapter then investigates possible challenges in new, automatic analyses of spelling change by analysing semantic ambiguity in the alternation between <u> and <w>, and discusses results which appear to support previous statements about the independence of spelling from word meaning. These results are pivotal for an assessment of the extent to which new methodologies can be used comparatively across corpora and variant pairs in future research. Chapter 12, co-written by myself and Anja Voeste, reflects on the effectiveness of using

---

[50] Cf. Hinrichs and White-Sustaíta, 'Global Englishes'; Lillis, *The Sociolinguistics of Writing*; Sebba, 'Orthography as social action'; 'Sociolinguistic approaches'; *Spelling and Society*; 'Spelling as a social practice'.

models and methods of analysis as a means to initiate future synergic discussions in the field. This chapter also touches on issues related to national philologies and comparability across languages, with the hope that some of these considerations will encourage more researchers to contribute to the field.

Overall, *Advances in Historical Orthography* attempts to take a step forward in the recognition of innovative changes occurring in the study of historical orthography as a field of enquiry across multiple languages, following a broad thread of discussion based on models and methods which are relevant to many languages. The book hopefully better informs our knowledge of early modern Europe, both for specialists in historical orthography and for those interested in European historical studies more broadly (e.g. historians, literary scholars and those interested in the history of the book). It is also hoped that the present volume will encourage others to contribute to building bridges and opening dialogues on research practices and policies across different nationalities and multiple geographical areas, at a particular moment in time when national and individualistic cultural choices across Europe and beyond may affect our perspectives on the long-sought unity of countries and peoples.

A Phonological–Graphemic Approach to the
      Investigation of Spelling Functionality, with
      Reference to Early Modern Polish

Tomasz Lisowski

Two independent editions of *Żywot Pana Jezu Krysta* (*Life of Our Lord Jesus Christ*), an apocryphal compilation by Baltazar Opec, were printed in Cracow in 1522. The voluminous text was published by two competing printing houses, Hieronymus Vietor,[1] on 5 May 1522 (according to the edition's title page), and by Florian Ungler,[2] in the summer or early autumn of 1522.[3] The editor of Vietor's version is unknown; it might have been Jan of Koszyczki, a graduate of the University of Cracow, who edited other texts for Vietor's publishing house at that time.[4] The edition printed by Florian Ungler and financed by Jan Haller was prepared for print by Jan Sandecki.[5] While the first text to be printed in Polish (three prayers attached to synodic decrees in Latin)[6] was published in 1475 in the city of Wrocław in Silesia, Cracow in Lesser Poland became the centre of Polish printing at the beginning of the sixteenth century (and remained so until the middle of the century). The two editions of *Żywot Pana Jezu Krysta* from the year 1522, as well as four extant minor books published by Vietor's printing house in 1521 and 1522, initiated an uninterrupted series of publications in the Polish language. From that moment, the number of books written in Polish and published by the Cracow printing houses began to increase.[7] The Polish printed texts (appendices to Latin books) published in Cracow between 1506 and 1520, and at least one book, *Raj duszny* (*Paradise of the Soul*, 1514), adopted graphic conventions from mediaeval manuscripts, in which spelling was not standardised.[8] In the Middle Ages, when scribes started adapting the Latin alphabet for transcriptions in Polish,[9] the number

---

[1] Hieronymus Vietor (Polish: Hieronim Wietor, alias Bütner), a Silesian and a graduate of the University of Cracow, founded his printing house in 1518. The house started printing Polish books in 1521 (Kawecka-Gryczowa, *Drukarze*, 325–6; 'Miejsce książki', 417).

[2] Florian Ungler, a Bavarian, opened a printing house in 1510 in Cracow. It operated, with a short hiatus (1515–17), up to the year 1551 (Kawecka-Gryczowa, *Drukarze*, 229).

[3] Wydra, 'Drukarstwo nasze', xi–xii.   [4] Wydra and Rzepka, *Chrestomatia*, 321.

[5] Ibid., 325–6.   [6] Wydra and Rzepka, 'Niesamoistne', 263.   [7] Ibid.   [8] Ibid., 263–4.

[9] The earliest extant manuscript mentioning Polish anthroponyms and toponyms dates back to the year 1136 (Walczak, *Zarys*, 66).

of Polish phonemes substantially exceeded the number of Latin letters.[10] Attempts to resolve this issue focused on solutions that increased the number of graphic units to make them as unambiguous as possible:[11]

(1) By expanding the Latin alphabet with additional characters. These included the Greek letter <φ>, used only in *Kazania świętokrzyskie* (*Holy Cross Sermons*),[12] and <ø>, used in manuscripts between the twelfth and the fifteenth centuries,[13] which in turn, according to Stanisław Rospond, was borrowed from the Irish and Scottish graphic tradition.[14] Both of these characters were used to transcribe nasal vowels;

(2) By developing a system of complex spelling,[15] that is, by introducing, under the influence of Romance, German and Czech languages,[16] combinations of characters (digraphs and trigraphs) that were to represent specific single phonemes;[17]

(3) By defining the phonetic value of a Latin alphabet letter on the basis of the graphic context in which it appears in the word,[18] e.g. the spelling of the phoneme /j/ with <i> in front of a vowel (*iego, kroluią*) and with <y> word-finally or in front of a consonant (*twey, troyce*).[19]

On the margins of these established spelling practices, there was a theoretical proposition formulated by Jakub Parkosz at the close of the manuscript era (around the year 1440). Parkosz was a professor and, for three terms, chancellor of the University of Cracow. He was aware of the variable character of manuscript spelling and wished to systematise it. Parkosz was also familiar with Jan Hus's orthographic treatise *De orthographia bohemica*,[20] which called for the introduction of diacritic spelling. However, for ideological reasons (Hus was considered a heretic and was burned at the stake for his views), Parkosz could not reference him directly. Thus, while advocating the standardisation of complex spelling, he also proposed diversifying the shape of the letters of the Latin alphabet, e.g. writing hard consonants with angular-shaped characters and palatalised consonants with

---

[10] Ibid., 66–8.

[11] Lisowski, 'The Polish printed book', 116–19; 'The beginning of the typographical era', 142.

[12] *Holy Cross Sermons* is a collection in Polish dating back to the late thirteenth or the early fourteenth century and is considered to be the oldest document written in prose. Among the preserved parts are one full sermon and fragments of five other sermons (Wydra and Rzepka, *Chrestomatia*, 89).

[13] Klemensiewicz, *Historia*, 95–6; Walczak, *Zarys*, 67.

[14] Rospond, *Dawność mazurzenia*, 69.   [15] Bunčić, 'The standardization', 220.

[16] Walczak, *Zarys*, 69.

[17] Cybulski, *Język*, 40–6; Kamińska, *Psałterz*, 22–6; cf. Lisowski, 'Ideographization', 97.

[18] Kamińska, *Psałterz*, 14; Lisowski, *Grafia*, 17; Lisowski, 'Ideographization', 96; 'The Polish printed book', 115.

[19] Lisowski, *Grafia*, 46–52.

[20] It is not well established who was the author of *De orthographia bohemica* (published between 1406 and 1412). The treatise is traditionally attributed to the theologian and philosopher Jan Hus (1372–1415) (Berger, 'Religion and diacritics', 259).

round-shaped characters. His propositions were not subsequently followed in the practice of handwriting.[21] Until the end of the fifteenth century, only two social classes were represented among the users (active and passive) of printed texts. A small number of Polish manuscripts (translations of Bible passages, sermons, lives of saints, religious songs) were used predominantly among the clergy,[22] whose real grapholect was mediaeval Latin, a learned, universal language.[23] The clergy constituted an elite group of educated individuals who had an excellent understanding of the conventions of reading Polish manuscripts.[24] For practical reasons, written texts were also gaining popularity among the urban citizens, as literacy made it possible for merchants and craftsmen to increase their incomes. However, the texts were predominantly written in languages other than Polish. In the case of German speakers, city chanceries created documents mostly in German, while documents for Polish speakers were written in Latin (much like those issued by the royal chanceries). A small number of these texts included single Polish words[25] or short Polish fragments intertwined with the main Latin text (e.g. court oaths). Thus, Polish-speaking urban citizens had contact with the written word, albeit in a foreign language. The situation began to change at the beginning of the sixteenth century, when one of the guilds in Cracow obtained royal approval of its status written in Polish.[26]

Books printed in Polish, which gradually came to be produced in multiple copies (in the sixteenth century some Polish titles were printed in as many as 500 to 800 copies), were to be read not only by clergymen or students of the University of Cracow, but also by less educated members of other classes and professions, including women.[27] Variants in spelling might have deterred them from buying books, and printed books were intended to generate profit through sales.[28] The cost of their production was also to be kept to a minimum.[29] The creators of the Polish spelling system for printed books understood these linguistic, technical, economic and sociological constraints[30] and faced the task of developing a system that would implement the phonological (phonetic) rules of alphabetic spelling in an unambiguous manner, while also not being too expensive for the producer (i.e. the owner of the printing house).[31] The task was further complicated by the fact that the sixteenth century was a time of change in the Polish vocalic and consonant systems: the disappearance of vowel length and the emergence of narrow

---

[21] Kucała, *Jakuba Parkosza Traktat*, 7–19.
[22] Walczak, 'Komu zawdzięczamy polski język literacki?', 38.
[23] Ong, *Orality and Literacy*, 104, 110–11.   [24] Lisowski, 'Geneza imiesłowu *reca*', 176–7.
[25] Bartoszewicz, *Piśmienność*, 276–7.   [26] Klemensiewicz, *Historia*, 219.
[27] Ibid., 253; Książek-Bryłowa, 'Uwarunkowania społeczne normy językowej', 141.
[28] Ulewicz, *Wśród impresorów krakowskich doby Renesansu*, 104–5.
[29] Lisowski, 'Economic calculation', 203; Wydra and Rzepka, 'Niesamoistne', 265.
[30] Rutkowska and Rössler, 'Orthographic variables', 213–14.
[31] Lisowski, 'Economic calculation', 203.

vowels,[32] the diversification of the tone of the two nasal consonants,[33] probably even the frontalisation of /ʊ/, the depalatalisation of /ʃ/, /ʒ/, /t͡ʃ/, /d͡ʒ/, /t͡s/, /d͡z/, /ʳʒ/, /ʎ/,[34] and the palatalisation of /k/ and /g/.[35]

In these circumstances, publishers sought spelling conventions that would be suitable for printed books produced as widely available goods. Stanisław Zaborowski prepared an orthographic treatise commissioned by Florian Ungler, entitled *Orthographia seu modus recte scribendi et legendi Polonicum idioma quam utilissimus* (1514–15), in which he proposed a system of diacritical spelling that increased the number of graphic units by adding diacritic marks like accents, dots and hooks (*ogonek*) to the Latin letters used to transcribe the Polish language (cf. Chapter 8 for a more thorough discussion of diacritic marks, with reference to Czech).[36] Zaborowski drew inspiration from the solutions proposed by Hus (as he believed) at the beginning of the fifteenth century in Hus's work *De orthographia bohemica*,[37] which focused on spelling in Czech manuscripts.[38] However, the system of diacritical spelling proposed by Zaborowski did not gain popularity in printing practice, as it proved expensive; it required publishers to purchase or cast new diacritic fonts that were not included in standard printing sets.[39] What is more, the excess of diacritic marks was a strain on the eyes.[40]

The publication of the two editions of *Żywot Pana Jezu Krysta* also coincided with the emergence of the Polish literary *koine*. The process occurred, among other means, through contact between Polish and borrowed languages.[41] As early as the Middle Ages, the Polish language had contact with two *étalon* languages[42] mainly through translations of religious texts, namely Latin[43] and Czech.[44] German, whilst not an *étalon* language, was the language of commerce and municipal law; the

---

[32] Klemensiewicz, *Historia*, 100–1, 285–90. 'Narrow vowel' ('*samogłoska pochylona*'), 'bright vowel' ('*samogłoska jasna*') and other definitions that might sound unusual to an English reader are terms used in diachronic studies in Polish phonology, but I prefer to use them as they better reflect the Polish terminology. Long vowels, i.e. /aː/, /ɛː/, /ɔː/ were shortened between the end of fifteenth and the beginning of sixteenth centuries and evolved into so-called narrow vowels as follows: /aː/ > /ɒ/, /ɛː/ > /e/, /ɔː/ > /o/. Bright (short) vowels, i.e. /a/, /ɛ/, /ɔ/, were typically lower than their parallel narrow vowels, cf. /a/ – /ɒ/, /ɛ/ – /e/, /ɔ/ – /o/ (cf. Klemensiewicz et al., *Gramatyka*, 23).

[33] Kuraszkiewicz, *Polski język literacki*, 59, 182, 223–4, 236.

[34] Klemensiewicz et. al., *Gramatyka*, 35; Rospond, 'Dyspalatalizacja spółgłosek funkcjonalnie miękkich'.

[35] Klemensiewicz, *Historia*, 103.

[36] Bunčić, 'The standardization', 229–30; Decyk-Zięba, 'Ortografia'; Lisowski, 'The Polish printed book', 116–18; Urbańczyk and Olesch, *Die altpolnischen Orthographien*, 17–18, 97.

[37] Šlosar, 'Diakritický pravopis', 200–1. See note 20 above.

[38] Kucała, *Jakuba Parkosza Traktat*, 31–3.   [39] Wydra and Rzepka, 'Niesamoistne', 273.

[40] Klemensiewicz, *Historia*, 362.

[41] Lehmann, 'An essay on crosslinguistic phenomena', 132–3.

[42] *Étalon* languages are languages considered as standard against which a language under examination is compared or evaluated (Ramat, *Linguistic Typology*, 7).

[43] Reutter, 'The language shift', 110–11, 124.

[44] Lewaszkiewicz, 'O potrzebie nowego spojrzenia', 215–16; 'Rola kontaktów', 133–4; 'Rola przekładów Biblii', 236–7.

Magdeburg legal code had been adopted in medieval times by many municipalities in Germany and Eastern and Central Europe, including Poland, and decisions (*ortyle*) based on the Magdeburg legal code were translated from German.[45] The influence that these languages had on the Slavic languages, including Polish, encompasses areas such as syntax and vocabulary.[46] Contact between German, Czech and Polish facilitated the adaptation of foreign conventions in Polish spelling.[47] Until the middle of the sixteenth century Czech, as an *étalon* language, had a strong influence on Polish,[48] and also served as a model for standardisation in Polish.[49] During the period in question, Silesia, the region between the Polish-, Czech- and German-speaking territories, served as a bridge between the Polish and Czech languages. The people of Silesia used three languages in their everyday lives, that is to say German, Czech and Polish; these languages therefore were in contact and formed a network of linguistic relations. The similarity between the two Slavic languages and the political status of Czech gave rise to a significant influence of the Czech language on Polish, which was further reinforced by the use of Czech in official contexts. Bohemian interferences were visible in formal language contact and permeated the Polish dialects of many regions.[50] Until the middle of the sixteenth century, the use of Czech was fashionable among the members of the Polish royal court and the Cracow intellectual elite. Knowledge of Czech (albeit superficial) was considered a sign of intellectual ability.[51] It is worth noting that Zygmunt Jagiellończyk (Sigismund I the Old), King of Poland and Grand Duke of Lithuania (1507–48), had been the governor (*Oberlandeshauptmann*) of Silesia and Lower Lusatia between 1504 and 1507, the years preceding his coronation. All of these circumstances may have helped to shape Sandecki's conservative linguistic views in his edition of the *Żywot Pana Jezu Krysta*; he also expressed these views in metalinguistic statements in his later works. Sandecki viewed the Polish language as imperfect and non-unified and believed that it would have remained imperfect if Polish people did not follow the example of the Czech language, which was characterised by 'revered antiquity'.[52]

In this context, analysis of the variants and standards of spelling in the two 1522 editions of *Żywot Pana Jezu Krysta*[53] provides a significant research perspective. The books featured two independent but internally consistent

---

[45] Lazar, 'Transfer des Rechts', 180.   [46] Reutter, 'The language shift', 121–3.
[47] Stęplewski, *Pismo i pisarze w średniowiecznej Polsce*, 51–81.
[48] Lewaszkiewicz, 'Rola kontaktów', 242; 'Rola przekładów Biblii', 136.
[49] Cf. e.g. Siatkowski, *Bohemizmy fonetyczne*; 'Wpływ języka czeskiego'; Stieber, *Świat językowy Słowian*.
[50] Malicki, 'Język czeski na Śląsku', 380–1; 'Slezské jazykové spektrum', 21–2.
[51] Walczak, *Zarys*, 141.
[52] Janów, *Jan Sandecki (Malecki)*, xl; 'O stosunku', 45; Rospond, 'Kultura językowa w Polsce XVI w. I'; 'Kultura językowa w Polsce XVI w. II'; *Studia*, 21–60.
[53] From this point, the names of the editions will be abbreviated: *WŻyw* for Vietor's edition, and *UŻyw* for Florian Ungler's Sandecki version.

spelling systems, designed especially for their readers.[54] The creators of the systems aimed to eliminate the variability in spelling that was typical of mediaeval manuscripts, using the most invariant graphical representation possible for the phonological (phonetic) reality of the Polish language at the beginning of the Middle Polish period. When developing the two spelling systems, they had to consider various technical and financial constraints. Thus, they needed to maximise the use of the fonts available in the standard printing sets and keep the number of typefaces with new characters to a minimum. Both of the systems were alternatives to the diacritic system proposed by Zaborowski, and gained so much popularity in the printing practice that they determined future graphic standards in printed Polish spelling.

In this chapter, the two spelling systems are analysed with reference to their functionality, defined as the assignment of the most unambiguous meaning possible to a specific graphic representation of a phoneme (phone).[55] The analysis also covers the degree of regularisation within the systems, defined as the elimination of opposing textual graphic variants that share the same function but differ in form, or as the assignment of new, specific functions to these variants. The methods used by the creators of the spelling systems are also discussed, together with the technical and economic conditions that may have influenced the shaping the spelling systems. Some of the spelling conventions employed in *Używ* show similarity to Czech spelling. Taking into consideration Sandecki's pro-Bohemian linguistic views, the similarity may not be a coincidence. The issue of the relationship between sixteenth-century Polish printed texts and Czech spelling has not yet been systematically and empirically explored, and the observations made here may serve as a starting point for further research on the matter.

To achieve the goals set out above, the analysis combines different perspectives, taking into account linguistic (phonological, phonetic and morphological) as well as non-linguistic (technical, economic and sociological) factors. The traditional structural description of graphophonemic correspondences proposed in this chapter enables the identification of graphemes and variants of the graphemes as comparable units existing in the two spelling systems. The selection of comparable variants on a phonological level justifies the use of the quantitative method proposed here. On the basis of the results generated, the degree of regularisation of graphemes and the degree of the functionality of the two spelling systems are assessed, and an attempt is made to

---

[54] The solutions proposed in the spelling system of *WŻyw* were also implemented in the four books published by the printing house in the years 1521–2, mentioned earlier (cf. Lisowski, *Grafia*). Thus, we can speak of a single spelling system used by Vietor's printing house, with *WŻyw* as an example of its realisation.

[55] Bunčić, 'Introduction', 20–5; Coulmas, *The Writing Systems of the World*, 223–41; Elmentaler, *Struktur und Wandel*; Leith, *A Social History of English*, 31–4; Lisowski, *Grafia*; Mathesius, *Jazyk, kultura a slovesnost*; Šefčík, 'K základním pojmům grafémiky', 31–2; Vachek, *Selected Writings*; *Written Language*; Wydra and Rzepka, 'Niesamoistne', 264.

trace the genesis of the variants in both spelling systems. The diachronic variants are discussed with reference to the use of the traditional complex spelling versus modern diacritic spelling, in addition to diatopic variants (e.g. textual opposition of the phonemes /s/, /z/ : /ŝ/, /d̂z/ : /ʃ/, /ʒ/ : /ŝ/, /d̂ʒ/) and, as an alternative, foreign (Czech) spelling patterns. The characterisation of the spelling systems also takes into account extra-linguistic variables, such as date of production, geographical location, demographics (gender of potential readers), social networks and medium (printed versus handwritten),[56] as well as technical and financial constraints that might have had an impact on the spelling conventions introduced in the two systems. The description of graphophonemic correspondences draws on the traditional structuralist assumption that the alphabetical graphic system is not a part of the linguistic plane *sensu stricto*, but rather a parallel entity to the phonological system as a graphic substitute for the phonic code.[57]

2.1   Creating Functionality in Two Spelling Systems from the Year 1522

2.1.1   *Textual Realisation of Bright and Narrow Vowel Phonemes*

The textual distinction between the graphemes of the long vowels /aː/, /ɛː/, /ɔː/, which evolved into the narrow vowels /ɒ/, /e/, /o/ at the beginning of the sixteenth century, and the graphemes of the short vowels /a/, /ɛ/, /ɔ/, which remained as bright vowels (/a/, /ɛ/, /ɔ/) in the sixteenth century, was not fully established in the Polish manuscript tradition. Nonetheless, it was represented in all major Polish manuscripts from the Middle Ages.[58] The division was sporadically marked by doubling the letter in the case where a variant stood for a grapheme of a long vowel.[59] Parkosz, who was aware of the distinctive phonological feature of long vowels, proposed this same spelling convention.[60] The disappearance of long vowels probably took a long time, and it can

---

[56] Rutkowska and Rössler, 'Orthographic variables', 219.

[57] Despite equating a phone (phoneme) with a letter, the writings of the early theoreticians of Polish orthography clearly prove that they had an understanding of the phonological character of alphabetical writing (Kucała, *Jakuba Parkosza Traktat*, 21–2; Urbańczyk and Olesch, *Die altpolnischen Orthographien*, 16). For useful references on the graphophonemic realm of investigation, see Bünting, *Einführung in die Linguistik*, 53–4; Hockett, *A Course in Modern Linguistics*, 609; Lisowski, *Grafia*, 16–17; Polański, *Encyklopedia*, 182; Ruszkiewicz, *Modern Approaches*, 48; Rutkowska and Rössler, 'Orthographic variables', 215–19; Šefčík, 'K základním pojmům grafémiky', 35–7; Vachek, *Written Language*; *Selected Writings*. The analysis was conducted on samples from the following sections: *WŻyw* 5v–7v, 44v–45v, 88r–90r, 123v–125r; *UŻyw* 2r–4r, 45v–47v, 88r–90v, 131r–133r, 173r–175v.

[58] Cyran, 'Ślady iloczasu'.   [59] Cybulski, *Język*, 31–3; Kamińska, *Psałterz*, 21–2.

[60] Kucała, *Jakuba Parkosza Traktat*, 21–2; Urbańczyk and Olesch, *Die altpolnischen Orthographien*, 16.

therefore be assumed that the newly formed narrow vowels might have initially been long. It is difficult to draw any definite conclusions as to their length at the beginning of the sixteenth century based on their spelling. Until the year 1520, Polish printed texts exhibited one of the following: (1) they did not make any textual distinction between the graphemes of narrow and bright vowels; (2) they combined the traditional, manuscript-based approach to marking these graphemes (by doubling the letter, <aa> and <ee>) with the solution proposed by Zaborowski (<é>, <ó>); or (3) they combined both methods (<eé>).[61] These spelling methods are considered to mark the last phase of the process of the long vowels' disappearance.[62] The methods of spelling (using diacritics or doubling letters) were dependent on technical factors and did not necessarily indicate the length of narrow vowels.[63]

In the material analysed in Table 2.1,[64] both graphic systems consistently differentiate only between the textual representation of the phonemes /a/ and /ɒ/, whereas the graphical difference between /ɛ/ : /e/ and /ɔ/ : /o/ is marked with varying consistency only in *Używ*. The use of characters with diacritic signs reflects the solution proposed in Zaborowski's treatise. The systems also differ in the manner of demarcating the opposition /a/ : /ɒ/. The system used by Vietor's printing house marked /a/ as <á>, and /ɒ/ as <a>. This solution, although contrary to the mediaeval tradition of graphic representation of the long vowel /aː/ (i.e. *aa*), or, later on, even of the narrow vowel /ɒ/ (i.e. *á* in *Używ*), made it possible to retain the original spelling of numerous Latin loanwords that ended in <yja> or <ija>, such as *fentencya*, pronounced with /ɒ/. On the other hand, in the system introduced by Sandecki, /a/ is spelled as <a> and /ɒ/ as <á>. This convention was used in Czech printing to mark the opposition /a/ : /aː/.[65] The optional use of the variants <aa> : <á> also exists in Czech manuscripts.[66] Sandecki used the textual oppositions of the phonemes /ɛ/ : /e/ proposed by Zaborowski. Once again, the solution was similar to contemporary Czech printing practices, which used all of the variants for /e/ featured in *Używ* as a parallel equivalent to the Czech phoneme /ɛː/.[67] The graphic representation of the difference in length between /ɛː/ : /ɛ/ was far less consistent in Czech.[68] The graphical variants of the phoneme /e/ may be a consequence of an insufficient number of *é* characters available to the

---

[61] Wydra and Rzepka, *Chrestomatia*, 317.   [62] Stieber, *Rozwój fonologiczny*, 26.
[63] Lisowski, 'Ideographization', 102–7.
[64] In Tables 2.1–2.8 the level of regularisation is calculated as the ratio of the sum of the textual realisations of the primary grapheme of a given phoneme to the sum of all textual variants of the phoneme. The primary variant is the only or the most frequent grapheme used to spell a given phoneme. The secondary variant is a less frequent grapheme used to spell a given phoneme. The quantitative data given in the tables are cited from Lisowski, *Grafia*, 23, 25, 27–8, 30–1, 34–7, 39–40, 44, 47–8, 53, 57–62, 65–8, 70–2, 76–7, 83–6, 96. The number of instances is shown in round brackets.
[65] Porák, *Humanistická čeština*, 77.   [66] Lazar, 'Transfer des Rechts', 189–91.
[67] Porák, *Humanistická čeština*, 74.   [68] Lazar, 'Transfer des Rechts', 189–91.

Table 2.1 *Textual opposition of the phonemes /a/ : /ɒ/, /ɛ/ : /e/, /ɔ/ : /o/*

Phoneme	Variant type	WŻyw	UŻyw
/a/		**Level of regularisation 98.53%**	**Level of regularisation 98.25%**
	Primary	<á> (1,139) *pánná* 46v	<a> (1,212) *krola* 174v
	Secondary	<a> (17) *ſyna* 89v	<á> (14) *á* 45v
/ɒ/		**Level of regularisation 99.2%**	**Level of regularisation 92.01%**
	Primary	<a> (493) *zwidzenia* 6v	<á> (315) *powiedá* 2v
	Secondary	<á> (4) *pełná* 124v (attributive)	<a> (25) *dla* 2v <aa> (1) *wolaa* 37r <aá> (1) *daár* 49v
/ɛ/		**Level of regularisation 100%**	**Level of regularisation 99.09%**
	Primary	<e> (all instances) *gdźie* 6r	<e> (1,523) *niebo* 175r
	Secondary	–	<é> (14) *ſié* 89r
/e/		**Level of regularisation 0%**	**Level of regularisation 82.32%**
	Primary	–	<é> (318) *zlégo* 45v
	Secondary	<e> (all instances) *milego* 45r	<e> (48) *milemu* 46v <eé> (19) *ſwięteégo* 47r <ee> (1) *blogoſlawionee* 4r
/ɔ/		**Level of regularisation 100%**	**Level of regularisation 99.78%**
	Primary	<o> (all instances) *owce* 44v	<o> (1,703) *nocy* 133r

Table 2.1 (cont.)

Phoneme	Variant type	WŻyw	UŻyw
	Secondary	–	<ó> (3)
			óytcze 175r
			<u> (1)
			iegu 89v
/o/		**Level of regularisation 0%**	**Level of regularisation 6.97%**
	Primary	–	<ó> (9)
			bóg 46r
	Secondary	<o>	<o> (160)
		krolewa 123v	*bog* 2v
			<uó> (2)
			buóg 174r
			<uo> (1)
			buog 2v

The data defining the variants of the phonemes /a/, /ɒ/, /ɛ/, /e/, /ɔ/ and /o/ were obtained through the observation of categories described in the following sources: Bajerowa, *Kształtowanie*, 46–7, 92; Klemensiewicz et al., *Gramatyka*, 83–4, 92, 95, 287.
See note 64 for other conventions.

typesetter,[69] which in turn led to partial solutions, either the use of the digraph <ee> or the forfeiting of the distinction with the use of the variant <e>.

By contrast, the attempt at introducing a distinction between variants for the phonemes /ɔ/ : /o/ in *UŻyw* seems experimental, as only 12 of 172 instances of the graphical representation of the phoneme /o/ are marked (<ó>, <uo>, <uó>; the variants <uo> and <uó> are introduced only in the nominative singular form of *buog*, *buóg*, 'God'). The variants <uo> and <uó> were used at the beginning of the sixteenth century in Czech printing as a graphical representation of the diphthong /uo/, which replaced /ɔ:/.[70] However, it was more frequent for Czech printed texts to spell the diphthong with the variant <o>.[71] Thus, the use of <ó>, which was unknown in Czech printing, is an original solution that implements the guidelines proposed by Zaborowski.[72] In Polish printing practice, <ó> was first used (together with <uo>) in the *Początek święte Ewanielije podług świętego Jana* (*Prologue to the Gospel According to Saint John*, 1518/19).[73] The decision not to differentiate the textual

---

[69] Wydra and Rzepka, 'Niesamoistne', 272–3.
[70] Lamprecht, *Vývoj fonologického systému*, 99; Porák, *Humanistická čeština*, 59.   [71] Ibid.
[72] Urbańczyk and Olesch, *Die altpolnischen Orthographien*, 18.
[73] Bajerowa, 'Zanik', 107–9; Wydra and Rzepka, 'Niesamoistne', 276.

realisations of the phonemes /ɛ/ : /e/, /ɔ/ : /o/ in the system used by Vietor's printing house might have been underpinned by economic reasons and also reinforced by the fact that mediaeval manuscripts rarely marked the length of /ɛ:/ and /ɔ:/. The decision above may also be a consequence of the phonological 'insignificance' of the phonemes /e/ and /o/.[74]

Another reason, apart from the fact that narrow vowels could also be long, may have been the unclear phonetic status of narrow vowels at the beginning of the sixteenth century.[75] Analysis of the variants of genitive singular feminine noun endings /ɒ/ or /i/ in *WŻyw* and *UŻyw* suggests that, at that time, the ending /e/ was pronounced as the diphthongs [ej] or [eʲ]. This ending is spelled in *UŻyw* as <ey> (2 instances), as <é>, <ee>, <eé> (108 instances), as <e> (32 instances), and as <i> (2 instances). In *WŻyw*, on the other hand, there are 105 instances of <ey> and only 14 instances of <e>.[76] When analysing this issue, however, we must take into consideration the origin of the ending /e/ in genitive singular feminine nouns in Polish, i.e. from Proto-Slavic *–ě₃, which changed into /ɛ:/. As early as the fourteenth century, /ɛ:/ was diphthongised (/ɛ:/ > /ɛ:ʲ/), while, in mediaeval Polish, the ending /ɛ:ʲ/ was generally used alongside the ending /ɛ:/.[77] It is also possible that the ending /ɛ:ʲ/ of the genitive singular feminine adjectives in complex declension was adopted from the dative singular feminine or locative singular feminine form of adjectives of the same declension. This was further reinforced by the similarities in pronunciation, and most of all by syntactic agreement, such as in the genitive singular feminine /bɔʒɛ:j vɔlɛ:/ > [bɔʒɛ:j vɔlɛ:ʲ] or [bɔʒɛ:j vɔlɛ:j]. Later, at the turn of the fifteenth century, when the vowel /ɛ:/ changed to /e/, the ending /ɛ:ʲ/ or /ɛ:j/ changed to /ej/.[78]

Thus, the spelling <ey> to indicate the genitive singular feminine of the /ɒ/ or /i/ paradigm nouns was probably the graphic representation of its morphological form established in the Middle Ages. The ending is spelled <ey> in all of the relevant instances in *WŻyw*, as the edition does not mark /e/ graphically. The morphological form of the ending /e/ of the genitive singular feminine of the /ɒ/ or /i/ paradigm nouns (spelled <é>, <ee> and <eé>), as used in *UŻyw*, may be interpreted as an attempt at restoring (in terms of morphology) the Old Polish style. It would be an example of *graphic fossilisation*, that is, of spelling limited to a specific morpheme, uncorrelated with pronunciation.[79] The variations of spelling of the groups /ir/, /er/ and /ɛr/ constitute another example of the graphic fossilisation of the allographs of /e/ or /i/ (/er/ or /ɛr/ in Polish sixteenth-century printed texts were created as a result of an etymological articulatory lowering of /ir/ in forms like *pirwszy*, *piérwszy* or *pierwszy* and *wirzba*, *wiérzba* or *wierzba*). Individual printing houses arbitrarily spelled the sounds either with <ir> or with the variant group <ér> and <er>.[80]

---

[74] Bajerowa, 'Zanik', 107–9.   [75] Lisowski, 'Ideographization', 110–12.
[76] Lisowski, *Polszczyzna początku XVI wieku*, 156–61.   [77] Kowalska, 'Końcówka -*ej*', 58–60.
[78] Klemensiewicz et al., *Gramatyka*, 288.   [79] Kuraszkiewicz, *Polski język literacki*, 623–30.
[80] Borecki, *Kształtowanie*, 148.

2.1.2 Textual Realisation of the Phonemes /ẽ/ and /ɔ̃/

At the turn of the fifteenth and the sixteenth centuries, the two old nasal vowels, which were identical in timbre but differed in length, i.e. /ã/ and /ã:/, changed to two nasal vowels that were both short but differed in timbre (/ẽ/ and /ɔ̃/).[81] The shift progressed at different rates in different Polish dialects.[82] As early as the middle of the fifteenth century, the Greater Polish dialect featured two nasal vowels, one of which was pronounced as /ẽ/.[83] Even at the beginning of the sixteenth century, in the Lesser Polish dialect (spoken in the Cracow region), two nasal vowels of identical (short) length were pronounced with only a slight difference in timbre, with /ɒ/ as the vocalic base for the back vowel and /a/ as the base for the front vowel.[84] The influences of the Lesser Polish dialect and the spelling tradition derived from manuscripts are the reason why most Polish publications used one character to denote the two nasal vowels.[85] Zaborowski however insisted on the distinction between the two nasal vowels in print spelling and proposed the use of <ǫ> for the back nasal vowel and <α> for the front nasal vowel.[86] Later printed texts, dating from 1518/19 and 1520,[87] featured the opposition of /ɔ̃/ spelled as <ǫ> and /ẽ/ spelled as <e>. The use of a graph identical to the textual realisation of /ɛ/, i.e. <e>, mirrored the regional, Lesser Polish timbre of the front vowel.[88] The letter <ę> originates from the Latin e caudata and was sometimes used in Classical and Renaissance Latin for <ae> or <æ>. The character was included in the printing sets owned by Vietor and Ungler, as shown in Table 2.2.[89] The letter <ą>, however, was designed as the analogue of the e caudata. Therefore, both systems represent nasal vowels in the 'modern' manner as used in Polish spelling to represent /ẽ/ as <ę> and /ɔ̃/ as <ą> up until today.

2.1.3 Textual Realisation of the Phoneme /u/

According to the manuscript tradition, which stemmed from the spelling tradition in Latin, the phoneme /u/ was represented either by <v> or by <u>, depending on its position.[90] The material analysed followed these practices, as shown in Table 2.3.

---

[81] /ɔ̃/ symbolises only a nasal back vowel. It is not certain what vocalic quality it had at the beginning of the sixteenth century.
[82] Kuraszkiewicz, *Polski język literacki*, 59. [83] Ibid., 236. [84] Klemensiewicz, *Historia*, 59.
[85] Wydra and Rzepka, 'Niesamoistne', 282.
[86] Decyk-Zięba, 'Ortografia'; Urbańczyk and Olesch, *Die altpolnischen Orthographien*, 17–18, 97.
[87] Wydra and Rzepka, 'Niesamoistne', 284. [88] Kuraszkiewicz, *Polski język literacki*, 223–4.
[89] Ibid., 226; Wydra and Rzepka, 'Niesamoistne', 283.
[90] Cybulski, *Język*, 26; Kamińska, *Psałterz*, 19.

Table 2.2 *Textual realisation of the phonemes /ɛ̃/ and /ɔ̃/*

Phoneme	Variant type	WŻyw	UŻyw
/ɛ̃/		**Level of regularisation 97.81%**	**Level of regularisation 98.99%**
	Primary	<ę> (223)	<ę> (294)
		głęboko 89v	*radę* 2r
	Secondary	(2)	<e> (3)
		głemboko 35r	*ogledatz* 2r
		<ęm> (3)	
		głęmbokie 31r	
/ɔ̃/		**Level of regularisation 100%**	**Level of regularisation 99.07%**
	Primary	<ą> (248)	<ą> (330)
		bożą 46v	*związán* 88v
	Secondary	–	<a> (1)
			panna-INSTR.SG.F 4r

See note 64 for conventions.

2.1.4   Textual Opposition of the Phonemes /i/ : /ɨ/

The textual realisation of the phonemes /i/ and /ɨ/ in mediaeval manuscripts is inconsistent. Both <i> and <y> are used as variants for the phoneme /i/, and, similarly, both <i> and <y> can serve as variants for the phoneme /ɨ/.[91] This feature was typical of manuscripts and was also replicated in Polish printed texts until the year 1520.[92] Zaborowski proposed to spell the phoneme /i/ as <i>, and the phoneme /ɨ/ as <î>. This idea did not gain popularity, however.[93] As shown in Table 2.4, both systems introduced the modern opposition between /i/ = <i> : /ɨ/ = <y>, thus deviating from the mediaeval spelling tradition in the printed texts. <i> = /ɨ/, which appears in the texts analysed (e.g. WŻyw: *trędowáti* 89v, instead of expected *trędowáty*; UŻyw: *dobrich* 2v instead of expected *dobrych*), may be a reflection of the manuscript tradition, or it may reflect the variational pronunciations of the consonants /pʲ/, /ʒʲ/, /bʲ/, /dʒʲ/, /tsʲ/, /dzʲ/, /ʳʒʲ/, which underwent depalatalisation,[94] and which caused the following palatalising /i/ to turn into a non-palatalising /ɨ/ (e.g

---

[91] Cf. Cybulski, *Język*, 16–19; Kamińska, *Psałterz*, 13; Rospond, 'Z badań', 45–9.
[92] Wydra and Rzepka, *Chrestomatia*, 309.
[93] Urbańczyk and Olesch, *Die altpolnischen Orthographien*, 61, 93, 107.
[94] Brajerski, *O języku polskim dawnym i dzisiejszym*, 123; Rospond, 'Dyspalatalizacja spółgłosek funkcjonalnie miękkich'.

Table 2.3 *Textual realisation of the phoneme /u/*

Phoneme	Position	Variant type	WŻyw	UŻyw
/u/			**Level of regularisation 100%**	**Level of regularisation 100%**
	word-initially	Primary positional[a]	<v> (all instances) *vczniowie* 89v	<v> (all instances) *vczynil* 131r
	not word-initially	Primary positional	<u> (all instances) *zamku* 6v	<u> (all instances) *początku* 173v

[a] A positional variant is a grapheme used to spell a given phoneme; its textual realisation is determined by its position, i.e. its graphic context, and it may be a primary or secondary variant. See note 64 for other conventions.

WŻyw: *vczinić* 45v, instead of expected *vczynić*; *UŻyw*: *vczinku* 2v, instead of expected/ *vczynku*).

The numerous variants of graphical realisation of the phoneme /i/ in word-initial positions reflects the difficulty in transcribing the pronunciation of a possible preiotation of /i/ in word-initial positions, as the preiotation of /i/ in these cases is a phonetic rather than a phonological phenomenon: [ʲi] (preiotated /i/) is an allophone of /i/. The hesitation visible in the manner of representing word-initial /i/ graphically in the system used by Vietor's printing house suggests that the creators of the system approached spelling from a phonological rather than a phonetic perspective. In *WŻyw*, <y> is the most frequent positional variant used to represent the conjunction *i* ('and'). Its occurrence in *WŻyw* is carried over from the manuscript tradition,[95] and appears to be an example of graphic fossilisation.[96] The contrastive introduction of <j> to spell word-initial, preiotated /i/ in some other lexemes might be considered an original feature of the *WŻyw* system. The inconsistent implementation of this solution may be explained by technical limitations, i.e. an insufficient number of *j* letter blocks in the printing sets of the printers. The spelling <ij> implemented in *UŻyw* to represent word-initial, preiotated /i/ was also used in Czech printing to spell long /iː/.[97] The digraph <ij> was also a spelling unit of Latin orthography.[98] Sandecki assigned a Polish phonetic representation to this Czech–Latin character combination. <ý>, indicating the phoneme /ɨ/, was seldom used in Czech printed texts to also represent long /ɨː/.[99] The variant <ý> is used in *UŻyw* only twice in the examined parts of the text; the other examples come from

[95] Lisowski, 'Ślady graficznej tradycji rękopisów', 73.
[96] Kuraszkiewicz, *Polski język literacki*, 623–30; Lisowski and Osiewicz, 'Leksykalizacja', 160–4.
[97] Porák, *Humanistická čeština*, 49.
[98] In his treatise, Zaborowski gives the following Latin examples: *pijs, vijs, eijtio* (Urbańczyk and Olesch, *Die altpolnischen Orthographien*, 94).
[99] Porák, *Humanistická čeština*, 48.

Table 2.4 *Textual opposition of the phonemes /i/ and /ɨ/*

Phoneme	Position	Variant type	WŻyw	UŻyw
/i/	word-initially (/i/ preiotated)[a]	Primary positional[b]	**Level of regularisation 93.64%** <y> (123) (conjunction, spelled always in the same way, in a total of 120 instances) *y* 5v	**Level of regularisation 94.22%** <ij> (259) (conjunction, spelled always in the same way, in a total of 150 instances) *ij* 2r
		Secondary positional	<i> (56) *iże* 7r <j> (16) *jmię* 44v	<i> (3) *iż* 88v
	in other positions	Primary positional	<i> (1,041) *pęgami* 89v	<i> (800) 47r *vzdrowil*
		Secondary positional	<y> (6) *dżyś* 7r <ij> (1) *śmierćij* 90v	<y> (2) *profyli* 4r <ij> (57) *tejkliwofcij* 3v <ii> (1) *rozliicznii* 175v
/ɨ/	irrespective of position	Primary	**Level of regularisation 96.61%** <y> (770) *rady* 44v	**Level of regularisation 95.82%** <y> (298) *fyna* 88r
		Secondary	<i> (27) *nátim* 6r	<i> (17) *dobrich* 2v <y> (15) *ijzbý* 2r

[a] From the spelling used in the analysed texts, it can be concluded that the etymological, word-initial /i/ was preiotated at the beginning of the sixteenth century.

[b] A positional variant is a grapheme used to spell a given phoneme; its textual realisation is determined by its position, i.e. its graphic context, and it may be a primary or secondary variant.

vivae paginae (headings repeated on every recto page of the book) and appear only in the form *Żywot*, e.g. 88r. Thus, <ý> should be regarded as an interference from the Czech spelling system, and one that has no functional justification.

2.1.5   Textual Realisation of the Phoneme /j/

Finding an appropriate graphical representation of the phoneme /j/ was a difficult task for mediaeval writers. In the *Psałterz floriański*,[100] the variants used for /j/ are <i>,[101] <y> and <g> or <gy>.[102] The problem was described by Parkosz, a theoretician of Polish manuscript spelling.[103] Zaborowski did not approve of the practice of using the variant <g> = /j/.[104] As shown in Table 2.5, both systems normalise the spelling of /j/ by introducing positional variants, <i> in front of a vowel grapheme (except for any textual variants of the phoneme /i/) and <y> in front of a consonant grapheme or word-finally. In the system used in Vietor's printing house, the spelling of the pronoun *ji* as <gi> or <gy> is a fossilised interference adapted from manuscripts.[105]

2.1.6   Textual Opposition of the Phonemes /l/ : /ł/

Polish manuscripts did not mark the difference between /l/ : /ł/ and used <l> freely, to indicate either sound. An exception was the fifteenth-century part of *Psałterz floriański*, which, under the influence of Czech spelling, employed <ll> for /l/ and <yl> or <il> for /ł/.[106] However, Parkosz proposed <l> for /ł/ and the character *l* with a loop in its upper part for /l/.[107] Zaborowski adopted the idea but insisted on using a diacritic mark similar to an apostrophe for the phoneme /ł/, i.e. <l'>.[108] In most cases, Polish printed texts created before 1520 represented the opposition with combined spelling, using the opposing pairs of variants <l> : <ll> or <li> : <l> to denote /l/ : /ł/.[109] As shown in Table 2.6, the system used in Vietor's printing house consistently implemented the opposition between /l/ : /ł/ with a diacritical spelling used to represent /ł/. Thus, the rule /l/ = <l> and /ł/ = <ł> was observed. The occurrence of the rare variant <li> may be a relic of manuscript spelling or an oversight on the part of the proofreader, possibly a consequence of the pronunciation of /l/ characteristic of the Lesser Poland region.[110] The absence of graphical

---

[100] The *Saint Florian Psalter* was written in three languages, and it contains psalms in Latin, German and Polish. The Polish translation was produced between the late fourteenth and the early fifteenth centuries (Wydra and Rzepka, *Chrestomatia*, 51).
[101] Kamińska, *Psałterz*, 20.   [102] Cybulski, *Język*, 34–9.
[103] Kucała, *Jakuba Parkosza Traktat*, 71–3, 102–4.
[104] Urbańczyk and Olesch, *Die altpolnischen Orthographien*, 92–3, 106–7.
[105] Lisowski, 'Ślady graficznej tradycji rękopisów', 73.   [106] Cybulski, *Język*, 69.
[107] Urbańczyk and Olesch, *Die altpolnischen Orthographien*, 95.   [108] Ibid., 27.
[109] Wydra and Rzepka, 'Niesamoistne', 278–9; Klimek, *Język polski*, 20.
[110] Karaś and Perzanowski, *Statuty kapituły norbertańskiej z r. 1541*, 15.

Table 2.5 *Textual realisation of the phoneme /j/*

Phoneme	Position	Variant type	WŻyw	UŻyw
/j/			**Level of regularisation 86.11%**	**Level of regularisation 98.89%**
	in front of a vowel grapheme (except <i>)[a]	Primary positional[c]	<i> (380) *kroluią* 124r	<i> (585) *przyiáciél* 133r
		Secondary positional	<j> (17) *jeść* 45r <y> (3) *Izáyaſſowe* 6r	<j> (3) *kije* 90v
	in front of <i>[b]	Primary positional	<y> (125) *y* 5v (the pronoun *ji*)	–
		Secondary positional	<i> (56) *ſtoi* 7r, *moich* 124v <j> (16) *jdąc* 45r <g> (13) *gi* 44v, *gy* 87v	<i> (3) *iż* 175r
	in front of a consonant grapheme or word-finally	Primary positional	<y> (146) *troyce* 5v	<y> (126) *pokoy* 46v

[a] <i> stands for any variant of the grapheme <i>.

[b] Assuming preiotation in word-initial positions.

[c] A positional variant is a grapheme used to spell a given phoneme; its textual realisation is determined by its position, i.e. its graphic context, and it may be a primary or secondary variant. See note 64 for other conventions.

opposition between the phonemes /l/ : /ł/ in *UŻyw* should be regarded as a conservative choice, which may have been reinforced by a practice emerging in Czech printing at that time. According to these new standards, the articulatory difference between the hard /l/ and the soft /ł/ was not marked, a feature which was also disappearing from most Czech dialects.[111]

2.1.7 Textual Opposition of the Phonemes in the Sequences /s/, /z/, /ŝ/, /d̂z/ : /ʃ/, /ʒ/, /t͡ʃ/, /d̂ʒ/ : /ɕ/, /ʑ/, /t͡ɕ/, /d̂ʑ/

Both of the spelling systems under discussion strived for an unambiguous representation of the graphical opposition between the three sequences of phonemes /s/, /z/,

[111] Porák, *Humanistická čeština*, 81–2.

Table 2.6 *Textual opposition of the phonemes /l/ and /ł/*

Phoneme	Variant type	*WŻyw*	*UŻyw*
/l/		Level of regularisation 99.56%	Level of regularisation 100%
	Primary	<l> (459) *krolu* 88v	<l> (all instances) *krol* 132r
	Secondary	<l> (1) *Slęknqwſſy ſie* 7v <li> (1) *alie* 46v	–
/ł/		Level of regularisation 98.79%	Level of regularisation 0%
	Primary	<l> (655) *golębie* 45v	–
	Secondary	<l> (8) *poſlan* 7v	<l> (all instances) *kochala* 46r

See note 64 for conventions.

/ts/, /dz/ : /ʃ/, /ʒ/, /t͡ʃ/, /d͡ʒ/ : /ɕ/, /ʑ/, /t͡ɕ/, /d͡ʑ/ (see Table 2.7), which mirrored the pronunciation of the Greater Polish dialect. Since then, this representation has become the norm in the spelling used in Polish printed texts.[112] Both systems display consistency in the distinction between the two series of phones /s/ : /ʃ/, /z/ : /ʒ/, /ts/ : /t͡ʃ/, /dz/ : /d͡ʒ/, which points to the absence of the so-called Mazovianism, a feature characteristic of dialects in Lesser Poland, Mazovia, Central Poland (Sieradzkie), and parts of Silesia, that entailed the loss of any distinction between the postalveolars /ʃ/, /ʒ/, /t͡ʃ/, /d͡ʒ/ and the dentals /s/, /z/, /ts/, /dz/.[113] Both systems use position to determine the phonological meaning of the variants. However, the system used in Vietor's printing house more frequently uses characters with diacritic marks, <ś>, <ż>, <ć> and <ź>, which was probably a result of Zaborowski's intention to make the system more functional. The spelling patterns detected in *WŻyw* consist either in the use of individual letters (<ſ>, <s>, <z>, <c>, <ś>, <ż>, <ć> and <ź>) or of characters combined with other letters to create digraphs (<ſſ>, <ſs>, <cz>, <dz>, <ſi>, <zi>, <ci>, <xi>, <śi>, <śy>, <źi>, <źy>, <dż> and <dź>) and trigraphs (<ſſh>, <dzi> and <dźi>) for the same purpose. The digraph and trigraph variants for palatal consonants (/ɕ/, /ʑ/, /t͡ɕ/, /d͡ʑ/) in front of a vowel grapheme except <i> (<śi>, e.g. *dźiśia* 7r; <źi>, e.g. *źiemi* 6r; <dźi>, e.g. *odźieniu* 88r) are

112 Rospond, *Dawność mazurzenia*, 467.
113 Bunčić, 'The standardization', 237; Stieber, *Rozwój fonologiczny*, 70.

Table 2.7 *Textual opposition of the phonemes in the sequences /s/, /z/, /ʦ/, /ʣ/ : /ʃ/, /ʒ/, /ʧ/, /ʤ/ : /ɕ/, /ʑ/, /ʦ/, /ʨ/, /ʥ/*

Phoneme	Position	Variant type	WŻyw		UŻyw	
/s/			**Level of regularisation 99.58%**		**Level of regularisation 95.93%**	
	not word-finally and not before a voiced consonant grapheme	Primary positional[a]	<ſ> (417)	ieſt 88v	<ſ> (425)	gloſem 131r
		Secondary positional	<z> (2)	rozpaloná 7r	<s> (12)	s tego 46r
	word-finally	Primary positional	<s> (53)	glos 88v	<s> (35)	glos 173v
/ʃ/			**Level of regularisation 97.71%**		**Level of regularisation 100%**	
	irrespective of position	Primary	<ʃʃ> (256)	wáʃʃ 88r	–	
		Secondary	<ʃʃh> (5)	dźiśieyʃʃhe 8v	–	
			<s> (1)	náuczas 45r		
	not word-finally	Primary positional	–		<ʃʃ> (206)	piʃʃe 131r
	word-finally	Primary positional	–		<ſs> (24)	znáſs 46r
/ɕ/			**Level of regularisation 80.68%**		**Level of regularisation 95.04%**	
	before <i>	Primary positional	<ſ> (8)	proſić 45v	<ſ> (19)	profila 2r

before a vowel grapheme (except <i>)	Primary positional	<ſi> (97)	*mieſiąc* 7v	<ſi> (126)	*kſiążęta* 3v
	Secondary positional	<si> (1)	*dźiśia* 7r	—	
		<ſy> (1)	*mieśyąc* 124r		
		<xi> (2)	*xięgi* 6r		
in front of a palatal consonant grapheme	Primary positional	<ſ> (132)	*cirpliwoſć* 124r	<ſ> (200)	*cirpliwoſz* 2r
	Secondary positional	<ś> (63)	*ſlicznego* 7v	—	
word-finally	Primary positional	<ś> (47)	*kondeś* 45v	—	
	Secondary positional	<s> (1)	*bogás* 125v	<s> (18)	*zwykles* 132r
		Level of regularisation 96.46%		**Level of regularisation 92.76%**	
/z/	Primary	<z> (191)	*zamek* 8v	<z> (269)	*zbawiciela* 45v
irrespective of position	Secondary	<ſ> (7)	*ſłożywſſy* 7r	<ſ> (12)	*ſmiłuycie* 131r
				<s> (9)	*s wami* 90r

Table 2.7 (cont.)

Phoneme	Position	Variant type	WŻyw		UŻyw	
/ʒ/		Primary	**Level of regularisation 99.06%**		**Level of regularisation 98.88%**	
			<ż> (210)	żony 88v	<ż> (267)	żądaią 131v
	irrespective of position	Secondary	<z> (1)	ize 43v	<z> (3)	polozyla 45v
			<ź> (1)	iźeś 123v		
/z/			**Level of regularisation 96.55%**		**Level of regularisation 100%**	
	before <i> or a palatal consonant grapheme or word-finally	Primary positional	<ź> (16)	źle 45r	<z> (2)	bliźniego 2r
	before a vowel grapheme (except <i>)	Primary positional	<zi> (12)	náleźiono 125v	<zi> (10)	naleziona 2v
		Secondary positional	<zy> (1)	żyemyęś 124r	–	
/ɕ/			**Level of regularisation 100%**		**Level of regularisation 99.69%**	
	irrespective of position	Primary	<c> (all instances)	mocny 124v	–	
	not before a frontal vowel grapheme	Primary positional	–		<tz> (212)	tznot 2r
		Secondary positional	–		<c> (1)	oblubieniec 3v
	before a frontal vowel grapheme	Primary positional	–		<c> (105)	ręce 2r

Phoneme	Context	Position	Level of regularisation (A)		Level of regularisation (B)	
/tʃ/	irrespective of position	Primary	**100%** <cz> (all instances)	*oblicze* 87v	**100%** <cz> (all instances)	*czynila* 2r
/tɕ/			**99.05%**		**57.23%**	
	in front of <i> or a palatal consonant grapheme or word-finally	Primary positional	<ć> (188)	*myflić* 6v	—	
		Secondary positional	<c> (3)	*mowic* 90v	—	
	in front of a vowel grapheme (except <i>)	Primary positional	<ci> (127)	*chcial* 8v	<ci> (105)	*zbawiciela* 45v
		Secondary positional	—		<tzi> (4)	*trzetzie* 2v
	in front of <i>	Primary positional	—		<c> (90)	*przeciw* 45v
		Secondary positional	—		<tz> (3)	*tzijchá* 2v
	in front of a palatal grapheme consonant or word-finally	Primary positional	—		<tz> (3)	*piętzdziefiąt* 175v
		Secondary positional	—		<tz> (140)	*vmrzetz* 173v
					<c> (1)	*czyftofc* 3r
/dʑ/	irrespective of position	Primary	**100%** <dz> (all instances)	*pieniądz* 88v	**100%** <dz> (all instances)	*ofądzon* 133r

Table 2.7 (*cont.*)

Phoneme	Position	Variant type	WŻyw	UŻyw
/ʣ̇/	irrespective of position	Primary	**Level of regularisation 100%** <dż> (1) *rożdżką* 125r	**Level of regularisation 33.33%** <dż> (1) *rożdże* 71v
		Secondary	–	<dz> (3) *rozdzka* 184v
/ʣ/	in front of a vowel grapheme (except <i>)	Primary positional	**Level of regularisation 98.59%** <dzi> (92) *ludzie* 125v	**Level of regularisation 96.96%** <dzi> (95) *dzień* 2v
		Secondary positional	<dzi> (1) *dziewicą* 7v	–
	in front of <i> or a palatal consonant grapheme or word-finally	Primary positional	<dż> (48) *bądż* 6v, *Dżiś* 8v, *ludżmi* 7v	–
		Secondary positional	<dz> (1) *Dzifia* 7v	–
	in front of <i> or a palatal consonant grapheme	Primary positional	–	<dz> (33) *ludzmi* 45v
	word-finally	Secondary positional	–	<dz> (4) *bądz* 88r

[a] A positional variant is a grapheme used to spell a given phoneme; its textual realisation is determined by its position, i.e. its graphic context, and it may be a primary or secondary variant.

See note 64 for other conventions.

redundant in the context of the full spelling system in question, as both ´ and *i* were used in parallel to indicate the same function.

The system created by Sandecki, on the other hand, relies more heavily on traditional, more complex spelling. It employs the spelling <tz>, which was common in German[114] and was also used in Czech printing.[115] The letter <ż> is the only diacritic unit used independently or in combination with other characters to form the discussed opposition. The decision not to mark the character representing /ɕ/, /ź/, /t͡ɕ/ and /d͡ź/ with diacritic marks might have been influenced by the spelling used in Czech printing.[116] The characters <ſ> and <s> used in both systems, recorded here as graphemes for simplicity, should in fact be regarded as allographs (the use of the latter was limited to word-final position and its shape was not functionally significant).[117] Both systems use <ſſ> as the primary variant for the phoneme /ʃ/, a variant used in manuscripts together with <ſch> and <ſz>.[118] Texts printed in the 1530s replace <ſſ> with <sz>, which remains in use today.[119]

2.1.8   Creation of Characters to Mark Palatal Consonant Phonemes

The practice of marking the palatal character of consonants was introduced into the Polish spelling tradition in the fifteenth century. Only a few examples of these practices are known from fourteenth-century texts, e.g. *zyele*.[120] In the fifteenth-century part of the *Psałterz floriański*, the frequency of occurrence of variants marking palatal consonants, especially in front of a vowel grapheme (except <i>), reaches 36%, which is a clear indication of the influence of Czech practices.[121] These include combinations of a hard (non-palatal) consonant letter with <y> (and, less frequently, <i>), e.g. in <py> or <pi>, <ny> or <ni>, <ſy> or <ſi>, and <dzy> or <dzi>.[122] Parkosz suggested that the variants of the parallel graphemes of soft and hard consonants should be represented in opposition with the use of different characters.[123] Zaborowski introduced a rule according to which the textual variants of graphemes for soft consonants were to be marked with diacritic signs, a double dot or a horizontal line above the letter.[124]

Both of the spelling systems proposed in 1522 represent the palatal character of consonants in the two aforementioned ways; see Table 2.8. The system used by Vietor's printing house appears to have found a complex way to represent palatal consonants in front of a vowel grapheme (except <i>) and diacritical spelling for palatal consonants in other positions, i.e. in front of a palatal

---

[114] Rospond, *Dawność mazurzenia*, 86.   [115] Porák, *Humanistická čeština*, 21.
[116] Ibid., 27–30.
[117] Twardzik, *O uważniejszym aniżeli dotychmiast tekstu staropolskiego czytaniu*, 17.
[118] Rospond, *Dawność mazurzenia*, 195–9.
[119] Urbańczyk and Olesch, *Die altpolnischen Orthographien*, 97.
[120] Kamińska, *Psałterz*, 29, 33–4.   [121] Cybulski, *Język*, 70–6.
[122] Rospond, 'Z badań', 145, 170.   [123] Kucała, *Jakuba Parkosza Traktat*, 65, 95.
[124] Urbańczyk and Olesch, *Die altpolnischen Orthographien*, 96, 110.

Table 2.8 *Creation of characters to mark palatal consonant phonemes*

Phoneme	Position	Variant type	*Wżyw*	*Używ*
/ɲ/			**Level of regularisation 99.10%**	**Level of regularisation 94.98%**
	in front of a vowel grapheme (except <i>)	Primary positional	<ni> (242) *niebá* 123v	<ni> (277) *niechcę* 3v
		Secondary positional	<ny> (3) *nyebo* 123v	<nij> (21) *przeſłanijá* 3r
	in front of <i>	Primary positional	<n> (81) *cieleſni* 45v	<n> (123) *czynila* 2r
	in front of a palatal consonant grapheme or word-finally	Primary positional	<ń> (16) *niepoſłuſſeńſtwa* 5v	<ń> (16) *kapłańcy* 4r
		Secondary positional	–	<n> (1) *poſłuſſeńſtwa* 2r
/vʲ/ /fʲ/ /pʲ/ /bʲ/ /mʲ/ /c/ /ɟ/			**Level of regularisation 99.45%**	**Level of regularisation 100%**
	in front of a vowel grapheme (except <i>) or word-finally [a]	Primary positional	<pi>, <bi>, <fi>, <wi>, <mi>, <ki>, <gi> (546) *człowiecze* 5v	–
		Secondary positional	<by>, <wy>, <my> (3) *zwyelkim* 123v	–
	in front of a vowel grapheme (except <i>)	Primary positional	–	<pi>, <bi>, <wi>, <mi>, <ki>, <gi> [b] (497) *biodra* 89v
	word-finally	Primary positional	–	<ṁ> (1) *ſiedm* 2r

[a] Palatalisation of the consonants /pʲ/, /bʲ/, /vʲ/, /fʲ/, /mʲ/, /c/, /ɟ/ as well as of /ɲ/ (/ɲi/ = <ni> as indicated in the table) caused by /i/ is not indicated graphically in any of the systems: /pʲi/ = <pi>, /bʲi/ = <bi>, /vʲi/ = <wi>, /fʲi/ = <fi>, /mʲi/ = <mi>, /ci/ = <ki>, /ɟi/ = <gi>.

[b] No examples of allographs of /fʲ/.

See note 64 for other conventions.

consonant grapheme or word-finally. The rule was predominantly applied to the analysed graphemes of the phonemes /ɕ/, /ʑ/, /t͡ɕ/ and /d͡ʑ/, as well as the phoneme /ɲ/, both of which are alveolo-palatal consonants articulated with the middle section of the tongue. Their relevant phonological feature is their place of articulation, i.e. the palate.[125] In the case of the phonemes of the labial consonants /vʲ/, /fʲ/, /pʲ/, /bʲ/ and /mʲ/ and the velar consonants /c/ and /ɟ/, their palatal character is an additional articulatory feature. Diacritical spelling in Sandecki's system was used only to mark the grapheme of /ɲ/ = <ń> (in front of a palatal consonant grapheme or word-finally) and the grapheme of /mʲ/ = <ḿ> (word-finally). Neither of the systems indicates palatalisation of the consonants /pʲ/, /bʲ/, /vʲ/, /fʲ/, /mʲ/, /c/, /ɟ/ or /ɲ/ in front of /i/: /pʲi/ = <pi>, /bʲi/ = <bi>, /vʲi/ = <wi>, /fʲi/ = <fi>, /mʲi/ = <mi>, /ci/ = <ki>, /ɟi/ = <gi>, /ɲi/ = <ni>. The systems also use <i>, which loses its vocalic value (and, exceptionally, <y> in *WŻyw* or <ij> in *UŻyw*), as a diacritic for palatal consonant graphemes. In this respect, both systems reflect the complex spelling known from manuscripts. The difference lies in the fact that manuscripts tended to use *y* as a diacritic. The change of the palatal diacritic in both systems may have been caused by economic factors: standard Latin printing sets contained many more <i> than <y>.[126] Additionally, the grapheme <y> had another phonological meaning, as both the systems used it to represent the phoneme /ɨ/. By using the type *i*, printers could avoid the costs of casting additional *y* types.[127]

2.2 Characteristic Features of the Two Spelling Systems from the Year 1522

The analysis conducted above has shown that the editors of both versions of *Żywot Pana Jezu Krysta* from the year 1522 simultaneously used individual spelling norms, and had an influence in deciding some of the spelling norms available in sixteenth-century Polish more broadly. The process of standardisation, which included the elimination of opposing spelling variants that shared the same function in both of the editions of *Żywot Pana Jezu Krysta*, eventually led to the creation of two spelling systems that were a complete innovation in the printing practice of that period. The methods of assigning specific phonological meanings to variants are identical in both systems. However, the systems radically differ in quality, scope of implementation of the proposed solutions, and degree of their functionality. The methods sometimes intersect, and, in some cases, they are overlaid with rules from mediaeval manuscripts, according to which the phonological meaning of a variant is determined by its graphic position. The methods used are generally as follows:

---

[125] Cybulski, *Język*, 75.   [126] Wydra and Rzepka, 'Niesamoistne', 276–9.
[127] Lisowski, 'Economic calculation', 202.

(1) redefining the meaning of Latin characters:
- *WŻyw* and *UŻyw*: /i/ = \<i>, /ɨ/ = \<y> (the spelling of /i/ in word-initial positions is an exception to this rule);

(2) traditional complex spelling:
- *WŻyw* and *UŻyw*: digraphs that were not analysed due to the lack of alternative variants: \<ch> = /x/, \<rz> = /ʳʒ/;
- *WŻyw*: /ʃ/ = \<ſ>, /ʧ͡/ = \<cz>, /d͡ʑ/ = \<dz>; *UŻyw*: /ʃ/ = \<ſ>, \<ſs>, /d͡ʑ/ or /d͡ʑ/ = \<dz>; /ɒ/ = \<aa>, /e/ = \<ee>, /o/ = \<uo>;

(3) assigning a new meaning to borrowed character combinations:
- *UŻyw* /t͡s/ = \<tz>;

(4) qualitative modifications to the traditional complex spelling:
- *WŻyw*: realisation of graphemes for labial-palatal consonants, velar-palatal consonants, and /ɲ/ in front of a vowel grapheme (except \<i>): /pʲ/ = \<pi>, /bʲ/ = \<bi>, /vʲ/ = \<wi>, /fʲ/ = \<fi>, /mʲ/ = \<mi>, /ɲ/ = \<ni>, /c/ = \<ki>, /ɟ/ = \<gi>;
- *UŻyw*: realisation of graphemes for labial-palatal consonants, velar-palatal consonants, and alveolo-palatal consonants in front of a vowel grapheme (except \<i>): /pʲ/ = \<pi>, /bʲ/ = \<bi>, /vʲ/ = \<wi>, /fʲ/ = \<fi>, /mʲ/ = \<mi>, /ɲ/ = \<ni>, /c/ = \<ki>, /ɟ/ = \<gi>, /ɕ/ = \<ſi>, /ʑ/ = \<zi>, /t͡ɕ/ = \<ci> or \<tzi>, /d͡ʑ/ = \<dzi>, /ɲ/ = \<ni>;

(5) defining the meaning of a variant through its positional features:
- *WŻyw* and *UŻyw*: realisation of the phoneme /u/ word-initially as \<v> and in other positions as \<u>; realisation of the phoneme /j/ in front of a vowel grapheme (except \<i>) as \<i> and in front of a consonant grapheme or word-finally as \<y>; realisation of graphemes of labial-palatal consonants, velar-palatal consonants and /ɲ/ in front of \<i> as \<p>, \<b>, \<w>, \<f>, \<m>, \<n>, \<k>, \<g>;
- *WŻyw*: realisation of the phoneme /j/ in front of \<i> as \<y> (fossilised spelling of the conjunction *i*) or as \<g> (fossilised spelling of the pronoun *ji*) or \<j>; *UŻyw*: realisation of the phoneme /j/ in front of \<i> as \<ij>; realisation of the phonemes /ɕ/, /ʑ/, /t͡ɕ/, /d͡ʑ/ in front of a palatal consonant grapheme as \<ſ>, \<z>, \<dz>; realisation of the phoneme /t͡ɕ/ in front of a palatal consonant grapheme or word-finally as \<tz>;

(6) diacritical spelling:
- *WŻyw*: /a/ = \<á>, /ɔ̃/ = \<ą>, /ɛ̃/ = \<ę>, /ɫ/ = \<ł>, /ʒ/ = \<ż>; realisation of the phonemes of alveolo-palatal consonants in front of a palatal consonant grapheme or word-finally as /ɕ/ = \<ś>, /t͡ɕ/ = \<ć>, /ʑ/ = \<ż>, /ɲ/ = \<ń>;
- *UŻyw*: /ɒ/ = \<á>, /e/ = \<é>, /o/ = \<ó>, /ɔ̃/ = \<ą>, /ɛ̃/ = \<ę>, /ʒ/ = \<ż>, /ɲ/ in front of a consonant grapheme or word-finally = \<ń>;

(7) mixing of complex spelling with diacritical spelling:
- *WŻyw*: the spelling of the phonemes of alveolo-palatal consonants in front of a consonant grapheme or word-finally: /d͡ʒ/ = \<dż>, /d͡ʑ/ = \<dź>;

realisation of the phonemes /ɕ/, /ʑ/, /t͡ɕ/, /d͡ʑ/ in front of a vowel grapheme (except <i>): <śi>, <źi>, <ći>, <dźi>;
– *UŻyw*: /ʧ/ = <cż>; /d͡ʒ/ = <dż>; /ɒ/ = <aá>, /e/ = <eé>, /o/ = <uó>.

The characteristics shared by the two spelling systems (*WŻyw* and *UŻyw*) are as follows:

(a) opposed graphic realisation of the phonemes /ɔ̃/ = <ą> and /ɛ̃/ = <ę> with newly designed typefaces;
(b) the use of <i> for the phoneme /i/ and <y> for the phoneme /ɨ/;
(c) position-dependent spelling of the phoneme /u/ word-initially = <v> and = <u> in other cases, in accordance with mediaeval practices;
(d) position-dependent spelling of the phoneme /j/ in front of a vowel grapheme (except <i>) = <i>, in front of a consonant grapheme or word-finally = <y>;
(e) realisation of the phoneme /ʒ/ = <ż>;
(f) the use of the diacritic <i> to mark palatal consonants in front of a vowel grapheme (except <i>);
(g) realisation of the phoneme /ɲ/ in front of a palatal consonant grapheme or word-finally as <ń>.

Both systems bear traces of spelling traditions derived from manuscripts, especially <y> = /i/ and <i> = /ɨ/. These also include the fossilised spelling borrowings stemming from mediaeval practices that were employed only by the Vietor printing house system: <gi> or <gy> as the pronoun *ji* 'him', and <ji> or <y> in the function of the conjunction *i*; <a> = /a/; the use of the letter *y* as a diacritic for palatal consonants in front of a vowel grapheme (except <i>); and <ſſh>. The analysis suggests that Sandecki's system was traditional and conservative, and largely used the complex spelling characteristics of manuscripts. In contrast, Vietor's system made frequent use of the more functional diacritical spelling. Some of the solutions proposed by Sandecki show similarities to Czech spelling. Apart from the diacritic spelling of the phonemes of the narrow vowels /ɒ/, /e/ and /o/ (which was also proposed by Zaborowski), the solutions include the use of <ij> to represent the phone combinations /ji/ and /ij/; the variants <ż> and <cż>; the use of <ij> as the realisation of the phoneme /i/; and the orthographic borrowings <eé>, <uo>, <uó> and <ý>.[128] Although the lack of differentiation between /l/ and /ɫ/ is similar to the spelling used in Czech printed texts, it should be seen as a convention derived from the tradition of Polish manuscript spelling. The solutions proposed by Sandecki made much greater use of standard printing font sets, for

---

[128] Lisowski, 'Jan Sandecki', 104.

financial reasons. At the same time, the limited funds provided by the printing house for the editing of the book had a detrimental effect on the functionality of the system.

By contrast, the system used in Vietor's printing house might have been more expensive to implement, but was more functional and closer to the phonetic reality of the Polish language of the period. The system became the basis for the new, Middle Polish typographical spelling system.[129] It survived, with only slight modifications, until the end of the eighteenth century.[130] This fact is proven not only by printing practices, but also by metalinguistic materials, such as the Introduction to the translation of the *Ewangelia Święta wedle Mateusza Świętego* (*Holy Gospel According to Saint Matthew*) by Stanisław Murzynowski, published in the mid-sixteenth century in Königsberg (a new, fast-developing centre of Polish printing). The book's preface is entitled *Ortografia polska* (Königsberg, 1551), and it contains remarks that indicate the rejection of the conventions proposed by Sandecki.[131] Murzynowski compiled and organised the as yet uncodified spelling rules used by Vietor's printing house to introduce his readers of the Gospels to the principles of reading a printed text.[132] Jan Seklucjan had a similar objective when he wrote the section entitled 'Krótka a prosta nauka czytania i pisania języka polskiego' ('A Short and Easy Lesson in Reading Polish') in his *Katechizm* (Königsberg, 1549).[133] At the end of the sixteenth century, *Nowy karakter polski* (*The New Polish Spelling*) was published in Cracow; it was a book containing treatises on orthography by Łukasz Górnicki and Jan Kochanowski, as well as a commentary by Jan Januszowski, a practising printer of the time. Górnicki's proposals, although the outcome of a thorough phonological analysis of the Polish language, were based entirely on existing printing practices. Among other things, Górnicki introduced a new diacritic mark (a reversed wedge ˆ) to indicate palatal consonants, and replaced <ł> with <ll>. Kochanowski, on the other hand, argued for limiting the use of diacritic marks in positions where the pronunciation was obvious and thus did not require graphic representation. Later, Januszowski expressed his approval of the printing practice that had been popular for more than 70 years and implemented the conventions proposed in Vietor's project.[134]

To return to the main focus of my analysis, this chapter has suggested that the two spelling systems under investigation were created as printing practices. At the moment of their creation, in the year 1522, they were not codified in a

---

[129] Bunčić, 'The standardization', 241–3; Jodłowski, *Losy polskiej ortografii*, 45; Kamińska, 'Pisownia druków polskich XVI wieku'; Kresa, 'Gramatyka dla szkół narodowych'; Lisowski, 'Economic calculation', 203; Urbańczyk and Olesch, *Die altpolnischen Orthographien*; Winiarska-Górska, 'Krótka a prosta nauka'; 'Ortografia polska'.
[130] Walczak, *Zarys*, 133–4.   [131] Rospond, *Studia*, 45, 91.
[132] Winiarska-Górska, 'Ortografia polska'.   [133] Winiarska-Górska, 'Krótka a prosta nauka'.
[134] Walczak, *Zarys*, 120.

metalinguistic manner. The systems had little impact on the spelling used in the manuscripts of that period, as the latter were heavily influenced by regionalisms,[135] and employed mediaeval, complex spellings (e.g. the manuscripts sporadically used variants for nasal vowels).[136] The two systems were developed by literate professionals, with a good grasp of the technicalities of printing, as well as an awareness of its scope and limitations. The spelling systems were largely designed for non-professional readers, and were shaped by linguistic (phonological, phonetic and morphological) as well as non-linguistic (technical, economic and sociological) factors. Some of the spelling conventions (especially those employed in *UŻyw*) show similarities to Czech patterns. Modern Polish spelling relies more heavily on the system created at Vietor's printing house (diacritical spelling), but it is largely based on the primary premises of both systems. In particular, modern Polish spelling features the following graphemes introduced by both spelling systems:

(i). <ą>, <ę>, <ń>, <ż>;
(ii). the combined digraph <dż>;
(iii). the characters introduced by Vietor's printing house: <ś>, <ź>, <ć>, <ł>, and the combined digraph <dź>;
(iv). the character <ó> introduced in Sandecki's system.

Polish orthography owes to both systems the practice of combining other characters with <i> to mark soft consonants in <pi>, <bi>, <wi>, <mi>, <ki>, <gi>, <si>, <zi>, <ci> and <dzi>. The character combinations <ch>, <sz>, <cz>, <dz> and <rz>, which are still in use today, were present in both systems and reflected the spelling traditions of the mediaeval period.[137]

---

[135] Bargieł, *Cechy dialektalne polskich zabytków rękopiśmiennych*; Cybulski, 'Na obrzeżach głównego nurtu', 183–5; Osiewicz, *Fonetyka listów polskich*; *Wariantywność leksemów*.
[136] Kuraszkiewicz, *Polski język literacki*, 595–9.
[137] Lisowski, 'The Polish printed book', 128–30.

3   Graphematic Features in Glagolitic and Cyrillic Orthographies

A Contribution to the Typological Model of Biscriptality

Per Ambrosiani

The typological model of biscriptality proposed in the recently published collective monograph by Daniel Bunčić et al., *Biscriptality. A Sociolinguistic Typology*,[1] is a recent step forward in the growing subfield of typological work, which promises to provide a rigorous framework of analysis. The model aims to describe and classify linguistic situations in which two or more writing systems are used simultaneously for one and the same language.[2] The model successfully introduces a clear distinction between scripts (e.g. the Latin and Cyrillic alphabets), glyphic variants of scripts (e.g. roman and italic) and orthographies, which can in turn be classified according to different relationships between the respective concepts; see Table 3.1.

As examples of different biscriptal situations Bunčić discusses three cases of the use of two scripts for one language: Hindi–Urdu, with Hindi written in Nāgarī script and Urdu in Arabic script; Old Norse, written in Runic or Latin script depending on the functional context; and Modern Serbian, with Cyrillic and Latin scripts, where almost any text can be written in either script. The Nāgarī/Arabic script situation is characterised as equipollent, the Runic/Latin as privative, and the Cyrillic/Latin as diasituative, that is, as neither privative nor equipollent.[3] While the biscriptality model represents a much-needed step forward in the typological analysis of scripts and orthography, there are still some issues which could be explored further in order to maximise the analytical potential of the typological model in specific linguistic contexts. In particular, the biscriptality model still lacks a thorough, well-developed discussion of *graphematic features* from a biscriptality perspective,[4] and also of how best to include the *grapheme* concept in the typological framework of biscriptality. A deeper understanding of the relationship between the graphematic features of historically attested Glagolitic

---

[1] Bunčić et al., *Biscriptality.*   [2] Cf. ibid., 54.   [3] See ibid., 54–68.
[4] Cf., however, ibid., 63–6, which introduces a distinction on the graphematic axis between *diglyphia, biglyphism* and *glyphic pluricentricity.*

Table 3.1 *Types of biscriptal situation*

Opposition types	Script	Glyphic variant	Orthography
privative	digraphia	diglyphia	diorthographia
equipollent	scriptal pluricentricity	glyphic pluricentricity	orthographic pluricentricity
diasituative	bigraphism	biglyphism	biorthographism

Simplified version of Bunčić et al., *Biscriptality*, 67, Figure 5.

and Cyrillic orthographies would further contribute to the elaboration of the model on a more detailed level. Both the factual and the methodological insights gained from such a study may, in turn, contribute to the general descriptive potential of the typological model, thus improving its applicability for further case studies. In the present chapter, I investigate the applicability of the biscriptality model to the analysis of the orthographies attested in two different editions of the *New Testament* printed in Glagolitic and Cyrillic letters during the mid-sixteenth century. Through the analysis of the orthographic features of the printed texts, I aim to elaborate on and further extend the following points:

(1) the definition of concepts like *letters, graphemes, allographs, variants* within the respective script contexts;
(2) the relationship between *form* and *function* of the relevant writing units within the respective script contexts, with special emphasis on the distinction between segmental and suprasegmental features;
(3) the relationship between the Glagolitic and Cyrillic script contexts, particularly the degree of graphematic *isomorphism* that can be observed for different classes of graphemes.

Thus, the overall aim of the present chapter is to provide a more detailed analysis of the relationship between two scripts in a biscriptal situation, and to show how such an analysis can be performed on different levels of 'biscriptal isomorphism'.

If the introduction of the grapheme concept into the analysis is to play any meaningful role, it must be clearly defined.[5] Historically, at least two main grapheme models have been proposed. According to one approach, the grapheme is seen as the written language expression of the spoken language *phoneme* concept: graphemes are defined by their function to distinguish between different phonemes. Thus, within this model, the definition of the grapheme is dependent on the definition of the phoneme. According to the other main approach, the written language grapheme is defined in the same way as the spoken language phoneme, that is, by the function of distinguishing between different meanings. This

---

[5] For a more detailed discussion of the use of the term *grapheme* cf., for example, Kohrt, *Problemgeschichte*, 390ff, and Zalizniak, 'O poniatii'.

'autonomous' grapheme concept is not dependent on any analysis of spoken language. When it comes to the analysis of historical texts, the autonomous grapheme concept seems more useful, as we have no direct access to the spoken language supposedly related to the texts under study: as our understanding of the spoken language features are as a rule dependent on any analysis of the extant written texts, conclusions on the specifics of the written texts that depend on the analysis of the spoken language exhibit an obvious risk of being circular.[6] Therefore, in the following I try to keep to a grapheme definition based on the distinction of meaning. In the context of the current investigation, the grapheme is defined as the minimal writing unit that can distinguish different meanings. In a written text, a specific grapheme may be represented by one or more concrete *allographs*, which can be defined as one or more written signs (graphs) that can occur in the same context without indicating any difference in meaning. Graphemes can be either *segmental*, that is, represented by segmental allographs, or *suprasegmental*. Suprasegmental graphemes are represented by modifications of segmental graphs within a specific *domain*, which can comprise two or more graphs (sometimes even a whole text); see further below, Section 3.2.2. Following Peter Gallmann, *Graphische Elemente*,[7] I discuss mainly the following types of segmental and suprasegmental graphemes and their function in the Glagolitic and Cyrillic orthographies of the sources at hand.

Among the segmental graphemes, Gallmann distinguishes between independent ('*selbständige*') and dependent ('*unselbständige*') graphemes. The most important groups among the independent segmental graphemes are *letters* and *numerals*. Among the letters, Gallmann[8] considers lowercase letters to be the unmarked allographs, whereas capital letters are seen as combinations of a lowercase letter graph with the supragrapheme *capitalisation* (cf. below). As far as numerals are concerned, both the Glagolitic and Cyrillic orthographies differ from modern German by using certain letter graphemes as numerals; cf. below, Section 3.2.1.[9] Among the dependent segmental graphemes, Gallmann

---

[6] For a recent insightful discussion of the applicability of different grapheme models to the study of historical texts see Palumbo, *Skriftsystem*, particularly pp. 63–79.

[7] Cf. Gallmann, *Graphische Elemente*, 11–16 on the 'formally defined grapheme classes'. Gallmann distinguishes between '*Grapheme (im engern Sinn)*' 'graphemes (in the narrow sense)', '*lineare Supragrapheme*' 'linear supragraphemes' and '*flächige Supragrapheme*' 'spatial supragraphemes'. Gallmann's first group includes the segmental graphemes *letters, auxiliary signs, empty sign(s), numerals, special signs* and *diacritical marks*, and is thus opposed to the two groups of supragraphemes. In the present chapter the discussion will be limited to segmental and linear suprasegmental graphemes.

[8] Gallmann, *Graphische Elemente*, 12.

[9] For modern German, Gallmann (ibid., 13) considers only figures (1, 2, 3, etc.) as a formally defined class of numeral graphemes, whereas he does not consider for example Roman numerals (I, II, III, etc.) to constitute a separate class. Within the Glagolitic and Cyrillic script contexts, the graphematic status of the numerals is less clearcut, and in the following they will be treated as constituting a separate class of segmental graphemes.

identifies only the *diacritical marks* class, including glyphs like diaeresis, macron, etc., which are often combined with an independent segmental grapheme such as, for example, a letter.[10] Among the linear suprasegmental graphemes (supragraphemes), Gallmann distinguishes between the concrete supragrapheme *underlining* and the abstract supragraphemes *initial* and *general capitalisation, emphasis, size, ligatures*, etc. In the following, the discussion is limited to three of the linear supragraphemes mentioned by Gallmann that are particularly important for the biscriptality discussion of the Glagolitic and Cyrillic orthographies: *capitalisation, superposition* and *ligature*. In addition, I also consider a fourth suprasegmental linear grapheme, *abbreviation*, which is not explicitly mentioned among the supragraphemes by Gallmann. However, as will be shown below, *abbreviation* can be analysed in a similar way, as a modification of a sequence of segmental graphemes within a certain domain.[11]

3.1   Two Croatian *New Testament* Editions

The material for the following graphematic analysis consists of two Slavic *New Testament* editions published in Tübingen in the mid-sixteenth century, one printed with Glagolitic letters in 1562/3 (Part 1, the Gospels and the Acts of the Apostles, was published in 1562; Part 2, the Epistles and the Revelation, in 1563), and the other printed with Cyrillic letters in 1563; see Figure 3.1.[12] Both editions were published by the short-lived South Slavic Bible Society, which printed Protestant editions of important Christian texts for use in the South Slavic area,[13] and have been extensively described and discussed in the scholarly literature (cf. also Chapter 9 for a study of the Glagolitic edition from the perspective of grapholinguistics),[14] and in 2007 and 2008 facsimile editions of both books were

---

[10] The graphematic status of certain diacritical marks is briefly discussed below in connection with the analysis of letter graphemes; cf. Section 3.2.1.

[11] Cf. also Miklas, 'Zur Struktur', 63, who discusses briefly the traditional Old Church Slavonic abbreviations in connection with the linear supragrapheme *superposition* ('*Supraskription*').

[12] In the following, the two editions will be referred to as **G** and **C**, respectively. Digital copies of both editions are available on the internet; see Bibliography under *Novi Testament*. There are also recent physical facsimile editions available, curated by Jembrih: see the Bibliography for details.

[13] For an overview of the approximately twenty-five editions published by the South Slavic Bible Society with Glagolitic, Cyrillic and Latin letters during the period 1561–4, see Bunčić et al., *Biscriptality*, 170; Jembrih, 'Pogovor uz pretisak glagoljičkoga *Novoga testamenta*', 20–2. According to Vorndran (*Südslawische Reformationsdrucke*, 5), the most important sources for the history of the Society are located at the Tübingen University Archives. For a more recent discussion of the history of the Society cf. now also Ehmer, 'Hans Ungnad'.

[14] Cf. for example, Bučar and Fancev, 'Bibliografija', 65–81; Damjanović, 'Kakav je jezik'; Fancev, 'Jezik hrvatskih protestantskih pisaca'; Kruming, *Svodnyĭ katalog*, 52–5, no. 24 (only

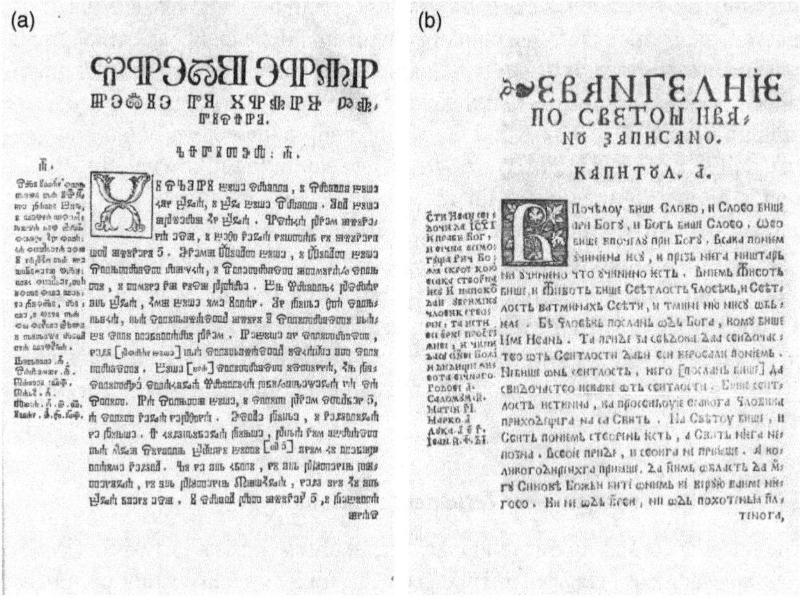

(a)

(b)

Figure 3.1 *New Testament* (1562/3), Gospel according to Saint John, Chapter 1 (beginning): (a) Glagolitic edition; (b) Cyrillic edition

Sources: (a) Bayerische Staatsbibliothek München, call no. ESlg/4 B.rel. 15 c-1, p. 304, http://daten.digitale-sammlungen.de/bsb00078762/image_304; (b) Württembergische Landesbibliothek, Stuttgart, call no. Ba kroat.156301, p. 300, http://digital.wlb-stutt gart.de/sammlungen/sammlungsliste/werksansicht/?no_cache=1&tx_dlf%5Bid%5D= 5084&tx_dlf%5Bpage%5D=300

published in Croatia, with extensive afterwords.[15] The language of the two editions differs in terms of details, but it is usually considered to constitute an early variety of a Croatian literary language as a whole,[16] encompassing both vernacular linguistic features originating in different dialect areas of the Croatian-speaking territory and the written Church Slavonic tradition. The Glagolitic text contains more vernacular features than the Cyrillic text, and several scholars argue that the Cyrillic text represents a reaction against the Glagolitic text published a year earlier, which could have been considered too

G); Kuštović, 'Jezik'; Nemirovskiĭ, *Slavi͡anskie izdani͡a*, vol. 2, 175–80 (only **C**); Vorndran, *Südslawische Reformationsdrucke*, 27–39.

[15] See Jembrih, 'Pogovor uz pretisak glagoljičkoga *Novoga testamenta*'.

[16] Kruming (*Svodnyĭ katalog*, 53), for example, describes **G** as the 'first edition of the New Testament in the Croatian language'.

innovative, and too vernacular.[17] From a biscriptality perspective, the relationship between **G** and **C** has been characterised as 'diatopic scriptal pluricentricity';[18] that is, the relationship between the two scripts is seen as equipollent, and dependent neither on any ethnic or confessional distinctions: both the Glagolitic and Cyrillic *New Testament* were published for a Protestant Croatian audience, the only difference being that some of the potential readers were literate in the Glagolitic alphabet, others in the Cyrillic alphabet.[19] In order to elaborate on the characterisation of this particular biscriptality situation, I now embark on a more detailed graphematic analysis of the respective Glagolitic and Cyrillic orthographies of the two editions.

3.2   Graphematic Analysis

The graphematic analysis of the respective Glagolitic and Cyrillic orthographies attested in **G** and **C** is divided into two parts: in Section 3.2.1, I discuss the segmental graphemes *letters* and *numerals*, and in Section 3.2.2, the analysis moves on to the four important suprasegmental graphemes *capitalisation*, *superposition*, *abbreviation* and *ligature*.

3.2.1   Segmental Graphemes

With regard to letter graphemes, both the Glagolitic and Cyrillic *New Testament* books are printed with types produced specifically for the South Slavic Bible Society. However, the design of the letters was based on similar letters used for printed Glagolitic and Cyrillic books from the preceding period.[20] The Glagolitic and Cyrillic letter graphemes that occur in **G** and **C** are shown in Table 3.2.

---

[17] Cf. Damjanović, 'Kakav je jezik', 137f, who bases his conclusions on the analysis of the language of the prefaces to the two editions, in which the influence of the *New Testament* textual tradition can be considered to be of only minor importance. Cf. also Kuštović, 'Jezik', who, based on an analysis of the verb forms in the Gospel according to Saint Mark, comes to a similar conclusion.

[18] Cf. Bunčić et al., *Biscriptality*, 171.

[19] However, this does not of course exclude the possibility that some potential readers were literate in more than one alphabet (for example, in Croatian Glagolitic sources the use of Cyrillic letters is well attested, albeit sporadically; cf. Gadžieva et al., *Hrvatski crkvenoslavenski jezik*, 55f). For a more detailed discussion of the intended readership of Glagolitic and Cyrillic Protestant publications, see Jembrih, 'Pogovor uz pretisak ćiriličkoga *Novoga testamenta*', 77–82.

[20] For general descriptions of early Cyrillic printed editions see Nemirovskiĭ, *Slavi͡anskie izdani͡ia*, vols. 1 and 2; for early Glagolitic printed editions see Kruming, *Svodnyĭ katalog*. The fonts used in **G** and **C** were created by Hans Hartwach and Simon Auer in Nürnberg in 1560 (Glagolitic) and in Urach in 1561 (Cyrillic); see Vorndran, *Südslawische Reformationsdrucke*, 5f, who also identifies the design sources as earlier Croatian Glagolitic books printed in Venice and Senj, and previous Serbian Cyrillic Church Slavonic books printed in Venice, as well as the famous Cyrillic Bible books printed in Prague earlier during the sixteenth century by Skorina. Kruming identifies seven different Glagolitic and Cyrillic fonts created by Hans Hartwach (*Svodnyĭ katalog*, 148f, nos. 13–14, 20, 32–5).

Table 3.2 *Glagolitic and Cyrillic letter graphemes in* **G** *and* **C**

Glagolitic letter	Transliteration	Cyrillic letter	Transliteration
ⰰ	a	Ⰰ	a
ⱂ	b	Ⰱ	b
ⱆ	v	Ⰲ	v
ⰳ	g	Ⰳ	g
ⰴ	d	Ⰴ	d
ⰵ	e	ⰵ	e
		ⰵ	ê
ⰶ	ž	Ⰶ	ž
ⰷ	ż	Ⰷ	ż
ⰸ	z	Ⰸ	z
ⱑ ⱑ	ï		
ⰹ	i	Ⰹ	i
		Ⰺ	ı
ⰻ	ĵ		
ⰽ	k	Ⰽ	k
ⰾ	l	Ⰾ	l
ⰿ	m	Ⰿ	m
ⱀ	n	Ⱀ	n
ⱁ	o	Ⱁ	o
		Ⱉ	ô
ⱂ	p	Ⱂ	p
ⱃ	r	Ⱃ	r
ⱄ	s	Ⱄ	s
ⱅ	t	Ⱅ	t
ⱆ	u	ⱆ, ⱆⱆ	u
		ⰲ, ⱛ	ẏ
		Ⱔ	ι̣
ⱓ	û	Ⱓ	û
ⱇ	f	Ⱇ	f
ⱈ	h	Ⱈ	h
ⱌ	c	Ⱌ	c
ⱍ	č	Ⱍ	č
		Ⱍ	ķ
		Ⱚ	ċ
ⱎ	š	Ⱎ	š
ⱋ	ĉ		
		Ⱋ	ŝ
ⰺ	ь	Ⱐ	ь
ⱑ	ě	Ⱑ	ě
		Ⱔ	â

Of these letters, the Glagolitic *ż* and *ï*, and the Cyrillic *ı*, *ẏ*, *ι̣* and *ķ*, are used only as numerals; cf. below, Table 3.4.

The transliteration of the Glagolitic letters follows Gadžieva et al., *Hrvatski crkvenoslavenski jezik*, 49f.

Table 3.3 *Glyph pairs that can be analysed as allographs of the same grapheme*

Grapheme	Transcription	Allographs	Transcription
<Ⰲ>	<v>	Ⰲ, Ⰲ	$\|v_1\|$, $\|v_2\|$
<Ⰰ>	<d>	Ⰰ, Ⰰ	$\|d_1\|$, $\|d_2\|$
<ⱃ>	<r>	ⱃ, ⱃ	$\|r_1\|$, $\|r_2\|$
<ⰻ>	<i>	ⰻ, ⰻ	$\|i_1\|$, $\|i_2\|$
<Ⱆ, оу>	<u>	Ⱆ, оу	$\|\bar{u}\|$, $\|o\ddot{y}\|$

For the use of the symbol | to indicate allographs (in contrast to graphemes), see Fuhrhop and Buchmann, 'Die Längenhierarchie', 135.

As a general trend, most Glagolitic letter graphemes in **G** have only one standard allograph, whereas the Cyrillic letters that are attested in **C** require a graphematic analysis in terms of graphemes versus allographs. A careful analysis of the printed text shows that there are at least five pairs of glyphs that can be analysed as exhibiting an allographic relationship, that is, as being allographs of a common grapheme. The graphemes with considerable allographic variation include <v>, <d>, <r>, <i> and <u>; cf. Table 3.3.

The distribution of the two <v> allographs, $\|v_1\|$ and $\|v_2\|$,[21] seems to be more or less random, with the same word spelled sometimes with $\|v_1\|$, sometimes with $\|v_2\|$: cf. *Slo$\|v_1\|$o* versus *Slo$\|v_2\|$o*, both 130v1; *Ži$\|v_2\|$otъ* 130v5 versus *Ži$\|v_1\|$otъ* 130v6; *I$\|v_2\|$anъ* 130v9 versus *I$\|v_1\|$anъ* 131r6. There is no reason to conclude that there would be any meaning or sound difference between the words printed with $\|v_1\|$ and $\|v_2\|$. Similarly, the distribution of the two <d> allographs, $\|d_1\|$ and $\|d_2\|$, also seems to be more or less random, with the same word spelled sometimes with $\|d_1\|$, sometimes with $\|d_2\|$: cf. *ô$\|d_1\|$ъ* 152r5, 152r23, 152v12 versus *ô$\|d_2\|$ъ* 152r1, 152r6, 152r15; *ka$\|d_1\|$a* 152v6 versus *ka$\|d_2\|$a* 152r22, 152v3; and so on. The same applies to the distribution of the two <r> allographs, $\|r_1\|$ and $\|r_2\|$: cf. *P$\|r_2\|$o$\|r_1\|$okъ* 131r21 versus *P$\|r_1\|$o$\|r_2\|$okъ* 131r26; *p$\|r_1\|$ide* 130v9, 130v16, 140v16 versus *p$\|r_2\|$ide* 140v12, 158v4; *$\|r_1\|$eče* 139v14, 141v8 versus *$\|r_2\|$eče* 139r24, 140r19, 140r27; and the like. The distribution of the two <i> allographs, $\|i_1\|$ and $\|i_2\|$, is similar to those mentioned above: cf. *lûd$\|i_1\|$* versus *lûd$\|i_2\|$* 139v19; *V$\|i_1\|$st$\|i_1\|$nu v$\|i_1\|$st$\|i_2\|$nu/* 140r19 versus *V$\|i_1\|$st$\|i_1\|$nu*, *v$\|i_1\|$st$\|i_1\|$nu* 140v6; *rad$\|i_1\|$* 141v5 *versus rad$\|i_2\|$* 141v4. From some of the examples given

---

[21] In the following examples, allographic variation is reflected in the transcriptions only where it is considered relevant for the discussion. In other cases, <v> indicates the presence of either $\|v_1\|$ or $\|v_2\|$, etc. Here and in the following examples, the symbol '/' indicates the end of a line.

here, there seems to be a tendency for $|i_2|$ to appear in the vicinity of the end of a line: cf., for example, $p|i_1|tat|i_2|/$ 144r15, $nev|i_2|$-$/deŝ|i_1|$ 144r21/2, $sagr|i_2|ŝ|i_2|$ $t|i_2|/$ 144r25. However, this does not appear to be anything more than just a tendency, as the examples also indicate that both $|i_1|$ and $|i_2|$ are printed at the end of a line, and there are many examples of $|i_1|$ in this position: cf. $hod|i_1|/$ 144v2, $uh|i_1|t|i_1|/$ 144v21, $uč|i_1|$-$/n|i_1|t|i_2|$ 145r23/4.

The distribution of the allographs of the grapheme <u> differs from the above in that one of the allographs, |оу̇|, is a digraph, that is, it consists of a sequence of two separate graphs, |о| and |у̇|. On its own, the graph |о| can also represent a separate grapheme <o>, but the graph |у̇| does not occur – except as a numeral – independently of |о|, and there are thus hardly any cases where it is unclear if an |о| represents the grapheme <o> or only the first part of the allograph |оу̇| of the grapheme <u>. The general impression is that the mono-graphic allograph |ū| occurs more frequently than the digraphic |оу̇|, which seems to have a tendency to occur in word-final position; cf. $bliz|$оу̇$|$ 139r22, $nêm|$оу̇$|$ 139v5, $hotiâh|$оу̇$|$ 139v13. However, the monographic allograph |ū| occurs in all positions, including word-final; cf. $sid|ū|$ 139v9, $bih|ū|$ 139v14, $vaistin|ū|$ 139v20. The remaining Cyrillic letters do not show any substantial allographic variation, that is, each grapheme can be assumed to be represented by a single allograph, much like the patterns in the Glagolitic version.[22]

With respect to numerals, both the Cyrillic and Glagolitic writing systems include the use of specific letters as numerals, a tradition that was inherited from Ancient Greek. According to Stephen Chrisomalis's typology, both the Glagolitic and the Cyrillic numerical notation systems are 'ciphered-additive and decimal'.[23] In **G** and **C**, the numerals indicated in Table 3.4 are used.[24]

The information contained in Table 3.4 indicates that the Glagolitic system follows the alphabetical order of the Glagolitic alphabet 'abvgde ... ', whereas the Cyrillic system is oriented towards the Greek alphabetical order 'αβγδε ... ', with the Greek letter *β* corresponding to Cyrillic *v* '2' rather than to *b*, which in the Cyrillic system has no numerical value. Consequently, there is a discrepancy between the two systems, with the Glagolitic letters' numerical values being one or two units higher than the corresponding Cyrillic letters' numerical values (cf.

---

[22] In **G**, the letters *i, n, o, t, ě* in certain cases occur together with the diacritical marks *dot* or *macron* < ¯ >. The graphematic status of these combined, composite graphs is not immediately obvious: they could be analysed as independent composite letter graphemes, or as a combination of separate graphemes (cf. Gallmann, *Graphische Elemente*, 12–14). In **C**, there is a similar problem with the analysis of the combination of the letters *n* with *macron* and *ŝ* with three dots above. Due to limitations of space, this problem cannot be analysed in detail here.

[23] See Chrisomalis, *Numerical Notation*, 13 (Table 1.1), 179f.

[24] In both systems, the letters' function as numerals is normally indicated by the presence of a diacritical mark, a 'titlo' < ˜ >, above the respective letter. For more details on the use of Glagolitic and Cyrillic letters as numerals see, for example, Đorđić, *Istorija*, 38–40; Gadžieva et al., *Hrvatski crkvenoslavenski jezik*, 54f; Karskiĭ, *Slavi͡anskai͡a*, 215–19.

Table 3.4 *Glagolitic and Cyrillic numerical notation systems attested in* **G** *and* **C**

Numerical value	Glagolitic numerals		Cyrillic numerals		
	Glagolitic letter	Transliteration	Cyrillic letter	Allograph	Transliteration
1	ⰰ	a	Ⰰ		a
2	ⰱ	b	В	ě	v ($\lvert v_2 \rvert$)
3	ⰲ	v	Г		g
4	ⰳ	g	Д	đ	d ($\lvert d_2 \rvert$)
5	ⰴ	d	Є		e
6	ⰵ	e	Ѕ		ż
7	ⰶ	ž	З		z
8	ⰷ	ż	И		i ($\lvert i_1 \rvert$)
9	ⰸ	z	Ѳ		t
10	ⰺ ⰺ	ï	І		ı
20	ⰻ	i	К		k
30	ⰼ	ĵ	Λ		l
40	ⰽ	k	М		m
50	ⰾ	l	Н		n
60	ⰿ	m	Ѵ, Ỿ	ẏ̄	ẏ
70	ⱀ	n	Ѻ, о		o
80	ⱁ	o	П		p
90	ⱂ	p	Ҁ	ȥ	ķ
100	ⱃ	r	Ρ	ā	r ($\lvert r_2 \rvert$)
200	ⱄ	s	Ϲ		s
500	ⱇ	f	Ф		f
1,000	ⱍ	č	҃А		₊a

The numerals '500' and '1,000' occur only in the numbers '1562' and '1563', indicating the respective publication years of **G** and **C**.

for example, Glagolitic *g* '4' versus Cyrillic *g* '3', Glagolitic *n* '70' versus Cyrillic *n* '50'). A particular feature of the Cyrillic numerals attested in **C** is the use of the letter *ẏ* for '60' both on the title page (where the year 1563 is written as ₊*a. f. ẏ. g.* [1,000 + 500 + 60 + 3]), and consistently also in the folio numbers. This use of *ẏ* with the numerical value '60' contrasts with the more common use of Cyrillic *ȥ ksi* for '60', and *ẏ* for '400'.[25]

Glagolitic and Cyrillic numerals are as a rule employed only in folio numbers and chapter headings, as well as in paratextual references to other Bible books; cf. the following examples: **G** 133r (first page of Jn 6): folio

---

[25] Cf. Jembrih, 'Pogovor uz pretisak ćiriličkoga *Novoga testamenta*', 107, who briefly mentions the use of Cyrillic *ẏ* for '60' in **C**, comparing it with the use of the more common *m* [sic] for the same numerical value in the Tübingen Cyrillic publications. For background on the use of *ķ* (*koppa*) for '90', see, for example Karskiĭ, *Slavianskaia*, 216.

number *rȳv* [133], chapter number *KAPITUL e* [6], paratextual references to: *Matei gï* [14], *Mar<u>ko</u> e* [6],[26] *Luka z* [9], *Ishod bï* [12], *g* [4], *Kral g* [4]; **C** 139r (first page of Jn 6): folio number *rl<u>t</u>* [139], chapter number *ż* [6] *KAP. ż.* [6], paratextual references to: *Rodove. g.* [3], *Devtero: ì* [18]. *la* [31], *Daniel v* [2]. *z* [7]. *t̲* [9]. However, in the main text of the Gospels, only spelled-out lexical numerals are normally used; cf. for example the following numerical expressions: **G** Jn 6:7 *Dvě sta pinez Kruha* 'two hundred pennyworth of bread', Jn 6:9 *pet kru<u>ho</u>v* [...] *i dvě Ribe* 'five loaves [...] and two fishes', Jn 6:10 *pet/ tisuĉi* 'five thousand', Jn 6:13 *od pet/ Hli<u>bo</u>v* [...] *i od dvěû Rib* 'of five loaves [...] and of two fishes'; **C** Jn 6:7 *Dvi sto pinezъ Kruga* 'two hundred pennyworth of bread', Jn 6:9 *petъ Hlebovъ* [...] *i dvi Ribě* 'five loaves [...] and two fishes', Jn 6:10 *petъ tisuŝъ* 'five thousand', Jn 6:13 *ôdъ petъ Hlibovъ* [...] *i ôdъ/ dvěû Ribъ* 'of five loaves [...] and of two fishes'.

3.2.2   Suprasegmental Graphemes

In the two sources, **G** and **C**, at least four different suprasegmental graphemes (supragraphemes) can be identified: {capitalisation}, {superposition}, {abbreviation} and {ligature}.[27] These supragraphemes can be described systematically with the help of two parameters, graphic effect and domain, where the latter includes graph sequence, word,[28] sentence, line, book chapter and book.[29]

In the earlier Slavic writing tradition, capitalisation is generally never attested; except for the presence of different types of decorative initials, neither the Glagolitic nor the Cyrillic letter inventories include any letter forms that can be classified as 'capitals'.[30] However, in the orthographic systems of both **G** and **C**, two varieties of the supragrapheme {capitalisation}, {initial capitalisation} and {general capitalisation} play prominent roles. For {initial capitalisation}, the graphic effect consists of the replacement of the first letter of the domain with its capital letter counterpart, whereas for {general capitalisation} all letters of the domain are replaced with their capital counterparts; cf. Table 3.5.

As the table indicates, {initial capitalisation} is normally applied to the domains *word* and *sentence*, and also to the domains *chapter* and *book*.[31] {General capitalisation}, on the other hand, seems to be applied only to the

---

[26] Here and in the following, the use of single underlining indicates the presence of a ligature.

[27] Here and in the following, names of supragraphemes are enclosed in curly brackets {}.

[28] The *word* domain is usually defined as a sequence of segmental graphs delimited by spaces or punctuation marks, that is, with no reference to the expressed meaning.

[29] The domains *book chapter* and *book* are here defined within the organisational context of the *New Testament*.

[30] For a general presentation of early Glagolitic and Cyrillic writing see, for example, Đorđić, *Istorija*; Ĭagich, 'Glagolicheskoe pis'mo'; Karskiĭ, *Slavi͡anskai͡a*.

[31] Obviously, in certain positions, the different types of {initial capitalisation} are neutralised: for example, the first letter of a sentence is also the first letter of a word. The domains *chapter* and *book*, however, at least in the investigated sources, take clear precedence, and no neutralisation is attested; cf. below.

Table 3.5 *Varieties of the {capitalisation} supragrapheme*

		Domain				
Supragrapheme variety	Graphic effect	Word	Sentence	Line	Chapter	Book
{initial capitalisation}	Replacement of the first letter of the domain with its capital counterpart	+	+		+	+
{general capitalisation}	Replacement of all letters of the domain with their respective capital counterparts	+		+		

domains *word* and *line*. {Word-initial capitalisation} occurs regularly in personal and geographical names, names of holidays, as well as (less regularly) in words indicating important concepts: *Svit* 'World', *Človik* 'Man', etc.; cf. the following parallel excerpts: **G** (Jn 1: 9–10) *Biše [ona] svitlost istinna, koě pro-/ svitlué svakoga Človika prihodečega na sa/ Svit. Na Světu biše, i svit poňem stvoren ě,/ a svit ňega nepozna*; **C** (Jn 1: 9–10) *Biše svit-/lostь istinna, va prosvičuê vsakoga Človika/ prihodešega na sa Svitь. Na Světu biše, i/ Svitь ponêmь stvorenь êstь, a Svitь nêga ne-/pozna*. The optional character of {word-initial capitalisation} is illustrated by its use in the **G** excerpt, above. Here, out of three instances of the word *svit* only one has (word-initial capitalisation}, whereas the **C** excerpt shows {word-initial capitalisation} for all three instances of *svit*.

When a main word is preceded by a preposition, different applications of {initial capitalisation} are possible:

(1) when there is a space between the preposition and the main word, normally the first letter of the main word is capitalised; cf. for example, **G**: Jn 2 *u Templu, iz Templa, od Templa/*, Jn 3 *u Enone*; **C**: Jn 2 *izь Templa*, Jn 5 *ka Ivanu*. However, at least in **C** (I have not been able to attest this use in **G**), there are also cases where {initial capitalisation} is applied to the preposition instead of the main word; cf. **C**: Jn 2 *V templu*;

(2) when there is no space between the preposition and the main word, {initial capitalisation} is as a rule applied to the graphic word as a whole (at least in **C**), which means that the first letter of the preposition is capitalised; cf. **C**: Jn 2 *Vkapernaumь*, Jn 5 *Vьtempli*, Jn 6 *Kfi-/lipu, Kьmoru*. In **C**, however, {initial capitalisation} can also be applied to the main word; cf. **C**: Jn 3 *kaIvanu, naNebo*, Jn 4 *vьGalileu*. The same phenomenon is occasionally also attested in **G**: cf. Mk 1 *uProrocih*.

{Sentence-initial capitalisation} occurs regularly in the first letter of every graphic sentence.[32] {Sentence-initial capitalisation} can be considered obligatory in both **G** and **C**; cf., for example: **G** (Jn 1: 9–11) *Biše [ona] svitlost istinna, koĕ pro-/svitlué svakoga Človika prihodečega na sa/ Svit. Na Svĕtu biše, i svit poñem stvoren ē,/ a svit ñega nepozna. Usvoe pride, i ñegoviga/ ne priěše*; **C** (Jn 1: 9–11) *Biše svit-/lostь istinna, va prosvičuê vsakoga Človika/ prihodešega na sa Svitь. Na Svĕtu biše, i/ Svitь ponêmь stvorenь êstь, a Svitь nêga ne-/pozna. Vsvoê pride, i svoiga ne priâše.*

{Chapter-initial capitalisation} and {book-initial capitalisation} occur in the first word of a Gospel book chapter and a Gospel book as a whole, respectively; cf. the following examples:[33]

(a) {Chapter-initial capitalisation}: **G**: Jn 2 (126v) *I NA treti dan*, Jn 3 (127v) *BIŠE Človik ot Fariseov*, Jn 4 (129r) *KADA pak Gospodin pozna*, Jn 17 (152v) *OVE riči govoril e ISUS*; **C**: Jn 2 (132v) *I NA treti dan'*, Jn 3 (133v) *BIše Človik*, Jn 4 (135r) *Kada paki Gospodinь pozna*, Jn 17 (159v) *OVE riči govorilь estь ISUS.*

(b) {Book-initial capitalisation}: **G**: Mt (1r) *KNIGA OD ROIST/va Isukrstova*, Mk (46v) *POČETAK EVANGELIA I/sukarstova*, Lk (105r) *U Dneh Iruda Krala Židovskoga*, Jn (124v) *I ISKONI biše slovo*; **C**: Mt (1r) *KNIGE ROISTVA ISUKR/stova*, Mk (49r) *POČETAK EVANGELьÂ ISU/krьstova*, Lk (79v) *BIše vadni Iruda Kralâ Židovskoga*, Jn (130v) *V Počelu biše Slovo.*

The application of these types of {initial capitalisation} results in capital letters with a particular design, as different types of 'initials'.[34] In both **G** and **C**, we can thus distinguish between three types of capital letters: a standard capital letter (which can occur anywhere in a line), a simple chapter-initial letter (with a height of two lines), and a more elaborately decorated book-initial character (with a height of four lines): cf. Tables 3.6 and 3.7.[35]

In addition to the main varieties of {initial capitalisation}, both **G** and **C** also feature an additional, optional 'one-letter-capitalisation' type, which is applied to the letter immediately following a character affected by {chapter-initial capitalisation}; cf. the following examples: **G**: Jn 5 (131r) *POtom bĕše dan Blagdana Židovskoga*, Jn 6 (133r) *POtom poide ISUS priko mora Galileiskoga*

---

[32] As a rule, a graphic sentence ends with a full stop <.>, whereas, for example, the comma <,> does not function as a divider between graphic sentences.

[33] Here and in the following, {chapter-initial capitalisation} is represented by a regular-sized bold italic capital (**B**), {book-initial capitalisation} by a bigger-sized bold italic capital (**B**).

[34] For a different analysis cf. Miklas, 'Zur Struktur', 62, who identifies a separate supragrapheme '*Schriftauszeichnung "Form"*', which is used in order to characterise formal differences between different types of initials.

[35] The use of the chapter and book initials are naturally limited to the letters that actually occur in these specific positions, and it is impossible to ascertain only on the basis of **G** and **C** whether all letter graphemes could in fact be represented by all three types of capital letter glyphs.

Table 3.6 *Types of Glagolitic capital letters attested in* **G**

Letter grapheme	Standard capital	Chapter initial	Book initial
b	Ⱎ	Ⱎ	
v	Ⱇ	Ⱇ	
i	Ⰻ	Ⰻ	Ⰻ
k	Ⰽ	Ⰽ	Ⰽ
p	Ⱂ	Ⱂ	Ⱂ
u	Ⱆ	Ⱆ	Ⱆ

Table 3.7 *Types of Cyrillic capital letters attested in* **C**

Letter grapheme	Standard capital	Chapter initial	Book initial
b	Б	Б	Б
v	В	В	В
k	К	К	К
p	П	П	П

ko / e Tiberiĕtsko, Jn 7 (135v) *POtom toga hoĕše ISUS u Galilei.* The same type of capitalisation also occurs at the beginning of Jn 8 (137v) *POide tada ISUS na goru Maslinsku*, Jn 10 (141v) *VIstinu, vistinu govoru vam*, Jn 11 (143r) *BĚše nĕki nemočnik imenom Lazar iz Betanie* and Jn 12 (145r) *PRed šestimi dni Vazma*; **C**: Jn 5 (137r) *POtomь biše danь Blagdana Židovskoga*, Jn 7 (142r) *POtomь toga hoâše ISUS Vgalilei*, Jn 8 (144r) *PÔide tada ISUS na Goru Maslinsku*, Jn 10 (148r) *VIStinu*[36] *vistinu govoru vamь*, Jn 11 (149v) *BIše niki nemočnikь imenomь Lazarь izь Be/tanie*, Jn 12 (151v) *PRedь šestimi dni Vazma*.

In both **G** and **C**, the {general capitalisation} supragrapheme is considerably less common than {initial capitalisation}, and is applied only to the domains *word* and *line*. Here, the supragrapheme results in the replacement of all letters

[36] In this example, two letters immediately following the initial are, exceptionally, capitalised.

within the respective domain by their standard capital letter counterparts. {Word capitalisation} occurs regularly in all forms of the name *ISUS* 'Jesus', as well as in possessive adjectives based on the same name (*ISUSOVE* etc.).[37] Occasionally, {word capitalisation} is also attested in the very first word of a chapter, where it is combined with {chapter-initial capitalisation}; cf. **G**: Jn 3 (127v) *BIŠE Človik ot fariseov*, Jn 4 (129r) *KADA pak Gospodin pozna*, **C**: Jn 17 (159v) *OVE riči govorilь estь ISUS*. {Line capitalisation} is attested only at the beginning of a book, and is then combined with {book-initial capitalisation}; cf. **G**: Mt 1 (1r) *K̲NIGA OD ROIST/va Isukrstova*, Mk 1 (46v) *P̲OČETAK EVANGELIA I/sukrstova Sina Božjega, kako je / pisano uProrocih.*; **C**: Mt (1r) *K̲NIGE ROISTVA ISUKR/stova*, Mk (49r) *P̲OČETAK EVANGELьÂ ISU/krьstova*. The consistent application of the {capitalisation} supragrapheme in the orthographies of both **G** and **C** should be considered an important innovation, compared to the earlier writing traditions. As shown, the different {capitalisation} varieties seem to function more or less similarly within the orthographies of our sources. In both systems, both {initial capitalisation} and {general capitalisation} are applied to the same domains, the only difference consisting in the different shapes of the actual letters. However, there are also some differences: the most important one seems to be the possibility in **C** of the strict application of {word-initial capitalisation} also to graphic words beginning with a preposition, such as, for example, Jn 2 *Vkapernaum'*; whereas in **G**, {word-initial capitalisation} seems always to be applied only to the main word in such combinations.

In contrast to {capitalisation}, the {superposition} supragrapheme is well attested in the earlier Glagolitic, and, more commonly, in the earlier Cyrillic writing traditions.[38] The graphic effect of the {superposition} supragrapheme is achieved by replacing the last letter of the domain with a smaller variant of the same letter, and placing this letter above the preceding letter. As a rule, the domain for this supragrapheme includes only two consecutive letters, both of which belong to the same graphic word. In both **G** and **C**, the {superposition} supragrapheme appears only rarely, but it is clearly much more productive in **C** than in **G**. In **G**, the only case of {superposition} seems to be attested with the letter sequence *ot*, in which the regular *t* is replaced by a smaller variant of the same letter placed above the *o* ꙩ (cf. the same letter sequence without {superposition}: ꙩꚍ); cf. Jn 1 (124v, line 9) *učini o̲t Svitlosti*, (125r) *o̲t Otca*, Jn 2

---

[37] {Word capitalisation} can be combined with the supragrapheme {abbreviation} (cf. below): thus, the abbreviated form of 'ISUS' ('IS') is also capitalised, including possible declensional endings, such as, for example, the genitive sg. ending -*a*; cf. **G** Jn 12 (145v): *i prideše ne listo ISA radi*.

[38] See, for example, Đorđić, *Istorija*, 186f; Gadžieva et al., *Hrvatski crkvenoslavenski jezik*, 60; IAgich, 'Glagolicheskoe pis'mo', 216.

(126v) *ot̲ Ga/lilee* etc.[39] As these examples indicate, {superposition} is common with the preposition *ot*, but the same preposition is also attested without {superposition}; cf. Jn 1 (124v, line 11/12 *iskaže ot svi/tlosti*. In sequences other than in the preposition *ot*, I have not found any examples of the use of the {superposition} supragrapheme.

In **C**, on the other hand, {superposition} is attested not only in the preposition *ôt* and the verbal prefix *ôt-*,[40] but frequently also in other letter sequences: *im, ih, mo, no, om, ho*.[41] The application of {superposition} seems to be at least partially conditioned by lexical and/or morphological factors: *im̲* seems to appear more frequently in case endings (instrumental sg.; dativ̲e pl.), *mo̲* in forms of the personal pronoun 'moi', *no̲* in forms of the pronoun 'on̲' and with the root *mnog-*, *ho̲* with the root *hoč-*. In addition, {superposition} seems to be more common in letter sequences placed near the beginning or end of a line than in letters placed in the middle of a line. Still, {superposition} is far from obligatory, and the majority of the *im, ih, mo, no, om, ho* letter sequences are not affected by {superposition}. Thus, in the orthographic systems of both **G** and **C**, {superposition} can be considered marginal.

Let us now move on to analyse patterns regarding the {abbreviation} supragrapheme. In both the Glagolitic and Cyrillic earlier writing traditions, abbreviations were frequently used, particularly, but not exclusively, in certain lexical items which were considered 'sacred' for Christianity, viz. *Isus* 'Jesus', *Hristos* 'Christ' and *Bog* 'God'.[42] However, in **G** and **C**, abbreviations are not very common, and the {abbreviation} supragrapheme, similarly to {superposition}, can be considered a marginal feature in both orthographic systems. The application of {abbreviation} consists in the deletion of certain letters in a graphic word, and, notably, is always combined with the supragrapheme {word capitalisation} in both **G** and **C**; cf. above. In **G**, the {abbreviation} supragrapheme is used mainly for the word *Isus*, but only optionally; in most cases the name *Isus* is spelled out entirely; cf. **G** 145v *ISA radi* (for 'ISUSA

---

[39] Here and in the following, {superposition} is indicated with <u>double underlining</u>.

[40] Cf. Jn 2 *ôt̲ Tĕmpla*, Jn 3 *ôt̲/ duha*, Jn 5 *ôt̲ Ôtca*, Jn 8 *ôt̲ vasь, ôt̲ počela*, Jn 9 *ôt̲/ Boga*, Jn 15 *ôt̲nimlêtь*, Jn 21 *ôt̲/govoriv*, etc. In the word *ôtac̲*, {superposition} is also sometimes combined with {initial capitalisation}, cf. Jn 6 *Ôt̲/acь, Ôt̲/ci*.

[41] Cf., for example, Jn 10 *ih̲, nih̲, slĕpih̲*, Jn 9 *mi vidim̲o*, Jn 8 *kam̲o*, Jn 21 *ka/mo̲*, Jn 16 *moi̲, mo̲/ga*, Jn 20 *mo̲/mu*, Jn 14 *sam̲omu*, Jn 10 *onom̲u/*, Jn 12 *ôno̲/ga*, Jn 18 *ôno̲ga*, Jn 5 *mno̲žstvo*, Jn 6 *Mno̲/zibo*, Jn 7 *ôt mno̲ž/stva*, Jn 8 *Mno̲ga*, Jn 20 *Ženo̲*, Jn 6 *pisano̲*, Jn 3 *Ženiho̲/va*. All types are noted also by Jembrih ('Pogovor uz pretisak ćiriličkoga *Novoga testamenta*', 107), who, however, does not provide any examples.

[42] See, for example, Đorđić, *Istorija*, 184f; Gadžieva et al., *Hrvatski crkvenoslavenski jezik*, 59f; IAgich, 'Glagolicheskoe pis'mo', 215f.

radi', 'for Jesus's sake'), versus *ISUS* passim. An indication of the functional equivalence of the abbreviated and non-abbreviated forms of *Isus* is attested at the break between 144v and 145r, where the name is spelled *ISъ* as a catchword at the bottom of 144v, but *ISUS* as the first word at the top of 145r. Occasionally, *IS* occurs together with *H*; cf. **G** 137r (Jn 7) *ISHъ* (for 'ISUS HRISTOS'). The root *Bog/Bož*- is abbreviated only as an exception; cf. **G** 147r (Jn 12) *BU* (for 'BOŽьÛ'; cf. the catchword *Božьû* at the bottom of 146v), but in most cases it is used in an unabbreviated form; cf., for example, **G** 141r (Jn 9) *Bog*, *Bog*, *Boga* (with two of the three unabbreviated examples on this page including the ligature *Bo*; cf. below). In **C**, {abbreviation} is even rarer than in **G**, but some isolated examples are attested; cf., for example, **C** 131r (Jn 1) *po ISHU* (for 'po ISUSU HRISTU'), 143v (Jn 7) *ISHT* (for 'ISUS HRISTOS').

Finally, the {ligature} supragrapheme has the graphic effect of joining two (or in some cases three) letters within the same graphic word into a combined graph.[43] Ligatures are attested in both the Cyrillic and Glagolitic earlier writing traditions, particularly in the Croatian Glagolitic tradition. Here, the earlier 'round' Glagolitic letter forms were replaced by 'angular' letter forms, which offered ample opportunities for the joining of letters.[44] In **G**, the use of the {ligature} supragrapheme does not seem to be obligatory in any particular context, but it is clearly a very important feature of the orthographic system, as it is attested at least once on nearly every line of the text in this source. In the orthographic system of **C**, on the other hand, the use of ligatures is not attested, and this is thus one of the most obvious differences between the two sources. For an example of the abundant use of the {ligature} supragrapheme in **G**, see Table 3.8, which includes the different ligatures attested in the first paragraph of the text of Jn 6 (26 lines on 133r plus the first four lines on 133v). In the thirty lines of the selected paragraph, there are altogether sixty-nine ligatures, which means that there are approximately two ligatures per line.

Table 3.8 suggests that the most common two-letter ligatures are *ko* ↗ (cf. the letter sequence *ko* 4ⴀ without {ligature}, attested only once in the same text

---

[43] Cf. Miklas, 'Zur Struktur', 63, who uses the designation '*Sonderligatur*' (special ligature) for this supragrapheme. From a typographical point of view, ligatures are of course individual, indivisible entities in the same way as ordinary letters, but from a functional point of view it is more fruitful to analyse these glyphs as combinations of a sequence of two or more segmental graphemes and the suprasegmental grapheme {ligature}; cf. also Gallmann, *Graphische Elemente*, 104.

[44] For detailed discussion of the use of ligatures in the Glagolitic writing tradition, see, for example, Gadžieva et al., *Hrvatski crkvenoslavenski jezik*, 60f; ĨAgich, 'Glagolicheskoe pis'mo', 216–26; Lunt, 'Ligatures'; Žagar, *Grafolingvistika*, 405–27.

Table 3.8 *Two-letter ligatures in **G**, Jn 6, first paragraph*

	a	d	o	r	û	Total
b			1	2		3
v			6	1		7
g		1	7	2		10
z	5					5
k			16			16
l					3	3
m			2			2
n			2			2
p	1		3	3		7
t			10	2		12
h			2			2
Total	6	1	49	10	3	69

excerpt) and *to* ⰞⰔ (cf. the letter sequence *to* ⰞⰞⰃ, which, however, is not attested in the same excerpt). These two ligatures are attested altogether twenty-six times in the analysed paragraph, and the {ligature} supragrapheme can be considered almost obligatory in these letter sequences. Outside of the selected excerpt, other ligatures are also not uncommon. These include, for example the two-letter ligature *tv* ⰞⰞⰁ (cf. without the ligature ⰞⰞⰁⰁ) and the three-letter ligature *tvo* ⰞⰔⰁ (cf. for example, Mt 6 ⰞⰔⰁⰀⰓⰔ *tvoĵe*).

3.3   Comparison of the Orthographies

Having surveyed the most important graphematic peculiarities in the respective Glagolitic and Cyrillic orthographies of **G** and **C**, we are now in a position to draw a number of conclusions for the different grapheme types. Among the segmental graphemes, the grapheme inventories of the two sources are in general quite similar. However, the Cyrillic system, similar to all early Cyrillic orthographies, includes the digraph *oy*. This digraph is made of two segmental glyphs, of which the second, at least in some orthographies, never occurs on its own.[45] More importantly, allographic variation is much more pronounced in the Cyrillic system than in the Glagolitic system, where it is virtually absent, and almost every letter grapheme has only one single allograph. As for the numerals, the

---

[45] The Cyrillic digraph is based on the similar Greek digraph <ου>, and is thus one more example of the close relationship between Cyrillic and Greek orthography.

Table 3.9 *Comparison of the orthographic systems in **G** and **C***

		G	**C**
Segmental graphemes	Letters	almost no allographic variation	considerable allographic variation
	Numerals	standard inventory	standard inventory (with certain exceptions)
Suprasegmental graphemes	{capitalisation}	attested	attested
	{superposition}	uncommon	regularly attested
	{abbreviation}	only particular cases	only particular cases
	{ligature}	very common	not attested

Glagolitic system is, as expected, based on the alphabetical order of the Glagolitic alphabet; whereas the Cyrillic numerals attested in **C** present a more idiosyncratic picture, including the consistent use of *ẏ* as the numeral '60', which contrasts with the more common use of Cyrillic ѯ *ksi* for the same numeral. However, when it comes to suprasegmental graphemes, the differences are more striking, particularly for {superposition} and {ligature}. The former is clearly more productive in **C** than in **G**, but for {ligature} the situation is reversed: no ligatures are attested in **C**, whereas **G** is characterised by an abundant use of ligatures. The {capitalisation} and {abbreviation} supragraphemes, on the other hand, appear to be applied more or less in a similar way in both sources, even if the possibility in **C** of a strict application of {word-initial capitalisation} also to graphic words beginning with a preposition should be mentioned as noteworthy. Also worth mentioning is the functional connection between {abbreviation} and {word capitalisation} in both sources. The overall similarities within and differences between the Glagolitic and Cyrillic orthographic systems attested in the two sources is summarised in Table 3.9.

After the comparative description of the Glagolitic and Cyrillic systems in the two *New Testament* sources, let us now return to the biscriptality discussion. As already stated above, the biscriptal situation between our two sources is characterised as 'diatopic scriptal pluricentricity', which means that two scripts are used for the same language.[46] The use of the term *scriptal pluricentricity* does not account for possible similarities or differences between the two scripts

---

[46] Bunčić et al., *Biscriptality*, 168ff argue convincingly that the reason for this use of two different scripts in publications aimed for the literate Croatian-speaking population can be assumed to be that the majority of this population was 'monoscriptal', that is, they knew only one script, either Glagolitic or Cyrillic. This, however, does not exclude other possibilities; cf. above, Section 3.1.

participating in this type of biscriptal situation. The differences between the situations of scriptal pluricentricity mentioned by Bunčić et al. (Nāgarī/ Arabic for Hindi/Urdu, Runic/Latin for Old Norse, and Cyrillic/Latin for Modern Serbian)[47] are analysed from an external, sociolinguistic perspective, but they are obviously also different from an internal, grapheme-systematic perspective. For example, in Modern Serbian there is almost complete biscriptal isomorphism between the Cyrillic and Latin orthographies, the only difference being the choice of glyphs. However, this is not the case for the sixteenth-century Glagolitic and Cyrillic systems attested in **G** and **C**, where, as discussed above, the biscriptal isomorphism differs considerably between the different grapheme classes.[48] For a more systematic discussion of biscriptal isomorphism, it is useful to distinguish between isomorphism on two different levels, the *system level* and the *grapheme level* (where the latter is understood to include both segmental and suprasegmental graphemes).

On the system level, most grapheme classes exhibit high degrees of biscriptal isomorphism. Among the segmental graphemes, both the Glagolitic and Cyrillic systems include similar types, and the letters are related in more or less the same way to both distinctions in meaning and distinctions in sound. The same situation can be observed for the numerals: in both the Glagolitic and Cyrillic systems numerals are structured the same way. Similarly, both {superposition} and {abbreviation} exhibit a high degree of isomorphism, as the relevant domains correspond almost exactly to each other. However, {capitalisation} seems to show a somewhat lower degree of isomorphism, as the Cyrillic domains for this supragrapheme in addition to the isomorphic *graphic word* domain also include at least an occasional use of a domain *semantic word*. Finally, as the {ligature} supragrapheme is attested only in the Glagolitic orthography under investigation, there can be no isomorphism with any comparable feature in the Cyrillic orthography of **C**. On the grapheme level the situation is more varied, with only {capitalisation} and {abbreviation} exhibiting a high degree of isomorphism, whereas {superposition} does not show isomorphism to the same degree: in **G**, {superposition} is attested only for the domain <ot>, whereas in **C** it is applied to several other graph sequences as well. For the letter and numeral graphemes, the presence of allographic variation in **C** entails a number of one-to-two relationships between **G** and **C** on the glyph level, and the use of different graphemes for the same numeral (or,

---

[47] Bunčić et al., *Biscriptality*, 54–68.
[48] However, in order to get a more comprehensive picture of the sixteenth-century Glagolitic and Cyrillic biscriptal situation, the current investigation should be complemented by similar studies of a broader group of sources.

Table 3.10 *Biscriptal isomorphism for six grapheme classes in* **G** *and* **C**

	System level	Grapheme level
Letter graphemes	high	medium
Numeral graphemes	high	medium
{capitalisation}	high	high
{superposition}	high	low
{abbreviation}	high	high
{ligature}	no	—

conversely, different numerical values of the corresponding graphemes) is an important characteristic of the Glagolitic and Cyrillic scripts in general. The biscriptal isomorphism degrees for the grapheme classes are summarised in Table 3.10.

The present analysis of graphematic features of the Glagolitic and Cyrillic orthographies in **G** and **C** and their mutual relationships has established the significance of biscriptal isomorphism for the characterisation of certain biscriptal situations. By analysing the correspondences between the two orthographies, both on the system and grapheme level, the concept of biscriptal isomorphism further describes details of the scriptal pluricentricity biscriptal situation. Possibly, the same concept could also be applied to other biscriptal situations, but this needs to be further investigated in separate case studies.

4 The Emergence of Sentence-internal Capitalisation in Early New High German

Towards a Multifactorial Quantitative Account

Lisa Dücker, Stefan Hartmann and Renata Szczepaniak

Capitalisation has recently enjoyed the attention of a growing number of scholars from around the world and different languages, especially thanks to the rise of new models of analysis and frameworks of investigation. In German historical linguistics, the diachronic emergence of capitalisation has attracted widespread interest, as sentence-internal capitalisation in nouns is a distinguishing feature in German orthography and emerged in Early New High German (c. 1350–1650).[1] Relevant research on the topic has unveiled the roles of part of speech, reverence and animacy as driving forces for the spread of sentence-internal capitalisation in the sixteenth and seventeenth centuries.[2] Generally, nouns were more prone to capitalisation than other parts of speech. Those referring to people with a high social status (such as *Herzog*, 'duke') were however more likely to appear with a capital letter than words referring to a person of lower social status. Things or abstract concepts such as *Krieg* ('war') or *Hoffnung* ('hope') were capitalised even less frequently. However, most of these previous studies (with the exception of Claudine Moulin, who analyses Martin Luther's handwritten letters)[3] have been conducted on printed texts. Thus, what we know about the emergence of uppercase spelling in German mostly comes from texts that were thoroughly proofread and typeset by printers, who might have changed the original manuscripts.[4] As such, they are most likely the result of a collaborative effort. In contrast, this chapter presents a corpus study based on fifty-six handwritten protocols of witch trials from the sixteenth and seventeenth centuries (the so-called SiGS corpus).[5] This time period is commonly seen as a decisive period for

---

[1] See e.g. Bergmann and Nerius, *Die Entwicklung*; Kaempfert, 'Motive'; Moulin, *Der Majuskelgebrauch*; Rössler, 'Die Großschreibung'.

[2] See Bergmann and Nerius, *Die Entwicklung*; Risse, *Untersuchungen*; Weber, *Das Aufkommen*, among others.

[3] Moulin, *Der Majuskelgebrauch*.

[4] For the influence of printers, see Voeste, 'Proficiency and efficiency'.

[5] This corpus was created within the framework of the project 'Development of Sentence-Internal Capitalisation in German' (*Entwicklung der satzinternen Großschreibung im Deutschen*, SiGS),

the emergence of sentence-internal noun capitalisation in German.[6] This gives us the opportunity to investigate whether the factors for capitalisation in printed texts also hold true for handwritten texts created spontaneously by individual scribes. Moulin's analysis[7] suggests that the development of noun capitalisation in handwritten texts was delayed and rather erratic compared to that in printed texts.

Our study shows that, on the one hand, factors such as reverence and animacy hold for handwritten texts as well. On the other hand, however, we argue that the development of sentence-internal capitalisation was driven by a multitude of different factors, some of which have not been sufficiently acknowledged so far: word frequency, agentivity, syntactic function and socio-pragmatic factors, i.e. factors relating to interactions between social structure and language use. This can be seen from the different rates of capitalisation for nouns that are thought to be part of the same animacy class, like *Mann* ('man') and *Kind* ('child') or *Junge* ('boy') and *Mädchen* ('girl'), and the fact that the same noun can be found written in both upper- and lowercase within the same text.[8] Furthermore, we argue that our multifactorial approach can be applied as a framework for studying the diachronic development (increase as well as decrease) of capitalisation in the historical development of other written languages, e.g. Dutch and English.

The remainder of this chapter briefly discusses the current orthographic rules for sentence-internal capitalisation in German and offers a review of linguistic and experimental research pointing to potential benefits of this system. This in turn can help us understand why German still uses sentence-internal capitalisation[9] and why it emerged in the first place. This latter question lies at the heart of our overview of previous research on the historical development of sentence-internal capitalisation (Section 4.1.2). In this chapter, we specifically focus on the socio-pragmatic and cognitive factors that have been shown to drive the use of sentence-internal capitalisation in its earliest stages, such as reverence and animacy.

4.1   State of the Art

4.1.1   *Sentence-internal Capitalisation in Present-day Orthography*

In standard orthography of present-day German, sentence-internal capital letters are used to mark not only proper names and titles of honour, but all

funded by the German Research Foundation (DFG) in 2013–14 (SZ 280/2–1 and KO 909/12–1) and 2017–19 (SZ 280/2–3); see https://www.uni-bamberg.de/germ-ling/forschung-und-lehre/forschungsprojekte/sigs/ [last accessed 13 April 2020].
[6] See e.g. Bergmann and Nerius, *Die Entwicklung.*   [7] Moulin, *Der Majuskelgebrauch.*
[8] See Barteld et al., 'The usage'.
[9] Despite some failed attempts to abolish it; see Ewald and Nerius, 'Die Alternative'.

heads of noun phrases. Consider the examples in (4.1): in (4.1a) the noun *Haus* 'house' is capitalised; in (4.1b), the nominalised conjunction *aber* 'but' is marked by a capital letter.

(4.1) a. *das große Haus*
            the   big   house
       b. *das große Aber*
            the   big   but

While the writing systems of many other Germanic languages as well as Polish and French developed sentence-internal capitalisation at some point of their history as well,[10] German (subsequently also Luxemburgish, which developed out of a Mosel-Franconian dialect) is the only language that has maintained this convention, and has even codified it as an orthographic rule.[11] Sentence-internal capitalisation is said to be reader-friendly, since it highlights the word with the highest lexical weight within a noun phrase and thus supports and accelerates the decoding process. Experimental support for the hypothesis that the visual aspect (the sheer size) of capital letters benefits text comprehension comes from a series of experiments.[12] The results vary (not least due to different experimental designs) but they do suggest that capitalisation has a positive influence on the decoding process. Michael Bock and Bock et al.[13] measured the reading time required by Dutch students of German and German students of English for decoding texts in German, Dutch and English. Interestingly, Dutch students read Dutch texts with sentence-internal capitalisation faster than those with other deviations from standard orthography (like continuous or reversed capitalisation). Stefan Gfroerer et al.,[14] who made use of eye-tracking, observed an even stronger influence of sentence-internal capitalisation: here, Dutch participants read texts in Dutch presented with sentence-internal capitals even faster than texts written in the usual Dutch orthography. The results of the recent eye-tracking experiment by Dennis Pauly and Guido Nottbusch[15] – with a different design based on the contrast between garden-path sentences and sentences with only one syntactic interpretation – also suggest a (moderately) positive effect of sentence-internal capitalisation.[16] Pauly and Nottbusch found that, in noun phrases with upper-case letters, the gaze duration on the preceding adjective was longer than on the

[10] For an overview see Nowak, 'A diachronic contrastive study'.
[11] For the historical process of the orthographic rule-setting see Mentrup, *Groß- und Kleinschreibung*.
[12] See Bock, 'Lesen'; Bock et al., 'Funktion der Groß- und Kleinschreibung'; Gfroerer et al., 'Augenbewegungen'; and, most recently, Pauly and Nottbusch, 'Groß- und Kleinschreibung'.
[13] Bock, 'Lesen'; Bock et al., 'Funktion der Groß- und Kleinschreibung'.
[14] Gfroerer et al., 'Augenbewegungen'.
[15] Pauly and Nottbusch, 'Groß- und Kleinschreibung'.
[16] See also Nottbusch and Jonischkait, 'Einzeluntersuchungen'.

capitalised noun. In contrast, the gaze duration was longer on the noun than on the adjective when the noun was not capitalised. In their view, this suggests that the initial capital letter shortens the fixation on the noun, which can be preprocessed in the parafoveal belt (i.e. seen 'in the corner of the eye'). These findings are relevant for diachronic studies of sentence-internal capitalisation in both printed and handwritten texts, where capital letters differ from small letters in size and form.[17]

4.1.2 Previous Research on the Historical Development of Sentence-internal Capitalisation

Sentence-internal capital letters appeared as early as in the Old High German period (AD 750–1050). According to Brigitte Labs-Ehlert and Walter Rudolf Weber,[18] capitalisation was used predominantly for proper nouns at that time. Extensive use of capital letters came only with the invention of moveable-type printing in the middle of the fifteenth century. The economic interest of book printers on the one hand[19] and the emergence of the modern state and bureaucratisation on the other contributed to the development of well-structured written communication.[20] Capital letters were used to make books more attractive and better comprehensible for the growing (and demanding) reading public. In the period from the sixteenth up to the eighteenth century, a steadily increasing use of capitalisation in printed books has been observed and analysed by Weber, Manfred Kaempfert, Rolf Bergmann and Dieter Nerius, and Paul Rössler,[21] among others. They assume that the spread of sentence-internal capital letters started with an initial period of pragmatic use for reverence, emphasis and evaluation. At a later stage, however, morphological and semantic factors become more important, especially part of speech and animacy. For example, in the corpus compiled by Bergmann and Nerius,[22] nearly 20% of all adjectives were capitalised in the seventeenth century (as compared to more than 90% of all nouns). Subsequently, however, sentence-internal capitalisation of parts of speech other than nouns fell out of use.[23] For nouns, it has been observed that words with a higher degree of animacy (e.g. referring to humans) were capitalised more often and earlier than those with a lower degree of animacy (e.g. referring to objects or abstract concepts).[24]

---

[17] See Szczepaniak and Barteld, 'Hexenverhörprotokolle', 48f.
[18] Labs-Ehlert, *Versalschreibung*; Weber, *Das Aufkommen*.   [19] See Maas, 'Grundannahmen'.
[20] See Barteld et al., 'The usage'.
[21] Bergmann, 'Herausbildung'; Bergmann and Nerius, *Die Entwicklung*; Kaempfert, 'Motive'; Rössler, 'Die Großschreibung'; Weber, *Das Aufkommen*.
[22] Bergmann and Nerius, *Die Entwicklung*.   [23] See Wegera, 'Zur Geschichte'.
[24] Bergmann and Nerius, *Die Entwicklung*; Moulin, *Der Majuskelgebrauch*; Weber, *Das Aufkommen*; Risse, *Untersuchungen*.

Moulin's study of Martin Luther's personal correspondence[25] reveals that the same mechanisms hold for handwritten texts but that the increase in use of capital letters took place more slowly than in printed texts. Proper nouns are capitalised considerably more often than common nouns, and, within the group of common nouns, those referring to superhuman and human beings are more often written with a capital letter than nouns denoting objects or abstract concepts. Additionally, loanwords show higher rates of capitalisation than native words. In comparison to printed texts from the same time, Luther's letters are not as progressive. Compared to his letters, the printed editions of Luther's Bible translation from the same time period show nearly twice the amount of capitalisation.[26] Furthermore, Moulin's analysis reveals that capitalisation was extensively used in Luther's letters to mark the beginning not only of main clauses, but also of subordinate ones. As noted above, with the notable exception of Moulin, most previous studies on the emergence of sentence-internal capitalisation have been conducted on printed texts, which were the joint work of an (often unknown) team of printers and, hence, the result of a planned collaborative effort. In contrast, we have shifted the focus onto the products of individual handwriting. Our corpus consists of protocols of witch trials from the sixteenth and seventeenth centuries. With a few exceptions, each protocol is written by one person only. Hence, we are able to show how scribes with a high level of experience in writing judicial texts behaved in this period, during which capitalisation was experiencing an increase in frequency while at the same time being subject to much variation. In a previous study that we conducted on a small corpus of eighteen protocols, we were able to identify additional significant factors.[27] Using binomial logistic regression, we demonstrated the influence of animacy, compositional complexity[28] and frequency. The latter seems to play a role in inhibiting the capitalisation of highly frequent inanimates (objects and abstract nouns). In the present chapter, we re-examine those findings on an extended corpus of fifty-six protocols. Additionally, we suggest the influence of agentivity, syntactic function and socio-pragmatic factors.

4.2   The SiGS Corpus: Handwritten Protocols of Witch Trials

4.2.1   Corpus Composition

For the present study, we used the SiGS corpus consisting of fifty-six hand-written protocols of witch trials edited by Jürgen Macha et al.[29] The protocols

---

[25] Moulin, *Der Majuskelgebrauch.*   [26] See Risse, *Untersuchungen.*

[27] See Barteld et al., 'The usage'.

[28] Compositional complexity refers to the question of whether the (graphemic) word is part of a compound. For a detailed analysis of the interaction between capitalisation and compositional complexity, see Dücker, 'Die Getrennt- und Zusammenschreibung'.

[29] Macha et al., *Kanzleisprache.*

were written between 1570 and 1665 and are distributed across the geographic area of present-day Germany.[30] The corpus texts are not distributed evenly; nor were the locations of the witch trials.[31] The entire corpus compiled by Macha et al. contains sixteen protocols from the North West dialectal area, five from the North East, thirteen from the Middle West, four from the Middle East, nine from the South West and nine from the South East. For our explorative study of socio-pragmatic factors in Section 4.4 we consulted our so-called 'core' corpus of eighteen protocols, as used by Fabian Barteld et al.[32] The core corpus is a selection of protocols balanced for region, time and length: the texts are evenly distributed across all six dialectal areas and three time periods (1580–99, 1600–19, 1620–40) and contain between 1,000 and 2,000 graphemic tokens. All fifty-six protocols can be classified as semi-spontaneously produced texts. They are either direct transcripts of trials or revised copies of direct transcripts, and were typically each recorded by one scribe. They comprise between 550 and 2,870 words and are written in German cursive, which allows for a distinction between uppercase and lowercase letters, except for the letters <h>, <v> and <z>. Since the upper- and lowercase variants of these letters can be distinguished only by the size of the letters, and not by different shapes, words that start with <h>, <v> and <z> were omitted from the present study. For the analysis, all texts were semi-automatically tokenised, lemmatised and tagged for parts of speech. Two different levels of tokenisation were used to account for Early New High German spelling conventions: compound nouns, which are written as one word in present-day German (*Teufelstanz* 'devil's dance'), tended to be written as two separate words in the corpus texts, even though they form one syntactic word (*Teufelß dantz*, Alme 1630).[33] Conversely, contracted forms like *im* (*in dem* 'in the') combine two (syntactic) words in one (graphemic) word. One annotation layer therefore captures *graphemic* words, another *syntactic* ones.[34]

4.2.2   Semantic, Syntactic and Socio-pragmatic Annotation

In addition to the semi-automatic annotation, all nouns in the corpus were hand-coded for animacy using a customised annotation scheme.[35] Each text was coded by at least two different annotators. Mismatches between the annotations were discussed and resolved. Cases that remained ambiguous after discussion were omitted from the present study. Our annotation scheme used eleven categories

---

[30]   In the preface, Macha et al. point out that they also collected witch trials protocols from Austria and Switzerland but decided to limit their edition to texts from places within the political boundaries of present-day Germany.

[31]   Voltmer, 'Hexenverfolgungen'.   [32]   Barteld et al., 'The usage'.

[33]   In this study, corpus texts are referred to by a combination of place name and the year in which they were written according to Macha et al., *Kanzleisprache*.

[34]   See Barteld et al., 'The definition of tokens', for details.

[35]   Different from e.g. Zaenen et al., 'Animacy encoding'.

Table 4.1 *Fine- and coarse-grained animacy coding schemes*

superhuman (positive)	superhuman	human
superhuman (devil)		
human	human	
human (collective)		
animal	animal	animal
concrete	concrete	concrete
concrete (body part)		
concrete (collective)		
concrete (place)		
abstract (measure)	abstract	abstract
abstract		

and distinguished between human and superhuman entities (such as *God*, *devil* or *spirit*) as well as between different concrete and abstract construals. The *superhuman* category was necessary because of the ubiquity of elements belonging to the religious world view in the discourse world of the protocols. The fine-grained scheme that we implemented in our annotation can be broken down into more coarse-grained categories, as shown in Table 4.1. For the regression analysis reported in Section 4.3.1, we used the five-way hierarchy in the middle column of Table 4.1; for all other analyses, we used the four-way hierarchy in the rightmost column.

The annotation of animacy was context-dependent; e.g. a noun such as *ding* 'thing', which may refer either to a concrete object as in (4.2) or to an unspecified process as in (4.3), was coded as concrete or abstract, respectively, according to its use in the specific context.

(4.2)   *vnd ihr die bösen dinger zugebracht* 'and brought the bad things [referring to worms] to her' (Leipzig 1640)

(4.3)   *saget auch ein schlecht vndt gering ding sey, einem verzauberten zu helffen* 'also says it was a bad and vain thing to help an enchanted person' (Schweinfurt 1616)

At the phrase level, the data were double hand-coded for the syntactic functions of subject and object[36] and agentivity. Our annotation of agentivity comprises five categories (see Figure 4.1), and is based on David Dowty's concept of proto-roles:[37] rather than working with a discrete inventory of a dozen or more

---

[36] Only noun phrases coded as subject or object were included in the present study. Prepositional phrases and phrases used as adverbials were not taken into account. Nouns included in lists and other structures that did not allow for a syntactic interpretation were omitted.

[37] Dowty, 'Thematic proto-roles'.

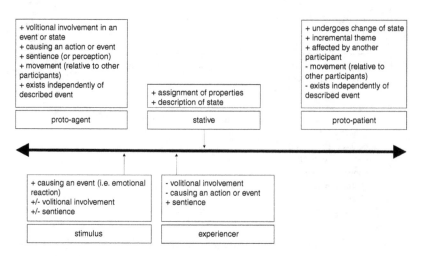

Figure 4.1 Overview of annotation criteria for semantic roles

semantic roles, we assumed that the multitude of semantic roles proposed in the literature cluster around a limited number of prototypes. This is in line with Dowty's idea that semantic roles can be seen as points on a continuum reaching from a proto-agent, which embodies all the attributes of a prototypical agent (volitional involvement, sentience or perception, causing an event or change of state, relative motion), to the proto-patient, embodying all the attributes of the prototypical patient (affected by the action, undergoing a change of state, incremental theme, stationary relative to other participants).[38] This means that a noun will be coded as a (proto-) agent even if it does not meet all of the criteria of the prototypical agent. To account for the special role of perception verbs,[39] we added *experiencer* and *stimulus* to the annotation scheme (see (4.4)).

(4.4)   *She*experiencer *likes books*stimulus.

(4.5)   *She*stative *is a linguist*stative.

(4.6)   *The picture*stative *is in the Louvre.*

While the experiencer is a sentient entity that does not cause any action, a stimulus is what causes the emotional reaction in an experiencer rather than any action and is often non-sentient. In addition to these, a fifth category *stative* was implemented; this category applies to nouns that are used to assign properties to

---

[38] See ibid., 572.   [39] Ibid., 579.

other participants of an event, since – in the absence of action – such nouns usually do not meet any of the criteria for either proto-agent or proto-patient. Consequently, the subjects in (4.5) and (4.6) do not cause any action, nor are they involved in any change of state, and whether they are interpreted as sentient or in motion is irrelevant. Hence, they are coded as stative.

The criteria that we employed in our annotation of semantic roles are summarised in Figure 4.1. For the socio-pragmatic analysis in Section 4.4, all nouns in the core corpus referring to human referents were additionally annotated for gender. For this annotation, we coded only nouns that could clearly be said to be female or male. Consequently, gender-neutral nouns such as *Kind* ('child') were not coded for gender. In the following section, we discuss the results of our corpus analysis. Section 4.3.1 first addresses the influence of animacy and frequency, replicating the results reported on in Barteld et al.[40] on the basis of a much larger dataset. Section 4.3.2 then adds a new explorative analysis that also takes semantic roles and syntactic functions into account.

4.3   Corpus Analysis

4.3.1   Animacy and Frequency

As mentioned above (Section 4.2.1), Barteld et al.[41] have shown the relevance of animacy and frequency for the use of sentence-internal capitalisation in the Early New High German witch trial protocols under investigation. This section replicates their analysis on the basis of the entire SiGS corpus. We fitted a binomial mixed-effects regression model to the data (all sentence-internal nouns) using lme4 package[42] for the R programming language.[43] Two variables were entered into the model as fixed effects: animacy and frequency. The fine-grained animacy annotation was broken down into a five-way distinction (*abstract, concrete, animal, human, superhuman*),[44] as too fine-grained a variable would lead to a rank-deficient model, i.e. a model that contains too few data points given the parameters that it is supposed to estimate. The reason for adding frequency as a factor is that we can expect more frequent words to have a fairly fixed graphemic form while we would expect a greater range of variation for low-frequency items.[45] In addition, random intercepts for lemma and protocol as well as random slopes for the fixed effect of animacy were

---

[40] Barteld et al., 'The usage'.   [41] Ibid.   [42] Bates et al., 'lme4'.   [43] R Core Team, *R.*
[44] The operationalisation of animacy here slightly deviates from that in Barteld et al. 'The usage', who distinguished between male and female humans. However, the natural gender of human entities is currently annotated only in the core corpus; we will return to this topic below.
[45] Cf. e.g. Kapatsinski, 'Lexical frequency effects'.

Table 4.2 *Coefficients of the fixed effects in the regression model*

	Estimate	Standard error	z value	Pr (> |z|)
(Intercept)	−2.01	0.25	−8.05	< 0.001***
Animacy – concrete	1.27	0.27	4.62	< 0.001***
Animacy – animal	1.7	0.59	2.87	< 0.001***
Animacy – human	1.82	0.38	4.81	< 0.001***
Animacy – superhuman	3.79	1.28	2.97	< 0.001***
$\log_{10}$(Freq)	0.39	0.2	1.9	0.06.
Animacy – conc × $\log_{10}$(Freq)	−0.85	0.26	−3.32	< 0.001***
Animacy – anim × $\log_{10}$(Freq)	−0.17	0.68	−0.25	0.8
Animacy – hum × $\log_{10}$(Freq)	−0.35	0.32	−1.11	0.27
Animacy – sup × $\log_{10}$(Freq)	−1.79	0.76	−2.36	0.02*

The z value is the quotient of standard error and coefficient estimate.
The p value is based on z.
*** < 0.001, ** < 0.01, * < 0.05, . < 0.1

added.[46] Table 4.2 shows the coefficient estimates of the model along with the standard error, the z value (the quotient of standard error and coefficient estimate), and the p value, which is calculated based on the z statistic: under the null hypothesis that the corresponding coefficient is zero (and, hence, has no effect), it indicates the probability (Pr) that the value of the predictor variable is bigger than the z value, in either direction (positive or negative), i.e. bigger than the absolute value of z, denoted $|z|$. In other words, it indicates how likely it is that a value as extreme as the respective estimate is observed under the null hypothesis that the variable has no effect. The asterisks and dot indicate the significance thresholds (*** < 0.001, ** < 0.01, * < 0.05, . < 0.1).

We used likelihood-ratio tests to assess the impact of the individual predictors. The idea behind the likelihood-ratio test is that a full model is compared against a reduced (= null) model that does not contain some of the terms. For instance, we can compare our model against a null model that has the same response variable and the same random effects, but only animacy or only frequency as fixed effects. Using the likelihood-ratio statistic, which, in a nutshell, compares the plausibility of two different models in the light of the given dataset, we can then check whether adding the predictor variable(s) that we left out in the null model significantly improves the performance of the model. A series of likelihood-ratio tests indicates that the use of the random intercepts and slopes mentioned above was warranted as the model performed

---

[46] Compositional complexity, which was used as a further predictor by Barteld et al., 'The usage', has not yet been coded in the entire SiGS corpus.

significantly better than models without the random effects for lemma and protocol. Importantly, the model also performed better than null models without animacy ($\chi^2 = 327$, $df = 22$, $p < 0.001$***) or without the interaction term between animacy and frequency ($\chi^2 = 15.7$, $df = 4$, $p = 0.003$**).[47] The index of concordance C, which assesses how well the model predicts the data,[48] indicated a very good fit ($C = 0.94$, considered 'outstanding discrimination').[49] All Variance Inflation Factors (VIFs) – which were used to check for potential multicollinearity, i.e. strong correlations between predictors that can severely influence the coefficient estimates – were below the threshold of 5, often mentioned as a rule of thumb in the statistical literature.[50] In sum, the present study confirms the results which Barteld et al. obtained on the basis of a much smaller sample: while the effect of animacy shown in earlier studies is clearly substantiated, animacy alone cannot explain the variation in the data.

The model indicates that there is an interaction between animacy and frequency that has an effect on capitalisation, but it does not tell us much about the nature of this interaction. Thus, it seems worthwhile to visually explore these variables in more detail. In general, the model suggests that highly frequent items are more prone to capitalisation than low-frequency items. This also becomes clear in the association plot in the lower section of Figure 4.2, which roughly distinguishes 'high-frequency' from 'low-frequency' items. This plot shows the so-called Pearson residuals obtained using a chi-squared test (used for measuring how the model results compare to the expectations under the null hypothesis that there is no influence of frequency). Pearson residuals indicate the extent to which the observed frequency differs from the expected frequency, which is calculated using probability theory (more specifically: by multiplying each column total with the respective row total and dividing the product by the grand total). The rectangles above the dashed line indicate observed frequencies that exceed the expected frequencies, while the rectangles below the dashed line indicate observed frequencies that are lower than expected frequencies.[51] The width of the rectangles in the lower section of the figure is proportional to the square root of the expected frequencies.[52] As the upper section of Figure 4.2 shows, items were considered

---

[47] The likelihood-ratio test assesses the difference between the two models by computing a chi-squared difference test over the likelihoods of the two models (the likelihood being a measure that quantifies the goodness-of-fit of the model to the data; the chi-squared test is explained in more detail below). The p-value, which quantifies how likely it is that the difference between the models is due to chance, is calculated on the basis of the chi-squared value χ^2 on the one hand and the degrees of freedom (df) on the other. The degrees of freedom, in this case, indicate the difference in variables between the model and a null model. A low p-value indicates that the two models differ significantly, which in turn suggests that the richer model fits the data better than the model with less variables.

[48] See Baayen, *Analysing Linguistic Data*, 204.

[49] Hosmer and Lemeshow, *Applied Logistic Regression*, 162.

[50] Levshina, *Linguistics with R*, 272.   [51] See Gries, *Statistics*, p. 188.   [52] Ibid.

Frequency and capitalisation

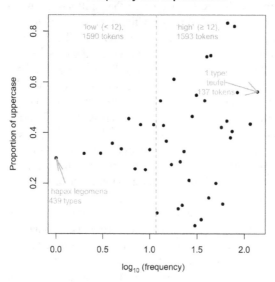

Case / frequency association plot

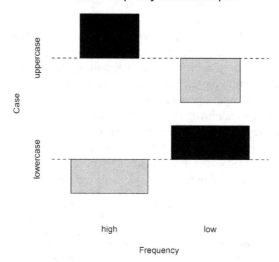

Figure 4.2 Upper half: proportion of uppercase tokens per (logarithmised) frequency value. Lower half: association plot for case/frequency in the SiGS data

Note: The plot in the lower half shows the Pearson residuals obtained using a chi-squared test. Black bars indicate that the observed frequencies are higher than expected; grey bars that they are lower. The vertical length of the rectangles indicates the extent to which the observed frequencies exceed the expected ones; the width of the rectangles is proportional to the square root of the expected frequencies.

members of the 'high-frequency' class if the respective lemma occurred twelve or more times in the data. This cut-off point is of course arbitrary but not entirely without basis. If we split the range of frequency values in our data – log-transformed to base 10, as in Figure 4.2 – in two halves, a cut-off point of 1.068 emerges. This logarithmised value corresponds to an absolute value of ~11.7. The upper section of Figure 4.2 shows, for each attested frequency value, the proportion of uppercase tokens for items that are attested with the respective frequency. For example, there are 439 *hapax legomena* in the corpus, i.e. types with a frequency of 1. As $\log_{10}(1) = 0$, they are represented by the leftmost point in the upper section of Figure 4.2. Of these 439 *hapax legomena*, 131 are uppercase, which corresponds to 30%. Unsurprisingly, the variance between the data points increases, especially so in the right half of the plot, where we find the 'high-frequency' tokens. Here, the number of *types* (lemmas) represented by each data point is much lower than in the left half of the plot. For instance, the rightmost data point represents only one single type, *teufel* 'devil', which occurs 137 times in the corpus (77 uppercase, which corresponds to 56%). As such, this visualisation is only marginally informative, which is why it is complemented by Figure 4.3, to which we will return shortly. Nevertheless, it can already give a first clue to an interpretation of the interaction between capitalisation and frequency. In the case of low-frequency lemmas, uppercase and lowercase tokens approximately counterbalance each other (with a slight tendency towards lowercase). In the right half of the plot, we arguably see more pronounced tendencies. For example, the highly frequent lemmas *gott* 'God' and *mann* 'man' show a clear tendency towards capitalisation, each occurring in uppercase in more than 80% of all instances. A chi-squared test (used for measuring how the model results compare to the expectations under the null hypothesis that there is no influence of frequency) shows that 'high-frequency' lemmas (i.e. lemmas occurring twelve or more times in the data) occur significantly more often in uppercase than 'low-frequency' ones ($\chi^2 = 22.5, df = 1, p < 0.001$), as shown in the lower section of Figure 4.2. Note, however, that the effect is fairly weak ($\varphi = 0.08$), which indicates that other factors are probably more decisive. Figure 4.3 spells out in more detail the interaction between frequency and capitalisation as presented in the upper section of Figure 4.2. In addition, it adds animacy to the picture.[53]

In order to increase readability, Figure 4.3 includes only nouns with a frequency ≥ 5. Interestingly, the higher-frequency abstract nouns all show a fairly clear tendency towards lowercase, while the picture is more nuanced in the remaining animacy categories. For concrete nouns, it is notable that *pulver* 'powder' and *trunk* 'drink' show a slight tendency towards capitalisation.

---

[53] Some lemmas appear in multiple panels as they can belong to several different animacy categories (see Section 4.2 above).

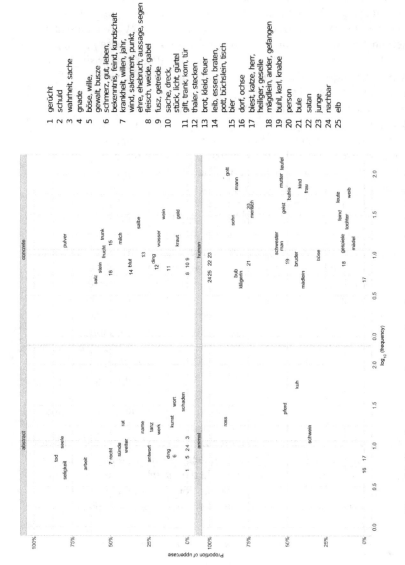

Figure 4.3 Log frequency and proportion of uppercase tokens per lemma, sorted by animacy

Note: For the sake of readability, some lemmas that share (approximately) the same frequency values have been replaced by numbers. The legend on the right-hand side of the plot shows the mapping between numbers and lexemes.

1 gerücht
2 schuld
3 wahrheit, sache
4 gnade
5 böse, wille,
   gewalt, busze
6 schmerz, gut, leben,
   bekenntnis, feind, kundschaft
7 krankheit, willen, jahr,
   wind, sakrament, punkt,
   ehre, ehebruch, aussage, segen
8 fleisch, weide, gabel
9 fusz, getreide
10 sache, dreck,
    stück, licht, gürtel
11 gift, trank, korn, tür
12 thaler, stecken
13 brot, kleid, feuer
14 leib, essen, braten,
    pott, büchslein, tisch
15 bier
16 dorf, ochse
17 biest, katze, herr,
    heiliger, geselle
18 mägdlein, ander, gefangen
19 buhl, kerl, knabe
20 person
21 bule
22 satan
23 junge
24 nachbar
25 elb

These words refer to items that often play a key role in the protocols. As such, the fact that these words are frequently capitalised could reflect the function of uppercase as a marker of thematic relevance. In the case of animals, the proportions of uppercase spelling cluster around 50% for the three high-frequency items (i.e. *ross*, *pferd* and *kuh*). The capitalisation of lemmas belonging to the *human* category seems to be highly variable. However, a closer look reveals that words referring to males like *junge* 'boy', *sohn* 'son' and *mann* 'man' almost exclusively occur with uppercase spelling, while some words referring to women, such as *weib* 'woman', show a clear tendency towards lowercase spelling. We return to this topic below (Section 4.4). Furthermore, words with a negative connotation like *böse* '(the) evil' and *gespiele* (roughly: 'mate'), which usually refer to the devil in the context of the witch trial protocols, tend to occur in lowercase.

These considerations show that high frequency alone probably cannot explain a scribe's choice for or against uppercase spelling. Nevertheless, the fact that some of the highly frequent nouns already show a clear tendency towards capitalisation may have helped pave the way towards establishing sentence-internal capitalisation as a general convention affecting all nouns in German writing. At this point, however, we still see much lexeme-specific variation even among the high-frequency items. We have already alluded to some potential explanations that go beyond the factors that were considered in the model reported above. In the following sections, we elaborate on further potential factors in more detail. First, we discuss the potential role of semantic roles and syntactic functions; then, we return to the socio-pragmatic factors just mentioned.

4.3.2   Agentivity and Syntactic Functions

As shown in the previous section, capital letters seem to be used to mark pragmatically, textually or semantically salient words. For this reason, we now consider the influence of the hierarchies of syntactic functions[54] and of agentivity. While these two aspects (syntactic functions and agentivity) often coincide, this is not always the case. This is why, for instance, Ronald Langacker[55] distinguished between role asymmetries, which belong to the level of conceptual content, and prominence asymmetries, which are imposed on events via linguistic coding. Passive constructions are a case in point: '*The man bit the dog* and *The dog was bitten by the man* represent alternate construals of the same conceived occurrence.'[56] In the passive sentence, syntactic prominence is assigned to the patient argument by virtue of occurring in sentence-initial position, which is

---

[54] See Dik, *Functional Grammar*.   [55] Langacker, *Cognitive Grammar*, 366.   [56] Ibid.

usually regarded as particularly salient.[57] If it is true that sentence-internal capitalisation is used to emphasise salient words and expressions in the period in question, then we can expect both 'role asymmetries' (operationalised here in terms of semantic roles) and 'prominence asymmetries' (operationalised in terms of syntactic functions) to be important determinants in capitalisation. It would be a highly questionable choice to add agentivity (operationalised by means of semantic roles) and syntactic function as further predictors in the model reported on in Section 4.3.1 above, since a high degree of correlation between the variables could be expected, which would violate one of the most important assumptions of the model.

Thus, we chose to use a more explorative method, namely hierarchical configural frequency analysis (see Appendix 4A).[58] This method computes multiple cross-tabulation tests over configurations of categorical data in order to identify 'types', i.e. configurations that occur with above-chance frequency in the data, and 'antitypes'.[59] The analysis was performed using a hierarchical configural frequency analysis script, known as *HCFA*, written by Stefan Gries for use with R.[60] The *p*-values were adjusted for multiple *post hoc* tests using Bonferroni correction, used to protect against false positives. Hierarchical configural frequency analysis computes chi-squared tests over all possible combinations of variables.[61] These combinations of factors are called configurations. As there are 540 configurations in total in our dataset, Appendix 4A shows only the significant types and antitypes involving the variable *case* (uppercase versus lowercase) and at least one more variable. The four leftmost columns in the Appendix indicate the respective configurations; the subsequent columns show the observed and expected values, the chi-squared value, the adjusted *p*-value, the significance level, and the effect size measure *Q*, which is used as a 'coefficient of pronouncedness'.[62]

When interpreting our results, it is important to keep in mind that the method starts from the null hypothesis that all configurations are equally probable. For obvious reasons, however, some configurations are more likely to occur than others; for instance, we tend to talk or write much more about humans than about other entities. More specifically, we tend to talk about what humans do, i.e. we talk about humans as agents. This is clearly reflected in the present data. For instance, the configuration *human – agent – subject*, exemplified in (4.7) and (4.8), is a highly significant type irrespective of case. If we assume a cline of animacy and agentivity as roughly sketched in Figure 4.4, with agentive humans in the subject position at one end and non-agentive abstract nouns in the object position at the other, we find that, in most cases, the configurations

[57] See e.g. Evans and Green, *Cognitive Linguistics*, 18.
[58] See e.g. von Eye, *Configural Frequency Analysis*; Hilpert, *Constructional Change*.
[59] See e.g. Gries, *Statistics*, 244.   [60] Ibid., pp. 248–9.
[61] See e.g. Hoffmann, *Preposition Placement*, 24.   [62] Gries, *Statistics*, 251.

'higher' on that scale tend to be more likely to occur in combination with *uppercase* than with *lowercase*, and vice versa. For instance, the observation that *human – agent – subject – uppercase* is a (slightly) more significant type than *human – agent – subject – lowercase* is very much in line with our hypothesis. On the opposite 'pole' of the animacy/agentivity scale, we find that *abstract – patient – object – lowercase* (exemplified in (4.9)) emerges as a highly significant type, while *abstract – patient – object – uppercase* does not (the latter is slightly more frequent than expected as well, but not significantly so; as such, it is neither type nor antitype).

(4.7)   *daruff **Clägerin** geantworttet* 'to which the **plaintiff** replied' (Schweinfurt 1616)

(4.8)   *wan **braut** vndt **brautgam** vor m Althar die handt zu samen geben* 'when **bride** and **groom** take each other's hands in front of the altar' (Friedberg 1620)

(4.9)   *damit sie die **wahrheit** sagen könne* 'so that she could tell the **truth**' (Augsburg 1625)

As we are interested in the potential influence of the individual factors irrespective of animacy, it seems promising to take a look at the distribution of uppercase and lowercase items across the different role and function categories for animates and inanimates separately, as shown in Figure 4.5. Again, the crucial impact of animacy shows up immediately; the average number of capitalisations is much lower in the *inanimates* category (which comprises the animacy levels *concrete* and *abstract*) than in the *animates* category (which consists of *humans* and *animals*). While the distribution of uppercase and lowercase items does not differ significantly between the role/function

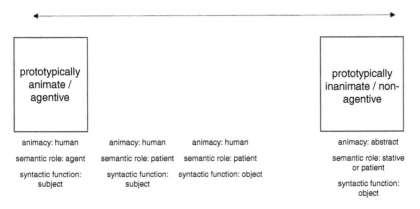

Figure 4.4 Idealised cline of feature configurations from prototypically animate/agentive to prototypically inanimate/non-agentive

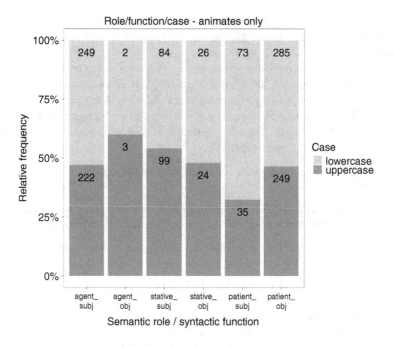

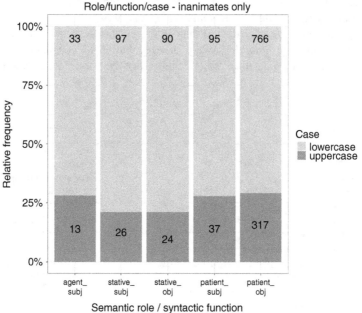

Figure 4.5 Distribution of uppercase and lowercase items across role/
function categories for animates (upper half) and inanimates (lower half)

Note: The combination agent/object is not attested for inanimates, which
is why the lower half has fewer variable levels than the upper half.

categories in the case of inanimates, there are at least slight differences in the *animate* category.

It is interesting to note, in connection with Figure 4.5, that, somewhat counterintuitively, the proportion of capitalised objects is higher than the proportion of capitalised subjects both for agentive and for patientive entities (but note that the absolute numbers are very small in the case of the former). This might point to the influence of at least two other factors. Firstly, the observation that, for example, 'patient_obj' has a higher percentage of capitalised nouns than 'patient_subj' might partly be explained by pragmatic factors. Some of the most frequent nouns referring to animates in the 'patient_obj' category refer to entities that play a key role in the accusations and testimonies reported in the protocols. For instance, *kuh* 'cow' (39 attestations, 15 uppercase; in object position: 25 lower, 19 upper), *pferd* 'horse' (23 attestations, 13 uppercase; in object position: 10 lower, 13 upper), and *rosz/ross* 'horse' (19 attestations, 17 uppercase; in object position: 2 lower, 17 upper) refer to animals that are often reported to be victims of spells cast by the accused persons. Secondly, as mentioned before, there is a certain amount of lemma-specificity. Some lemmas almost exclusively occur with a capital letter, others hardly at all. The most frequent items in the 'patient_obj' category are *gott* 'God' and *teufel* 'devil', which, as we have seen, show a strong tendency towards capitalisation. This is hardly surprising given the fact that they refer to supernatural entities, which also shows, once again, that the different factors discussed in the present chapter are closely intertwined.

4.4   Socio-pragmatic Factors in the Emergence of Capitalisation

Over time, the use of sentence-internal capitalisation became more systematic, to the degree that there are fairly clear capitalisation rules in present-day German. This is why Utz Maas uses the term 'grammaticalisation' to describe the diachronic development of sentence-internal capitalisation of German nouns.[63] In the time period investigated here, however, we have seen that we still find a large amount of variation. We have already seen that capitalisation is lexeme-specific to some degree. We argue that this lexeme specificity partly reflects what can be seen as the original function of capitalisation, namely pragmatic emphasis. Some lexemes are capitalised earlier and more consistently as authors tend to lay emphasis on the concepts that they denote. Conversely, some lexemes show a strong tendency towards lowercase spelling. As Figure 4.3 shows, terms denoting men are often very prone to capitalisation, while lexemes referring to women like *mädel* 'girl', *tochter* 'daughter' or *weib* 'woman' show a strong tendency towards lowercase spelling. This tendency

---

[63] Maas, 'Grundannahmen'.

can hardly be explained by the above-discussed factors of animacy, frequency, agentivity or syntactic functions. The distribution of *mann* 'man' and *weib* 'woman' across agent and patient roles as well as across subject and object position do not differ significantly. Thus, it seems plausible to assume that the differences in the use of uppercase spelling reflect a socio-pragmatic difference related to gender. From a patriarchic perspective, women rank lower in the social hierarchy than men. In texts going back to a context that is characterised by a strongly patriarchic society, it is hardly surprising that terms denoting men are emphasised more often than terms denoting women. In the SiGS core corpus, all nouns referring to humans were annotated for gender. Figure 4.6 shows the distribution of uppercase versus lowercase spelling for those nouns that are clearly identifiable as referring to a male or female person; (4.10) gives an example.

(4.10)   *Auch viel **Menner** vnnd **weiber*** 'Also many **men** and **women**' (Georg-
          enthal 1597)

The data from the SiGS core corpus suggest that terms denoting men are more systematically capitalised than terms denoting women. A mixed-effects logistic regression model was fitted to the subset of data annotated for gender (583 tokens, 251 female, 332 male), with capitalisation as response variable, gender as fixed effect, and the protocol as random effect. A likelihood-ratio test against a null model without 'gender' shows that the model fit decreases significantly if we omit this predictor ($\chi^2 = 30.03$, $df = 1$, $p < 0.001$). Further evidence for the influence of gender comes from a study by Lena Schnee[64] on the basis of the SiGS core corpus. She systematically distinguished the gender-specified nouns according to the roles in the trial played by the persons they referred to (defendant, witness, etc.). She was able to show that lowercase spelling was used significantly more often for females who appeared as defendants/accused persons than for females who were victims, witnesses, or plaintiffs. For nouns referring to male persons, by contrast, no such difference could be found.

4.5   Towards a Framework for Capitalisation
         in Early Modern Languages

At the beginning of our chapter, we made brief reference to research in capitalisation across languages, an issue to which we can now return. Existing work on the topic has shown that sentence-internal capitalisation emerged in other languages as well, e.g. Dutch, English and Danish, though it did not last there for a long time. Jessica Nowak presented the first empirical study on the spread of sentence-internal capitalisation in Dutch.[65] Her analysis

---

[64] Schnee, 'Gender und Großschreibung'.   [65] Nowak, 'A diachronic contrastive study'.

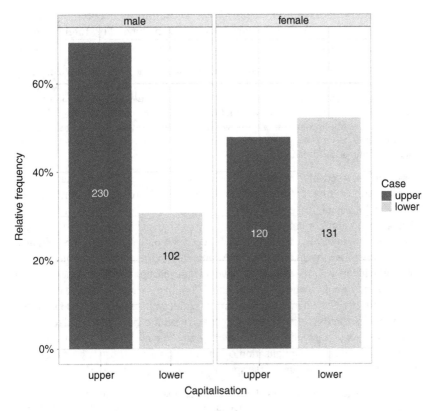

Figure 4.6 Capitalisation by gender

was based on translations of Genesis, Chapter 2 (*Old Testament*) in a corpus of 26 Dutch Bible editions from the fifteenth to the eighteenth century. Even though the Bible section under investigation comprises only approximately 750 graphematic words, Nowak's study yields some interesting results. Firstly, the earliest printed editions of the Bible from the late fifteenth century and the first quarter of the sixteenth century show almost complete absence of sentence-internal majuscules. Only in the second quarter of the sixteenth century was there a slow increase in the use of capital letters, mainly for reverence (capital-isation of *God*) and for emphasis in words of special thematic importance. While the use of capitalisation in this initial period – similarly to German – was pragmatically driven, the subsequent spread affected mainly nouns. Over time, capitalisation of concrete nouns became stable and reached more than 80% in the second half of the eighteenth century, while abstract nouns developed in the opposite direction. At the end of the period of investigation, the proportion of capitalised abstract nouns lay below 10%. Thus, the gap between higher and lower degrees of animacy became greater over time. For English, Noel Osselton observes

a steady rise in the use of initial capitals until about the year 1720, with a sudden drop after 1750. What evidently happened was that around the first decades of the eighteenth century printed English prose virtually achieved the situation which exists in present-day German, with all nouns given initial capitals. This meant that the 'extra' initial capital had clearly become a marker of word-class. Since it was then generally redundant, it could be dropped without inconvenience; and this is indeed [...] what was to happen within a few decades.[66]

Osselton analysed fifty randomly chosen prose passages from first editions of London printers from 1500 to 1800.[67] There is no information about the genre of the texts. Interestingly, he observed a development similar to German and Dutch. According to him, capital letters were either used to make a word more 'prominent' (i.e. pragmatically driven) or they depended on semantics, with animates being more prone to capitalisation than concretes and abstracts. A gradual spread of capital letters is observable in the seventeenth and eighteenth centuries, only to be followed by a dramatic decline around 1760. In his study on the use of capital letters in Early Canadian English from the eighteenth century, Stefan Dollinger analysed three texts (a diary, a newspaper and a semi-official letter).[68] He arrives at the conclusion that animacy did not play any role in the use of capitalisation. Interestingly, the rare capitalisation of common nouns in those texts indicates a socio-pragmatic use of uppercase spelling. As Dollinger observes,

we may hypothesize that the capitalized nouns are somehow 'more important' or 'higher valued' than the ones on the left [which are written in lowercase]. The interpretation may be as follows: a girl does not have the [same] social prestige as a lady does and friends are not one's social superior[s], whereas one's parents are.[69]

A more systematic and thoroughly corpus-based investigation of sentence-internal capitalisation in English as well as in other (not only Germanic) languages can therefore be seen as an important *desideratum* for future research. It could shed light upon the spread and possibly also upon the decline of capitalisation. Drawing on a corpus of handwritten protocols of witch trials, we have suggested a number of factors that influenced the variation between lowercase and uppercase spelling in the Early New High German period, i.e. at a time when the now-standard convention of sentence-internal capitalisation was just emerging. Our results lend further support to the findings of Bergmann and Nerius, who showed on the basis of printed texts that animacy was among the most important determinants of

---

[66] Osselton, 'Informal spelling systems' (1984), 127f.
[67] Osselton, 'Spelling-book rules'; Osselton, 'Informal spelling systems'.
[68] Dollinger, 'Capitalisation'.   [69] Ibid., 35.

capitalisation in that period. In addition, we investigated the potential influence of syntactic functions and semantic roles. Our results suggest that they might actually play a role within the *animate* subcategory. Furthermore, we discussed the role of socio-pragmatic factors. These can hardly be underestimated given that, in the time period in question, sentence-internal capitalisation was on its way to becoming a 'grammaticalised' marker of word class, rather than a pragmatic marker of emphasis. Bergmann and Nerius highlighted the importance of reverence (another pragmatic factor) in the emergence of sentence-internal capitalisation. Words denoting deities or persons of high social rank are capitalised first and most consistently. This finding is confirmed by our data. In addition, however, we have shown that there are clear gender differences in the use of sentence-internal capitalisation. In our data, many lexemes denoting men are consistently capitalised, while many terms denoting women are hardly ever capitalised. This suggests that the use of sentence-internal capitalisation reflects both cognitive factors such as the construal of entities as animate or inanimate, agentive or patientive, and socio-cultural conceptualisations.

However, the question as to what extent these findings are generalisable remains unanswered. Three important limitations have to be mentioned. Firstly, while the homogeneity of the SiGS corpus regarding the text type can be considered an important advantage, it also entails a number of problems. Some aspects are quite specific to the text type, with regard to both form and content. Potentially, some aspects of the use of sentence-internal capitalisation might therefore turn out to be text-type specific. Secondly, even though the complete SiGS corpus (fifty-six protocols) is much larger than the SiGS core corpus (eighteen protocols) used by e.g. Barteld et al., it is still a fairly small database. Thirdly, the time span covered by the corpus is too small to allow the thorough investigation of diachronic developments in the use of sentence-internal capitalisation, as carried out by Bergmann and Nerius for printed texts. As such, *desiderata* for future research on sentence-internal capitalisation in Early New High German include more systematic investigation of the above-mentioned factors beyond animacy on the basis of larger corpora, and the construction and investigation of larger and more heterogeneous corpora of handwritten texts that ideally should cover a longer time span than the SiGS corpus. In addition, the explanatory framework discussed in the present chapter could also be fruitfully applied to the investigation of sentence-internal capitalisation in other languages, as the above-mentioned factors could help explain the variation between upper-case and lowercase spelling there too. Testing this hypothesis, however, would require a much broader and more systematic investigation, which might also address why almost all languages eventually abandoned sentence-internal capitalisation – and why only German has taken a different path.

Appendix 4A Results of Hierarchical Configural Frequency Analysis on the SiGS Corpus

Types (observed > expected)

Animacy	Role	Syntactic function	Case	Observed	Expected	χ^2	$p_{adj.}$	Significance level	Q
human	agent	subj.	upper	141	17.19	891.84	2.96E-76	***	0.048
human	agent	subj.	lower	176	31.83	653.07	9.40E-70	***	0.056
human	agent	subj.	upper	231	72.28	348.51	4.39E-50	***	0.057
	patient	obj.	lower	1,014	695.02	146.40	5.15E-39	***	0.147
abstract	patient	obj.	lower	386	196.03	184.11	3.05E-34	***	0.079
	patient	subj.	lower	277	124.00	188.82	1.51E-32	***	0.056
human	agent	subj.	upper	272	121.84	185.04	2.59E-32	***	0.059
human	agent	subj.	upper	145	49.13	187.08	1.86E-27	***	0.034
human	stative	subj.	upper	84	19.88	206.84	9.25E-25	***	0.025
concrete	patient	obj.	lower	359	203.39	119.10	5.32E-23	***	0.065
abstract		obj.	lower	452	306.69	68.85	1.32E-15	***	0.061
human	agent		lower	178	91.60	81.52	1.44E-14	***	0.031
abstract	patient		lower	437	304.64	57.50	1.19E-12	***	0.052
	patient	obj.	upper	539	405.17	44.20	1.56E-10	***	0.054
human		obj.	lower	326	224.27	46.15	3.19E-10	***	0.042
human		subj.	upper	494	380.05	34.17	7.26E-09	***	0.045
	stative	subj.	upper	120	64.25	48.37	9.53E-09	***	0.02
	stative	subj.	lower	179	110.21	42.93	2.27E-08	***	0.025
concrete		obj.	lower	421	320.08	31.82	1.06E-07	***	0.043
animal	patient	obj.	upper	65	28.56	46.48	5.27E-07	***	0.014
human	experiencer	subj.	upper	13	1.46	91.29	1.06E-06	***	0.004
human	stative		upper	125	74.47	34.28	2.33E-06	***	0.018
human	stative	subj.	lower	74	36.81	37.58	6.76E-06	***	0.014
concrete	patient		lower	400	313.61	23.79	2.21E-05	***	0.034
animal	patient		upper	76	42.68	26.01	0.00014	***	0.012
abstract	patient		lower	603	516.53	14.48	0.00017	***	0.036

concrete	stative	subj.	lower	57	28.72	27.84	0.00035	***	0.011
concrete	patient	obj.	upper	160	109.84	22.91	0.00049	***	0.02
animal		obj.	upper	74	44.55	19.46	0.00069	***	0.011
	experiencer	subj.	upper	17	5.07	28.05	0.0011	**	0.004
	agent		upper	235	188.19	11.65	0.0060	**	0.016
human	experiencer		upper	14	4.20	23.28	0.007	**	0.003
human	stim.	obj.	upper	14	3.88	26.42	0.010	*	0.004
human	experiencer	subj.	lower	11	2.70	25.49	0.023	*	0.003
animal			upper	96	72.16	7.88	0.03	*	0.008

Antitypes (observed < expected)

	agent	obj.	lower	2	199.86	195.88	1.18E-84	***	0.074
	patient	subj.	lower	165	431.19	164.33	3.08E-53	***	0.11
			upper	1,172	1,591.5	110.58	1.78E-50	***	0.264
	patient	subj.	upper	65	251.37	138.18	8.30E-46	***	0.071
	agent	obj.	upper	3	116.51	110.59	3.22E-45	***	0.041
human		obj.	lower	205	409.61	102.20	9.36E-32	***	0.09
human	patient		lower	224	413.86	87.10	4.80E-26	***	0.078
human	agent	obj.	lower	2	57.5978	53.67	1.75E-20	***	0.022
concrete	agent	obj.	lower	0	44.95	44.95	3.93E-18	***	0.017
human	patient	subj.	lower	51	144.03	60.09	1.14E-17	***	0.038
abstract	agent	obj.	lower	0	43.32	43.31	2.05E-17	***	0.017
concrete	agent		lower	14	69.41	44.23	2.29E-14	***	0.02
concrete	patient	subj.	lower	41	112.39	45.35	6.04E-13	***	0.029
human	patient	subj.	upper	21	77.78	41.45	2.30E-12	***	0.022
abstract		subj.	upper	31	91.23	39.76	3.03E-12	***	0.023
abstract	agent		lower	19	67.42	34.78	1.40E-10	***	0.017
abstract	patient	subj.	upper	14	58.50	33.85	4.22E-10	***	0.017
abstract	stative	obj.	upper	44	103.56	34.26	8.00E-10	***	0.022
concrete		subj.	upper	41	95.21	30.87	4.19E-09	***	0.021

(cont.)

Antitypes (observed < expected)

Animacy	Role	Syntactic function	Case	Observed	Expected	χ^2	$p_{adj.}$	Significance level	Q
concrete	agent	obj.	upper	0	24.27	24.27	4.93E-09	***	0.009
human	stative	obj.	lower	21	66.61	31.23	8.37E-09	***	0.018
abstract	agent	obj.	upper	0	23.39	23.39	1.20E-08	***	0.009
concrete	agent		upper	6	37.23	26.20	1.60E-08	***	0.011
human	agent	obj.	upper	3	31.11	25.39	2.82E-08	***	0.011
abstract	agent		upper	6	36.16	25.16	3.97E-08	***	0.011
abstract	agent		upper	192	278.47	26.85	4.86E-08	***	0.033
concrete	patient	subj.	upper	19	60.70	28.64	5.35E-08	***	0.016
abstract	patient	subj.	lower	51	108.32	30.33	6.36E-08	***	0.023
human	patient	obj.	lower	173	260.64	29.47	1.76E-07	***	0.037
human			lower	591	704.95	18.41	2.27E-06	***	0.052
	stative	obj.	lower	113	177.65	23.52	2.92E-06	***	0.024
abstract	stative	obj.	upper	4	27.06	19.65	8.01E-06	***	0.009
concrete		subj.	lower	115	175.24	20.71	9.02E-06	***	0.024
abstract		subj.	lower	109	167.91	20.67	9.26E-06	***	0.024
human	patient		upper	156	222.00	19.61	4.97E-05	***	0.025
abstract	stative		upper	24	54.82	17.32	0.0001	***	0.011
animal	agent	obj.	lower	0	11.69	11.69	0.002	**	0.004
animal	stative		lower	9	26.70	11.72	0.004	**	0.006
concrete			upper	238	289.33	9.11	0.005	**	0.02
human		obj.	upper	175	222.54	10.16	0.008	**	0.019
human	stative	obj.	upper	15	35.97	12.23	0.012	*	0.008
	experiencer	obj.	lower	3	14.03	8.67	0.022	*	0.004

Columns 1–4 indicate the respective configurations; Columns 5–10 show the observed and expected values, the chi-squared value, the adjusted *p*-value, the significance level, and the effect size measure *Q* (used as a coefficient of pronouncedness).

5 Punctuation in Sixteenth- and Seventeenth-century French and Spanish Grammars
A Model of Diachronic and Comparative Graphematics

Elena Llamas-Pombo

The history of the punctuation of modern languages from a linguistic point of view is a recent contribution to historical linguistics since it has been developed only over the last four decades. During this development, traditional scholarship has inevitably tended to concentrate on issues related to punctuation with a preference for a single-language focus.[1] As a result of this traditional attitude to the diachronic study of punctuation, patterns across languages have remained largely unknown. The aim of this chapter is twofold: a general goal to advocate for a comparative approach to the history of punctuation in Western European languages, and a more specific goal to illustrate this approach with a case study based on a description of the French and Spanish uses of the point during the sixteenth and seventeenth centuries. Despite advances in the history of punctuation, those who want to venture on a cross-linguistic analysis of the topic are still confronted by a lack of analytical examples or a proven

Research for this chapter was supported by a research project on 'Enunciation and Orality Marks in French Historical Linguistics' from the Ministerio de Ciencia, Innovación y Universidades, Spain (Research Project FFI2017-84404-P).

[1] The most insightful contributions to the history of punctuation in Europe deal almost solely with self-standing analyses of individual languages. The great *Storia della punteggiatura*, directed by Mortara Garavelli, is oriented towards individual languages and geographical areas. Catach, in *La Ponctuation: histoire et système*, locates the origins of French punctuation in the Greco-Latin tradition (12–14) and cites the strong Italian influence on marks introduced towards the end of the fifteenth century in French printing presses (29), but her important handbook concerns only the French language. For Spanish, see Real Academia Española (RAE), 'La puntuación a través de la historia'; for English, see Crystal, *Making a Point*; Medina-Sánchez, 'Punctuation'; Medina-Sánchez and Rodríguez-Álvarez, 'Estudio'; Salmon, 'Orthography and punctuation'. Some of the most important studies on Spanish punctuation during the sixteenth and seventeenth centuries are: Bédmar Sancristóbal, 'Problemas'; Blecua, 'Notas'; Esteve Serrano, *Estudios*; Maqueira, 'Teoría y práctica ortográficas'; Martínez Marín, 'La ortografía'; 'La estandarización'; Santiago, 'Apuntes'; Sebastián Mediavilla, *La puntuación en el Siglo de Oro*; *La puntuación en los siglos XVI y XVII*; *Puntuación, humanismo*; *La puntuación del* Quijote; *Fray Luis y Santa Teresa*; 'A propósito del *Persiles*'.

methodology. In this chapter, I propose a model for the study of *diachronic variation in punctuation* and a definition of *linguistic invariants* common to the punctuation of several languages to advance the discussion of a comparative graphematic perspective. My diachronic and comparative analysis of punctuation firstly draws on the theoretical remarks made by orthographers.[2] Subsequently, I investigate whether or not their prescriptions are reflected in printed and handwritten examples of punctuation, particularly in books by grammarians and orthographers themselves. To complete this descriptive analysis fully, it is necessary to subject old practices to conceptual tools of graphematics and current variational linguistics. In order to explore the degree of standardisation or variation within and across punctuation in French and Spanish during the sixteenth and seventeenth centuries, I propose to test the operability of two concepts regarding graphic variation – the concepts of *persistence* and of *potential normative variance* – by examining the specific case of the variable uses of the point in Early Modern French and Spanish.

5.1   A Model for Diachronic Graphematics

5.1.1   A Comparative Perspective

The existence of diachronic comparative graphematics in parallel to diachronic comparative phonetics or diachronic comparative grammar has been accepted by contemporary linguistics.[3] In the history of punctuation, some scholars have opened the way for such a perspective. The first comparative description was that of the famous palaeographer Malcolm Parkes, whose monumental *History of Punctuation in the West*, whilst covering a broad study of Latin manuscripts,

---

[2] French primary sources: (a) Most of the French grammars from the fourteenth to the seventeenth centuries are available in Colombat et al., *Grand corpus*, which includes both digital and facsimile formats. (b) Some of these grammars and orthographic treatises are also available in *Gallica*, the official digital library of the Bibliothèque nationale de France. (c) French treatises on punctuation of the sixteenth century are available in Baddeley, 'Sources'. Spanish primary sources: (a) Facsimile copies of Spanish grammar are available in Gómez Asencio, *Antiguas gramáticas*. (b) Facsimile copies of all Spanish treatises on orthography are available in Martínez Alcalde, *Textos clásicos*. Some of them are also available in the Biblioteca Digital Hispánica of the Biblioteca Nacional de España. (c) A study of Spanish treatises on punctuation from the sixteenth and seventeenth centuries is presented in Sebastián Mediavilla's important book, *Puntuación, humanismo*, an updated and revised edition of two previous, and similarly important, works by the same author: *La puntuación en el Siglo de Oro* and *La puntuación en los siglos XVI y XVII*. (d) See especially Santiago, 'La puntuación según Nebrija', for ideas about punctuation expressed by Antonio de Nebrija, author of the first Spanish grammar.

[3] For example, Weingarten, in 'Comparative graphematics', has discussed *comparative graphematics* as a linguistic approach within research on writing systems and typology, through a discussion of the relationship between the gemination of consonant letters and the graphemic representation of long consonants.

also considers the standardisation of the forms of marks due to the *disseminatio* of printing types in English, French, Italian and Spanish texts.[4] Similarly, the Hungarian linguist Borbála Keszler developed a diachronic and synchronic analysis of Hungarian punctuation based on a comparative orthotypography of European languages, all the while underlining the unitary nature of punctuation as a remarkable occurrence in European cultural history.[5] More recently, a broadly comparative graphematic perspective of the history of typographical marks has been undertaken by Keith Houston.[6] Fidel Sebastián Mediavilla, a specialist in the history of Spanish punctuation during the sixteenth and seventeenth centuries, has also covered in various historiographical works a comparison of Hispanic theory with the output of European orthographers and printers like Estienne Dolet and Aldo Manuzio.[7] The hypothesis that I have attempted to prove in recent works is that the practices of punctuation in mediaeval Europe reflect implicitly the existence of a veritable 'treatment of text', applicable to several languages, from which we can extract some linguistic patterns that are significantly more unitary than has been previously stated and which bear witness to cultural unity in mediaeval Europe.[8] Yet this idea is not new, as, between the sixteenth and eighteenth centuries, it was expressed, more or less explicitly, by important punctuation theorists in France and Spain.

(1) It is commonly accepted that if Antonio de Nebrija, author of the first modern grammar within the Romance languages – the *Grammatica de la lengua castellana* (1492) – did not cover the subject of punctuation in this work nor in his *Reglas de ortographia* (1517), it was because, implicitly, the rules set out in his Latin grammar, *Introductiones in latinam grammaticem* (1502),[9] were equally valid for Castilian, a language that should, in his view, 'acquire the same degree of standardisation as the Greek and Latin languages'.[10]

(2) The *Tractado de orthographia* (1531) by Alejo Venegas contains the first theoretical exposition of punctuation written in Spanish.[11] Although

---

[4] Parkes, *Pause and Effect*.

[5] For current punctuation in European languages, see Keszler, 'A magyar írásjelhasználat'; for the diachronic perspective, see Keszler, *Írásjeltan*.

[6] Houston, *Shady Characters*.

[7] Sebastián Mediavilla, *La puntuación en el Siglo de Oro*; *La puntuación en los siglos XVI y XVII*; *Puntuación, humanismo*.

[8] Llamas-Pombo, 'Variación gráfica'; 'Administración, cultura escrita'; 'Pour une étude'.

[9] The treatise 'De punctis clausularum', part of Nebrija's *Introductiones*, did not figure in the first issue of the first edition (Salamanca, 1481); it was printed only in the 1482 and 1483 issues of that edition. The third edition, printed in, among other cities, Seville in 1501, 1502 and 1503, provides the version that is nowadays the reference for specialists: see Santiago, 'La puntuación según Nebrija'; Sebastián Mediavilla, *La puntuación en los siglos XVI y XVII*, 7 and *Puntuación, humanismo*, 23.

[10] Nebrija, *Grammatica*, a3v.

[11] Venegas, *Tractado*. See Sebastián Mediavilla, *Puntuación, humanismo*, 23.

writing in the vernacular, he displays the theory of Latin punctuation as a model for Spanish to imitate. In doing so, he illustrates his theory mostly by using examples in Latin and only a few rare examples in Spanish. Thus, Venegas seems to imply, like Nebrija, the 'translinguistic' character of punctuation marks.

(3) The French humanist (and printer) Dolet first stated explicitly, in 1540, that 'languages do not have more than one punctuation and you will not find any difference in punctuation among Greek, Latin, French, Italian and Spanish speakers'.[12]

(4) Around 1552, the Spanish humanist Antonio de Torquemada wrote a *Manual de escribientes*, a work on the virtues of the good scribe and appropriate orthography in manuscript writing. In it he states, like Dolet, that 'orthography is different because languages are different, but there are also many general rules which can be applied to all languages'.[13]

(5) Some years later, the anonymous author of a Castilian grammar known as *Anónimo de Lovaina* (1559) expressed the same idea as Dolet: 'I will not say anything on punctuation because it entails applying natural common sense and the requirements of the art, as it is the same for all languages.'[14]

(6) The French school of thought in the seventeenth century reinforced the notion of common structures in languages. In the early 1660s, the Jansenist circle at Port-Royal propagated the influential idea 'that the various syntactical features of different languages could be regarded as independent manifestations of an underlying structure common to all languages, which mirror the structure of thought'.[15] For Parkes, this idea encouraged the use of punctuation for the balance between logical and rhetorical analyses of discourse.

(7) A century later, the first 'official' orthographic treatise on the Spanish language, published in 1741 by the Real Academia Española (RAE), reiterated the same idea: 'Punctuation marks are common to all languages and nations and, consequently, everyone understands them without difficulty.'[16]

---

[12] Dolet, 'De la pvnctuation', 17: 'Si toutes langues generalement ont leurs differences en parler, et escripture, toutesfoys non obstant cela elles n'ont qu'une punctuation seulement: et ne trouueras, qu'en ycelle les Grecs, Latins, Francoys, Italiens, ou Hespaignolz soient differents.'

[13] Torquemada, *Manual*, 39: 'Puesto caso que la orthographía en muchas cosas sea diferente, como lo son las lenguas en que se escrive, no dexa de aver muchas reglas generales que sirven y se guardan en todas.'

[14] Anónimo, *Gramatica*, 4r: 'Del puntuár no diré nada, porque solo consiste en buen juizio natural, i de lo que requiere el arte, por ser cosa general a todas las lenguas.'

[15] Parkes, *Pause and Effect*, 89.

[16] RAE, *Orthographía*, 262: 'Estas notas son comunes á todas las lenguas, y Naciones, y por consiguiente sabidas de todos sin dificultad alguna.'

According to Marie-Luce Demonet,[17] in the sixteenth century the possibility of transferring punctuation from one language to another presupposed a 'universally' implicit conception of punctuation marks and of general grammar. Yet, there is also a technological factor, highlighted by Susan Baddeley,[18] which may explain the perception of unity of punctuation: the technology of printing has influenced the standardisation of the marks. As Parkes noted, since, in the sixteenth century, 'punches for the marks of punctuation were cut along with those for the rest of the fount, forms of punctuation were disseminated with the types'.[19] This perception of the unity of European punctuation on the part of Dolet and other sixteenth-century orthographers should of course be viewed with caution and is, above all, a hypothesis that seems to be worth studying at length.[20] I therefore propose a model for the study of diachronic variation in punctuation to advance the discussion of a comparative graphematic perspective. This model comprises the contrast between theory and practice (see Section 5.1.2) and the consideration of seven parameters of variational linguistics (see Section 5.1.3).

5.1.2   Variation between Theory and Practice

The history of punctuation should consider both historiographical and descriptive data in order to contrast theoretical treatises with variation in writing practices. There is often a certain degree of divergence between the theory of grammarians and orthographers and the writers' practices, so we cannot limit the 'history of punctuation' to a 'history of theories about punctuation'. For example, studies on mediaeval punctuation in Romance languages following linguistic models have proven that the 'reading units', or the 'syntactic punctuable units' distinguished as such by scribes, correspond to writing traditions that linguists uncover, but which have not for the most part been the object of any mediaeval grammatical theorisation.[21] In the sixteenth century, the task of

---

[17] Demonet, 'Ponctuation et narration', 41.

[18] Baddeley, 'Sources', 195; 'Accents, signes auxiliaires'.   [19] Parkes, *Pause and Effect*, 51.

[20] My comparative and diachronic perspective on *linguistic invariants* of punctuation of European languages is compatible with other investigations of synchronic linguistics into the specificity of punctuation of current languages of all origins (including Chinese, Arabic, Hindi, Japanese, Turkish and Romance and Germanic languages). In fact, a recent study by Markov et al. has explored how 'punctuation is specific to each language and is part of the indicators that overtly represent the manner in which each language organizes and conveys information' ('Punctuation as native language interference', 3456).

[21] The biggest corpus of theoretical treatises on punctuation written in Latin from antiquity to the fifteenth century is Hubert's 'Corpvs'. For French practice, following the pioneering study on the linguistics of mediaeval punctuation by Marchello-Nizia ('Ponctuation et unités'), the 'grammar' of the punctuation of mediaeval scribes has been described by Lavrentiev, 'Tendances'; 'Ponctuation française'; Llamas-Pombo, 'Ponctuation médiévale' and Mazziotta, *Ponctuation et syntaxe*, amongst others. I am not able to provide an exhaustive bibliography on punctuation here as it is rather voluminous; I present a state-of-the-art, comprehensive bibliography in Llamas-Pombo, 'Ponctuer, éditer, lire' and in Parussa et al., 'Introduction'.

punctuation and segmentation of texts was still most commonly in the hands of print workshops and not in those of the authors.[22] Yet, as Baddeley reminds us,[23] printers could use different punctuation marks, as physical objects, only if they had the relevant punches in their own matrix. Hence, we find that there sometimes exists a surprising dissociation between the theory and the practice of some humanists.[24] The first treatise on punctuation to be printed in France, the *Compendiosus dialogus de arte punctandi*, was written in Latin and edited with the punctuation marks of the humanist tradition. This treatise was included in France's second printed book, Gasparino Barzizza's *Orthographia* (1470).[25] Its Paris printers (Gering, Crantz and Friburger) scrupulously followed the marks and rules advised by this treatise for the punctuation of their edition. However, as Baddeley again reminds us,[26] at the time of the second edition of the *Compendiosus dialogus*,[27] in 1482, its printer, Pierre Hongre, did not have the founts for the punctuation marks described in the treatise, which resulted in a discrepancy between the theoretical recommendations and the punctuation of his edition of the text.

In his brief treatise, 'De la pvnctvation de la langve francoyse' (1540), Dolet applies the same principles that he himself formulated, even if one can occasionally observe slight disparities.[28] However, as Demonet points out,[29] in 1529 Geoffroy Tory quoted, in his work *Champ Fleury*,[30] a list of punctuation marks extracted from the work of the Italian grammarian Aulus Antonius Orobius,[31] none of which truly corresponded to their use in his own text, a use which was at the discretion of its printer, Giles Gourmont. Additionally, the marks that he listed are engraved like drawings and not printed like the punctuation in his text.

Turning to the history of the Spanish language, José Luis Girón Alconchel has established a model for analysing Spanish Golden Age grammars by

---

[22] Baddeley, 'Accents, signes auxiliaires'; 'Sources', 192; Catach, *L'Orthographe*, 295–309; *La Ponctuation: histoire et système*, 29. In a recent work, Chartier analyses this divergence between the hand of the author and the mind of the printer in Spanish, French and English literature (*La Main de l'auteur*, 15). Arellano ('La puntuación', 20) and Azorín and Provencio ('La puntuación') study an interesting case of punctuation of a text first established by a printer and later corrected by the author.

[23] Baddeley, 'Sources', 193.

[24] See Huchon, 'Pour une histoire'; Lavrentiev, 'Ponctuation française'.

[25] Barzizza, *Gasparini Pergamensis orthographia*, 474–7 (page numbers from the digital version; see Bibliography). The *Compendiosus dialogus de arte punctandi* was composed by Guillaume Fichet, summarised by Jean Heynlin and later included in Barzizza's *Orthographia*; for the authorship of this treatise, see Baddeley, 'Sources', 193; Beltrán, 'Un traité', 286; Veyrin-Forrer, 'Aux origines', 173–4. Gasparino Barzizza (c. 1370–1431) was a Lombard teacher of rhetoric; see Section 5.2.1.1.

[26] Baddeley, 'Sources', 193.   [27] Guarino Veronese, *In presenti libro*, 5.

[28] Baddeley, 'Sources', 198; Lavrentiev, 'Tendances', vol. 1, 433.

[29] Demonet, 'Ponctuation et narration', 40.

[30] Tory, *Champ Fleury*, 65v–66r; see further Section 5.2.2.   [31] Orobius, *Libellus*.

distinguishing at least three levels of language variation: 'prescribed uses', 'described uses' and 'written uses' for each theoretician.[32] This model has recently been applied to the punctuation of Marcos Fernández, a teacher of Spanish in Europe during the seventeenth century and author of a grammar which includes the rules of punctuation and, in the case of Fernández's grammar, Daniel Sáez Rivera has analysed the divergence between the theory about marks of direct speech and the variable practices for quotation.[33]

Thus, my analysis of punctuation from the sixteenth century draws on the orthographers' theory, and I then investigate whether or not their prescriptions were applied in practice.

5.1.3 The Parameters of Variational Linguistics

The 'variational' and 'diasystemic' model established by Eugenio Coşeriu (1966)[34] provides the most innovative and up-to-date methodological basis for the study of Old French grammar. Following the theoreticians of Old French diasystemic grammar[35] I aimed, in a recent work, to establish a graphematic theory of mediaeval French writing and to demonstrate that graphic signs, like any other level of language, allow for a diachronic analysis through the parameters of variational linguistics.[36] This work defined several areas of language where spelling and punctuation variation occurs, and presented examples in manuscripts from Old and Middle French. My theoretical framework, developed for mediaeval French punctuation, can be applied to other languages and periods, including the sixteenth and seventeenth centuries, given that in this period variability in writing practice characterised the process of graphic standardisation.[37]

---

[32] Girón Alconchel, 'Las gramáticas', 285–6 and 304–5.

[33] Fernández, Olla; Sáez Rivera, 'Discurso referido y puntuación'. See also Sáez Rivera, 'La lengua', 907.

[34] Coseriu, 'Structure'; Principios, 118–22.

[35] Buridant, Grammaire; 'Prolégomènes'; Schøsler, 'The importance'; Völker, 'Linguistique variationnelle'; 'La Linguistique'.

[36] Llamas-Pombo, 'Graphie et ponctuation'.

[37] Rutkowska and Rössler (in 'Orthographic variables') have established a linguistic framework for categories of orthographic variants: diachronic, diatopic, diaphasic, diastratic, diasituative and aesthetic variants. Variability as a key factor for understanding mediaeval scripts is a subject that has recently begun to be analysed empirically: for example, Stutzmann ('Variability', 2–3) observes that 'Variability has always been a key concept in the humanities, as a factor of change and historical evolution as well as the core phenomenon between normativity, social control and individuality [...] Nevertheless, the very notion of variability has not been clearly defined for medieval scripts and there is no acknowledged method to measure intra-scribal or inter-scribal variation.' My variationist approach to mediaeval spelling and punctuation is an attempt to contribute to developing such a theorisation on mediaeval variation, through the definition of its different parameters and relevant linguistic frameworks (Llamas-Pombo, 'Graphie et ponctuation').

5.1.3.1   The Diachronic Axis

Diachronic variation shapes the tension between the opposing forces of the inertia of conservative writing and graphic innovation. For example, the spellings *francoys/francois, françois, français* constitute diachronic variants of the same word that emerged during the history of the French language. In order to explore the degree of standardisation or variation within and across punctuation in French and Spanish in the sixteenth and seventeenth centuries, I propose to test the validity of two concepts regarding graphic variation.

(1)   The Concept of *Persistence* (French: rémanence)
The concept of *persistence* has begun to be considered by French diachronic linguists, most notably by Claire Badiou-Monferran,[38] an author who stresses that 'histories of languages tend to give strong precedence to "change" (as grammaticalisation, metaphor, disappearances, etc.), but not to "endurance" or "persistence"'. Yet since the 2000s, 'study of the factors of linguistic stability has been considered to be just as important as that of the modalities of change'. *Persistence*, as Badiou-Monferran maintains, 'has reached the status of an emerging study' and is a concept that should be developed in language sciences, as it affects all elements of language. Such a concept seems highly pertinent to the graphic framework of language in the sixteenth and seventeenth centuries, because the orthography of European languages was subjected not only to processes of innovation and standardisation but equally to varying degrees of conservative forces, which the linguist must also analyse.

(2)   The Concept of a Potential Normative Variant
In my model of variational graphematics, I propose to pay particular attention to graphic variants which, although infrequent or unusual at any given moment, have the potential to become the norm. Just as in the framework of the internal evolution of language, diachronic graphematics should consider certain minor graphic devices that are often forgotten by the history of orthography and which were never defined by theoreticians, because it is in these rare devices that we sometimes find outlines of norms that were later accepted as standard.

5.1.3.2   The Diatopic, Diastratic and Diaphasic Axes

The three parameters of variation of area, register of language and stylistic properties can also play a part in punctuation. *Diatopic variation* is inherent in Old French just as it was in the Old Iberian Romance language, given the great dialectal variability of both. This 'polycentrism' of the norm was rooted in

---

[38] Badiou-Monferran (*La 'Rémanence'*) proposes the development of this concept on the basis of the difference between 'genetic stability' and 'persistence', established by Nichols ('Diversity and stability in language').

mediaeval *scriptae* and lasted until well past the Middle Ages in the Romance languages. For the period before standardised systems of writing, it is important to consider whether or not there also existed a certain degree of specialisation in punctuation in different regions of Europe, in contrast to the unity of punctuation systems of European languages. Parkes stresses, for example, that there was variation in the form of marks: 'the form of the *virgula stroke* of the *punctus elevatus* was [...] subject to regional variations'.[39]

The *diastratic parameter*, related to the variation in registers between prestigious or less valued graphs, is more relevant to the history of punctuation because in French, just as in Spanish, two systems of punctuation, one formal and the other more informal, coexisted in the same period. For example, the palaeographer Gilbert Ouy demonstrated that the first French humanists, from the fourteenth and fifteenth centuries, used two sets of punctuation; a more common one for drafts or for dictated texts and another, more magnificent and archaic.[40] Jacqueline Hamesse confirms that study notes at this time had either rudimentary or even non-existent punctuation.[41] A double usage such as this lasted until the sixteenth century in France. For example, as Demonet highlights, the writer and philosopher Michel de Montaigne, in his marginal notes to the 1558 edition of his *Essais*, used the most simplified punctuation; however, his corrections of punctuation in the printed part of the text were extremely precise.[42] Equally, autograph manuscripts of Spanish writers from the sixteenth and seventeenth centuries do not evince careful punctuation, as a recent study by Ignacio Arellano on the punctuation of *El Quijote* proves.[43] Nevertheless, for writers, just as much as for orthographers, the best punctuation was in fact that applied by good printers. For example, the Spanish theoretician Juan de Ycíar, in his *Orthographia pratica* of 1548, maintains that the distinction between the six punctuation marks must be based on printers' practices, 'given that they are the professional specialists on the best punctuation'.[44] In 1614, Bartolomé Jiménez Patón maintained, in his *Epitome de la ortografia*, that the best examples of his theory about punctuation can be found in the editions published by the most modern printers.[45]

Lastly, the *diaphasic axis* – or 'graphic variation with stylistic purposes' – is a parameter which has proved to be pertinent in explaining the numerous cases of alternation of marks in mediaeval and Renaissance punctuation, but it will not be discussed here.[46]

---

[39] Parkes, *Pause and Effect*, 43.   [40] Ouy, 'Orthographe', 169–70.
[41] Hamesse, 'Reportations', 141.   [42] Demonet, 'Ponctuation et narration', 39.
[43] Arellano, 'La puntuación', 19–20.   [44] Ycíar, *Orthographia*, I5r.
[45] Jiménez Patón, *Epitome*, 78; see Azorín and Provencio, 'La puntuación', 444–5.
[46] On *diaphasic* or *stylistic variation in spelling*, see Llamas-Pombo, 'Variación gráfica' and 'Gratiam varietatis'.

5.1.3.3 The Diamesic Axis

The *diamesic axis* refers to the medium of language and concerns the relationship of correspondence or autonomy between the phonic and the graphic codes of language. This relationship constitutes one of the essential *variables* in the linguistic analysis of punctuation and in the history of its theorisation, given that, from Latin grammar up to current pragmatic linguistics, the theories take either one or other polar stance: punctuation as the notation of suprasegmental features or the functional autonomy of writing. This parameter, which considers mediums of language and oral–written relationships, should be radically distinguished from another parameter, which concerns *enunciative types of discourse*.

5.1.3.4 The Enunciative Parameter

The *enunciative parameter* concerns the relationship between the written form and the recording of reported speech. In practice, current diachronic studies of French favour the study of the representation of oral language (*l'oral représenté*, in French terminology), focusing on what is presented as oral language in written texts.[47] In this domain, the history of quotation marks is fundamental and has yet to be studied in depth, specifically in the sixteenth and seventeenth centuries, a period when there were attempts to establish several methods for marking citations, direct discourse or 'the discourse of others'.[48] This parameter also concerns the relationship between punctuation marks and enunciative modalities (declarative, interrogative, exclamative, etc.).

5.1.3.5 The Conceptional Parameter

The *conceptional parameter* allows for the classification of the different styles and needs of punctuation in relation to the communicational typology established by Peter Koch and Wulf Oesterreicher, which opposes linguistic forms proper to *immediate communication* and those specific to *language of distance*.[49]

The framework and seven linguistic parameters mentioned above concern any of the three levels of graphic segmentation of texts by punctuation markers, namely *word punctuation* or *word sequencing*, *statement punctuation* and *text punctuation*.[50] In fact, the variational axes and parameters outlined are not mutually exclusive. We can simultaneously detect, for example, the *communicational* properties and *diatopic* traits of the same graphic phenomenon. Let us examine a representative case of this kind of co-occurrence of variational parameters: some

---

[47] For a definition of the concept of *oral représenté*, see Marchello-Nizia, 'L'Oral représenté'.

[48] I have embarked on a history of quotation marks and other marks of speech in French in Llamas-Pombo, 'Marques graphiques' and 'Ponctuer, éditer, dire'. Sáez Rivera has recently analysed the practices of the punctuation of reported speech in Spanish during the seventeenth century, particularly in Fernández's works; see 'Discurso referido y puntuación'.

[49] Koch and Oesterreicher, 'Gesprochene Sprache und geschriebene Sprache'.

[50] Catach, 'La Ponctuation'.

French poems written in England in the twelfth and thirteenth centuries are characterised by the fact that they are accented; slightly accented in some cases, such as the *Chanson de Saint Alexis* or the *Chanson de Roland* in the Oxford manuscript, or heavily accented in others, such as *The Oxford Psalter*.[51] Its editor, Ian Short, notes the fact 'that such diacritics were intended to facilitate the reading aloud of the texts, presumably to a collective audience, has long been recognised, and they prove to be a particular feature of Anglo-Norman manuscripts'.[52] Graphic variants with diacritics consist of an inscription denoting an accent of intensity (*séntes, medésme, voluntét*), a mark of hiatus (*áasme, meésme*) and other distinctions of phonemes. All these spelling variants allow the text to be read aloud correctly and represent the orality of the words; and simultaneously they constitute a set of *diatopic variants*, proper to the Old French of England.

Let us consider another example relating to the period in question. The works of the Spanish writer Juan Boscán were published by several printers during the sixteenth century; their different punctuation traditions have been analysed by Dolores Azorín Fernández and Herminia Provencio Garrigós.[53] In this context of graphic variation in the successive editions, proper to the pre-standardised written form, we know, thanks to printer Carles Amorós's contract with the bookseller Joan Bages, that the first edition (1543) was partially corrected and generously punctuated by Boscán himself.[54] Azorín and Provencio's hypothesis is that the pause and intonation marks are so abundant because Boscán wanted to note down the prosody necessary for the correct recitation of his verse. It means that the printed version was punctuated for the purpose of an *immediate communication*. In this same edition from 1543, Amorós, a Provençal printer working in Barcelona, also made frequent use of the *hedera* (❦) and the *manicule* (☞) to mark paragraphs, a technique that is considered 'archaic', 'provincial', 'individual' and characteristic of Amorós. In summary, in the same text, there coexist *diachronic persistent variants* of punctuation, probably marked *diatopically*, with spellings determined by *immediate communication*.

5.2   The Variable Uses of the Point in French and Spanish in the Sixteenth and Seventeenth Centuries

In the current systems of punctuation, the full point's main role, in addition to others, is that of an *organiser of sequentiality* of the written text, and it works as a *syntagmatic indicator*,[55] given that its function is that of the syntactic organisation

---

[51] *Chanson de Roland; Chanson de Saint Alexis; Oxford Psalter.*
[52] Short, *The Oxford Psalter*, 139, 142, 143.   [53] Azorín and Provencio, 'La puntuación', 465.
[54] Boscán, *Las obras;* Azorín and Provencio, 'La puntuación', 441.
[55] In French, *organisateur de la séquencialité; indicateur syntagmatique*; here I follow the terminology and concepts established by Anis ('Pour une graphématique', 42), Anis, Chiss and Puech (*L'Écriture*, 122, 245) and Dahlet (*Ponctuation*, 23).

of the text. For the contemporary user, the point is a mark that is essentially used to denote the end of a sentence; it is a full stop that represents a pause. This specialisation of the point for the end of a sentence was established progressively between the fifteenth and seventeenth centuries, a period in which modern stand-ardised systems were formed and during which time the point had different functions originating from the mediaeval usage. It is commonly accepted by punctuation specialists that, during the Middle Ages, the point had a high level of 'polysemy' in manuscripts.[56] In effect, in mediaeval Romance language manu-scripts, the point followed by uppercase usually denotes the end of a statement or the end of a text (this full stop separates different verses, denotes the end of a charter, distinguishes between sentences, etc.). Yet, for centuries, the point has also accom-plished another equally important *syntagmatic function*, not of 'separation', but of 'connection' or 'union' between two linguistic elements. Said value constitutes a prototypic case of *persistence* of a mediaeval use that was defined by some Renaissance theoreticians of the *ars punctandi* ('art of punctuation'). It presents a clear case of divergence between the theory and the writing practices in Spanish just as much as in French. Perhaps it is because of this divergence that the connective value of the point has been almost entirely forgotten by the history of French and Spanish orthography, which explains why editors often have difficulty with the interpretation of some texts. Let us read, as an example, some mediaeval sentences which imply the connective usage of the point. This may seem strange to present-day readers but it demonstrates the most stereotypical and constant value of the point in Latin and in the writing of mediaeval Romance languages. In these cases, it can be seen that the dot does not serve to represent 'a pause' or to 'separate' elements but rather to highlight a 'nexus' between verbal elements that have the same syntactic hierarchy or that present a parallelism or an identity, independently of whether it implies a pause or not. The point before coordinating conjunctions (*et, ne, ou*, in French; *e/et/i/y, ni, o*, in Spanish) is constant in mediaeval texts:[57]

sisaluaraieo cist meon fradre karlo · & in ad iudha · & in cad huna cosa · (tenth-century French manuscript, *Serments de Strasbourg*)[58]

'I shall help this my brother Charles both with aid and in all other things'[59]

dueno *christ*o . dueno salbatore
enos sieculos . delosieculos (tenth- to eleventh-century Spanish glosses, *Codex Aemilianensis* 60)[60]

---

[56] Hubert, 'Notes', 87, 94; Parkes, *Pause and Effect*, 42, 75, 77.
[57] On the connective value of the point, see Llamas-Pombo, 'Réflexions méthodologiques', 15–23 and 'Ponctuer, éditer, lire', 143.
[58] *Serments*, fol. 13r; the height of the points in this and the following quotations preserves palaeographical fidelity. The use of the ampersand <&> is also maintained.
[59] Translation from Ayres-Bennett, *A History*, p. 18.
[60] *Codex Aemilianensis* 60, fol. 72r. I have expanded the manuscript abbreviation *xp̄* for *christ*. In the remaining quotations in this chapter I have silently expanded original abbreviations.

Our Lord Christ, Our Lord Saviour
forever and ever

Peres . et fils . et esperis .
Terre . mers . et airs ce me semble (fourteenth-century French manuscript, *Ovide moralisé*)[61]

The Father, the Son and the Holy Spirit,
earth, sea and air, this appears to me

5.2.1   The Point and Medial Punctuation: The Theory in the Fifteenth and Sixteenth Centuries

As the Renaissance punctuation specialist Demonet reminds us,[62] the main debates and differences of opinion concerning systems of punctuation between 1530 and 1540 in France were specifically about the definition of *medial punctuation*. In this period, this medial function could be represented by three marks:[63] by the *comma*, which symbol was at that time formed of two points <:>, by the comma <,>, or by a point that was generally followed by lowercase <. m>[64] (which Demonet calls *le point non final*, that is to say 'the non-full stop point'). These divergences, Demonet also states, are not specific to French; we are aware of similar vacillations in Latin punctuation and in that of other European languages. In mediaeval Latin, one of the functions of the *punctus* or *low dot* <.> was the 'distinction' or 'separation' between units of a statement corresponding to an oral pause: this was a *minor medial pause* (in Latin, *distinctio media sive constans*), according to Parkes.[65] This point was used, after a main clause, when this followed on from one or a number of subordinate clauses. In the next section, we see how the theoreticians of the fifteenth century defined and exemplified this, whilst we keep in mind that, until the first written treatises in Romance languages, humanists understood that the precepts that they applied in Latin were equally valid for the French and Spanish languages.

---

[61] *Ovide moralisé*, fol. 6vb, 7ra.   [62] Demonet, 'Ponctuation et narration', 41.

[63] In this chapter, the word '*comma*' in italics corresponds to the Latin name of a punctuation mark the mediaeval symbols for which were <,> or <:>. The word 'comma' in roman corresponds to the English name of the modern punctuation mark <,>. Equally, the term '*colon*' in italics corresponds to the Latin name of a point whose symbols were a middle or a lowercase point <·> or <.>.

[64] In this chapter, *graphemes* and spellings are represented by angle brackets. A point followed by lowercase is represented by the symbols <. m>. A point followed by uppercase is represented by the symbols <. M>.

[65] Parkes, *Pause and Effect*, 42, 69, 70, 71.

5.2.1.1   Connection of Coordinate and Subordinate Clauses

The theory of punctuation taught around 1400 at the Sorbonne in Paris, following Barzizza's *Liber de arte punctandi*,[66] included the *colon* (<.>) in the list of marks considered old, i.e. of Latin tradition. This mark was defined in the following terms:[67]

Colon est punctum sine virgula / quando constructio est perfecta in se / sed adhuc pendet animus dictatoris / et talis distinctio vocatur media sive constans · ꟾ

A *Colon* is a single point without a comma, which should be used when the construction has ended but the author still has something to say. We call a mark like this *medial punctuation* or *constans*.

Ouy has noted that this point was mostly used in very carefully written manuscripts but that, in copies written in cursive, this function was carried out at this time by the *virgula recta* or forward slash </>.[68] However, as will be seen later, in practice, the point used as *medial punctuation* had a persistent and valid use in manuscripts and even in printing. Observe that the mark ending a sentence that is presented in the manuscript itself of this citation is not a point but a mark called *periodus*, which corresponds not to medial, but to terminal punctuation. Barzizza defines this mark in the following way:[69]

Pariodus [*sic*] est punctus cum virgula deorsum ducta / quando nec constructio nec sententia amplius dependet . et talis distinctio dicitur finitiua . de quibus omnibus distinctionibus traditur hoc exemplum · ꟾ

Periodus is a point with a comma underneath, which should be used when there is nothing left to add to the construction or to the sentence, and we call it *terminal punctuation*, as in this example.

Note also, in this definition given in the manuscript copy, the use of the point or *colon* followed by a lower-case letter, as *medial punctuation* to add coordination through the conjunction *et* or a subordinate relative clause.

5.2.1.2   Connection and Enumeration

Barzizza himself in his treatise gave a second list of marks and typical uses of them by 'modern authors', that is to say, his contemporaries around 1400. In this list, he defines the term *punctus copulativus*, which means 'linking point' and serves to connect elements of equal hierarchy. Observe that, in this case, today's orthography requires a comma in French, just as it does in Spanish.[70]

---

[66] Ouy, 'La Ponctuation', 65, 89; Parkes, *Pause and Effect*, 49, 135. See Section 5.1.2 above for Barzizza's *Orthographia*, printed in Paris in 1471.
[67] Barzizza, *Liber de arte punctandi*, fol. 37v; italics added.   [68] Ouy, 'La Ponctuation', 67.
[69] Barzizza, *Liber de arte punctandi*, fol. 37v; italics added.   [70] Ibid., fol. 38r; italics added.

Punctus copulativus est qui complet viam copule . vt *ferro . peste . fame . vinclis . algore . calore* · ⌐ punctus enim ponitur inter omnia ista substantiva loco copule

The linking point is that which is used to unify, as in *ferro . fame . vinclis . algore . calore*; between all these nouns, the point functions as a link.

In Nebrija's Latin grammar (1502), this same syntactic structure was named *articulus* and defined as a series of words of the same grammatical class linked without conjunctions:[71]

Colum quoque ponimus inter singulas partes orationis: quae per articulum aut dissolutum sine coniunctione annectuntur: ut *Grammaticus . rhetor . geometres . pictor . aliptes .*

We also use the *colum* between those parts of a clause which we join by the *articulus*, that is to say, without conjunctions, such as: *Grammaticus . rhetor . geometres . pictor . aliptes .*

In Nebrija's Castilian grammar (1492), the point is also usually employed in enumerations, as in these sentences:[72]

No tienen esso mesmo plural las cosas umidas que se miden i pesan. como *vino. mosto. vinagre. arrope. azeite. leche.* [...] No tienen tan poco plural estos. *sangre. cieno. limo. colera. gloria. fama. polvo. ceniza. arena. leña. oregano. poleo. tierra. aire. fuego.*

Wet things which are measured and weighed do not have plural, such as *wine, must, vinegar, grape syrup, oil, milk.* [...] Nor do these have plural: *blood, silt, slime, anger, glory, fame, powder, ash, sand, wood, oregano, pennyroyal, earth, air, fire.*

Sebastián Mediavilla notes that this use of the point is more frequent in manuscripts than in printing throughout the sixteenth century.[73] Such a divergence seems to remain reflected in punctuation theory. Indeed, in 1531, Venegas, in the first treatise on punctuation written in Castilian, uses the term *entreuallo* ('interval') to describe each of the 'divisions' of discourse, which we call in graphematics 'graphic sequences that can be distinguished by a punctuation mark'. One of these syntactic patterns defined by Venegas is precisely the *articulus* or *articulo*, already cited by Nebrija, a term which designates the position of the mark as much as its form:[74]

Otro entreuallo ay que se dize articulus: que es en señal el mismo que el de la comma: saluo que este articulo se pone en lugar de la coniunction copulativa. y es quando se juntan muchas partes de vna misma manera: sin conjunción que las ligue. Entonces entre parte y parte ponemos dos puntos como diziendo. *Cardinales virtutes sunt quattuor fortitudo: justicia: temperantia: prudentia. Item del hombre prudente es acordarse de lo passado: mirar lo presente: proueer en lo por venir.*

---

[71] Edition by Santiago, 'La puntuación según Nebrija', 282–4; italics added.
[72] Nebrija, *Grammatica*, e4r; italics added.
[73] Sebastián Mediavilla, *Puntuación, humanismo*, 24.
[74] Venegas, *Tractado*, d6r; italics added. See also Sebastián Mediavilla, *Puntuación, humanismo*, 90.

There is another *interval*, which we call *articulus* and whose mark is the same as that of the *comma*, although this *articulus* is used as a substitute for a copulative conjunction. This occurs when elements of the same status are joined together without a conjunction that ties them together. So, between two of these elements we use the mark <:>, like in the sentences: *There are four cardinal virtues courage: justice: temperance: prudence. A prudent man should remember the past: look at the present: prepare for the future.*

Within fifty years of the first publication of Nebrija's treatise,[75] the university professor and orthographer Venegas had already substituted the point <.> for the symbol <:> as the punctuation mark used for *medial punctuation* in enumerations.

In France, between 1546 and 1553, the mark formed by two points <:>, named in Latin *comma*, was in turn equally substituted by the comma <,>, named in French *virgule*. Louis Meigret, in his *Tṛetté de la grammẹre françoẹse* (1550), had by this time presented a very advanced theory of punctuation, which integrated the uses and terminology of printing. In the mid-sixteenth century, Meigret established the use of the comma <,> (for which he used the name of the musical term *soupir* – 'rest' – and which he said was named *point a cúe* – literally, 'point with tail' – by printers) to the detriment of the mark <:>. In this way, he prescribed the comma <,> for enumeration ('this mark is used for various words of the same class') and for punctuating the different clauses of a sentence ('le soupir aosi conjoint la claoz a la claoze', that is to say 'the comma joins a clause to another clause').[76]

5.2.1.3   Medial Punctuation and Connection

The most interesting element to highlight in all these definitions (see Sections 5.2.1.1 and 5.2.1.2) is the value of 'connection' or 'union' that Italian, French and Spanish Renaissance theoreticians attribute to the marks of *medial punctuation* (the point <.>, the *comma* <:>, the *articulo* <:> or the comma <,>). This connective value is often ignored by current philologists, since they generally attribute to all marks the function of 'separation' and so that of a 'pause'. This is important from a linguistic point of view because, semiotically, 'linking' is precisely the opposite of 'separating' or 'pausing'.[77] We cannot overlook the terms used at the time: Barzizza (around 1400) used the term *punctus copulativus*, 'linking point'; Nebrija (around 1502) used the expression *partes orationis* [...] *annectuntur*, meaning 'parts of the sentence [which are] linked',[78] and Meigret, in 1550, highlighted the function of *soupir* <,> as a union of clauses through the verb *conjoindre* ('to join'), as noted above, Section 5.2.1.2.

---

[75] See note 9 for the publication history of Nebrija's 'De punctis clausularum'.

[76] Meigret, *Le Tṛetté*, 142v; *Le Traité*, 139. See also Baddeley, 'Sources', 208 and Pagani-Naudet, 'Ponctuer en 1550'.

[77] For example, Sebastián Mediavilla identifies the *articulus* with 'the point as a separation of a series of words' (*La puntuación en los siglos XVI y XVII*, 8).

[78] Nebrija, 'De punctis clausularum', in edition by Santiago, 'La puntuación según Nebrija', 284.

5.2.2   The Point as Medial Punctuation: A Persistent Use
in the Sixteenth Century

Throughout the sixteenth century, the mark named at that time *comma* (repre-resented by the symbols <:> or <ʔ> in manuscripts, by the symbol <:> in printed texts and subsequently by the comma <,>) were substituting the point in its role of *medial punctuation* and, above all, in its connective qualities. This occurred to such an extent that, as Demonet observed, between 1546 and 1553, the point followed by lowercase (<. m>) as *medial punctuation* was appearing less and less.[79] Appearing less and less, but not completely disappearing. Curiously, the memory of this point serving as *medial punctuation* would remain explicit amongst grammarians in the sixteenth, seventeenth and even eighteenth centuries. When they established the use of the *comma* <:> or the comma <,> in French just as in Spanish, they insisted that the use of the point followed by lowercase, instead of the comma, be banned. Indirectly, the censuring of the *connective point* confirms to us that some people were still using it in a traditional or 'persistent' practice. In 1540, Dolet, whose treatise on punctuation would be used as a reference for the subsequent main theories, banished use that was not sentence-final for the following marks: *colon* in Greek, *punctum* in Latin and *point, point final* or *point rond* in French, that is to say 'full stop':[80]

Quant au poinct final, aultrement dict poinct rond, il se mect tousiours à la fin de la sentence, et iamais n'est en aultre lieu. Et apres luy on commence uouluntiers par une grand letre.

With regard to the full point, also called the *point rond*, it is always placed at the end of a sentence and never in another place. And after it comes an uppercase letter.

The Spaniard Ycíar, in his *Orthographia pratica* (1548), took as a model for the rules of punctuation the Italian printer Manuzio and restricted the point, as did his French contemporary Dolet, to its terminal value:[81]

Punctum clausulare, siue Periodi [...] punto (que llamamos clausular, por que se pone en fin de clausula, que es vna principal parte de nuestro razonamiento: despues del qual siempre se sigue letra capital, o dicha maiuscula) [...]

We call the *punctum clausulare* or *Periodi* [...] 'terminal' because it is placed at the end of a sentence as a complete part of our reasoning. After it, there is always a capital letter, also called uppercase.

The grammarian Jean Bosquet mentioned in 1586 the fact that 'the French and speakers of other languages, in Latin just as in other common languages, substitute the linking value of the *comma* <:> for a point'; following earlier

---

[79] Demonet, 'Ponctuation et narration', 44.   [80] Dolet, 'De la pvnctuation', 23.
[81] Ycíar, *Orthographia*, I5r; italics added.

learned orthographers, Bosquet disapproved of this use.[82] The definition of the *virgule* <,> in Richelet's *Dictionnaire*, written in 1680, still retains the impossibility of using a point in its stead:[83]

Virgule [...] C'est une maniére de petite marque en forme de *c* renversé qu'on met à la fin des parties des periodes quand il n'y faut pas un point seul, & cela pour en distinguer les divers sens.

A comma [...] is a small mark in the shape of an inverted *c*, which we place after those parts of a sentence where we cannot use the full stop. This serves to distinguish between its differing meanings.

Throughout the seventeenth century, the theoreticians of Spanish orthography also insisted on the rule of using the point only as an end to a sentence, followed by uppercase: Jiménez Patón, in 1614, affirmed that it was a question of 'good printing';[84] Miguel Sebastián, in 1619, observed that the rule in question was typically observed by 'the very scholarly'; Juan Bautista de Morales in 1623 and Juan de Palafox y Mendoza in 1662 repeated identical rules.[85] And still, in 1741, the first *Orthographia* of the RAE continued to insist on banning the use of the point followed by lowercase:[86]

Punto final, que se figura assi (.) (despúes del qual siempre se escribe letra mayúscula) sirve, para denotar que está acabado el sentido de lo que queremos decir.

The *full stop*, which is represented like this (.) and after which there must always be uppercase, serves to indicate that the meaning of what we want to say has been completed.

If the point followed by lowercase <. m> was so often censured as *medial punctuation*, it is logical to suppose that it was still in use. In effect, said graphic tradition was considered habitual in manuscript writing: this can be deduced from the *Manual de escribientes* by Torquemada. This author specified around 1552 that there were different uses as between 'those who read and write in printing forms' and 'those who write by hand'. He acknowledged that it was more correct to use the mark <:> to distinguish parts of the sentence but that, in handwriting, the mark <.> was used for the same function. Thus, we detect a case of *diastratic variation* in the uses of punctuation. Torquemada identifies two different 'language registers' determined by technology: an accurate and technical register, proper to printed writing and contemporary rules, and another common and traditional register, proper to manuscripts:[87]

---

[82] Bosquet, *Elemens*, 138.   [83] Richelet, *Dictionnaire*, s.v. *virgule*.
[84] Jiménez Patón, *Epitome*, 78.
[85] Morales, *Pronvnciaciones*; Palafox, *Breve tratado*; Sebastián, *Orthographia*. See also Sebastián Mediavilla, *Puntuación, humanismo*, 120–39.
[86] RAE, *Orthographia*, 262.   [87] Torquemada, *Manual*, 66–7.

En lo que de mano escrevimos [...] todas las vezes que acaváremos noticia o oración, que es donde avemos de hazer un poco de pausa, deteniendo un poco el aliento, o donde acavamos la oración deteniéndonos un poco más, acavaremos con poner un punto, porque no somos tan curiosos o cuidadosos que nos queramos detener a poner dos puntos en la pausa.

When we write by hand, upon finishing a clause, which is when we have a slight pause, briefly holding our breath, or where we stop for a bit longer, we put a point because we are not so careful as to put two points in this pause.

In 1582, Juan López de Velasco explained a similar idea in his treatise *Orthographia y pronunciación castellana*. He distinguished two series of punctuation marks: a formal series and a simpler one, proper to 'ordinary handwriting', which needs fewer punctuation marks because, in López de Velasco's words, 'it is difficult to divide the parts of a sentence correctly'.[88] Indeed the use of the point as distinction between clauses remained in Spanish manuscript writing. It can be seen, for example, in the extant manuscript of the *Diálogo de la lengua* (1535) by the humanist Juan de Valdés:[89]

M. Pues los moços son ydos a comer y nos an dexado, solos antes que venga alguno que nos estorve. tornemos a hablar en lo que començe a deziros esta mañana [...]
V. ya me acuerdo. no tenia cosa mas oluidada.

MARCIO.— As the youngsters have gone for lunch and left us alone, before anyone comes to bother us, let us return to the topic of this morning [...]
VALDÉS.— Now I remember; I had forgotten.

Observe that the 'respiratory' value that Torquemada attributed to the point in *medial punctuation* was also highlighted by French humanists. For example, Tory, in the classification of marks that he presents in his *Champ Fleury* (1529), affirms that he is setting forth the list of the Italian grammarian Orobius (1518),[90] in which two types of points are distinguished: the *colon* or *point respirant* ('respiratory mark'), represented by a point at middle height <·>, which is different to the *periodus* or *point concluant* (a full point represented by a low dot <.>). In reality, Tory's *Champ Fleury* was punctuated by its printer, so that the punctuation of his book did not correspond to Orobius's classification of marks nor to the distinction in Latin between a dot placed at middle height and another below. Curiously, although Tory affirmed that 'the point is the mark of a complete sentence' ('le point est le signe d'une sentence parfaite'),[91] we can see that, in his printed book, the point <.>, the *comma* <:> and the comma <,> alternate constantly in the function of *medial punctuation*. Here I give several examples without exhausting the high rate of graphic variation in the punctuation of *Champ Fleury*.[92]

---

[88] López de Velasco, *Orthographia*, 299.   [89] Valdés, *Diálogo*, fol. 1r.
[90] Orobius, *Libellus*; Tory, *Champ Fleury*, 66r; see Section 5.1.2.
[91] Tory, *Champ Fleury*, 65v. See also Demonet, 'Ponctuation et narration', 40.
[92] In the quotations from *Champ Fleury*, the use of the ampersand <&> in the print original text is maintained.

(1) Distinction between a conditional or temporal subordinate clause and the main clause:

(a) Use of the point followed by uppercase <. M>
Si nous voulons user de Grec ou de Latin. Vsons en / en allegations dautheurs seullement [...] (12r)

Quant ie voy vng Francois escripre en Grec ou en latin. Il me semble que ie voy vng masson vetu dhabits de Philosophe [...] (12v)

(b) Use of the *comma* followed by lowercase <: m>
Et si on me repliquoit que ce sont metres & non pas lettres : ie dirois que [...] il a faict metres en nombre .XXIII. (27v)

(2) Enumeration or connection of lexical units of the same hierarchy:

(a) Use of the point followed by uppercase <. M> in enumerations
Treze diverses facons de Lettres. Cest a scavoir. Lettres Hebraiques. Greques. Latines. Lettres Francoises. & icelles en Quatre facons, qui sont. Cadeaulx. Forme. Bastarde, & Torneure. Puis en suyuant sont les Lettres Persiennes. Arabiques. Africaines. Turques. & Tartariennes. qui sont toutes cinq en vne mesme Figure Dalphabet [...] (A1v)

(b) Connection of parts of discourse at two levels: primary connection <. Et>, secondary connection <, &>
Ce Livre est [...] a vendre [...] par Maistre Geofroy Tory de Bourges / Libraire, & Autheur du dict Liure. Et par Giles Gourmont aussi Libraire (A1r)

(c) Connection of parts of discourse at three levels: primary connection <: &>, secondary connection <, &> and tertiary connection without a mark <&>
FRancois, par la grace de Dieu, Roy de France, aux Preuost de Paris, Baillis de Rouen, & Senechal de Lion: & a tous noz autres Iusticiers & Officiers, ou a leurs Lieuxtenans, & a chascun deulx sicomme a luy apartiendra, salut. (A2r)

(3) The point also appears as a *mark of discourse hierarchy*,[93] with a distributive value, to share out, on either side of the mark, the *theme* and the *rheme* of the statement in question (this is the typical function of the colon <:> in contemporary French, just as in Spanish orthography).

Doncques icelles Quatre sont. Beth, Gimal, Vau, & Mem (68r)

Les Noms des Poincts [...] sont telz quil sensuyt. Pathach, Cames, Hatheph [...] (68r)

[...] ie vous ay cy ensuyuant mis lesdictes Trois sortes de letres. Cest a savoir. Hebreu, Grec, ... Latin (67r)

Iay cy dessoubz pourtraict & designe deux figures dhomme. Lune pour le logis des lettres & lautre pour lesdites Muses & leur sequele. (22r)

---

[93] I follow the terminology used in Dahlet, *Ponctuation*, 91.

(4) As a *mark of discourse hierarchy*, the point can also highlight the introduction of a direct discourse or a new enunciator:

Au contraire les Dames de Paris, en lieu de A pronuncent E. bien souuent, quant elles disent. Mon mery est a la porte de Peris, ou il se faict peier. En lieu de dire. Mon mary est a la porte de Paris ou il se faict paier (33v)

(5) The metalinguistic connector *cest a dire* (modern spelling *c'est-à-dire*) is punctuated according to differing criteria:

(a) With a point <.> after the connector, when a sentence follows:

Punctum, est sententiae perfectae signum. Cest a dire. Le point est le signe dune sentence perfecte. (65v)

Car il les fault lire a Gauche / & en retrogradant. Cest a dire. Il fault commancer a lire a la fin dune chascune ligne (67v).

(b) With a comma <,> after the connector, when a complement follows:

[...] le secret dun nombre Per, & Imper. Cest a dire, de unze points [...] (66r)

(c) With no mark <Ø>, when a nominal or verbal lexeme follows the connector:

Parenthesis (). Cest a dire Point suspensif (66r)

5.2.3   The Point and Punctuation of Enunciation

The *punctuation of enunciation* displays, by graphic signs, the enunciative activity of a writer.[94] One of its modalities is 'semantic reorientation': a punctuation mark highlights the autonymous use of a word, namely its metalinguistic value. Current orthographies mark this value by different types of *quotation marks* (for example: *I like the word 'rain'*). Following on from the mediaeval tradition of using two points (an opening and a closing point), diverse symbols for this type of enunciation mark were used during the sixteenth and seventeenth centuries. In the *Grammatica* of Nebrija (1492), letters and sounds are enclosed between two points:[95]

la .ç. puesta debaxo aquella señal que llaman çerilla

enel verso siguiente. Paro nuestra vida ufana. callamos la .a. e dezimos Paro nuestra vidufana.

In Tory's *Champ Fleury* (1529), when a grapheme is used as the name of a letter and not as its phonetic value, the point <.> and the uppercase allograph highlight this change of code. The point can appear either after the letter, for example <le I.>, or with a double form (opening and closing point), for

---

[94] Following the definition in ibid.   [95] Nebrija, *Grammatica*, b3v, c8r.

example <.E.>. Note that, in the following examples, the punctuation mark does not carry out any possible respiratory pause function, but provides only a visualisation function of the metalinguistic use of the letters:

la iambe de le I. est accordant a la grosseur de la teste (18r)

O. en sens moral.
O. Adverbe Vocatif.
[...]
P. est tire du B.
[...]
Q. torne en C.
Q. nest pas Lettre finalle. (Table of contents, A7r)

No explicit rule about the autonymous use of words can be found until the seventeenth century in treatises on Spanish punctuation. The first definition of metalinguistic marks is that of Juan de Robles, who prescribed the use of the comma (called *inciso* <,>) for this function in 1631:[96]

[El inciso] tambien se ha de poner por señal de cualquiera cosa que particularizamos; como: *La A, es más sonorosa que la E.* Aquellas dos letras han de estar cada una entre dos incisos. *Pedro, es nombre propio.* La diccion *Pedro* ha de estar entre incisos, para que se entienda que hablan della, y nó de hombre que se llame Pedro.

[The comma] should also be used as a sign of anything that we specify. For example: *La A, es más sonorosa que la E.* These two letters should appear between two commas. *Pedro, es nombre propio.* The word *Pedro* goes between commas because it is understood that we are talking about the word itself and not about a man who is called Pedro.

However, some printers had previously trialled more specialised printed characters for the autonymous use of words. This is the case with the Castilian grammar known as *Anónimo de Lovaina* (1559), which does not explicitly mention this type of enunciative punctuation but does include it amongst its graphic resources for dealing with words. Instead of using italics, its printer used two variants of a double mark (an opening and a closing mark). This practice was not yet standardised or defined, but its innovation outlined a 'potential standard', given that, centuries later, inverted commas would become part of widespread linguistic standard as a visual mark of the autonymous use of words (for example, in current Spanish: *Me gusta la palabra "lluvia"*; in English, *I like the word 'rain'*). These are the two graphic variants in the *Anónimo de Lovaina*:[97]

---

[96] Robles, *Primera parte*, in Sebastián Mediavilla, *Puntuación, humanismo*, 128–9.
[97] Anónimo, *Gramatica*, 6v, 15r.

(1) A straight double quotation mark and a point <". >:

como " rei, lei, teneis. también es latino este ditongo
como " hei. es Italiano
como " lei, fei. es Frances

as *rei*, *lei*, *teneis* this diphthong also is Latin
as *hei* is Italian
as *lei*, *fei* is French

(2) A dash and a point <– . >:

Como –faia, vaia, malicia, presencia. en las lenguas Latina i Francesa

As *faia*, *vaia*, *malicia*, *presencia* in Latin and French

El primero dellos es aquel, que se dize de la primera persona, es a saber –io. en Latin
–ego. en Italiano –io. en Frances –ie.

The first of those is the one for the first-person singular pronoun *yo*, *ego* in Latin, *io* in
Italian, *je* in French.

Observe in this last case that the point used as a closing mark 'absorbs' the
presence of the comma <,> to distinguish between the units of an enumeration.
Thus, it becomes a point followed by lowercase with the value of a *minor medial
pause*. The concept of 'absorption', used by Claude Tournier and Véronique
Dahlet,[98] plays a role in explaining some mechanisms of punctuation. In the lineal
combination of some adjacent marks, contact implies the disappearance of one of
them. As an example: there is a law of 'absorption' in current standards, according
to which the question mark <?> 'absorbs' the full stop of the sentence and makes it
disappear. We write <*What time is it?*> and not <*What time is it?.*>. Straight double
quotation marks are innovative in this context; but the point here corresponds to an
old mediaeval tradition common to Latin and vernacular texts. The point does not
function as a respiratory pause; it is a mark proper to the functional autonomy of
writing, which visually distinguishes a category of enunciation.

5.2.4   *Connection and Punctuation Marks 'For the Eye'*

I outlined above (see Section 5.2.1.3) the value of 'connection' or 'union' that
punctuation theorists of the fifteenth and sixteenth centuries attributed to the
marks of *medial punctuation*. This value refutes the preconceived idea that all
marks of punctuation that Renaissance systems presented still had the rhetoric
quality of representing respiratory pauses of different lengths: brief pause,
medium pause, long pause. In addition to the metalinguistic function that has
just been mentioned, there are other functions of the point which demonstrate

---

[98] Tournier, 'Histoire', 39; Dahlet, *Ponctuation*, 26.

its connection value more than its use for the notation of supposed respiratory pauses.

5.2.4.1 Connection of Grammatical Morphemes

A representative case is one which Petrus Ramus theorised in his *Grammaire* of 1572: he reported a Latin system of punctuation marks which was already obsolete at this time, but that reflected clearly the old connective value of medial punctuation. This system included four marks for the segmentation of discourse: the *soupir* </> (a forward slash), the *demipause* (or *demipose*) <·> (a middle point), the *pause* <'> (a high point) and the *periode* <.> (a low point). This middle point <·> represented for Ramus the connection between an incomplete part of the discourse and the elements that completed its meaning; for example, subordinate adjective clauses (*ce · qui est juste*) or subordinate completive clauses (*conclurre · que ...*). It was replaced by a simple comma <,> by the 'new grammarians' – as Ramus called them – and represents, in my view, not a pause, but a link between two units of syntax:[99]

Demipose cest vne distinction de sentence imparfaicte, & se marque par le poinct moyen, ainsi · [...] Vous auez toutes ses distinctions en ceste exemple. [...] *Car ils estiment estre prouffitable tout ce · qui est juste ' Aussi iugent ils estre iuste tout ce · qui est honneste ' Dont il fault conclurre · que tout ce · qui est honneste ' que cela mesme soit vtile.*

Demipose is the punctuation mark of an incomplete sentence and is represented by a middle point <·>. You can see all these distinctions in this example: *Car ils estiment estre prouffitable tout ce · qui est juste ' Aussi iugent ils estre iuste tout ce · qui est honneste ' Dont il fault conclurre que tout ce · qui est honneste ' que cela mesme soit vtile.*

Note that, in the structure *ce · qui est juste*, the point does not represent any pause but functions as a nexus, similar to the hyphen which currently joins grammaticalised sequences such as *c'est-à-dire* in modern French spelling. Demonet reminds us that, following the typical alternation between the point and the comma in the sixteenth century, Tory used the comma for this same function (for example: *en ce, que daucuns escrivent*).[100] Demonet also observes that the point was occasionally used with this value in the English language during the seventeenth century.[101]

5.2.4.2 Connection and Coordination

According to the current norm, coordinated words do not require punctuation, given that there is already a conjunction that semantically denotes the

---

[99] Ramus, *Grammaire*, 207–8. I have standardised spacing before and after punctuation marks even though, as is usual in sixteenth-century printing, it is not consistent in the original; italics added.
[100] Tory, *Champ Fleury*, A3r; see Demonet, 'Ponctuation et narration', 45.
[101] Referring to Ben Jonson (1620), following the study by Salmon, 'English punctuation', 290ff, quoted by Demonet, 'Ponctuation et narration', 45.

connection and that, in principle, there is not an obligatory pause. We usually write *blanco y negro, noir et blanc, black and white* and not *blanco, y negro; noir, et blanc; black, and white*. However, in Latin, French and Spanish, the most intensive and long-lasting use of *medial punctuation*, which had a function of 'connection' and not a pausal value, was the reinforcement of coordinating conjunctions (in Latin *et*, in Spanish *e/et/y/i* and *o*; in French *et, ou* and *ne*) by means of a point <.> or a slash </> in manuscripts, and a *comma* <:> or a modern comma <,> in print texts. In the brief examples presented above (see Section 5.2), we can see the most characteristic punctuation of coordinated words: *Peres . et fils . et esperis, Terre . mers . et airs*. It consists of a secular tradition in manuscripts, inherited from Latin and already mentioned in the fourth century by the Latin grammarian Diomedes,[102] but which was also common among French and Spanish printers of the sixteenth century, although it was not considered in French orthographic treatises until 1540 and until the seventeenth century in Spanish: some authors banned its use, others recommended it and others still accept either the presence or the absence of a comma in coordinate structures.

(1)   Coordination in the French Language

Dolet was one of the orthographers to accept the tradition of placing a punctuation mark before the conjunctions *et* and *ou* in French. He stated in 1540:[103]

Deuant que de uenir aux aultres poincts, ie te ueulx aduertir, que le poinct à queue se mect deuant ce mot, ou : semblablement deuant ce mot, &.

Before addressing other marks, I want to advise you that the comma <,> is placed before the word *ou* and equally before the word *et*.

However, the grammarian Meigret was the first French theoretician, very early on, in 1550, to prefer non-punctuated coordination and, citing proper linguistic arguments, highlighted that the comma is optional just as pausing is optional for speakers and writers:[104]

Or faot il ęntęndre qe qant a la copulatiue ę, ę a la disjonctiue ou ęlles sont ao plęzir du pononçant quant il' ne conjoiñent point clauz' a claoze: de sorte q'il ęt ęn nous de lę' prononçęr sans soupir preçedant, ę lors l'apostroph' y ęt neçessęre: come *Pięrr'ę Ian*: ou *Pięrr'ou Ian*: ou bien avęq soupir come, *Pięrre, ę Ian*: *Pięrre, ou Ian*: combien qe le premier ęt plus vzité tant ęntre lęs aotres partíes, q'ęntre lę' noms

We have to understand that, when they are not used to link clauses, the linking conjunction *et* and the disjunctive conjunction *ou* are used according to the will of the speaker. Thus, we must decide whether to pronounce them without a preceding pause, as an apostrophe, such as in *Pierr'et Jean* or in *Pierr'ou Jean*, or to make a pause before

---

[102] Hubert, 'Corpvs', 34. See also Sebastián Mediavilla, *Puntuación, humanismo*, 71.
[103] Dolet, 'De la pvnctuation', 21.   [104] Meigret, *Le Tretté*, 140v–141r; italics added.

them, such as in *Pierre, et Jean* or in *Pierre, ou Jean*. In any case, the first option is more frequent as much with words belonging to the same grammatical category as with nouns.

In 1692, the grammarian Nicolas Andry de Boisregard also suggested that 'if there is a conjunction, there is no need to use a comma, for example, in this coordination: *science et erudition*'.[105] Nevertheless, the conservative force of graphic tradition seems to have prevailed over Meigret's early and accurate observations because we find the use of a comma before conjunctions in French in all manner of written and printed texts. The practices of grammarians themselves can serve as examples. Robert Estienne wrote in 1557: '*s* entre deux voyelles se prononce doulcement, & mollement'. Vaugelas, a century later, in 1647, continued by writing: 'la commodité, & l'utilité de ces Remarques'.[106] Even in the eighteenth century, the *Encyclopédie d'Yverdon* (1770–80) explicitly stated that a comma must be placed 'without exception' before the conjunction *et* in enumerations that reach three or more elements, for example in *Le roi, les grands, et le peuple*; *La vertu, et l'esprit, et la science.*[107]

(2)   Coordination in the Spanish Language
In Spanish, until the seventeenth century, the tradition of placing a comma before the conjunctions *e/y* and *o* was not explicitly noted. It was first mentioned by Felipe Mey in 1607, Morales in 1623, the orthographer Palafox in 1662 and the printer Víctor de Paredes in 1680.[108] Such a tradition was generally practised in printed texts, although, it must be noted, punctuation of the conjunctions *e/y/o* is often a graphic variant. We can see, therefore, that an individual printer would either use or avoid a punctuation mark in identical syntactic and semantic structures. Conjunctions were punctuated in this way in the following significant examples: Nebrija's *Grammatica de la lengua castellana* of 1492.[109]

para los que enseñan a leer : i para los que quieren leer las cifras

la .n. pertenece ala vocal primera : i se desata dela siguiente i assi la tenemos de escrivir. deletrear. i pronunciar.

assi tenemos de escrivir como pronunciamos : i pronunciar como escrivimos.

figura por la cual se representa la voz : i pronunciacion.

veinte i tres figuras de letras

---

[105] Andry de Boisregard, *Réflexions*, 423.
[106] Estienne, *Traicté*, 10; Vaugelas, *Remarques*, Préface.
[107] *Encyclopédie d'Yverdon*, s.v. *ponctuation*.
[108] Mey, *De ortografía*; Morales, *Pronvnciaciones*; Palafox, *Breve tratado*; Paredes, *Institución*. See Sebastián Mediavilla, *Puntuación, humanismo*, 71.
[109] Nebrija, *Grammatica*, b7r, b7v, c1r, b1v, b1v, a5r, c1r.

a los professores i maestros della llamaron grammaticos

aunque la lengua griega i Latina puedan doblar las consonantes

or Miguel de Cervantes's *Quijote*, published in 1605.[110]

Que tuue ausente, y desdeñado sobre

Y alçandote la plata, estaño, y cobre (*Amadis de Gaula a Don Quixote. Soneto*)[111]

Despite the apparent insignificance of this tradition, I believe that it concerns a graphic criterion that is very important for the history of Western punctuation. Firstly, it is perhaps the most long-standing punctuation 'rule' in space and time: it lasted a millennium in Latin and, in French, for example, it can be found from the tenth century until the nineteenth. Secondly, it demonstrates clearly that, in the practice of punctuation, from the Middle Ages until the modern age, not all marks had an oratorical and pausal value or a suprasegmental correspondence. Punctuation marks before conjunctions are often visual marks of connection and not notations of pauses. I have tried to demonstrate this assertion with strictly linguistic criteria, through the analysis of metrics in proverbs and poems of the sixteenth and seventeenth centuries.[112] For example, the version of the *Proverbios de gloriosa doctrina* by the Marqués de Santillana glossed by Pero Díaz de Toledo and published around 1500 presents coordinated words, synonyms or near-synonyms, with marks of *medial punctuation* or, equally, without marks:[113]

(a) Conjunction with punctuation
Con estudio: e diligencia
Distinguir: e conocer

(b) Conjunction without punctuation
Ca sus lineas e senderos
De punir e castigar

The proverbs in question are composed in octosyllabic verse. In those in which coordination is punctuated, the marks of punctuation cannot represent any internal pause. One can prove this in cases of *synalepha* (a phonetic phenomenon that consists in the union of two or more contiguous vowels of different words into one syllable). When there is a *comma* <:> between two contiguous vowels pronounced in a single syllable, this *comma* cannot be a pausal mark. It reflects a long-standing tradition of punctuating conjunctions with marks that imply not a pausal or a respiratory value but a visual reinforcement of the copulative sense of a conjunction. Let us look at some more examples:[114]

---

[110] Sebastián Mediavilla, *La puntuación del* Quijote; 'A propósito del *Persiles*', 355.
[111] Cervantes, *El ingenioso hidalgo*, [Xr].
[112] Llamas-Pombo, 'Metro, ritmo y puntuación', 469–74.
[113] Santillana, *Los Prouerbios*, 10va, 11vb, 7vb, 14rb.   [114] Ibid., 11ra, 12ra.

Ha fecho: e faze por nos

A synalepha takes place in this octosyllabic verse: *ha-fe-**cho:e**-fa-ze-por-nos* (syllable boundaries are shown by hyphens and the synalepha in bold; note that the last stressed syllable *nós* implies an additional syllable in Spanish metrics). The phonic sequence ***cho:e*** makes a single syllable; thus the *comma* cannot represent a pause.

Del mundo: e la monarchia

Equally, in this octosyllable, the synalepha ***do:e*** joins two vowels between which there cannot be a pause: *del-mun-**do:e**-la-mo-nar-chi-a*.

Upon publishing the first edition of Hernán Núñez de Toledo's *Refranes o proverbios* in Salamanca in 1555,[115] the printer did not use medial punctuation with conjunctions (for example: *Ajo y vino puro, y luego veras quien es cada vno*; *Abril frio, pan y vino*; *Agua y sol para las huertas*). However, the subsequent edition, published in Lérida in 1621, presents the traditional punctuation of the conjunction *y*, although it used the comma <,> and not the *comma* <:>, which was more frequent in the sixteenth century. The cases of synalepha equally confirm that the comma could not have represented a pause.[116]

Agua fría, y pan caliente
nunca hicieron buen vientre

Manda manda, Pedro, y anda.

The first octosyllable is read with synalepha: *a-gua-frí-**a,** y-pan-ca-lien-te*. The latter octosyllable is also read with synalepha: *man-da-man-da-pe-**dro,** y-an-da*. Thus the comma <,> cannot have a pausal value. Similarly, in the hendecasyllabic verses of Cervantes's sonnets cited above, the comma does not have a pausal value because a synalepha is obligatory between the conjunction *y* and the preceding vowel, to count eleven syllables (synalepha shown in bold):

Que tuue ausen**te, y** desdeñado sobre

Y alçandote la plata, esta**ño, y** cobre (*Amadis de Gaula a Don Quixote. Soneto*)[117]

Rompi, cortè, abollè, y di**xe, y** hize

Fui comedi**do, y** regalado amante (*Don Belianís de Grecia, a Don Quixote de la Mancha. Soneto*)[118]

---

[115] Núñez, *Refranes* 1555 ed.   [116] Ibid., 1621 ed., 4r, 70r.
[117] Cervantes, *El ingenioso hidalgo*, [Xr].   [118] Ibid., [Xv].

5.3   Conclusions

European thought on written language appears to reflect great currents that cannot be understood as proper to only one language but must be seen as part of the history of linguistic ideas common to modern Europe, beyond differences between languages. This hypothesis has been shown to be true following this 'case study' on the theory and practice of the point in the fifteenth, sixteenth and seventeenth centuries, because its history is paralleled in the evolution of French and Spanish orthographies. The degree of graphic variation between orthographers and printers was still considerable in that period, but the comparative study of the testimonies of the two Romance languages allows us to better understand which syntactic and discursive units were distinguished by writers of that period, and to prove the degree of European unity in the theory of punctuation. Consequently, this case demonstrates the potential for a *comparative graphematics of European punctuation* to analyse the history of punctuation marks and to study the development of punctuation theory in Romance languages and other languages like English from a contrastive point of view. It could also be fruitful to study in the future the punctuation of Spanish works published abroad during the sixteenth and seventeenth centuries, in France and above all in the Netherlands (modern Holland and Belgium). A comparative study on punctuation across languages could be of interest, in the observation of graphic practices in multilingual works published during the sixteenth and seventeenth centuries, like dictionaries, dialogues for learning languages[119] or religious and technical texts.[120]

The *comparative perspective* gives us precise and novel insights into aspects of the history of orthography:

(1) It underlines the influence of the different *writing technologies*, hand or printed, in the processes of variability and standardisation.
(2) It also reveals the progressive *diastratic perception* distinguishing between more or less correct forms, which was especially developed over the sixteenth and seventeenth centuries in the face of the wide freedom and variability of mediaeval graphical marks.
(3) It proves that both graphic 'persistent' practices and printers' and orthographers' innovation are the same in French and Spanish.

If punctuation is, in Parkes's words, 'one of the contributions to literate civilization',[121] it would be pertinent to continue with the investigation of a common history of European punctuation, as a unique and significant object in

---

[119] For example, Fernández's dialogues for learning foreign languages. See Sáez Rivera, 'Marcos Fernández'.
[120] For a repertory of multilingual religious works during the sixteenth and the seventeenth centuries, see Pablo Núñez, 'El español de los *Emblemas*'. For multilingual technical works, see Pablo Núñez, 'Las *Machinæ Novæ*'.
[121] Parkes, 'Punctuation', 127.

the history of the European written heritage. Over the last two decades, editors of French and Spanish texts from the sixteenth and seventeenth centuries have shown a greater interest in maintaining the original punctuation of the edited works. Additionally, theorists of current linguistic punctuation often allude to its diachronic perspective. It is essential for both philologists and linguists to bear in mind various methodological principles that I have exemplified in this chapter and summarise below.

(a) Complementarity of theory and practice
None of the systems of punctuation of edited texts from these two centuries can be explained exclusively by reference to the theoretical treatises of the period: firstly, as there is a notable divergence between the theory and practice of the orthographers themselves and, secondly, because there were persistent rules or traditions of punctuation that came from mediaeval practice and were not recorded by theorists. An additional reason is that there were innovative practices that had never been the object of any theorisation. The uses of punctuation go beyond the contents of orthographic treatises. Only a parallel and comparative analysis of both theory and practice can complete the history of punctuation of the sixteenth and seventeenth centuries and explain the linguistic competence of writers from the past.

(b) Punctuation for the voice and punctuation for the eye
The history of modern punctuation cannot be simplified as if it were an easy step from the respiratory, pausal and oratorical function of marks to a visual function of the logical ordering of syntax, what Sabine Boucheron-Petillon has aptly called 'the oral myth'.[122] The evolution of ideas on punctuation has never been limited to a progressive mutation of prosodic notation to syntactic notation.[123] It is also the analysis of punctuation practice that shows us that, in all periods, there are punctuation marks 'for the eye', i.e. graphic criteria that express syntactic notions. An exemplary case is that of *medial punctuation* through the use of various marks (the point <.>, the *comma* <:> and the comma <,>) as was used in the sixteenth and seventeenth centuries in French and Spanish. The common link between these marks was the *persistent value of connection between linguistic units* as an autonomous use of graphical marks, not determined by the representation of pauses. This value constitutes a *linguistic invariant* that manifests itself in different languages and throughout almost a millennium (this invariant can be defined as 'graphical mark that

---

[122] The introduction to Boucheron-Pétillon's punctuation theories (*Les Détours*, 24) evaluates, within the history of French grammar and lexicography, this unresolved tension between oral expression and syntactic–semantic articulation. See also Anis ('Les Linguistes français', 5–6).

[123] For example, in English linguistic historiography, Bruthiaux ('Knowing when to stop', 35) highlights authors from the sixteenth century who explain the structural values of punctuation, as well as subsequent authors who continued to invoke its prosodic values.

indicates a connection between graphic segments'). Numerous authors have continued to refer to the function of 'separating' units, when those marks do not 'separate' nor do they represent 'pauses' but, on the contrary, they join syntactically linked words for the reader.

(c) Complementarity between old theory and contemporary graphematics
In order to study the history of punctuation it is appropriate to complement our analysis based on parameters, concepts and linguistic terminology with ideas and terms used in old texts. The two perspectives complement and illuminate each other. I have illustrated this principle with the case of the connective value of the point and the comma, which has endured for centuries: my definition of *marks of connection* was already in use by some fifteenth-century theorists with terms such as *punctus copulativus*.

(d) Reading and editing Golden Age Spanish and preclassical French
Diachronic graphematics can contribute to our textual heritage by explaining the value of punctuation in Golden Age Spanish and preclassical French texts: it allows us to read them faithfully and therefore to edit them better.

6 Orthographic Variation and Materiality of a Manuscript

Pre-standard Lithuanian Spellings in Simonas
Daukantas's 'History of the Lithuanian Lowlands'
(1831–4)

Giedrius Subačius

The literary activity of Simonas Daukantas (1793–1864) was of the utmost significance to the development of the Lithuanian national consciousness in the nineteenth century. More than any other public figure of the first two-thirds of the
century, Daukantas and his work are considered to have been charged with national
revivalist meaning. Today, Daukantas is credited with being the first to define the
Lithuanian *nation* in linguistic terms and is acknowledged for his efforts to connect
the Lithuanian majority in western Imperial Russia with the minority population in
East Prussia. He wrote the earliest histories of Lithuania in Lithuanian, the second
of which is the subject of this chapter. In addition to his three impressive manuscripts on Lithuanian history, Daukantas published an ethnographic history, which
is considered to be the first scholarly book ever printed in Lithuanian.[1] He wrote
Lithuanian grammars and dictionaries, translations of authors from antiquity,
literature for young adults and popular agricultural pamphlets. Today, schools,
streets and squares are named after him in several Lithuanian cities. The hundred-
litas bill was even decorated with Daukantas's portrait (the litas was the currency of
Lithuania from 1993 to 2014, before the introduction of the euro).

The emergence of the standard Lithuanian language is usually dated to
between 1883 and 1885, with the appearance of the national newspaper
Aušra. Lithuanian is a late (nineteenth century and later) dialect (norm) selection standard language, in line with patterns of standardisation in numerous
other European languages including Albanian, Belarusian, Bulgarian, Catalan,
Estonian, Faroese, Latvian, Luxemburgish, Finnish, Nynorsk, Romanian,
Serbian, Slovak, Slovene and Ukrainian. These standard languages were for-
malised considerably later than the early dialect selection languages that
emerged between the fifteenth and seventeenth centuries such as Danish,
Dutch, French, German, English, Italian, Polish, Spanish and Swedish.[2] The

---

[1] Daukantas, *Budą Senowęs-Lëtuwiû Kalnienû ïr Žámajtiû*, in 1845.
[2] See Subačius, 'Two types'.

period in which Daukantas lived preceded the standardisation of Lithuanian, so there were multiple ways in which the language could be written, and authors were often inconsistent in their dialect and spelling preferences. One traditional way of spelling (that of a western Highland dialect) was used in Prussia; another (that of a different branch of the same western Highland dialect, based on the speech of the town of Kėdainiai and its environs) was used in Lithuania, which was part of the Russian Empire at the time. There were also various attempts to write in the Lowland dialects of western Lithuania. In his early career, Daukantas had largely followed the most traditional way of spelling, that used for the Lowland dialects. In the year 1827, however, he initiated some remarkable modifications, which mark the beginning of his unique orthography. This chapter examines the orthography in the most extensive of Daukantas's manuscripts: 'Istoryje Żemaytyszka' ('History of the Lithuanian Lowlands'),[3] compiled in approximately 1831–4, while Daukantas was living in Rīga, Latvia (then also part of the Russian Empire). The manuscript consists of 553 leaves (1,106 pages) in folio, and it describes the history of Lithuania from the earliest times to the union with Poland in 1569. The orthography of the 'History' is rich in variation and often incongruous. Before attempting to describe and explain this diversity, I present examples of graphemic variants that represent the Lowland Lithuanian diphthong /əi/ in root position (the phoneme /ə/ is a mid central vowel here).

6.1   Lowland Lithuanian Diphthong /əi/

Daukantas selected complex patterns of graphemes to express his dialectal diphthong /əi/ in roots (the current standard Lithuanian equivalent, based on a Western Highland dialect, has a different diphthong, /ie/).[4] Had Daukantas followed a generalising phonetic rule, he could have opted to represent it by a single uniform digraph. Instead, he employed at least seven different graphic renderings of the diphthong /əi/ (or its equivalent /ie/ in Highland dialects) in his 'History': <ei>, <ęi>, <yi>, <ij>, <ie>, <iei>, <iey>, of which only the <ie> variant may be interpreted as a Highland feature. Of these, the most frequently used were <ei>, <ęi>, <yi>, <ij>. There is no doubt that Daukantas readily identified the diphthong /əi/ of his own dialect, as he represented it uniformly in certain concrete words (roots). For instance, hundreds of times in the 'History' he wrote <ei> in the words *deina*, 'a day' (*diena* in standard Lithuanian), *deiws*, 'God' (standard Lithuanian *Dievas*), *weita*, 'place, location' (standard Lithuanian *vieta*) and in their derivatives. He applied different strategies to

---

[3] Daukantas, 'Istoryje Żemaytyszka', inaccurately named thus by someone other than the author.
[4] See Subačius, 'Simono Daukanto dvibalsio [ęi]'.

many other words, however, and these strategies of change and transformation led to ample variation.

6.1.1   /əi/ after Palatal /kʲ/

One comparatively simple pattern of spelling variation of /əi/ may be reconstructed when it occurs after the palatal consonant /kʲ/ (grapheme <k>). These sounds occur in such words as (in standard Lithuanian) *kiek*, 'how many; how much', *kiekvienas*, 'everybody, everyone', *kiemas*, '(court)yard', *kietas*, 'hard', *skieda*, 'shingle' and *skiesti*, 'separate; detach'. In the first half of his manuscript, Daukantas used many variants (<kei>, <kyi>, <kie>, <kiei>, <kiey>) interchangeably to spell such words, but from fol. 256v he began using the single spelling <kiey>. This was Daukantas's firm decision, and he adhered to it not only to the end of the 'History', but in many of his later texts as well. The spelling <kiey> was an older feature of Polish orthography to denote palatalisation of /k/, indicating the mute letter <i> after <k> and before <ey> = <kiey>. The Poles used the same spelling after <g>, <giey> (cf. early-nineteenth-century Polish spellings *wielkiey*, '[of] huge', fem. sg. and *drugiey*, '[of] second', fem. sg.). Daukantas, however, decided to use only the <kiey> variant in his Lithuanian texts and not <giey>, which suggests his intention was not simply to follow Polish orthography. Indeed, Daukantas's use of <kiey> was connected to the name of the famous Grand Duke of Lithuania, Kęstutis (1297–1382),[5] which was pronounced with the same diphthong /əi/ in Daukantas's dialect. Daukantas found this name spelled 'Kieyſtutus' in a history of Lithuania, written in Latin, by Alberto Wiivk Koialowicz.[6] (Roughly two-thirds of the 'History' was in fact a loose translation of Koialowicz's history.)[7] Daukantas began writing extensively about Grand Duke Kęstutis on fol. 256v, at which point he also began to employ the <Kiey>, <kiey> spellings both in that name and in root position of other words with /kʲəi/ in Daukantas's dialect, e.g. *Kieystauts* and *kieykweiname*, *neskieydies*, *kieymû*, etc. As Figure 6.1 clearly demonstrates, the <kiey> variant predominates in the 'History', almost to the exclusion of all others after fols. 251–60.

6.1.2   The First Variational Group of /əi/ Representation: *<ei>* and *<ęi>*

I have distinguished two other abundantly represented variational groups of lexemes containing /əi/ in their roots. Words in the first variational group are

---

[5] See ibid., 69.   [6] Koialowicz, *Historiae Litvanae pars prior*, 347, 348, 349.
[7] See Bončkutė, 'Veikalo *Historia Lituana* recepcija'.

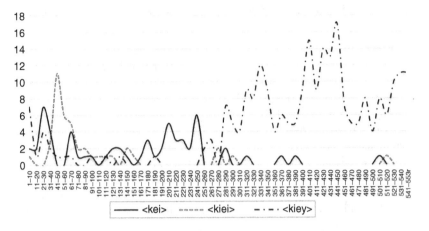

Figure 6.1 Dynamics of three major spelling variants of the diphthong /əi/ after palatal /kʲ/ in the 'History'

Note: Occurrences of <ei>, <iei>, <iey> (excluding the data for the name 'Kęstutis'). The vertical axis shows the number of occurrences; the horizontal axis indicates folio numbers.

mostly spelled with the <ei> digraph, or, less often, with the diacritical variant <ęi>. Compare the two variants when /əi/ is after a single initial consonant:

> *teis*, 'by; at' : *tęis*; *teisa*, 'truth' : *tęisa*
> *weiszes*, 'feast' : *węisznes*, 'guests' (fem.)
> *geiżdams*, '[one that] is craving revenge' (masc.) : *gęiżdams*
> *żeiba*, 'lightning' (pl.) : *żęima*, 'winter'
> *meiktante*, '[one that] sleeps' (acc. fem.) : *męigtanti*, '[one that] sleeps' (acc. masc.)
> *apreite*, '[they] bent [it] down' : *apręista*, '[one that] is bent down' (fem.)
> *deiga*, 'a sprout' (acc.) : *dęiga*, '[of] a sprout' (gen.)

Or after two consonants:

> *greite*, 'to plunder; to spoil' : *gręite*
> *sukweites*, '[one that] invited' (masc.) : *sukwęite*, '[he, she] invited'
> *pleinù*, '[with] steel' (instr.) : *plęinù*
> *sneigas*, 'snow' : *snęigas*

In this first group of lexemes, the variant <ei> dominates (occurring 735 times); the diacritical variant <ęi> is also fairly common (occurring 244 times). Both variants appear throughout the 'History', with no specific area of concentration in either case. Some other variants also appear, but so rarely that their inclusion could be accidental and is of minimal importance (e.g. <yi>, occurring 43 times).

6.1.3   The Second Variational Group of /əi/ Representation: <ei> and <ęi> plus <yi> and <ij>

The second variational group features the same variants <ei> and <ęi> (both of which are present throughout the 'History'), but also includes the 'additional' variants <yi> and <ij>. These, however, are concentrated only in specific sections of the manuscript, as follows: both <yi> and <ij> on fols. 31r–43r, only <yi> on fols. 319r–421r, and only <ij> on fols. 421v–553r. Thus, for instance, on fols. 319r–421r, the dominant variants of <ei> and <ęi> can be seen in addition to <yi>, but on fols. 421v–553r, <ei> and <ęi> alternate with the digraph <ij>, as if the variant <yi> from fol. 421v were substituted for <ij>. Daukantas continued to employ the variants <ei> and <ęi> as well as these, so at least three variants competed simultaneously in the sections under consideration. Examples of the second variational type include:

> *leipe*, '[he, she] ordered, directed' : *lęipe* : *lyipe* : *lijpe*
> *paleikt*, '[he, she] remains' : *belęikt*, '[it] remains only' : *lyipas*, '[of] a linden tree' (gen.); '[of] the month of July' (gen.) : *lijpu*, '[of] linden trees' (gen.)
> *paseikte*, 'to reach out' : *pasęikte* : *pasyikte* : *pasijkte*
> *teikte*, 'to render; to distribute' : *tęikies*, '[he, she] rendered; distributed' : *tyikę* : *tijkies*
> *teik*, 'that much' : *tęik* : *tyik* : *tijk*
> *peitus*, 'dinner' : *pęitu*, '[of] dinner' (gen.) : *pyitus* : *pijtu*

The variants in this second group appear with the following frequency in the manuscript: <ei> 376 times, <yi> 331 times, <ij> 169 times and <ęi> 136 times. All these variants appear after a single consonant (roots having two or more consonants before the diphthong /əi/ belong only to the first variational group). The common root *liep-* (*liepti*, 'to order, to command') can serve as an example of the second variational group: <leip> 199 times, <lęip> 45 times, <lijp> 54 times, <lyip> 90 times. As shown in Figure 6.2, the variant <lyip> dominates from roughly fol. 311 to fol. 400; the variant <lijp> becomes dominant from roughly fol. 443r.

6.1.4   Aesthetic Principle in the Second Variational Group of /əi/ Representation

The difference in spellings of the two variational types (graphemic rendering of the diphthong /əi/) begins roughly at fols. 31r–43r, after which point the first group loses the rare variant <yi>. The second group retains <yi>, which occurs with particular frequency between fols. 236v and 425v. Given that the variant <yi> was specific to texts written by Daukantas prior to 1827,[8] it can be argued

---

[8] See Subačius, 'Pirmasis', 210, 219–20.

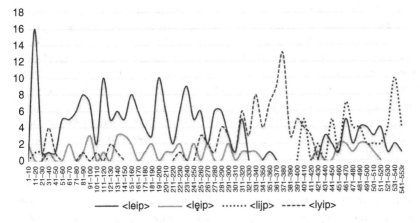

Figure 6.2 Dynamics of the four major spelling variants of the diphthong /əi/ in the common root *liep-* (*liepti*, 'to order, to command') in the 'History'

Note: <leip> 199 times, <lęip> 45 times, <lijp> 54 times, <lyip> 90 times. The vertical axis shows the number of occurrences; the horizontal axis indicates folio numbers.

that the second variational group was initially less modernised, and was possibly more susceptible to the orthography of Daukantas's lost drafts. Daukantas later began modernising the second group differently, by substituting <yi> for <ij> (this change was not applied to the first group). No other writer could possibly have discerned such orthographic groups; the groupings were unique to Daukantas. Neither palatalisation (velarisation), vowel assimilation, intonation, accentuation patterns, nor any other phonetic feature helps to explain the principle upon which Daukantas based his distinction between the two groups. The question of why the digraphs <yi> and <ij> were conspicuous only in words of the second group can be satisfactorily answered solely in terms of graphic representation (and highlights the importance of graphotactics). One graphic feature that unites the <yi> and <ij> variants is the *visual length*: <y> and <j> both have long descenders. The length of strokes in these letters seems to have mattered. In the second group, many roots begin with a long grapheme (containing either a long descender or ascender). For instance, common words with the elongated initial letter <l> (in standard Lithuanian) include *liepti*, 'to order, to direct', *lieka*, '[he, she] remains', *lieknas*, 'grove', *liemuo*, 'torso', *liepa*, 'linden tree; month of July', *liepsna*, 'flame', *liesas*, 'skinny' and *lieti*, 'to pour', all of which Daukantas often spelled with a <lyi> or a <lij>. Another letter with a long ascender, <t>, was also often followed by <yi> and <ij> in the common words *tiekti*, 'to render; to distribute' and *tiek*, 'that much' (<tyi> and <tij>). The third long grapheme (with a long descender) that must have affected

Daukantas's graphic choices was <p>: cf. <pyi> and <pij> in the words *piemuo*, 'shepherd', *pienas*, 'milk', *piestu*, 'prancingly (of a horse)', *piešti*, 'to draw', *pietūs*, 'dinner; south', *pieva*, 'lawn'. This spelling pattern is not absolute, and there are examples that do not follow it. For instance, Daukantas spelled some other roots after <t> without a long letter (*ties*, 'by; at', *tiesus*, 'straight'); these therefore belong to the first variational group. Also, some words in the second group have a long <y> or <j> even after the 'short' grapheme <s>: *prisiekti*, 'to swear (an oath)', *siekis*, 'month of January', *sieksnis*, 'fathom (unit of length of approx. 2 m)', *siekti*, 'to reach; to seek'.

Nevertheless, the correlation between the long initial graphemes <l>, <t>, <p> and the long variants of digraphs <yi> and <ij> in different sections of the manuscript is frequent and obvious. Daukantas must have been correlating the shapes of the graphemes, choosing certain letters because of their graphic form. The length of <l>, <t>, <p> inspired him to use the long graphemes <yi> and <ij>; on the other hand, two (rather than one) consonant-signifying letters before the diphthong /əi/ unequivocally discouraged the use of <yi> and <ij>. Graphotactics mattered. Daukantas was ornamenting his manuscript orthographically; the aesthetic composition of the signs also mattered to him. Daukantas must have perceived the graphic variants <ei>, <yi>, <ij> for the same diphthong as indivisible units (only the variant <ęi> might have been perceived as a variety of <ei>). In 2004, the psychologists Marie J. Tainturier and Brenda C. Rapp found evidence in modern English orthography, based on two cases of acquired dysgraphia, to the effect that digraphs are represented in subjects' minds 'in a different manner than other grapheme sequences' and therefore, in order to account for their pattern of results, they proposed 'that digraphs are represented as units with an internal structure that specifies the identity and ordering of their constituents'.[9]

Daukantas also manipulated the digraphs <ei>, <yi>, <ij> as inseparable elements with an internally structured order. In his view, the digraph <ei> and its variant <ęi> may have been short, graphic versions of the indivisible representation of /əi/, with <yi> and <ij> functioning as long versions. Anja Voeste has described the spelling variation in Early New High German (1350–1650) manuscripts as a token of aesthetic variation, which she categorises as an *aesthetic principle*:

Spelling variability may often be considered as a search for new visual word schemata, arising from variation being seen as a stylistic imperative. I take spelling variation as an aesthetic principle, comparable to today's variations as a lexical imperative. [...]
Looking at the beginning of the early modern age, there seems to be strong evidence for the fact that it was not appropriate to repeat words in the same monotonous spelling. This would explain why heterogeneous spellings occur on the same page, and why

---

[9] Tainturier and Rapp, 'Complex graphemes', 130.

common words are written in different shapes. *Variatio delectat* meant more than just giving pleasure to the eye. It meant demonstrating one's writing skills through the calculated use of alternation.[10]

Such orthographic variability largely disappeared in the centuries that followed, a trend for which, according to Voeste, the 'developing professionalism of type-setters was partly responsible'.[11] Variation in the way William Shakespeare signed his name, for example, has been documented by Peter Ackroyd: 'In each of six of his authenticated signatures he spells his surname differently. He abbreviates it too, as if he were not happy with it.'[12] Shakespeare could, of course, have produced a more uniform signature had he wished to. Ornamentation and a preference for diversity are more likely reasons for the variation than an inability to sign uniformly. Commenting on the textbook *Right Spelling Very Much Improved*, published anonymously in London in 1704, Noel Osselton observed that

in his treatment of the large category of adjectives such as *happy* and nouns such as *mercy* [the author] clearly has manuscript practice in mind: having observed that the *-y* has of late become the usual ending, he adds (p. 4) the interesting comment that the alternative ending in *-ie* 'may still very well be retained for Ornament Sake, at the Pleasure of the Scribe'.[13]

Daukantas, a historian familiar with a range of older manuscripts, was undoubt-edly aware of their orthographic heterogeneity. A similar preference for ortho-graphic ornamentation and the pleasure of scribing were known to Daukantas, as evidenced in his 'play' with the variants <lyi> and <lij>, <tyi> and <tij>, <pyi> and <pij>. The long <l>, <p>, <t> were the first to exhibit variation and to induce changes, suggesting they were the more expressive. In contrast, the short graph-emes may have been associated with a certain lack of expressiveness. Overall, the rationale for the distinction between the first and second variational types of the graphemic rendering of the diphthong /əi/ could have been the length of graphic strokes, the palpability of the graphemes, and Daukantas's aesthetic approach. The most surprising aspect of these choices is that Daukantas applied the aesthetic principle this late, in the nineteenth century, as no other attempts to adhere to this principle are evident in Lithuanian manuscripts of the time. Whether printed or handwritten, Lithuanian orthographies typically contained a significantly higher degree of uniformity, even if these uniformities were not considered standard orthographies *per se*.[14]

Ultimately, the four major variants <ei>, <ęi>, <yi>, <ij> in Daukantas's 'History' can be characterised as follows:

---

[10] Voeste, 'Variability', 303.   [11] Ibid.   [12] Ackroyd, *Shakespeare*, 199.
[13] Osselton, 'Informal spelling systems' (1984), 126.
[14] It can be argued that the modern standard Lithuanian orthography was launched in 1890 by Vincas Kudirka via the newspaper *Varpas*, which he edited, and his manual for contributors to the paper, 'Statrašos ramsčiai'.

(1) diachronic <yi> : <ei> : <ęi, ij> (following approximately one after another);

(2) diaphasic <yi> : <ei, ęi, ij> (characteristic of different periods in Daukantas's life);

(3) diaprecise <ei, ij> : <ęi, yi> (having varying degrees of precision of phonetic representation);

(4) aesthetic <ei, ęi> : <yi, ij> (correlation of graphemes embedded with elongated elements).

6.2   Scope of Variation in the 'History'

The spelling of /əi/ in root position is only one example of variation in spelling systems in the 'History'. I have counted forty-three such modifications by Daukantas in this manuscript, including seven changes in the rendering of the diphthong /əi/. Thirty of these forty-three changes may be grouped in clusters, dividing the manuscript into at least six segments of spelling variation (Figure 6.3).

The first segment, for example, can be characterised by the unique letters <ɥ> and <å>, which are almost entirely absent from Segment 2 on. In Segment 3, the spellings *kuryi*, 'which, what' (masc. pl. ending), <kiey> /kʲei/, *sauo*, 'own' and <ay> *kursay*, 'which, what' (masc. sg.) appear or begin to dominate. In Segment 5, <y> no longer appears in the five positions in which it had been present previously, and the innovations *i*, 'him', <ɨ> acc. sg., and <ł> (non-palatal position) are introduced. In Segment 6, <ą> (acc. sg.) and <ijs> (in some endings) are introduced, and the graphemes <ɨ> (acc. sg.), <ł> (non-palatal position), <è> (adv. ending) and <û> (gen. pl. ending) are reinforced. The general direction of Daukantas's orthographic innovation is toward a merger of traditional spelling practice in Lithuania and the way Lithuanians spelled in Prussia. At the time, understanding of nationhood was often based on the commonality of language, and, in Daukantas's case, this commonality was

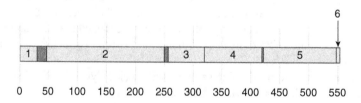

Figure 6.3 Six segments of orthographic variation in the 'History'

Note: The horizontal axis indicates folio numbers. The hatched areas indicate segments written in transitional orthography, which contained features of both the preceding and the following segments. Where there is no hatched area between the segments, the change is quite abrupt.

expressed in his attempts to link at least two Lithuanian orthographic traditions. He kept firmly to his own Lowland Lithuanian dialect, however; the orthographic levelling took place ahead of the dialectal. In practical terms, Daukantas introduced various diacritical marks, many of which were being used in Lithuanian texts in Prussia; for example, some diacritical letters he introduced shortly before he began writing the 'History' and in the manuscript itself: *ę, ë, ů, ų, û, ô, ù, è, à, i, ǫ, å*.[15] Daukantas was, however, quite creative; he often modified the meaning of these borrowed graphemes according to his own dialectal particularities. In the 'History', Daukantas's spelling rules frequently had a low degree of generalisation;[16] therefore they might be labelled as *lexical–phonetic* (or *logographic*, not merely *phonographic*).[17] Additionally, Daukantas not only created new rules; he also repeatedly modified them. The level of orthographic variation in this manuscript is extremely high; Daukantas's orthography must have been one of the most variational in the history of the Lithuanian language. At this stage in the development of Lithuanian spellings, such high variation is a surprising departure from the general trend. In a sense, the 'History' contained a partly experimental orthography. It was a loose attempt to merge different orthographic trends in Lithuanian, with which Daukantas blazed a trail through previously uncharted territory. The experimentation and ornamentation that produced such variety does not appear to have troubled Daukantas, who evidently was comfortable with orthographic diversity.

6.3   Contextualisation

Daukantas could read, write and speak at least eight languages, presented here in alphabetical order: French, German, Latin, Latvian, Lithuanian, Polish, Russian and (Church) Slavonic. At the time Daukantas was compiling the 'History', many of these languages (French, German, Polish and Russian – being early dialect selection languages – and Latin) had been generally standardised, and their orthographic variation relatively well suppressed. Many speakers of various languages perceived uniformity as advantageous for an orthography. Given his proficiency in so many standardised languages, Daukantas cannot have been unaware of this. Nevertheless, the analysis of the spellings conducted so far has proved the point that Daukantas did not follow the path of uniformity in his orthography. The remaining part of this

---

[15] Subačius, 'Pirmasis'.
[16] See Rutkowska and Rössler, 'Orthographic variables', 214: 'The degree of generalization can be low, as in the spelling of individual words in orthographic dictionaries. High degrees of generalization are found in the general rules which are intended to establish a norm for the spelling of large classes of linguistic items'.
[17] See Baddeley and Voeste, 'Introduction', 8.

chapter contextualises Daukantas's spelling choices drawing on the physical characteristics, potential readers and materiality of the volume as three key factors to explain the variation.

6.3.1   Physical Characteristics of the Volume

The 'History' is a huge volume bound in leather. Its paper is of high quality and must have been expensive. Daukantas possessed a very beautiful longhand; he had been praised for it since childhood. In the volume, this beautiful longhand is obvious (see Figure 6.4). Moreover, in addition to being the most extensive of Daukantas's manuscripts, the volume was by that time the most voluminous secular text ever composed in Lithuanian. Daukantas was well aware of the extraordinariness of his manuscript (see Figure 6.5). It is certain that he could not seriously consider publishing it. The cost would have been prohibitive, as even the publication of much smaller books and pamphlets had placed a substantial financial burden on him. For instance, after the publication of his first and second books in 1837 and 1838 (small format in octavo, 236 [130 + 106] pages in total), Daukantas paid 1,200 assignation roubles and 5 imperial gold coins to the printer Christian Hintze;[18] in 1838, that sum was equivalent to approximately 388 silver roubles (SR).[19] Daukantas worked in the Senate in Saint Petersburg, and at the time his annual salary was SR 285.92, plus a food allowance of SR 57.18,[20] or SR 343.10 in total. These figures indicate that he paid approximately thirteen months' salary to publish these books. We can estimate that publication costs for the 'History' would have been at least ten times higher – 130 months or more than ten years of Daukantas's salary. Additionally, the censors were unlikely to have looked favourably on such a history of a formerly independent nation that was now part of the Russian Empire. Mindful of these pressures, Daukantas must have tried to make an impression on readers with the *unpublished* manuscript. We know that he allowed his manuscript to travel between two Lowland Lithuanian locations, from a monastery to a mansion. The manuscript lived its own life in the form in which it is preserved today. Daukantas treasured his manuscript, and when eventually it returned to him, he reused the information contained in it in the preparation of some of his other texts.

6.3.2   Potential Readers

When addressing his readers in the volume, Daukantas sometimes called them 'educated' and 'men of science'. At that time, in Lithuania, the most prestigious

---

[18] Daukantas, *Prasmą Łotinû Kałbôs, Lhomond, Epitome*; Hintze, 'Signed receipt'.
[19] See Grimalauskaitė and Remecas, *Pinigai Lietuvoje*, 308; *Russkiĭ rubl'*, 41.
[20] Merkys, *Simonas Daukantas*, 73.

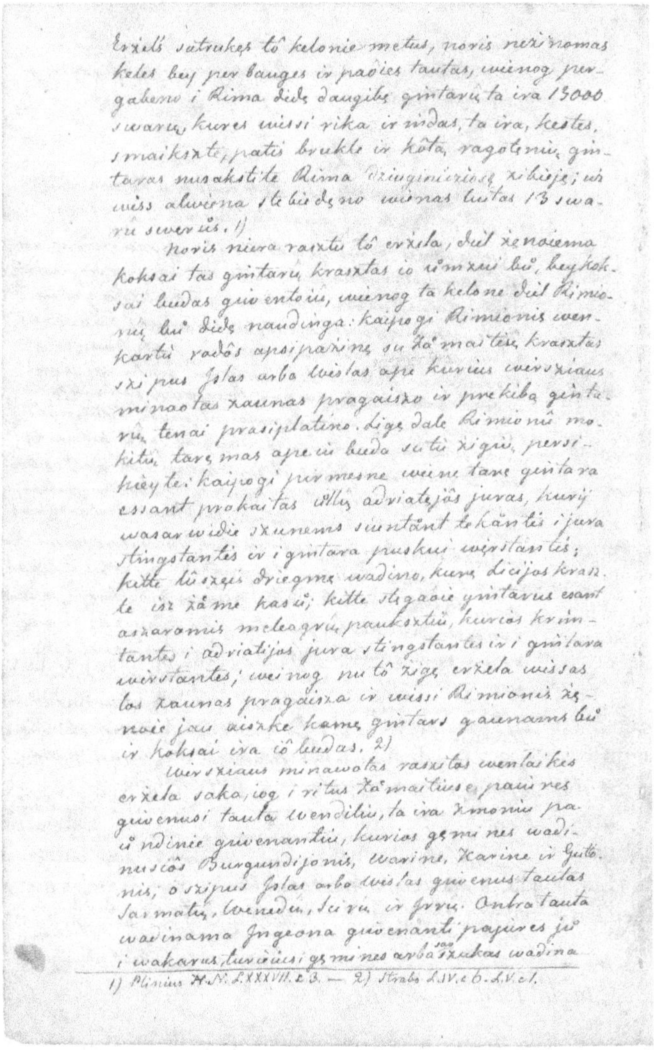

Figure 6.4 Daukantas's spectacular longhand ('History', fol. 5v)

cultural language was Polish; for instance, the then-recently closed (in 1832) Vilnius University had been a predominantly Polish-speaking milieu. Most of Daukantas's readers would have been fluent in Polish. It is somewhat ironic that Daukantas wrote in Lithuanian for *readers of Polish*. Daukantas formulated his

Figure 6.5 Daukantas's 'History'
Note: Photograph by Daukantė Subačiūtė.

arguments primarily to persuade those who somehow preferred to disregard texts in Lithuanian. There were, of course, readers of Lithuanian, too, but they would have been rather few in number. As previously noted, a significant portion of the manuscript is a loose translation of Koialowicz's *History of Lithuania.* Thus, in a sense, the volume is only partly an original text; Daukantas translated a text that many of his educated readers could access in the original Latin. These well-educated readers of Polish could neither have received Daukantas's arguments written in Lithuanian, nor noticed that the majority of the text was a translation, nor could they have paid any attention to or even noticed the orthographic variation.

6.3.3   Materiality of the Manuscript

Readers of Polish (many of whom disagreed with Daukantas's nationalist views) could have perceived and valued only the *material aspects* of the manuscript. The impressive size of the manuscript itself sent the message that the history of Lithuania existed and was being transmitted in the Lithuanian language, that it had a concrete, material shape, that one could see it, touch it, thumb it, that it was solid and undeniable, and laid out in even lines of beautiful words and sentences. The desire to impress readers of both Polish and Lithuanian with the sheer visuality, sheer *materiality* of the volume was more important to Daukantas than orthographic uniformity. *Ipso facto,* that there was such a thing as Lithuanian orthography must have been enough. Marshall McLuhan argued that 'environments are not just containers, but are processes that change the content totally. [...] That is why the media are the message.'[21] The material volume was not a mere container for Daukantas's message; it *was* his message. The *idea* of the orthography, as far as it was a Lithuanian orthography, was part of his message. Orthographic particularities and *variation*, however, were beyond the scope of his main communication. As Gosewijn van Beek put it, traditionally 'we are supposed to know that matter doesn't matter'.[22] However, his own approach to the materiality of things is different:

It is ultimately a gut feeling that leads me to accept that material culture significantly contributes to our construction and perception of the world and that presumably this must have to do with the most superficial aspect (appearance) of objects: the materiality, tangibility of things. That is to say that material objects contribute something special that is different from the textual attributes of cultural meaning.[23]

If his 'History' had been written in an ugly longhand on sheets of torn wrapping paper, it could not have had the impact Daukantas intended. The matter mattered greatly for Daukantas's volume and its readers. As Daniel Miller has pointed out,

a key question is to determine when, where and for whom the material attributes of things matter. Materiality like nature is mainly a potential presence. The solidity of the branch comes to matter mainly when you hit your head on it.[24]

Daukantas did not feel obliged to produce a uniform orthography; he felt at ease searching, experimenting, ornamenting and merging various orthographic traditions with no significant detriment to the validity of his *opus magnum* via its *materiality*. The orthographic diversity did not obstruct his core message. Daukantas knew that once you beheld, touched and opened the manuscript, you hit your head on a literary branch planted for that special purpose. The *political* message regarding the solidity of Lithuania's past conveyed through the *material volume* was more important to Daukantas than the orthographic needs of a few potential readers of Lithuanian. The history of Lithuania was *materialised* in this lengthy and neatly written manuscript. Daukantas behaved like a politician: he used history and language as tools to spread Lithuanian ideology, but he was not a zealous codifier of the Lithuanian language or its spellings. In other words, his manuscript includes demonstrative features; it prioritises appearance and externality; the orthography and even the content of the volume had less potential for impact. Daukantas's priorities while writing the volume were many. At the top, in rough order of precedence, were the following: (1) Lithuanian ideology (history,

---

[21] McLuhan, 'Address at Vision 65', 200.   [22] Van Beek, 'On materiality', 15.   [23] Ibid., 10.
[24] Miller, 'Why it's safer to build', 27.

Figure 6.6 Manuscript of Daukantas's 'Great Polish–Lithuanian Dictionary'
(1852–6, 1858)

language), followed by (2) thickness (number of pages), (3) skilled penmanship
(longhand), (4) special paper and (5) luxurious binding. At the bottom, in order of
diminishing priority, were (1) content, (2) dialect and (3) orthography.
Daukantas's relative unconcern for the latter gave him the freedom to experiment,
ornament, play and even ignore inaccuracies. In the books which he printed
subsequently, orthographic variation was also present, but not on the scale of
the volume under discussion. Generally, manuscript culture might have been far
friendlier to variation than print.

Daukantas's unfinished manuscript, 'Great Polish–Lithuanian Dictionary'
(1852–6 and 1858; see Figure 6.6),[25] is another example of his political approach
to the Lithuanian language. One particularly striking feature of this manuscript is
the lack of grammatical markers. By the mid-nineteenth century, dictionaries in
various languages in Lithuania and in neighbouring countries were including
such markers (to note, for instance, a noun, its gender, different endings of
adjectives according to gender, etc.). Daukantas compiled his dictionary using
the Polish list of words from Stanisław Ropelewski's *Polish–French
Dictionary*,[26] which generally included grammatical information. Daukantas's

[25] Daukantas, 'Didysis lenkų–lietuvių kalbų žodynas'.
[26] Ropelewski, *Słownik polsko-francuzki*.

decision to omit such information implies it held no significance for him. He reproduced only a minority of the illustrative sentences and phrases from Ropelewski's work. On the other hand, he did attempt to translate the majority of Ropelewski's words. The three volumes of Ropelewski's dictionary contained numerous rare poetical and even obscure Polish words (such as *Chłopobyk*, 'Minotaur' and *Chłopokoń*, 'Centaur') that Daukantas tried to translate (as *žmogjautis* and *žmogžirgas* respectively). In total I have counted approximately 3,800 neologisms that Daukantas created in this dictionary alone, suggesting he wished to prove that the Lithuanian language had equivalents for all Polish lexemes and contained just as many words as Polish. Demonstration of the wealth and, hence, the prestige of Lithuanian and its vocabulary was Daukantas's primary focus. Practicality and the needs of potential users of his dictionary were, obviously, of secondary importance. Here again the *materiality* of the compiled manuscript seems to have a premeditated significance: having beheld the three enormous volumes of the manuscript, the viewer will be convinced of the strength and power of the Lithuanian language. The *materiality* might make a stronger impact on a person's beliefs than the content itself.

6.4   Conclusions

It is customary to expect a new orthography to follow a phonetic path; ideally, each sound (phoneme) will be rendered by a single grapheme (letter, digraph, etc.). Daukantas chose a different path. This chapter has shown that when using the diphthong /əi/ of his Lowland Lithuanian dialect, Daukantas regularly employed four major orthographic variants <ei>, <ęi>, <yi>, <ij> (and in some cases also <ie>, <iei>, <iey>). It was not inattention that caused such significant diversity. There were several *important aspects* to such orthographic variation.

(1) As discussed previously, *the manuscript nature* of the volume is highly significant. On the one hand, Daukantas aimed for a certain visual perfection with his manuscript, as if imitating printed books; these were usually more orderly in appearance, and a higher prestige was attached to them. The concept of a printed book itself implied a certain uniformity: the shapes of the printed letters were usually alike, many copies were produced, and all were identical. It was expected that print would be more standardised. On the other hand, Daukantas did not achieve the (relative) orthographic uniformity of printed texts of that time; the diversity in spelling in his manuscript is significantly higher than what we would expect in printed works and even in manuscripts by many other authors. Manuscripts are generally more individual, their letter shapes always vary somewhat, and more space is available to the author for experimentation (e.g. with diacritics, combinations of letters); the limits of

graphemic variation are imposed only by the author himself and his willingness to comply with tradition. Manuscript form gave Daukantas freedom to improvise more easily.

(2) Daukantas did not focus on making his orthography uniform. He was in search of new ways of expression; old orthographic features blended with his new ideas of reforming Lithuanian orthography, merging the traditions of Lithuania with those of Eastern Prussia. Daukantas varied his orthographic patterns while writing, while producing the text – on the hoof, so to say.

(3) In some cases, for example, when rendering the diphthong /əi/ in script, Daukantas purposefully diversified his orthography, for the sake of *ornamentation*. In certain segments of the manuscript, he matched long ascenders and descenders of the graphemes <l>, <p>, <t> to the long descenders of the digraphs <yi>, <ij>. These trends represent a conscious diversification to achieve an *aesthetic* result.

(4) The majority of educated potential readers of Daukantas's volume must have been readers of Polish, yet his manuscript was composed in Lithuanian. Presumably, disarray in the orthography of a language with which such readers were only vaguely familiar would likely have escaped their notice. Having a limited audience, Daukantas lacked any incentive to make his orthography more uniform.

(5) On the evidence, Daukantas considered his orthography of less importance than the material aspects of the manuscript: he chose special paper, wrote in a precise, almost calligraphic longhand, and bound the volume luxuriously in leather. Visually, it was an impressive (intellectual) product. The *materiality* of the manuscript must have made a greater impression on the readers than did the Lithuanian orthography on the pages within: the large, heavy volume impressed before it was even opened. The *materiality* of such a manuscript may have had much greater influence than that of the average printed book.

(6) Impressing his readers with the physical aspects of his manuscripts must have been Daukantas's political strategy. By producing his 'History' and his 'Great Polish–Lithuanian Dictionary' in such visually imposing manuscripts, he was declaring that the Lithuanian language was valuable, that it contained an abundance of words and that the nation using this language was vibrant and had a very long history. In Imperial Tsarist Russia, the political goal of an independent Lithuania could not be openly discussed, so Daukantas spoke indirectly.

7   Investigating Methods
Intra-textual, Inter-textual and Cross-textual Variable Analyses

Anja Voeste

Even after several years of research, orthography – and in particular its core problem of spelling variation – is and still remains a challenge for those in search of explanations. If we assume that variation does not occur randomly and arbitrarily, we need to identify possible causal factors: which internal (linguistic) or external (non-linguistic) variables influenced spelling in its historical setting? Since this chapter deals with different methods of data collection, one might assume that it has little to do with explanations. However, an assessment of methods of data collection is of key importance for the formation of explanatory hypotheses. Each method has its advantages and disadvantages for discovering and dealing with typical data problems. Each method also permits a specific approach to analysing data and provides a basis for its interpretation. In any empirical study, one is confronted with problems related to data selection from the very beginning. Some of the problems involve the choice of the textual material that the investigation will be based upon, as well as which variables or variation phenomena to analyse more closely. The two issues are in fact interrelated.

When starting from the material, one will in consequence examine the text or texts with regard to some of the variants which are contained in them. When starting from the variation phenomena that one wants to explore, on the other hand, one has to find an adequate textual basis for the investigation of the variable in question. Whilst this may sound easy, the latter set-up confronts us with important decisions, such as the following: which variation phenomena should be analysed in relation to our textual basis? Are they the variants typical of the time, the variants characteristic of the text, those that are particularly prominent and unusual, or perhaps merely the variants that have already been annotated in other corpora? And also: which texts are particularly suitable for documenting and analysing the type of variation in which we are interested? Do the texts have to have a minimum size or a given form, and should they belong to a specific text type or genre, for the results to be reasonably representative?

Are there any hypotheses regarding which external variables are more likely to influence variation (format, place of printing, level of education, and the like), and should these be taken into account when selecting the text(s)? Should new findings be sought out with controlled random experiments or should generally accepted hypotheses be critically questioned?

In the context of these possible problems, it seems paramount to decide on a suitable method of data collection and analysis. Depending on the approach chosen, one will tend to focus either on the variants of a single text copy or on a comparative analysis of different text copies. In the present chapter, I aim to discuss three methods of data collection and analysis. The methods as such are well known, although perhaps not always by the names given in this contribution, and one could argue that they are fairly traditional. However, the angle chosen for this chapter aims to provide a new and useful comparative discussion for scholars of orthography. The terms used to identify the three methods under discussion here are drawn from an overview of grammatical variables[1] and have been used by other scholars:[2] these are intra-textual, inter-textual and cross-textual variable analyses. The three methods are discussed in order below.

Intra-textual variable analysis (TRAVA) involves an investigation of the frequency and range of variants in a single text copy. Since the external variables remain constant for a single text copy, this method is particularly helpful if one is interested in the influence of internal variables on orthography. By focusing on a single text, one may be able to uncover a scribe's or typesetter's spelling system. For instance, one could show that the scribe or the typesetter opted for a different consonant grapheme in derivational suffixes compared to word stems, or that they preferred the consonant cluster <dt> (rather than <d> or <t>) after sonorant graphemes. *Inter-textual variable analysis* (TERVA), on the other hand, aims to compare the results of two or more intra-textual investigations. This method of analysis is especially useful if one wants to investigate the influence of an external variable on spelling. For example, one would choose TERVA to find out whether the spelling in Albert Einstein's private letters differs from that of his correspondence with colleagues (addressee specificity), or if one wants to investigate whether his handwritten drafts and his typescript drafts show spelling differences (writing implement). The third method, *cross-textual variable analysis* (CTVA), examines the variants of different versions of the same text. One would choose this method to compare, for example, the punctuation in one of Einstein's drafts with that in the published edition of the same text. Since it also deals with

---

[1] Auer and Voeste, 'Grammatical variables', 259–61.
[2] Rezetko and Young, *Historical Linguistics*.

a comparison of intra-textual investigations while including an additional constraint, CTVA could be categorised as a subtype of TERVA.

The following sections discuss each method in greater detail by exploring the facets that each of them shows and considering their usefulness for forming individual hypotheses. My examples stem from German-speaking territories of the fifteenth, sixteenth and seventeenth centuries, a period and place of significant spelling variation. It was not until the seventeenth century that grammarians initiated a metalinguistic discourse,[3] heralding the first epoch of codification and pointing to an incipient norm consciousness. The spelling irregularity in the centuries and geographical areas of focus in this chapter therefore provide some excellent material for the application and discussion of each of the three methods.

7.1   Intra-textual Variable Analysis (TRAVA)

Data capture with TRAVA and its usefulness as the basis for hypothesis formation will be illustrated by a pamphlet from 1522, entitled *Hie kompt ein Beüerlein zu einem reichen Burger*, printed in Speyer by Johann Eckhart.[4] TRAVA reveals some characteristic variants typical of early German printed texts, as can be seen in the lemma 'beüerlein' (diminutive form of *Bauer* 'peasant') also mentioned in the title of the pamphlet, and occurring forty-six times in eight variants (cf. Table 7.1).

The first step to explain the multitude of variant forms in a single text would be to compare the individual instances of their occurrence. TRAVA is primarily useful as a preliminary step for detecting possible internal factors which trigger the choice of a variant, such as syllable boundaries,[5] sonority,[6] word shape (weight)[7] or lexical category.[8] This approach by no means excludes external variables as determining factors, but elements like time and place are simply less probable when we encounter variability within a single text copy. Instead, variants which are likely to have been triggered by the differing origins, qualifications or individual preferences of the involved parties (such as scribes or compositors) are definitely accounted for in the analysis.[9] Here, due to the brevity of the text (eight pages in quarto), it can be assumed that only one compositor was involved; it is therefore unlikely (although it cannot be ruled out entirely) that

---

[3] Cf. Takada, *Grammatik und Sprachwirklichkeit*.
[4] *Hie kompt ein Beüerlein*, VD 16 H 3466 in the Verzeichnis der im deutschen Sprachbereich erschienenen Drucke des 16. Jahrhunderts (Bibliography of Books Printed in the German-Speaking Countries of the Sixteenth Century).
[5] Cf. e.g. Voeste, *Orthographie und Innovation*, 132–224.
[6] Cf. e.g. Elmentaler, *Struktur und Wandel*, 292–8.   [7] Cf. Evertz, *Visual Prosody*.
[8] Cf. e.g. Rutkowska's description of the use of <i> in function words and <y> in content words in *Orthographic Systems*, 101–30.
[9] Cf. Fujii, 'Zur Methode'.

Table 7.1 *Variants of BEÜERLEIN in* Hie kompt ein Beüerlein

Main variant	Secondary variant	Other variants
Beüerlein (16)	*Beuerlein* (3)	*Bewerlein* (2)
beüerlein (13)	*beuerlein* (8)	*beuerlin* (2)
		Beüerlin (1)
		Beüwerlein (1)

spelling variants were caused by the presence of different contributors. Apart from the most traditional factors like time and space, there may be other external variables that should be considered, even if the focus tends to remain on internal variables. For example, macro- and micro-typographic factors may have an influence on variant selection. Imposition, casting off and text alignment (typographical stages of book production) are external factors that should be considered seriously. In the following paragraph, I discuss the Table 7.1 variants in greater detail.

For the lemma 'beüerlein' (cf. the variants in Table 7.1), we encounter six different variants (in upper- and lowercase),[10] and we do not know whether they were free, arbitrary variants (e.g. *bairn/bayrn* 'Bavaria', *heute/heüte* 'today') or whether they were chosen because they displayed relevant additional markers (special syllabic, morphological or graphotactic features, such as *jahr* 'year', *länder* 'lands, countries', *ratt* 'council'). In the early sixteenth century, German scribes and compositors often used both free and regulated variants in order to avoid unvarying spelling in close succession (cf. *Burger. Gutz **jar** Beüerlein gutz **iar**;* 2r; literally: 'Burgher: good year! Peasant: good year!', emphasis added).[11] As long as the written word forms were re-codable[12] and matched the correct phonic correlate, compositors enjoyed liberty to come up with new spellings. The dominant variant (cf. Table 7.1) is *Beüerlein* (twenty-nine times), occurring on all pages, while a second variant, *Beuerlein* (eleven times), is numerically superior only on pages 6 and 7, starting with the last third of page 6. The spellings without umlauts can be found on the penultimate two pages, but not on the last page, where only *Beüerlein* was chosen. There are no phonetic differences between the correlates

---

[10] The variants of 'beüerlein' are written in upper- and lowercase, but without regard to factors such as semantic animacy or their respective syntactic role. Capitalisation is limited to the title and to *inquit* formulas, indicating direct speech.

[11] Cf. Voeste, *Orthographie*; for English cf. Blake, 'Manuscript to print'; Shute, 'Pressed for space'.

[12] 'Recoding' is explained by Martin Neef: 'The primary goal of linguistics of writing is to model how written forms allow us to recode the content of [oral] language system forms': *Die Graphematik*, 11–12, translated in Bellosta von Colbe, 'Role and reference grammar', 246.

of the two spelling forms,[13] nor are there any differences in word shape (weight) or syllable boundaries, which might tend to favour possible external factors. One can argue that, after having set the second third of page 6, the compositor encountered a shortage of the type <ü>. He may have limited its use and reserved it for more important (otherwise underspecified) words such as *würdt* or *müſt*, indicating the subjunctive. If this was the case, however, how was it possible that umlauts were added again on page 8? Differences such as these may have been caused by the so-called process of imposition: the front of a sheet (quarto: pages 1, 4, 5, 8) may have been finished before its back (pages 2, 3, 6, 7) and the chase (the frame) with the front delivered to the printer before the back. This could explain why there were not enough umlaut types on the last two pages of the back and why they seem to reappear on page 8 in the bound version.

Apart from the elements described above, there is at least one other example of the influence of possible external print-related factors, concerning the words' width in *beuerlin* and *Beüerlin*. During the process of casting off, the compositor or editor had to estimate the quires and the lines per page by counting the words of the manuscript and comparing the full lot to a typeset sample page. According to Lotte Hellinga-Querido[14] the space requirement was rounded up rather than down, often allowing the compositor to set more text than previously estimated. In any case, the text at the end of one page had to match the beginning of the next, regardless of whether it was actually set before or after the next page. In order to adjust the lines and to ensure the correct connection to the next page, the compositors reduced or expanded the words' widths by using abbreviations and tittles, that is, letters with a raised bar/small stroke (e.g. *vñ* 'and'), or by adding segments (e.g. <n> and <t> to *lanndt* 'land') to the words. In the pamphlet from 1522, we find a possible example of this process in the variants *beuerlin* and *Beüerlin*, both of which end with <lin> (without diphthongisation of the suffix). Although the use of an older spelling here could indicate the origin of one or more of the contributors from a language region without diphthongisation (for example, the Low German or Alemannic areas), the accompanying tittles in two of the three cases point to justification as a decisive external factor. Both instances appear in the penultimate line on page 7, in which six tittles were also used to delay the line break and to include more text (see the first and last two lines of the paragraph in question in Example 7.1, where '*beuerlin*' is underlined). This means that the compositor was well aware of the older spelling and may have chosen its abridged form in favour of a better page break. However, as convincing as

---

[13] The second part of the diphthong is a front vowel and is therefore indeed better represented by <ü>.

[14] Hellinga-Querido, 'Methode en praktijk', 94.

the interpretation above may be, it does not explain the third <lin> example (*Beüerlin*) (not shown in Example 7.1), where there would definitely have been enough space for additional segments. Is this third case an exception, possibly even a typographical error? Contradictions such as these are quite frequent and often cannot be resolved satisfactorily. Nevertheless, the advantage of TRAVA is that it helps to reveal this kind of variation in the first place.

Example 7.1 Line justification compared (*Hie kompt ein Beüerlein*, fol. 4r)

Münch. Liebß beuerlein ſchweig ſtill wir haben genug ge
redt von diſen dingen. Beuerlein. Ja ich weyß woll das
[...]
ſachē eins vñ ſprachē zu dē beuerlin wolā beuerlin wir wolē
vnß ſcheidē vñ alle ding alſo laſen beſtō vñ ſchweig alſo ſtil.

For the remaining cases, namely *Bewerlein* and *Beüwerlein*, both variants have equivalents with <w> in their base word (*bauwer, bawern, bawren*), which could have served as templates. In *bauwer*, an epenthetic velar semivowel (svarabhakti) could actually occur in the phonic correlate /bauwɐ/, while in the correlate of *Beüwerlein*, only the palatal semivowel /j/ may be inserted. Here too the interpretation is difficult: are these random, arbitrary transfers of *bauwer/bawer*, or are they consciously chosen morphological spellings which confirm a linguistic awareness on the part of the compositor? Is *Beüwerlein* spelled with a <w> an unusual phonological spelling referring to a semivowel (<w> for /j/) while following the pattern of *bauwerlein*? Or are we again dealing with a micro-typographic, extended spelling variant? Regardless of the potential answers to these questions, the examples show that TRAVA affords detailed insights into a single text copy. The often chaotic distribution of variants and especially the idiosyncrasies, exceptions and contradictions generate a plethora of explanatory problems, an issue which was well expressed by Karl Kraus: 'The closer you look at a word, the further it looks back [at you].'[15] Nevertheless, TRAVA's detailed and painstaking approach offers a chance to identify decisive factors that are not always apparent at a first glance, but, rather, often lie relatively silently in the background. The factors identified may then be further investigated in larger groups of texts.

7.2   Inter-textual Variable Analysis (TERVA)

TERVA is a method that encompasses at least two intra-textual investigations to examine the influence of a specific variable. The comparison is designed in such a way that only one variable, called the independent variable, is

---

[15] Kraus, *Pro Domo et Mundo*, 164.

investigated as a possible determinant. The independent variable is usually an external variable such as time or place. TERVA is difficult to carry out because it is based on the premise of *ceteris paribus* ('all other things being equal'). The independent variable, for instance the place of printing (or rather the local spelling customs), influences the dependent variables (the so-called *regressands*) and it must be ensured that no potentially disturbing variables interfere with the analysis. Consequently, all other variables, such as the text type or the year of publication, should be the same. This is more than just advantageous; it is a fundamental prerequisite for examining only a single independent variable. However, the main problem with TERVA is that we cannot tell with certainty to what extent the *ceteris paribus* condition is met. When are our independent variables really the same? When is the same printing site sufficient, and are we always able to gather material from the same printing shop, the same typesetter or even in the same format? When is a time match possible or acceptable? Since chronological studies often compare decades, is 1522 really more similar to 1525 (falling within the same decade) than to 1519 (falling within a different decade)? Or, more abstractly, does *ceteris paribus* mean that there must be a perfect match (100%)? Would 75% also entail a convincing significance level? In the following, I will discuss some typical problems related to hypothesis formation when dealing with TERVA, with reference to two catechisms by the Protestant reformers Johann Meckhart and Nicolaus Han (Gallus), printed in 1554 in Augsburg by Hans Zimmerman and in Regensburg by Hans Kohl (Khol).[16] Here, *ceteris paribus* was fulfilled insofar as the text type, the denominational background, the size of the printing shop[17] and the year of publication were the same.

For TERVA, the printing site was chosen as an independent variable, and the spellings of the Middle High German vowels /ei/ and /i:/ as dependent variables. The Early New High German spellings of the two Middle High German vowels are of interest because, in the two printing sites in question, the old diphthong was often represented by <ai> or <ay>, while the old monophthong was instead written as <ei> or <ey>, following Early New High German diphthongisation. The objective is to examine, on the basis of a selective sample of the spellings of Middle High German /ei/ and /i:/ (about 100 items in each catechism, counted from the beginning of the text), whether and to what extent the two catechisms maintained historical differences in their spellings, as well as how much the local spelling customs in Augsburg or Regensburg influenced the typesetters. Analysis of the c. 100 instances reveals fundamental differences between the two printing shops (cf. Table 7.2). For both Middle High German /ei/ and /i:/, the compositor in

---

[16] Han, *Catechismvs* (VD 16 G 277); Meckhart, *Catechismus* (VD 16 M 1803).
[17] Cf. Künast, *Getruckt zu Augspurg*, 136 and 231; Pangkofer and Schnegraf, *Geschichte*; Reske, *Die Buchdrucker*.

Table 7.2 *Spelling variants of /ei/ and /i:/ in two sixteenth-century Protestant catechisms*

	Meckhart (Augsburg: Zimmerman)	Han (Regensburg: Kohl)
MHG /ei/	<ei> [21] (38%)/<ey> [19] (34%) <ai> [14] (25%)/<ay> [2] (4%)	<ei> [49] (100%)
MHG /i:/	<ei> [46] (90%)/<ey> [5] (10%)	<ei> [50] (98%) <i> [1] (2%) in *ferblin* 'colours'

Regensburg used exclusively <ei> as a digraph.[18] The Augsburg compositor, however, distinguished between the corresponding Middle High German vowels in about 30% of the old diphthongs and chose <ai> or <ay>. Moreover, his spellings are generally more variable (digraphs with <i> and <y> alternate). In the next step, we would have to compare the findings of TERVA with the results of previous studies in order to determine how much the findings differed from each other.[19]

The spellings of the Augsburg copy are by no means surprising: the peaceful coexistence of *e*- and *a*-variants,[20] as well as of <ei> and <ey>,[21] fit well into the picture described so far. Apparent regularities are the use of <y> in final position (*fey, bey*) and of <ei> in the case of possessive determiners (*mein, deine, feines*). Differing spelling variants for both /ei/ and /i:/ could similarly be expected in the Regensburg copy. However, surprisingly, the compositor adhered to a uniform spelling for both historical vowels. As a result, it is rather the exclusive use of <ei> in Regensburg that needs to be explained. One possible explanation could be proximity to the adjacent East Central German region. Both printing sites are located in the Upper German region (Augsburg in Swabia and Regensburg in Bavaria), about 70 miles apart but, in contrast to Augsburg, Regensburg is closer to the East Central German region, where *e*-graphemes (<ei, ey>) are typical for both corresponding historical vowels. Paul Rössler argues that geographical proximity to the East Central German region favoured the adoption of <ei> and <ey> in northern Bavaria.[22] This would imply that spelling variants could spread more easily from one region to the other if the regions were situated in the immediate vicinity of each other

---

[18] Outside the sample, however, there are individual spellings such as *Oberkait*.
[19] Cf. Rössler, *Schreibvariation*, 33–74; Glaser, 'Zu Entstehung und Charakter', 72–3; Keller, *Die deutsche Sprache*, 378–9.
[20] E.g. *arbeiten / Arbayt, ein / ain, einander / aingebornen, gemeinfchaft / gemayn, -keit / -kait.*
[21] E.g. *eiferer / eyfer, fleiß / fleyß, Geiftes / Geyft, heilige / heylige, vnterweifung / vnterweyfen.*
[22] Rössler, *Schreibvariation*, 34.

(this is by no means a foregone conclusion, however, as printed works could potentially be transported faster to more distant locations along major trade routes). In addition, the East Central German region from which the *e*-variants originated had been Luther's domain, so the variant may have been treated like a Protestant shibboleth. Since both printers in both cities were Protestant,[23] one could at best argue that the Regensburg compositor was more aware that the <ei>/<ey> variants (or rather, in his view, the <ei> variant only) had a Protestant character.

In order to validate or to challenge these assumptions, one would theoretically have to analyse a Catholic printed text from Kohl's workshop (which does not exist). Nevertheless, one can first of all ascertain whether the exclusive use of <ei> is an anomaly, or whether it can be found in Kohl's other publications as well. In order to investigate the choice of <ei>, I analysed a second Protestant text from Kohl's workshop, namely *Ein gebet aus heiliger Göttlicher geschrifft gezogen*, printed in 1555, a year after the catechisms.[24] If we compare the Regensburg printed texts in a second TERVA, we notice some similarities, but also considerable differences. With regard to the *e*-variants for both /ei/ and /i:/, the findings are consistent[25] and prove that the preference for <ei> in the catechism was no exception. However, the copy of 1555 also contains a great number of typically Bavarian features such as <p>, <kh>/<ckh>, <ue> or -*nus* and *nit* instead of (East Central German) <b>, <k>/<ck>, <ü> or -*nis* and *nicht*. We can use these incidental, additional findings as the basis for formulating an hypothesis. The findings tend to support the view that the compositor of 1555 did not regard <ei> as an East Central German variant, because otherwise he would not have used it so readily alongside the distinctively Bavarian ones. He probably did not interpret <ei> as a Protestant shibboleth either, because then he should have been aware of the other, more Catholic variants such as <kh>/<ckh> or -*nus* as well. Obviously, for some unknown reasons, <ei> remained, in contrast to other variants, 'below the radar' and was easily adopted from the East Central German region. However, the second TERVA also raises new questions: how can one explain that two printed texts from the same printing shop display such an uneven number of regional features only a year apart? Why does the copy of 1555 show so many other Bavarian characteristics? And here again the question of *ceteris paribus* arises, as we cannot rule out that some other compositor or proofreader was involved, or that the drafts of the two authors differed greatly in this matter. In order to avoid similar problems and to abide by *ceteris paribus* even more strictly, cross-textual variable analysis becomes the most relevant tool.

[23] Augsburg was in fact a mixed Protestant–Catholic city; cf. Warmbrunn, *Zwei Konfessionen*.
[24] *Ein gebet aus heiliger Göttlicher geschrifft gezogen* (VD 16 G 574).
[25] /ei/: <ei> [46] (94%); <ai> [2] (4%); <ey> [1] (2%). /i:/: <ei> [49] (91%); <ey> [5] (9%).

7.3   Cross-textual Variable Analysis (CTVA)

CTVA is a subtype of TERVA which involves a comparison of different versions of the same text. As a precondition, this approach requires different copies or editions or successive textual records, such as a concept, a draft, a first manuscript and a fair or final copy. CTVA adheres even more strongly to the principle of *ceteris paribus* because it sets the author and the text not just as similar but as identical factors. CTVA is particularly suitable if one wants to investigate changes that appear to have been made intentionally (and perhaps even systematically) from one version to the next, possibly inserted by the scribe, the editor, the proofreader or the compositor. Such changes may indicate a sound change or regional and local specifics, but also – and this would be particularly interesting – a re-evaluation of spelling variants, which is often accompanied by an increase in grammatical knowledge. Example 7.2 shows an extract with a focus on punctuation (underlined). The excerpts are taken from two Frankfurt editions of Thüring von Ringoltingen's translation (1456) of *Melusine*, printed by the Egenolff heirs (approx. 1580) and Feyerabend (1587).[26] We do not know which printing templates the printers used, but we can see that the versions differ in their sentence-terminal use of punctuation marks and the capitalisation of the first word (sentence case).[27]

Example 7.2 Punctuation (full point or *virgula suspensiva*) and sentence case in two versions of *Melusine* (Egenolff heirs, c. 1580; Feyerabend, 1587)

Egenolff heirs	*an dem morgen frü. Da er nun hinein kam ...* (B4v)
Feyerabend	*an dem morgen frü/ Da er nu hinein kam ...* (264v)
Egenolff heirs	*Reymund zohe mit dem Graffen in feinn herberg/ Jnn dem ward die Cappell ...* (C4v)
Feyerabend	*Reymund zohe mit dem Graffen in fein Herberg/ in dem ward die Capell ...* (265v)

The examples suggest that the Egenolff version may have used more explicit punctuation marks (full stop/period and capitalisation after virgule/slash). This convention requires additional work and grammatical knowledge from the editor, typesetter or proofreader, i.e. a level of syntactic parsing and planning that often goes beyond a single line.[28]

Particularly with Bible editions, CTVA has been profitably applied to types of enquiry with different dependent variables, such as morphological spellings, vowel graphemes and punctuation.[29] However, what is still pending is a thorough investigation of the independent variables of textual mode

---

[26] *Melusina. Von Lieb und Leyd* (VD 16 ZV 28676); '*Historia* und Geschicht von Melusina' (VD 16 B 8959).

[27] Cf. Voeste, 'Den Leser im Blick'.   [28] Cf. Voeste, 'Interpunktion'.

[29] For German, cf. e.g. Besch, 'Entstehung'; 'Sprachliche Änderungen'; Günther, 'Eine Etüde'; Hatz, 'Die Durchführung'; Rieke, *Studien*. For Hebrew, cf. Rezetko and Young, *Historical Linguistics*.

Table 7.3 *CTVA comparison of variants in four pilgrim guides*

No.	Munich 1482	Nuremberg 1491	Rome 1500	Strasbourg 1500
1	*kirchen*	*kirchen*	*kirchen*	*kirchen*
2	*püchlin*	*püchlein*	*buechlein*	*büchlin*
3	*räte*	*rete*	*rette*	*rette*
4a	*nach*	*noch*	*nach*	*nach*
4b	*nach*	*nach*	*noch*	*nach*
5a	*deſ*	*des*	*des*	*des*
5b	*was*	*was*	*waſ*	*was*
6	*land*	*land*	*land*	*landt*
7	*dem*	*dē*	*dē*	*dieſem*

(manuscript, woodcut, print), format (duodecimo, octavo, quarto, folio) and composition[30] (number of columns; flush right, ragged right). The following example demonstrates how to record and collate variants in order to determine distribution patterns that can serve as a basis for tentative hypotheses on the impact of format. The variants in question were taken from four editions of the German translations of the pilgrim guide *Mirabilia urbis Romae*, namely Munich: Johann Schaur, 1482 (quarto); Nuremberg: Peter Wagner, 1491 (octavo); Rome: Stephan Plannck, 1500 (octavo) and Strasbourg: [Matthias Hupfuff], 1500 (quarto).[31] The variants are compared as single items, line by line; Table 7.3 provides examples of the resulting distribution patterns of corresponding variants.

The variants can be identical (No. 1); each of the variants can be different (No. 2); they can differ in more than one edition (No. 3), or only in a single version (No. 4a). Their distributions are often not congruent (No. 4a/b), which points to an equivalence in spelling across the respective editions. The particular advantage of CTVA is that it supports the search for *possible* and *actual* spelling variants of a variable. If we take a look at No. 3, we can determine the 'possible space' and the 'actual space' of 'räte' across all four copies. The possible space is the sum of all imaginable combinations of those graphemes that were actually used in the spellings of a word, e.g. <r+ä/e+t/tt+e> = {*räte, rete, rätte, rette*}. The possible space is usually larger than the actual space: the variant *rätte* would potentially be possible (possible space) but it is not documented in actual space {*räte, rete, rette*}. Furthermore, the possible space is smaller than the sum of the theoretically possible combinations

---

[30] Cf. Shute, 'Pressed for space'.
[31] *Item in dem püchlin stet geschriben*, Incunabula Short Title Catalogue no. (ISTC) im00607300; *Item in dem püchlein stet geschriben*, ISTC im00608500; *In dem buechlein steet geschriben*, ISTC im00612000; *HIe yn diesem büchlin vindet man*, ISTC im00613100.

(the combinations *räthe* or *rhete* would also be logically possible). The possible space is based solely on the sum of the variants collected in a historical setting. In the case of rarely occurring variants, it is useful to compare the actual space of a copy with the possible space of all copies in question. This way, for example, one can rule out more easily the situation that rarely occurring spellings are typesetting errors (cf. <ſ> in final position in No. 5a/b). Assuming that the format (or, more precisely, the ratio of the width of the types and the width of the type area) as an independent variable influences the choice of spelling variants, one could now focus on those items that were expanded or reduced, e.g. *landt* instead of *land*, or abbreviated or contracted, such as *dē* instead of *dem* (No. 6 and 7).[32] In the pilgrim guides in question, we do indeed encounter a correlation between the use of calibrated (expanded or abridged) variants on the one hand and the format on the other hand. A comparison of 1,000 lines suggests that, in the octavos, expansions were the preferred means of coping with the small format, while the quartos contain more abbreviations.[33] Results such as these provide a first insight into the connection between typographical requirements and the occurrence of regulated spelling variants. CTVA is an excellent method for investigating these issues more closely.

7.4   Assessment

All three of the methods discussed here are useful for data capture and preparation, and belong to the descriptive level of analysis. They are by no means explanatory approaches, but they provide support in collecting and pre-structuring the data in a methodical manner. Although this overview was provided as objectively as possible, descriptions can never be completely neutral; rather, they focus on selected parts or features of the historical linguistic reality and not on others, thereby at least implicitly making judgements about relevance. These judgements may also be based on specific research interests, because scholarly expertise filters our view of the data and influences their selective description. Therefore, while description can be analytically separated from the process of hypothesising and explaining, both are in fact closely intertwined. Data capture is not only influenced by previous studies; it is also a necessary prerequisite for subsequent analytical processes. The objective of the analyses is to answer the 'whys' and 'wherefores' by linking the described phenomena to causative variables. At first, there are only hypotheses (or in criminological terms, 'grounds for suspicion'), which later have to be

---

[32] It might even be possible to consider lexical changes (*diefem* instead of *dem* in No. 7).

[33] In the pilgrim guides studied, the quarto editions show 99% more abbreviations, while the octavos have 48% more expansions; cf. Voeste, 'Variantenbildung'.

tested against other texts in order to be verified, modified or falsified. This leads in the long run (if one is given enough time and also a little luck) to the identification of regularities, but not to rules in their strictest sense. The formation of hypotheses for the purpose of explanation is thus the *raison d'être* of all descriptions, but since descriptions always pre-form their data material, the work of explanation is also implicated *a priori*. Positively stated, this means that different methods of analytical description favour certain types of hypotheses. What does this imply for the three methods presented? In principle, TRAVA takes all variants of a text into account in their full scope, although the variants are generally narrowed down to certain subsets (such as *Beüerlein*). The repertoire of explanatory hypotheses is initially not limited; in principle, all internal and external variables can be considered as *explananda*. The advantage of TRAVA is, as a consequence, a potentially high productivity in forming hypotheses. If you work thoroughly with this method and if you study the variants in detail, you may come up with innovative hypotheses about variable correlations.

TERVA, on the other hand, is a much more stringent method controlled by theoretical pre-assumptions, since it is based on a defined test arrangement and aims to test a pre-determined explanation. The independent and dependent variables in question have previously been determined and are then brought together for testing. Therefore, TERVA as a description technique can be described as a more restricted and more focused method. In terms of research logic, everything said about TERVA applies *a fortiori* to CTVA. The problem of *ceteris paribus* is reduced, though not eliminated. The comparative investigation of temporally and spatially different versions of one and the same text inevitably draws attention to different material modes and to the different socio-cultural contexts of an identical text. CTVA thus particularly stimulates the formation of hypotheses regarding the impact of external determinants. All three methods have their specific advantages and disadvantages, and none of them possesses an inherent superiority over the others. However, perhaps there is a logical sequence for their application. One can start with TRAVA to gain a multitude of hypotheses; then one can select the most plausible hypotheses and continue by using TERVA, focusing on a selected set of possible correlations. CTVA would then be an additional instrument to determine the impact of external determinants. Some scholars might call this final focus on external variables a bias; but since we are part of a historical discipline, we should consider this bias entirely welcome.

8   Orthography and Group Identity

A Comparative Approach to Studying Orthographic Systems in Early Modern Czech Printed and Handwritten Texts (c. 1560–1710)

Alena A. Fidlerová

Differences in spelling systems between early modern printed and handwritten texts can be distinguished across various European languages.[1] However, until the second half of the twentieth century, printers' orthography was usually described as standard or at least as 'more important',[2] and scribal usage was either ignored or dismissed as 'chaos', full of 'idiosyncratic variation' or simply following 'ancient tradition'.[3] Only relatively recently have authors started to refer to the 'dual standard', which is usually described as 'a public one [and] a private one'.[4] However, as I have demonstrated elsewhere,[5] the differences between printers' and scribal orthographies were more subtle than that: the scribal system, for example, can also be found in manuscripts written by professional or semi-professional scribes, which were intended for repeated reading or community use, such as copies of (printed) municipal law and hymn and prayer books. This chapter discusses selected orthographic variables[6] perceived as characteristic of the Czech printers' and scribal spelling systems between the late sixteenth and early eighteenth centuries and documents them with examples from selected printed and handwritten texts. On this basis, it aims to re-evaluate the character and mutual relations of these two orthographic systems and discusses them not as isolated, abstract systems but takes into

This study was supported by the Charles University project Progres Q10 'Language in the shiftings of time, space, and culture'.

[1] For Polish, see Bunčić, 'The standardization', 225; for French, see Cazal and Parussa, *Introduction*, 198–206; for English, see Görlach, *Eighteenth-Century English*, 78–9; Osselton, 'Informal spelling systems'; Salmon, 'Orthography and punctuation'; for German, see Voeste, 'Die Norm'; for Swedish, see Zheltukhin, 'Variable norms'.

[2] '[T]he printed texts are much more important for the further development, so that modern Polish orthography is based exclusively on the printed tradition' (Bunčić, 'The standardization', 225). Similarly Porák, *Humanistická čeština*, 102.

[3] Bunčić, 'The standardization', 225; Görlach, *Eighteenth-Century English*, 79.

[4] Osselton, 'Informal spelling systems' (1998), 33–4.   [5] Fidlerová, 'Ke vztahům'.

[6] Cf. Rutkowska and Rössler, 'Orthographic variables', 219; Zheltukhin, 'Variable norms', 194.

consideration selected material characteristics[7] of extant handwritten and printed books, and the social context of their creation and circulation. Thus, the chapter formulates and assesses several possible explanations for their long-time coexistence, both new and proposed previously for orthographies of Czech and other languages. I will combine traditional philological and (socio-)linguistic approaches with methods commonly used to study the history of the book, focusing on the materiality and the social role of a text (materiality is also discussed in Chapter 6). Finally, the chapter will propose its own, multi-layered explanation for the coexistence of the systems, based on the sociolinguistic approach to orthography as a 'dynamic interaction between extra- and intralinguistic processes and pressures'.[8]

8.1   Czech Printers' and Scribal Orthographies

The Early Modern Czech writing system[9] was quite strongly phonographic,[10] preferring the phonemic principle of writing to the etymological principle and orthographic conservativism. As with other European languages, the invention of printing in Czech 'brought about a strong impetus for the fixing of spelling habits'.[11] By the end of the sixteenth century, the orthography of Czech printed texts had reached a high degree of standardisation and, during the following two centuries, it underwent only minor changes.[12] Printers' orthography (also known as 'Brethren's orthography') featured diacritics to mark consonants that were non-existent in Latin and long vowels (e.g. <č> /t͡ʃ/, <ž> /ʒ/, <á> /aː/, <é> /ɛː/),[13] presented a low number of digraphs, and distributed <y> and <i> (both representing the vowel /ɪ/ in spoken standard Czech and the majority of dialects) mostly on an etymological basis.[14] However, the degree of licensed variation was considerably higher than today, even in printed texts, partly for technical reasons – the compositors did not always have all the required letters in their cases; they had to justify lines[15] and to ensure that the text fitted into the

---

[7] These include palaeography and layout, paper analysis and codicology (watermarks, collation, binding etc.), physical evidence of provenance or transmission, analysis of hybrid artefacts featuring both manuscript and printed texts, and the like. See e.g. Burke, 'Let's get physical'.

[8] Smith, *An Historical Study*, 60.

[9] Early Modern Czech, also called Middle Czech, signifies the language of the sixteenth to eighteenth centuries. See e.g. Vintr, *Das Tschechische*, 143, 166–77.

[10] Baddeley and Voeste, 'Introduction', 8.

[11] Llamas-Pombo, 'Variation and standardization', 36.   [12] Kučera, 'Vývoj účinnosti', 183–4.

[13] In this chapter, I use standard notation to mark phonemes (/p/) and graphemes (<p>). However, for the sake of readers not familiar with Czech phonology, I do not use the standard Czech way of writing phonemes based on Czech graphemes (e.g. /č/; see Bičan, 'Fonématika'), but provide the IPA symbols for their basic allophones instead (/t͡ʃ/).

[14] Berger, 'Religion and diacritics', 263–4; Kosek, 'Bratrský pravopis'; Porák, *Humanistická čeština*.

[15] Cf. e.g. Koupil, 'Druhé vydání'.

given number of pages, etc. Thus, unlike today,[16] there were in many cases two or more variants for the compositors to choose from.

The difference between the orthographies of manuscript and printed texts became apparent as early as the 1530s[17] and, during the following decades, the two systems developed partly independently. So-called scribal orthography showed much more variability, but was quite consistent in displaying digraphs (e.g. <cz> /t͡s/, <cž> /t͡ʃ/). Long and short vowels were not habitually distinguished (with the possible exception of /iː/ spelt as <j>), and the alternation between <y> and <i> either occurred completely or partly in free variation (the greatest variability usually occurring after the 'ambiguous consonants' /b/, /l/, /m/, /p/ and /v/), or one of them was completely substituted by the other.[18] Thus, certain digraphs and letters with diacritics functioned as orthographic variables both in printers' and scribal orthographies, but were usually perceived as unmarked in only one of these systems, and thus the choice between them created space for conveying social meanings. The fact that the scribal system displayed a preference for digraphs (e.g. <rž> /r̝/) over single letters with diacritics (<ř> /r̝/) contradicted the recommendations made at the beginning of the fifteenth century in the treatise *De orthographia bohemica* ascribed to Jan Hus,[19] which explicitly set out the goal of providing an efficient writing system for scribes.[20] As Karel Kučera has shown, the diacritical orthography proposed by this treatise was, with some modifications, accepted by the writers of many mid-fifteenth-century manuscripts, but not much later it was at least partly abandoned – both in manuscripts and in early printed texts – in favour of older digraphs. Kučera ascribes this change to the advent of the letterpress, which in its early stages was not able to systematically implement letters with diacritics and resorted to digraphs. This was particularly so in the case of majuscules or passages set in special type such as titles and headings, and the letterpress quickly became the prestigious graphical medium imitated by the scribes.[21] Nevertheless, while printers returned quite early to diacritics, at least in the case of minuscules, the scribes did not.

---

[16] '[W]hat users are led to want and expect is a "set of rules", not a licence to choose among different forms' (Sebba, *Spelling and Society*, 108).

[17] Porák, *Humanistická čeština*, 104.

[18] Cf. Berger, 'Užívání češtiny'; 'Religion and diacritics'; Čejka, 'Srovnání'; Kosek, 'Bratrský pravopis'; Porák, *Humanistická čeština*; Stich, 'Všechno je jinak'.

[19] Jan Hus (c. 1369 – 6 July 1415) was a Czech theologian, Catholic priest and church reformer condemned as a heretic and burnt at the stake during the Council of Constance. His teaching, especially popularised in his Czech sermons and edifying writings disseminated in manuscript (now published in the first four volumes of Hus, *Magistri Iohannis Hus Opera omnia*), inspired Hussitism and led to the Bohemian Reformation. On his life and thoughts see e.g. Soukup, *Jan Hus* or Šmahel and Pavlíček, *Companion to Jan Hus*.

[20] Cf. Schröpfer, *Hussens Traktat*.   [21] Kučera, 'Vývoj účinnosti', 182–3.

The scribal habit of using digraphs instead of diacritics is also recorded in contemporary grammars.[22] Some of those who mention it (Beneš Optát and Petr Gzel, and Jan Blahoslav) criticised it because it did not render the sounds correctly.[23] However, Optát and Gzel, in their slightly later school textbook (the *Isagogicon* of 1535), acknowledged and accepted the fact that the scribes would not follow all the orthographic rules strictly and would end up using digraphs because they had to take into account their readers' expectations and also had to write quickly – and what they wrote most often were letters, i.e. texts to be read only once. For letters or books intended for repeated reading, the authors required scribes to use printers' orthography.[24] Similarly, Blahoslav allowed certain concessions to 'letter scribes' hastily writing private documents to be read only once or twice.[25] A hundred years later, however, Matěj Václav Štajer (1668) dismissed scribal digraphs as a purely superfluous habit, although he tolerated the lack of vowel length marking.[26] Jiří Konstanc (1667), on the other hand, wanted not only printers, but also scribes, to distinguish between short and long vowels 'for the pure and correct writing, and, consequently, the appropriate pronunciation and speaking of the national language'.[27] However, rather surprisingly, their contemporary Václav Jan Rosa (1672),[28] and Rosa's anonymous younger admirer in the *Alphabetum Boëmicum* (1718), treat the differences between scribal and printers' orthography in detail and mention the digraphs with understanding. *Alphabetum Boëmicum*, for instance, distinguishes between scribal 'errors' (*errores*, can cause misunderstanding), and 'licence' (*licentia*, also called *parvi errores*, can cause some minor misunderstanding, but help to avoid large errors), and places the use of digraphs <cz> /$\widehat{ts}$/, <cž> /$\widehat{t\int}$/ and <rž> /$r̝$/ and the lack of vowel length

---

[22] For detailed descriptions and digital copies of all the sources mentioned in this paragraph, see the website Vokabulář webový (details in the Bibliography).

[23] Optát et al., *Grāmatyka czeſka*, B1r, B2r; Blahoslav, *Grammatica čeſká*, 33r–34r.

[24] Optát and Gzel, *Iſaǵogicon*, B3v–B4r, C2v, D1rv (where they even claim that scribes writing letters must write <rž> because custom requires it).

[25] Blahoslav, *Grammatica čeſká*, 10v.

[26] Štajer, *Wýborně dobrý způſob*, 71–3, 84–5; see also Koupil, 'Psáti, neb tisknouti?'

[27] Konstanc, *Lima lingvae Bohemicae*, 230: 'pro čiſtotu a zpráwné pſáng / y z toho náležité wyſlowowánj wlaſtenſkého yazyka a mluwenj'.

[28] Rosa, *Grammatica linguae Bohemicae*, 10–11; English translation in Rosa, *Czech Grammar*, 27: 'The consonants *c, č, ř* at the present time are written in printed books without the addition of the letter *z*, but scribes and secretaries are always accustomed in writing to add *z*, viz *cz, cž, rž* [...] Others, however, completely condemn this practice and say that *z* should never be added to *c, č, ř* [...] I approve of *c, č, ř*, without *z* as *z* is superfluous in print and should not be added. I do not, however, condemn the normal practice of scribes, who can justify themselves since printers formerly used an added *z*, as the books of Bartholomaeus Netolicensis, which were printed a hundred years ago, show. I also feel obliged to tell learners not only what should be done but also what is followed by others in practice.' Bartholomaeus Netolicensis, or Bartoloměj Netolický z Netolic, was a Prague printer who published, amongst other works, an important edition of the Bible in 1549: Voit, 'Netolický z Netolic, Bartoloměj'.

marking in the second group.[29] All of this shows that, at the beginning of the eighteenth century, scribal orthography had not merged with the printers' system but existed as a relatively focused and stable system with its own generally known rules differing from printers' usage, and that it became partly tolerated, if not fully approved of, even by the grammarians.[30]

The above-mentioned features also imply that scribal and printers' orthographies probably differ from one other in the quantitatively measured complexity of orthography, as calculated by Kučera.[31] He identified four constituent parts in this complexity, each considered from the point of view of the scribe and the reader: unambiguity (the percentage of one-to-one correspondences between a phoneme and a grapheme), standardisedness (the percentage of standardised, fixed correspondences between a phoneme and a grapheme), irregularity (the percentage of irregular, non-standard correspondences between a phoneme and a grapheme), and asymmetry (the average number of phonemes corresponding to one grapheme or vice versa).[32] Based on these parameters, Kučera assessed the level of difficulty of individual stages of Czech orthography for the writer and for the reader, and concluded that its main determinative feature was the development towards lesser reading difficulty caused by the quantitative rise of the reading public, which demanded a more easily decodable graphic record. It would be complicated to replicate his calculations, but even without them we can presume that the higher number of digraphs occurring in scribal orthography would increase the complexity of orthography as a whole only slightly. Many of these digraphs can indeed also be found in printed texts, especially in the case of majuscules and in passages set in special type.[33] The overall complexity however is increased by the lack of marking of vowel length, which, in turn, means increased difficulty for the reader and decreased difficulty for the writer. Since 1550, Czech printers' orthography had been, according to Kučera, considerably more difficult for the writer than for the reader; we can therefore infer that failure to mark vowel length probably only entailed narrowing of the gap between levels of difficulty for reader and writer, rather than favouring the latter over the former.

---

[29] *Alphabetum Boëmicum*, 24–5, 28, 104–7, 154–5, 203–6. Also see Koupil, '*Alphabetum Boëmicum*', 372–3, 376–7.

[30] This is not specific to Czech: scribal orthography was accounted for in English language textbooks providing separate advice to printers, and to scribes (Osselton, 'Informal spelling systems' (1998), 35–8), Fabian Frangk emphasised in *Cantzley vnd Titel büchlin* (1531) that his orthographic rules were not intended for informal and private use (Voeste, 'Die Norm neben der Norm', 6–7); etc.

[31] Cf. Kučera, 'Vývoj účinnosti', 184–95; see also his 'Dodatek'.

[32] Types, not tokens, were counted. The historically arisen phoneme (e.g. /jɛ/ written <ě>) or grapheme (e.g. <ch> for /x/) groups were counted as one phoneme/grapheme.

[33] Kučera ('Vývoj účinnosti') himself observes that there is no marked difference in this respect between mediaeval digraphs and early modern printers' orthography.

8.2   Examples of Printers' and Scribal Orthographies

There is not enough space in this chapter to address all the differences between printers' and scribal orthographies in minute detail. As previously mentioned, some digraphs, as well as a lack of vowel length marking, were perceived as 'recognition signs' of scribal orthography. Therefore, I will primarily focus on the graphic expression of several consonants (originally) unknown to the Latin phonological system, i.e. /t͡s/, /t͡ʃ/, /ʒ/[34] and /r̝/, which were respectively represented by <c>, <č>, <ž> and <ř> in printers' orthography, but were usually (also) spelt using various digraphs (<cz>, <cž>/<čz>/<cži>, <zi>/<ži> and <rz>/<rž>/<řz>/<rzi>/<rži> etc.) in scribal orthography. This prominent feature of scribal orthography was very persistent (the digraphs can even be found in early nineteenth-century texts) and cannot solely be explained by ignorance or negligence. The convention entails writing two or three graphs instead of one, and it appears to be contrary to one of the key principles – according to Jeremy Smith – of the evolution of script (if one can also apply this to orthography), namely the principle of 'least effort'.[35] In addition, as Anja Voeste has shown through the example of two texts (one printed and one manuscript) in German by the poet Martin Opitz from the same year (1637) and of similar genre (a dedication and a letter, both addressed to the members of high nobility), similar digraphs cannot be explained by an attempt to make the text longer (and, consequently, attract a larger remuneration) nor by the scribe's lack of education.[36] Therefore, the explanation of their ongoing popularity among scribes represents an interesting problem.

A rather similar problem is posed by the grapheme <ě>, which in printers' orthography replaced the older digraph <ie> (in Old Czech also <ye>), and thus its diacritic was often regarded as a 'remnant' of the <i>,[37] which was also supposed to be rudimentarily present in the pronunciation. The grapheme <ě> continues to be used either to mark palatalisation of the preceding consonant (in <dě>, <tě>, <ně>, pronounced /ɟɛ/, /cɛ/, /ɲɛ/ respectively),[38] or the positions of the Old Czech vowel *jat'* /i^e/ after labials /b/, /p/, /v/, /f/,[39] /m/ (since the fifteenth century these

---

[34] Since the fourteenth century, /ʒ/ has been pronounced [ʃ] if followed by a voiceless consonant or a glottal stop, but all the Early Modern Czech orthography systems generally follow the morphophonological principle here and use some of the orthographic variables of <ž>. Consequently, I also count these positions here.

[35] Smith, *An Historical Study*, 46.   [36] Voeste 'Die Norm', 5.

[37] See e.g. *Alphabetum Boëmicum*, 35. At least partly for this reason, <ě> was sometimes not a separate letter in early modern printed texts but a constituent part of the ligatures <bě>, <pě>, <wě>, <mě>, <dě>, <tě>, <ně>. In some early printed books, the diacritic was, in fact, positioned not above <e>, but in the middle between the two letters, e.g. in Optát et al., *Grāmatyka cžeſka*.

[38] If the consonants /ɟ/, /c/, /ɲ/ occur syllable-finally or in front of other vowels, the diacritic is positioned on the consonant letter (<ď>, <ť>, <ň>) in today's usage.

[39] This consonant is extremely rare in Czech and does not occur in the texts analysed here.

grapheme combinations have been pronounced /bjɛ/, /pjɛ/, /vjɛ/, /fjɛ/, /mɲɛ/). However, early modern scribes often replaced <ě> with <ie>, although most grammarians did not approve of this.[40]

Additionally, I will pay some attention to the marking of vowel length. In Czech, five vowels are used (/a/, /ɛ/, /ɪ/, /o/, /u/, spelt today as <a>, <e>/<ě>, <i>/<y>, <o>, <u> respectively), all of which have long counterparts (/a:/, /ɛ:/, /i:/, /o:/, /u:/, spelt today as <á>, <é>, <í>/<ý>, <ó>, <ú>/<ů>; before the mid-nineteenth century, /i:/ was spelt <j>/<ý>). Although one cannot exclude the possibility that the scribes were not always sure about the distribution of long and short vowels (which varied to some extent both regionally and diachronically), these were obligatorily distinguished in printed texts, and the (partial) absence of this distinction in most pre-nineteenth-century manuscripts requires some explanation.

Regarding the other prominent features of scribal orthography, I will not linger on those which are not represented in speech – most importantly the irregularities in the distribution of <i>/<y> (and <j>/<ý>) – as these may have resulted from the scribe's lack of education. In the period studied, despite the statements of some grammarians, only the /ɪ/ and /i:/ sounds were pronounced in the vast majority of the Bohemian territory, and the graphic difference was preserved partly due to tradition and partly in order to distinguish homophones. Moreover, the failure to place <i> and <y> correctly was perceived by contemporaries as an error rather than as a licensed feature of scribal orthography.[41] Variables pertaining not to individual sound–grapheme correspondences but to larger units, such as punctuation and capitalisation, will also be left for future discussions, as these often varied, even in printed texts, and represent a separate, more complicated problem.

In order to demonstrate the differences between scribal and printers' orthographies, I will focus on the orthography of a very common text category, namely books of municipal and provincial law. Such books were owned by the majority of town councils in Bohemia, and therefore have been preserved in numerous copies dating from the late sixteenth to the early eighteenth centuries. They were first published in print (and, with the exception of Ferdinand II's *Obnowené Práwo a Zřjzenj* [Reformed Law and Constitution], reissued repeatedly) and were subsequently often copied by hand, probably because of the shortage or high price of copies or because the councils wanted to own copies supplemented with later additions and cross-references. For my analysis, I used five printed editions and eight manuscript copies of these texts (randomly chosen), as listed below, with their brief identifiers.

---

[40] Even *Alphabetum Boëmicum* (203) requires the scribes not to omit the diacritic of <ě> (and does not mention the possibility of writing <ie> at all).
[41] Ibid.

(1) Printed books:

(a) Constitution: *Práwa a Zřijzenij zemſká Králowſtwj Cžeſkého* [Law and Constitution of the Kingdom of Bohemia] (Prague, 1564).

(b) Koldín, Code I: Pavel Kristián z Koldína,[42] *Práwa Měſtſká Králowſtwij Czieſkého* [Municipal Law of the Kingdom of Bohemia] (Prague, 1579).

(c) Koldín, Code II: Pavel Kristián z Koldína, *Práwa Měſtſká Králowſtwij Cžeſkého / w krátkau Summu vwedená* ... [Short Summary of the Municipal Law of the Kingdom of Bohemia] (Prague, 1582).

(d) Koldín, Constitution: Pavel Kristián z Koldína, *Práwa a Zřijzenij Zemſká Králowſtwij Cžeſkého w krátkau Summu vwedená* ... [Short Summary of the Law and Constitution of the Kingdom of Bohemia] (Prague, 1583).

(e) Renewed Constitution: Ferdinand II, ... *Obnowené Práwo a Zřjzenj Zemſké Dědjčného Králowſtwj Cžeſkého* ... [Reformed Law and Constitution of the Hereditary Kingdom of Bohemia] (Prague, 1627).

(2) Manuscript copies of these texts (or of other contemporary editions), randomly chosen:

(a) NKP XVII G 18: Pavel Kristián z Koldína, *Artykulowe Praw Meſtſkých* [Articles of the Municipal Law] (1619).

(b) KNM IV C 15: Pavel Kristián z Koldína, *Práwa Měſtſká Králowſtwij Czieſkého. Práwa a Zřijzenij zemſká Králowſtwj Cžeſkého* [Municipal Law of the Kingdom of Bohemia. Law and Constitution of the Kingdom of Bohemia] (Nový Bydžov, 1624).

(c) KNM V C 45: Pavel Kristián z Koldína, *Prawa Měſtſka Kralowſtwj Czieſkého* [Municipal Law of the Kingdom of Bohemia] (Hřešihlavy, 1661).

(d) KNM IV C 2: Ferdinand II, ... *Obnowene Prawo a Zřizeni Zemſke. Diedičneho Kralowſtwj Cžeſkeho* ... [Reformed Law and Constitution of the Hereditary Kingdom of Bohemia] (Solnice, 1672).

(e) Pardubice Rkp 393: Ferdinand II, ... *Obnowene Prawo a Zržizenj Zemſke Dědiczneho Kraloſtwj Czeſkeho* ... [Reformed Law and Constitution of the Hereditary Kingdom of Bohemia] (second half of the seventeenth century).

(f) KNM IV C 22: Pavel Kristián z Koldína, *Prawa Mieſtſka Kralowſtwy Cžeſkeho* ... [Municipal Law of the Kingdom of Bohemia] (1682).

(g) NKP XVII C 39: Pavel Kristián z Koldína, *Prawa Mieſtſka Kralowſtwi Cžeſkeho, wkratkau Summu Vwedena* ... [Short Summary of the Municipal Law of the Kingdom of Bohemia] (before 1685).

(h) Rychnov 562/74: Pavel Kristián z Koldína, *Prawa Mieſtſka Kralowſtwj Cžeſkeho w Kratkau Summu Vwedena* ... [Short Summary of the Municipal Law of the Kingdom of Bohemia] (early eighteenth century).

[42] Pavel Kristián z Koldína (1530–89), Bohemian jurist.

The most important characteristics of the two categories of texts are summarised in Table 8.1. Texts are ordered chronologically; manuscripts consisting of more than one part or written by more than one scribe are listed separately as (a, b) and (A, B) respectively.

The orthographic features of these texts are summarised in Table 8.2. Only minuscule letters were included in the analysis; in the case of capital letters, digraphs are also present in printed books, which excludes them from the group of features distinguishing between the two orthographies.[43] In each book, only the script of the body text (i.e. no titles, headings, incipits, marginalia, quotations etc.) was taken into account. Poorly legible letters were also excluded, and the length of the samples was chosen so that they comprised approximately 150 instances of <ě> (and its variants) and 70 instances of each consonant. Percentages were used to simplify comparability. All of the printed books were analysed together as a group because, unlike the manuscripts, they do not display any differences among the selected variables. In the case of consonants, I considered the digraphs <cž>/<čz>, <rž>/<řz> together. It is usually quite difficult to tell them apart, because the diacritics tend to be placed very imprecisely, and I did not distinguish between different shapes of diacritic (dot, hook, apostrophe, etc.); however, I did distinguish between <ě> and <ė> because the latter may have represented a strongly reduced variant of <ie>.

The above sample is admittedly quite small, but it will suffice for a concise analysis as part of this chapter. It confirms that printers' and scribal orthographic systems are really quite different. Unlike printed texts which use single letters with diacritics and mark vowel length consistently, the manuscripts are far from uniform, and some of them are further from printers' orthography than others. The manuscripts generally use two or more digraphs, most often <cž> and <rž>, in positions where contemporary printed books consistently feature letters with diacritics, and they generally do not (consistently) mark vowel length. The digraphs mostly include a diacritic mark, for which reason it is impossible to assume that they represent an attempt to reduce the number of diacritics. The only exception is represented by the scribe of KNM IV C 15, who is not fully consistent in different parts of his text – most of the time he strives to avoid digraphs, but occasionally he fails to do so. However, even this scribe marks vowel length only exceptionally. This (KNM IV C 15) is a rather

---

[43] Printers often did not have at their disposal (enough) capital letters with diacritics and so they resorted to digraphs. This practice was very common and was allowed for even by some grammarians (see e.g. Optát et al., *Grāmatyka cžeſka*, B1r, B2rv, B3r; Optát and Gzel, *Iſagogicon*, D1r; Štajer, *Wýborně dobrý způſob*, 73–4); however, other grammarians censured it (e.g. Blahoslav, *Grammatica čeſká*, 33r–34r; Konstanc, *Lima lingvae Bohemicae*, 282–3). Consequently, digraphs replacing capital letters with diacritics do not really represent any difference between printed books and manuscripts. Thus, although the decision to disregard majuscules proved problematic for some manuscripts where the majority of words featured an initial capital letter, I decided to keep to it.

Table 8.1 *Details of the sources selected*

Identifier	Medium	Content	Date	Scribe or printer	Script of the body text
Constitution	print	provincial law	1564	Jiří Melantrich z Aventýna senior	*Schwabacher* [a]
Koldín, Code I	print	municipal law	1579	Daniel Adam z Veleslavína, Jiří Melantrich z Aventýna senior	*Schwabacher*
Koldín, Code II	print	municipal law	1582	Jiří Černý z Černého Mostu	*Schwabacher*
Koldín, Constitution	print	provincial law	1583	Jiří Černý z Černého Mostu	*Schwabacher*
NKP XVII G 18 A	manuscript	municipal law	1619	unknown	Czech Gothic semi-cursive
NKP XVII G 18 B	manuscript	municipal law	1619	unknown	Czech Gothic cursive
KNM IV C 15 a	manuscript	municipal law	1624	Mikoláš Výborný (Nový Bydžov)	Czech Gothic semi-cursive
KNM IV C 15 b	manuscript	provincial law	1624	Mikoláš Výborný (Nový Bydžov)	Czech Gothic semi-cursive
Renewed Constitution	print	provincial law	1627	Jan Schumann	*Schwabacher*
KNM V C 45	manuscript	municipal law	1661	Georg Christoph Schultz (Jihlava)	Czech Gothic cursive
KNM IV C 2	manuscript	provincial law	1672	Jan Doubravský (Solnice)	Czech Gothic semi-cursive
Pardubice Rkp 393	manuscript	provincial law	2nd half C17	unknown	Czech Gothic cursive
KNM IV C 22 A	manuscript	municipal law	1682	W. F. E. H. Nedomský	Czech Gothic semi-cursive
KNM IV C 22 B	manuscript	municipal law	1682	unknown	German Gothic cursive
NKP XVII C 39 a	manuscript	municipal law	before 1685	Václav Vilém Patoč junior (Dvůr Králové)	Czech Gothic semi-cursive
NKP XVII C 39 b	manuscript	provincial law	before 1685	Václav Vilém Patoč junior (Dvůr Králové)	Czech Gothic semi-cursive
Rychnov 562/74	manuscript	municipal law	early C18	unknown	Czech Gothic cursive

[a] *Schwabacher* is a style of blackletter typeface.

Table 8.2 Orthographic characteristics of the sources selected

Identifier	/ts/						/tʃ/				/ʒ/			
	<cz>	<cż> or <cz>	<cži>	<czi>	<tcz>	<c>	<cz>	<čži>	<cž> or <cz>	<č>	<ži>	<zi>	<ži>	<ž>
Printed books (a)–(e)	0%	0%	0%	0%	0%	100%	0%	0%	0%	100%	0%	0%	0%	100%
NKP XVII G 18 A	76%	0%	0%	0%	0%	24%	0%	0%	98%	2%	0%	0%	0%	100%
NKP XVII G 18 B	100%	0%	0%	0%	0%	0%	0%	0%	100%	0%	0%	7%	0%	93%
KNM IV C 15 a	16%	1%	0%	0%	0%	83%	13%	0%	53%	34%	10%	7%	4%	79%
KNM IV C 15 b	0%	0%	0%	0%	0%	100%	6%	0%	10%	84%	2%	0%	0%	98%
KNM V C 45	99%	1%	0%	0%	0%	0%	9%	21%	70%	0%	0%	12%	0%	88%
KNM IV C 2	4%	0%	0%	0%	0%	96%	0%	0%	100%	0%	0%	0%	2%	98%
Pardubice Rkp 393	95%	5%	0%	0%	0%	0%	23%	0%	77%	0%	14%	0%	23%	63%
KNM IV C 22 A	83%	0%	0%	0%	17%	0%	3%	0%	97%	0%	10%	6%	0%	84%
KNM IV C 22 B	100%	0%	0%	0%	0%	0%	10%	0%	90%	0%	0%	0%	8%	92%
NKP XVII C 39 a	100%	0%	0%	0%	0%	0%	0%	0%	100%	0%	0%	19%	0%	81%
NKP XVII C 39 b	100%	0%	0%	0%	0%	0%	0%	0%	100%	0%	0%	8%	0%	92%
Rychnov 562/74	100%	0%	0%	0%	0%	0%	0%	3%	97%	0%	0%	5%	0%	95%

Identifier	/r̝/						/ɛ/ following /j/, /c/, /ɲ/, /ɟ/; /jɛ/ following /b/, /p/, /v/; /ɲɛ/ following /m/				Vowel length
	<řz>	<řž> or <řz>	<řži>	<řzi>	<ř>	<ě>	<ie>	<ě>	<e>	<ě>	
Printed books (a)–(e)	0%	0%	0%	0%	100%	0%	0%	0%	0%	100%	yes
NKP XVII G 18 A	0%	0%	0%	0%	0%	1%	2%	0%	0%	97%	unsystematically (only <á> and word-final <ij>)
NKP XVII G 18 B	0%	0%	0%	0%	0%	0%	100%	0%	0%	0%	unsystematically (most often <á>, sporadically also <é>, <ý> and <ó>)
KNM IV C 15 a	67%	8%	1%	0%	23%	1%	80%	0%	16%	3%	exceptionally
KNM IV C 15 b	1%	3%	0%	0%	96%	2%	1%	0%	90%	7%	exceptionally
KNM V C 45	0%	70%	30%	0%	0%	14%	82%	0%	1%	3%	no
KNM IV C 2	0%	100%	0%	0%	0%	3%	11%	0%	86%	0%	exceptionally
Pardubice Rkp 393	31%	68%	0%	1%	0%	0%	100%	0%	0%	0%	no
KNM IV C 22 A	0%	98%	2%	0%	0%	0%	99%	0%	1%	0%	no
KNM IV C 22 B	1%	98%	0%	0%	1%	75%	5%	98%	13%	7%	no
NKP XVII C 39 a	0%	100%	0%	0%	0%	1%	0%	98%	0%	1%	no
NKP XVII C 39 b	0%	100%	0%	0%	0%	0%	0%	100%	0%	0%	no
Rychnov 562/74	0%	98%	2%	0%	0%	2%	35%	0%	62%	1%	no

special manuscript, as not only its orthography, but also its overall layout, reveal an effort to imitate the printed exemplar as closely as possible, including the layout of the title page, partial imitation of the typeface, and use of pilcrows and fleurons. Thus, the relative closeness to printers' orthography may be interpreted as a constituent part of the scribe's attempt to imitate a printed book, and thus cannot act as evidence for or against two distinct orthographic systems.

8.3   Explanations

Although the existence of the 'dual standard' of printers' and scribal orthography has already been known for several decades in Czech, only rather sketchy and partial explanations for it have been proposed so far. In this section, I summarise some of these possible explanations, divide them into groups, and discuss their strengths and weaknesses. I also propose a new and multi-layered socio-cultural explanation.

8.3.1   Diachronic Explanation

A seemingly logical explanation for the differences between the two orthographies is the possibility that scribal orthography may be a remnant of mediaeval spelling resistant to the ongoing development of printed texts. For example, Jaroslav Porák ascribes 'strong conservativism' to Czech scribal orthography and a 'dislike for adopting the changes that were taking place in printers' orthography';[44] while Mirek Čejka calls scribal orthography 'considerably more archaic and primitive'.[45] Noel Osselton describes individual features of scribal orthography in English as conventions surviving from the more or less distant past, already abandoned by printers, and tentatively suggests that there seems to be 'a time-lag of between 50 and 100 years between epistolary and printers' spelling'.[46] A more sophisticated version of this approach would be to see printers' and scribal orthographies as *Gleichzeitigkeit der Ungleichzeitigen*,[47] the simultaneity of the non-simultaneous, 'diachronic variants used at the same point in time'.[48] This well-known concept has been used in different ways by different authors, Reinhard Koselleck's approach being probably the most relevant to our case. According to Koselleck, any historical moment represents a section through the historical continuum, which reveals different time layers featuring the phenomena of very different age and duration.[49] This concept differs from the previous,

[44] Porák, *Humanistická čeština*, 104.   [45] Čejka, 'Srovnání', 37.
[46] Osselton, 'Informal spelling systems' (1998), 42.
[47] Cf. e.g. Burkhard, 'Zur Ungleichzeitigkeit'; Schlögl, *Alter Glaube und moderne Welt*.
[48] Llamas-Pombo, 'Variation and standardization', 41.
[49] Koselleck, *Vergangene Zukunft*, 132.

'remnant' approach as it views the contemporary existence of old and new phenomena and their mutual relations not as accidental (and thus unimportant), but as a determinative feature of each epoch, which can be adequately understood only in its complexity. However, whichever approach to the diachronic explanation is adopted, it is not without problems. First, as mentioned above, there was a period in the history of Czech orthography immediately preceding the advent of print when letters with diacritics seem to have temporarily superseded the digraphs.[50] Thus, the development was not straightforward in this respect and there is no easy and unequivocal way to label these variables as 'old' and 'new'. Second, as can be seen from the example of sixteenth-century Sweden, scribal orthography may not be always more conservative than printers' orthography. In some cases, scribal features can present innovations which challenge the accepted printed standard.[51] Similarly, Voeste is convinced that specific graphic features used in seventeenth-century German handwritten correspondence have primarily pragmatic or stylistic functions (see Section 8.3.5) and do not necessarily represent older ways of writing.[52]

8.3.2   Technical Explanation (Scribe-oriented)

Another possible explanation takes into account the fact that the technologies of the composition of printed and handwritten texts differ fundamentally, as do the orthographies ideally suited for them. Rosa mentioned in his grammar the claim of some scribes that the addition of <z> enabled them to make writing more 'beautiful' by helping to cope with the problem of the imprecise placement of diacritics: 'The reason is given by some that the letter z seems [...] to produce a more beautiful script since, in writing, diacritics cannot be added in as orderly a way as in print.'[53] This statement was confirmed by the author of the *Alphabetum Boëmicum*, according to whom it was more expedient to use the digraph <rž>, thus allowing the scribe to position the diacritic less precisely than above the sole <ř>: 'It should be noted that in cursive script, (rž) instead of (ř) with a diacritic is generally used, e.g. "ržeka; zwěrž", and this is usually because, when writing fast, the diacritic above (r) is not readily positioned precisely, but can easily happen to be positioned elsewhere, which can cause major confusion for the reader.'[54] The same author added that this problem never occurred in print because there, the diacritic was a constituent part of the

---

[50] Kučera, 'Vývoj účinnosti', 182–3.   [51] Cf. Zheltukhin, 'Variable norms'.
[52] Voeste 'Die Norm', 10.
[53] 'Rationem aliqui dant hanc: quod illa litera z/ videtur [...] pulchriorem fcriptionem efficere, cum in fcriptis non poffunt accentus ita ordinatè poni, ficut in impreffis': Rosa, *Grammatica linguae Bohemicae*, 10; English translation: Rosa, *Czech Grammar*, 27.
[54] 'Quòd in currenti fcriptura locò punctuati (ř) paffim fcribatur (rž) út: ržeka/ zwěrž/ idque ideo fieri folet, quia celeriter fcribendo non facile illud punctum fupra (r) directè, fed citiùs aliò poneretur, & hinc etiam major confufio legenti caufaretur': *Alphabetum Boëmicum*, 104.

letter: 'It should be noted that this is different in the case of printed texts, where the letter (ř) is already available with its diacritic; therefore, the printer is not allowed to use (rž) instead of (ř).'[55] For digraphs without diacritics, when striving to write fast and legibly, it was easier to put down <cz> rather than the sole <c>, which in Gothic cursive closely resembled <i>, <e> or a stem of <n>, <m> or <u> etc.: '[...] however, in manuscripts [<cz>] might be excused because when writing the cursive script fast, it is easier to put down well and legibly than simple <c>'.[56]

As the cursive letter <z> has the form with a descender (similar to <ʒ>), the 'z' digraphs can also add visual emphasis to words containing them, much like an added <h> in Early Modern German.[57] What was also of significance was that using diacritics could considerably slow down the writing process '[w]hich is associated with a major retardation impeding writing of cursive script because it is quicker to put down two or three lines than a single line if due reflexions are distracted by the problems with the correct placing of accents'.[58] Thus, it seems rational that the scribes tended to write only those diacritics they deemed necessary for correct decoding. In the Gothic cursive (used in two variants, Czech and German, the German variant being also called *Kurrent*), these included diacritic marks (hook, dot etc.) used to distinguish <u> and sometimes also <c> from other letters of similar shapes, and the diacritic of <ž>. This last letter was used both on its own and in digraphs which, in turn, enabled the scribe to position the diacritic (pertaining not to a single letter, but to two) less precisely. Other letters with diacritics seem to have been regarded as unnecessary, potentially confusing and slowing down the writing process. However, the last-mentioned argument was of much less importance for formal, 'book-like' variants of Gothic script (imitating *Schwabacher* or *Fraktur*), where each letter was written with several strokes of the pen, and thus so slowly that using diacritics probably did not make much difference. Moreover, Gothic printed letters of this type were normally used to code texts in printers' orthography and thus were more strongly associated with a different orthographic practice (i.e. a different set of orthographic conventions) from Gothic cursive. Therefore, it is not surprising that handwritten *Schwabacher* or *Fraktur* (and to some extent also semi-cursive script) showed a stronger tendency to be understood as related to the typeface of printed books and could be

---

[55] 'Quod cùm in typis aliter ſe habeat, & littera (ř) jam cum ſuo puncto prae manibus ſit, idcirco Impreſſori (rž) locò (ř) ponere non licet': ibid., 104.

[56] '[...] [<cz>] nihilominus tamen in manuſcriptis excuſari poteſt; quia hoc in celeri ſcriptione faciliùs venit, quàm; ut ſolum (c) in currenti charactere bene & legibiliter exprimatur': ibid., 25; similarly, about <cž>, ibid., 28.

[57] Voeste, 'The emergence of suprasegmental spellings', 181.

[58] 'Cui adſtipulatur magna retardatio currentem ſcripturam impediens, cùm citiùs duae, vel tres lineae deſcribi, quàm de accentibus in una linea rectè apponendis debitae reflexiones diſcuti poſſint': *Alphabetum Boëmicum*, 204.

occasionally used together with printers' orthography, as I have explained elsewhere.[59]

Thus, as the manuscript writing process differs technically from the composition of a printed text, the suitability of diacritics to mark certain distinctions was assessed differently by printers and scribes. In fact, it may be presumed that marking vowel length never became customary among Early Modern Czech scribes precisely because of diacritics. If other means had been widely adopted in printed books (e.g. vowel doubling, occurring occasionally in early-sixteenth-century printed texts and also mentioned in the oldest Czech grammar),[60] the scribes would probably have adopted them. The history of English orthography can serve as a comparison: in late-sixteenth-century English printed texts, vowel length already tended to be indicated by doubling vowels or by adding a final <e> to the word, and shortness was marked by doubling the following consonant. Unlike in Czech, this practice was later followed to a certain extent in English manuscripts, though much less systematically than in print.[61]

8.3.3   Technical Explanation (Reader-oriented)

Until the early nineteenth century, reading of printed and manuscript texts was taught as two distinct skills, the latter being usually considered more difficult and thus better suited for advanced pupils. However, because of the lack of printed textbooks before the Enlightenment school reforms, and also at the request of some parents, especially craftsmen, instruction may have sometimes started with handwritten rather than printed texts.[62] At any rate, as some pupils (especially girls) often left school quite early, it was not surprising that they, as readers later in life, were not well-versed in both printed and handwritten texts and that they were consequently not familiar with their respective orthographic systems. As mentioned above, some of the scribal 'licences' were aimed at facilitating decoding by the reader, or, as *Alphabetum Boëmicum* puts it, 'to avoid mixing up adjacent letters'.[63] In this respect, most arguments previously discussed are also relevant here: if the digraphs enabled the scribe to write more legibly, they simultaneously made reading easier. Additionally, according to Elena Llamas-Pombo, when writing digraphs 'the scribe is using the letters of the Latin alphabet not simply to transcribe a phoneme, but as an instrument of analysis of something similar to a third articulation: it could be thought that he is seeking to transcribe each individual phonetic characteristic of the consonant'.[64] Thus, scribal digraphs can be understood as easier to read for

[59] Cf. Fidlerová, 'Ke vztahům'.   [60] Optát et al., *Grāmatyka čžeſka*, A3v.
[61] Salmon, 'Orthography and punctuation', 27, 30, 42.
[62] Cf. Messerli, 'Das Lesen von Gedrucktem'.
[63] 'ad evitandam confuſionem litterarum invicem cohaerentium': *Alphabetum Boëmicum*, 204.
[64] Llamas-Pombo, 'Variation and standardization', 23.

less-skilled readers in just another way: these readers do not have to remember how to pronounce all the letters with diacritics or digraphs; if they do not know the phonetic value of a digraph, they can simply guess it from its composition.

8.3.4   'Informal'/ 'Private' / 'Intimate' Explanation

The explanation mentioned most often in the secondary literature is that scribal orthography, with its increased variability, is simply the 'informal' or 'private' way of writing.[65] This approach is based on the assumption that handwritten texts are most often of an informal and private character and, therefore, may be spelt less systematically than printed texts, which are public. Accordingly, Vivian Salmon bases her description of the orthography of early modern manuscript English texts almost exclusively on the use of private documents, predominantly private correspondence.[66] Similarly, Čejka calls Czech scribal orthography the orthography *pro foro interno*, as opposed to the *pro foro externo* of printers' orthography.[67] This hypothesis appears to be supported by the opinions of various grammarians. I have already mentioned the statements of Jan Blahoslav regarding 'letter scribes' whose way of writing may be accepted if approved by the author and by the recipient;[68] scribes writing letters to be read only once are also explicitly mentioned by Optát and Gzel.[69] However, the presupposition of fewer readers of a manuscript than of a printed book may be connected not only with the lesser importance or greater intimacy of the handwritten text, but also with the assumption that the readers are probably native speakers who can make up for minor ambiguities by pronouncing the text correctly: 'Because [texts in] cursive script are intended for a small number [of readers] who already know the Czech language perfectly, and thus are able to understand the meaning intended by scribes despite small errors and to compensate for the lack of diacritics by correct pronunciation.'[70] Printed texts, on the other hand, not only existed in hundreds or thousands of copies and were to be read for hundreds of years, but might be read by a very diverse readership including beginners[71] or even non-native speakers.[72]

---

[65] Cf. Cazal and Parussa, *Introduction*, 198–206; Osselton, 'Informal spelling systems'.

[66] Salmon, 'Orthography and punctuation'.   [67] Čejka, 'Srovnání', 37.

[68] Blahoslav, *Grammatica čeſká*, 10v.   [69] Optát and Gzel, *Iſagogicon*, B3v–B4r, C2v, D1v.

[70] 'Nam currens Scriptura [...] pro paucis, ijsque aliunde jam perfectis Boëmis, qui non obſtantibus parvis erroribus ſenſum ſcriptorum intelligunt, & per rectam pronunciationem defectum accentuum ſupplere ſciunt [...]: *Alphabetum Boëmicum*, 205.

[71] 'At verò libri in typis edendi [...] per centena, aut millena exemplaria in uſum plurimorũ, etiam adhuc diſcentium coṁunicantur, atque ad annos ſaeculares aſſervantur': ibid., 205–6.

[72] Štajer, *Wýborně dobrý způſob*, 85.

However, some advocates of the 'informal' explanation are aware of the fact that scribal orthography is not chaotic but a system with its own rules. As Osselton says in reference to mid-eighteenth-century English:

I would then maintain that, at least at this stage in the development of English, epistolary spelling is a graphic system, which leads its own linguistic life; it has its own rules and tendencies: it is independent of, though it stands in a clear relationship to, the system of spelling used by the printers. Furthermore, this graphic system is a part of the educated English of its day.[73]

The emphasis is placed not only on the informality of the text, which allows the scribe to overlook some orthographic rules, but also on the more intimate relationship between the scribe and the reader (being sometimes one and the same). Čejka mentions in his analysis of a manuscript copy of a printed songbook the 'greater intimacy of the *manu propria* record for private use'.[74] Elaborating on this and on the concept of *Sprache der Nähe* ('language of immediacy') and *Sprache der Distanz* ('language of distance') developed by Peter Koch and Wulf Oesterreicher,[75] Daniel Bunčić et al. label the situation of the Early Modern Czech orthographic system as *diamesic diorthographia*, where printers' orthography pertained to the language of distance and scribal orthography to the language of (relative) immediacy.[76] Similarly, Voeste explains the archaic features of German scribal orthography 'as contrastive ornaments inserted in order to emphasise the personal, intimate character of a letter' or 'as signs of a private standard (of handwritten texts) distinct from the public standard (of printed texts)'.[77] This way, the author was aiming to establish a relationship of closeness and familiarity with the addressee, which was not attainable by means of printers' orthography.[78]

The main weakness of these explanations is demonstrated above: scribal orthography is not (exclusively) a system intended for private use nor for the language of communicative immediacy. It is used in the majority of early modern manuscript texts, even in copies of printed books written by professional or semi-professional scribes and intended for community or long-term use. The copies of municipal or provincial law analysed above clearly belong to the sphere of language of distance,[79] but they mostly follow the conventions of scribal orthography. If some of them partly tend toward printers' orthography (as does the manuscript KNM IV C 15), it is not because they contain different text or are intended for different use from others. Rather, they appear to be the products of an attempt to willingly change the register (and suppress the

---

[73] Osselton, 'Informal spelling systems' (1998), 35.   [74] Čejka, 'Srovnání', 37.
[75] Koch and Oesterreicher, 'Language of immediacy'.   [76] Bunčić et al., *Biscriptality*, 140–3.
[77] 'als kontrastive Ornamente eingesetzt, um den persönlichen, vertrauten Charakter des Briefs zu betonen [...] als Hinweis auf eine private Norm (der Handschriftlichkeit) neben der öffentlichen Norm (des Drucks)': Voeste 'Die Norm', 1.
[78] Ibid., 10.   [79] Cf. Bunčić et al., *Biscriptality*, 59.

scribe's habit of using scribal orthography), because their scribe, unlike others, perceives this type (or this particular copy) of handwritten text as functionally close to print culture. However, the clear predominance of scribal orthography in my sample confirms that, put in Bunčić et al.'s terms, it is not the *diamesic* but the *medial* dimension that is determinative here.

8.3.5   Stylistic / Pragmatic Explanation

According to Voeste, scribal digraphs used in German handwritten correspondence may have been understood as stylistically marked, and 'selected' in two ways: first, they may have served as an 'ornament', a means to express respect or politeness towards the addressee (*Mittel der Respektbekundung oder als Höflichkeitsmarker*). The fact that they represented an older way of writing may have contributed to this function, as it is usual for archaisms to be perceived as belonging to a higher register and being more prestigious. Second, the scribes may have used them to show off their erudition, in being able to switch between scribal and printers' orthographies.[80] Additionally, as Llamas-Pombo suggests for mediaeval Spanish[81] and Voeste for sixteenth-century German,[82] the scribes may have been following the classical rhetorical principle of variation not only on the level of morphology, vocabulary and syntax but also of orthography, and used orthographic variation as a stylistic device for aesthetic reasons. Thus, digraphs may have been used intentionally by educated scribes for stylistic purposes. Such a hypothesis has also been formulated for Czech: Kučera considers digraphs more (stylistically) marked and even ostentatious or ornamental than letters with diacritics.[83] Even today, some Czech aristocratic families use them in their family names, e.g. 'Czernin' or 'Lobkowicz', differing visibly from the spelling of the names of ordinary people (which would be 'Černín', 'Lobkovic'). This interpretation of digraphs may have also been supported by the fact that, in printed texts, digraphs were used in place of majuscules with diacritics – often representing the initials of personal names, honorary titles, forms of address to high-ranking people and the like, which could have strengthened the association between digraphs and names of noble or respectable persons. Although the stylistic explanation could well apply to handwritten books intended for community use, letters to important or beloved correspondents, historical records and so on, it seems incompatible with the explanation (advanced by some contemporary grammarians) that scribal orthography primarily represents a way of writing characterised by particular carelessness with respect to orthographic rules.

---

[80] Voeste 'Die Norm', 6–7, 10.   [81] Llamas-Pombo, 'Variation and standardization', 26–8.
[82] Voeste, 'The emergence of suprasegmental spellings', 171.
[83] Kučera, 'Vývoj účinnosti a složitosti českého pravopisu', 183.

8.3.6   Socio-cultural Explanation

Even the famous eighteenth-century English lexicographer Samuel Johnson found it 'inappropriate [...] to adopt for the purposes of writing a private letter the pattern of spelling used by the compositors'.[84] Given all the above-listed tentative explanations, a few questions may be asked: what does 'inappropriate' mean here? Does it simply mean 'unnecessarily complicated', 'not habitual', or, rather, should it be understood as 'improper', 'not in accordance with the social norm'? And if so, why? To answer these questions and to propose my own, more complex hypothesis, I will follow the concept of orthography as a set of social practices also conveying symbolic meanings, described in detail by Mark Sebba.[85] He claims that 'any explanatory account of orthography-as-practice must be sociocultural in nature'[86] and that in such a model 'the practices involving literacy in which a community engages are inevitably related to the type of orthography which will emerge as one of the technologies underpinning those practices'.[87] In other words, orthography is 'a practice which is bound up with other practices to do with literacy, which are themselves embedded in the social and cultural practices of a society or group'.[88]

One important concept to expand upon here is the idea of early modern print and manuscript cultures. The concept of the print (or Gutenberg) revolution and the print culture resulting from it was first introduced in the seminal publications of Marshall McLuhan and Elizabeth Eisenstein[89] and elaborated on in numerous later works. According to these, the invention and fast dissemination of letterpress brought about not only a fundamental change in the production and circulation of texts but irreversibly changed all domains of European culture, both public and private, and even the way Europeans perceived and interacted with the surrounding material world. Consequently, within this concept, manuscript dissemination of texts after Gutenberg was not denied but it was seen as a mere remnant of the mediaeval world, alien to the fundamentals of (early) modern culture. However, authors working with early modern manuscripts (e.g. H. R. Woudhuysen, Harold Love, Margaret Ezell and others)[90] soon started to object that, for several centuries after the invention of printing, manuscript culture still flourished, defined as a distinct communicative sphere characterised by the intentional dissemination of particular types of texts from some authors/scribes to some recipients by manuscript rather than by print. These texts were handwritten but mostly were not private: they often existed in more than one copy, were bought and sold or

---

[84] Osselton, 'Informal spelling systems' (1998), 35.   [85] Sebba, *Spelling and Society*.
[86] Ibid., 14.   [87] Ibid., 23.   [88] Ibid., 24.
[89] Eisenstein, *The Printing Press*; McLuhan, *The Gutenberg Galaxy*.
[90] Woudhuysen, *Sir Philip Sydney*; Love, *Scribal Publication*; Ezell, *Social Authorship*. For further details, see Fidlerová, 'Rukopisná kultura'.

custom-made by (semi-)professional scribes, were used by several generations of a family or a community and can be considered 'published'. The culture of manuscript dissemination of texts did not cease to exist in the first decades after the advent of the printing press; in fact, the notion of a manuscript as a specific medium developed only gradually, together with the notion of letterpress as a revolutionary and distinctive means of replicating texts (such a clear distinction was not common at the time of incunabula, which were usually created by a combination of these two techniques).[91]

Thus, the early modern print and manuscript cultures are generally regarded today as existing in parallel and functioning sometimes in cooperation and sometimes in competition, though at times without clear boundaries, at least until the early decades of the nineteenth century.[92] If we agree with Sebba that the choice of orthographic convention carries social meaning,[93] then scribal orthography can be understood as the deliberate distinguishing mark of the manuscript culture as opposed to the print culture. Similarly to unlicensed spellings used today, e.g. in graffiti, which demonstrate sub-cultural identity,[94] scribal orthography used by professional scribes may have demonstrated their identity as distinct from the identity of printers. This is why the 'Pupil' in Štajer's 1668 orthography textbook objects to his 'Master' that he cannot use printers' orthography: such practice would be sociolinguistically stigmatised; other scribes would laugh at him and say that this was not the scribal way of writing.[95] If the manuscript circulation of texts is perceived as a social practice distinct from, and partly also delimiting itself against, publication by print, then it is logical to expect that it was connected to different literacy and orthography practices, because graphic structures often serve as a 'linguistic boundary-marking device',[96] i.e. they secondarily display an emblematic and demarcating function.[97] It seems natural that it is the digraphs that became customary for this purpose, given their above-mentioned greater 'markedness' and 'ostentation'. The potential argument that they violate the principle of economy or 'least effort' does not hold up: first, because of their ability to improve readability as mentioned above, and second, because 'the acceptance or rejection of the orthography rests on *social* factors, not on its "efficiency" as an orthography'.[98] With their visually marked 'z' element, the

---

[91] As further evidence, it can be mentioned that manuscript and printed books started to be separated in private and corporate libraries only in the course of the sixteenth century (Saenger, 'The impact of the early printed page', 388).

[92] See also e.g. Crick and Walsham, *The Uses of Script and Print*; Ezell, *Social Authorship*; Hall, *Ways of Writing*; Richardson, *Manuscript Culture*; Woudhuysen, *Sir Philip Sidney*.

[93] Sebba, *Spelling and Society*, 32.   [94] Ibid., 40.

[95] 'Žáček. [...] Pročež budau ſe mi ſmáti / buduli yá pſáti tak / yako ſe má tiſknauti / a řeknau / že to nenj po pjſařſku pſáti': Štajer, *Wýborně dobrý způſob*, 72–3.

[96] Jaffe, 'Introduction', 505.   [97] Maas, 'Geschriebene Sprache', 642.

[98] Sebba, *Spelling and Society*, 75.

digraphs serve well to create a distinctive overall 'look', to function as a vehicle 'of differentiation and alliance'.[99] Thus, they probably served as a deliberate deviation from printers' usage, acquiring the status of iconic representations of the group identity of scribes[100] and providing them with a focused but also distinct (sub)cultural norm opposed to the printers' standard. Such a norm could have helped to strengthen the scribes' social identity and demarcate group boundaries while bridging the gap between professional scribes and their readers, who were often also non-professional scribes. Thus, as in the case of mediaeval English Chancery usage, the advantages of adopting the scribal standard may have been both communicative and sociolinguistic.[101]

It is not surprising that, in scribal orthography, the gap between the difficulty for the writer and for the reader is less than in printers' orthography. Unlike in print culture, where a small group of professionals compose texts for the general public, groups of writers and readers largely overlap in the manuscript culture. The positions of the producer and recipient are much closer to each other, they usually dispose of a higher level of shared knowledge,[102] and, thus, it is logical that similar amounts of effort be required from each of them. As Sebba puts it: 'Where texts are produced by a small group for large-scale consumption, the orthography may be different from the case where all "literates" are expected to engage in writing as well as reading.'[103] Printed texts were, for the vast majority of Czech speakers, read texts only and consequently were better served by a different orthography from handwritten texts, which at least some of these people also produced themselves. It is also not a coincidence that scribal orthography ceases to be used in the period when early modern manuscript culture gradually comes to its end, falling victim to educational, administrative and church reforms launched by the Enlightened Habsburg monarchs in the second half of the eighteenth century and continued by their successors in the early decades of the nineteenth. The beginning of the modern approach to orthography as an area of control, authority and conformity,[104] where 'invariance [...] is seen as satisfactory or even essential' and 'what users are led to want and expect is a "set of rules", not a licence to choose among different forms',[105] coincided with a period of increased state and church control, which was aimed at both manuscript dissemination of texts (escaping censorship) and the orthographic variation connected to it (escaping the control of uniform, state-guaranteed education). As a result, manuscript copying or publishing of book-length texts became extremely rare, professional scribes (other than those writing administrative documents) ceased to exist as a group, and handwritten documents acquired the predominantly private character known today. In this time of

---

[99] Jaffe, 'Introduction', 510.   [100] Sebba, *Spelling and Society*, 82–3, 161.
[101] Cf. Smith, *An Historical Study*, 58.   [102] Cf. Ezell, *Social Authorship*.
[103] Sebba, *Spelling and Society*, 24.   [104] Kress, *Early Spelling*, x.
[105] Sebba, *Spelling and Society*, 107–8.

the formation of the modern European nations, unified orthography began to serve as a tool of national identity, representing the Czech language, among others, 'as a unified and autonomous code'.[106]

According to Sebba, orthography 'touches on matters of social identity, national identity, cultural politics, representation and voice'.[107] Even today, orthography serves 'as one of the public symbolic spaces in which language identity, unity and legitimacy is displayed'.[108] This chapter represents an attempt to take these statements seriously and use them as explanatory tools to solve one of the most intriguing problems of early modern orthographies across many European languages, namely the parallel existence of distinct scribal and printers' orthographies. The chapter presents them not only as two different norms or practices, as Voeste calls them,[109] but also as two focused systems utilised by two partly distinct social groups, printers and (professional) scribes, engaged in different practices connected to different media of text dissemination. To a certain extent, the two systems can be understood as diasituative variants[110] used to express intimacy and respect. However, they are more than that: each of the two systems is not only better suited for its purposes in terms of composing and reading texts but also displays iconic features expressing the identity of each group and demarcating it against the other. This is why they did not merge soon after the advent of print but remained quite distinct until the onset of modernity, with its ideals of standardisation and attempts to replace group identities with a more generic national identity.

---

[106] Jaffe, 'Introduction', 502.   [107] Sebba, *Spelling and Society*, 6.   [108] Ibid., 108.
[109] Voeste, 'Die Norm', 2: 'eine (kontextuelle) Norm neben der Norm oder eine Praxis neben der Praxis'.
[110] Cf. Rutkowska and Rössler, 'Orthographic variables', 218.

9 Orthographic Solutions at the Onset of Early Modern Croatian

An Application of the Grapholinguistic Method

Mateo Žagar

The Middle Ages, as well as a significant part of the modern era (up to the nineteenth century), saw the use of three alphabets in Croatia: Glagolitic, Cyrillic and Latin. These alphabets were used for all literary varieties of the Croatian literary language: for Old Church Slavonic, for the varieties based on the Čakavian, Štokavian and Kajkavian dialects, as well as for mixed varieties.[1] From the early modern era onwards, however, this diversity waned as fewer texts were written in Slavic alphabets (Glagolitic and Cyrillic), and the Latin alphabet gradually took precedence over the other two for all registers of Croatian.[2] During the Middle Ages, texts in the Glagolitic and Cyrillic alphabets were written according to traditional orthographic principles handed down from the early period of Slavic literacy. The Glagolitic alphabet, from which the Cyrillic was later derived, was created by Saints Cyril (born Constantine) and Methodius in roughly AD 860, according to Greek orthographic principles of the time, and was based on the ideal principle that each one-letter grapheme should represent a single phoneme. This continuity was retained in Glagolitic texts for centuries and had a strong influence on the great reform of Croatian Latin-script orthography in the mid-nineteenth century. At that time, a phonologically based alphabet was adopted for the official Croatian Latin orthography, which has been in continuous use until today, with the exception of some minor deviations in certain periods of history. However, the influence of the Latin

This research was carried out within the framework of the project entitled 'Language of the Glagolitic editions of the Croatian Protestant printing house in the context of literary and linguistic principles in the 16th century', which was financed by the Croatian Science Foundation from 2015 to 2019.

[1] Cf. Hercigonja, *Tropismena i trojezična kultura*.

[2] A few other liturgical books were printed in the Glagolitic alphabet at the turn of the twentieth century (e.g. Blažević Krezić, *Književnimi radnjami*); since then, however, the Glagolitic alphabet has been used in Croatia only for commemorative purposes, as an expression of tradition and in design, especially in its appealing Croatian minuscule form (Kovačević, 'Neki novi glagololjupci', 37–9).

alphabet on Glagolitic and Cyrillic texts was subtler in the Middle Ages; it was mostly implemented on the level of the visual presentation of the texts.

Despite prestigious Latin source texts (such as lectionaries) in which orthographic practice was significantly more complex, the single-letter ideal was never abandoned. In fact, phonemic transparency (i.e. single-letter usage and consistency) in graphemic presentation was insisted on to an even greater extent. Although such influences are already apparent in texts written in the Middle Ages, especially because of the prestige of Latin, the dominant language of the Catholic Church, much stronger influences appeared after the invention of printing at the end of the fifteenth century. The prestige and dominance of Latin writing, which increased with the rise of humanism in literary production and in cultural tendencies in general, halted any influence in the opposite direction (i.e. of Slavic orthographies on Latin orthography) in texts written in the Croatian language during the Middle Ages or even at the time of the incunabula. Croatian texts written in the Latin alphabet did not have a unified spelling system, and the common practice was to borrow graphemic solutions for 'non-Latin' phonemes from neighbouring writing systems (Italian, German, Hungarian), which were fairly familiar to well-read Croatian speakers.[3] The formative influence of Slavic (Cyrillic and Glagolitic) literacy on Croatian Latin orthography was not accepted until the nineteenth century, a period of growing 'Austro-Slavism' (in the territories of today's Czech Republic, Slovakia, Slovenia and Croatia). The influence of Austro-Slavism meant a conscious departure from non-Slavic influences and a decisive search for a functional relationship between letters and phonemes that was the simplest to write and read.[4]

Between 1561 and 1565, in the town of Urach near Tübingen, a group of Croatian Protestants, under the aegis of the so-called South Slavic Bible Society, printed more than 30,000 copies of twenty-eight books written in the Croatian language (Čakavian dialect) in three alphabets, Glagolitic (fourteen books), Cyrillic (eight books), and Latin (six books). From the long diachronic perspective of the history of the Croatian language and its alphabets, the work of the Croatian Protestant printers and editors, who included the Glagolitic monks Stipan Konzul (Istrianin) and Anton (or Antun) Dalmatin, appears to have left no significant trace on the process of standardisation in Croatian in the early modern era. However, the 'folk language' of these books, especially that of the Bible, served as a turning point in some central European cultures

---

[3] Maretić's *Istorija* provides a thorough and still-relevant historical overview of Croatian Latin orthography, describing the many different orthographic solutions for pairing Latin with Croatian phonemes.

[4] The great Czech reformer Jan Hus (c. 1369 – 6 July 1415) is renowned in the history of Czech orthography for his attempt to apply a phonological, single-letter principle of writing, almost certainly under the influence of texts written in Slavic alphabets, including the Croatian Glagolitic alphabet, well known in Prague during Hus's time (Mareš, 'Die kyrillo-methodianischen Wurzeln').

(especially Slovenian) from the beginning of (early) modern standardisation processes all the way to the nineteenth century. This would also have been the case in Croatian, had Protestantism put down more significant, lasting roots there, as it did in neighbouring Slovenia. Regardless of their long-lasting effects on the process of standardisation, the quality of the Croatian Protestant books was remarkably high, with a well-developed and consistent grammar, nuanced style and skilful literary expressions founded on tradition.

The focus of this chapter is on the orthographic achievements in early printing at the time of the Croatian Protestants (cf. also Chapter 3). Previous analyses have attempted to explore the ways in which the Čakavian dialectal foundation at the onset of Early Modern Croatian was enriched with typical features of the Štokavian dialect, which is far more widespread throughout the Balkans.[5] It is still unclear, however, which graphemic system was estimated to be of sufficient quality to preclude any difficulties in reading, and thus serve as optimal (in terms of efficiency) for these early publications, which were intended for a large number of readers.[6] The ratio of titles (14:8:6) printed in the three alphabets, Glagolitic, Cyrillic and Latin, is a good reflection of the extent to which they were used in the Croatian language in the early sixteenth century. Most of the Latin Protestant works were published with Glagolitic and Cyrillic versions (e.g. *Katekizam* 1564, *Postilla* 1568),[7] and mutual influences on orthography were therefore inevitable. These suppositions are even more true if we take into account the fact that no noticeable steps were taken in early printed Latin-alphabet works (and in the Protestant project in general) to simplify the many digraphic or trigraphic solutions; this would imply an influence of Glagolitic and Cyrillic texts, of which the Croatian tradition had many. This chapter attempts to estimate the level of functional orderliness in the works published in Urach, primarily in the Glagolitic editions and through the occasional comparison with the Cyrillic and Latin editions, using the methodology described in the following section.

9.1   Methodological Framework

With the invention of printing, the Glagolitic, Cyrillic and Latin alphabets entered a new developmental phase; the task of finding a graphemic and

---

[5] See Žagar, 'Contesto filologico'.

[6] Facsimiles of the Glagolitic and Cyrillic editions: Jembrih, *Novi Testament* (1562/3) and (1563) respectively. Digital copies of both editions are available on the internet; see Bibliography under *Novi Testament*. Part 1 of the Glagolitic *New Testament* (the four Gospels and the Acts of the Apostles, 1562) was printed in a run of 2,000 copies, while Part 2 (Epistles and Revelation, 1563) was printed in 1,000 copies. These were significantly longer runs than those of earlier Venetian Croatian editions, which were printed in runs of roughly 200 copies (Stipčević, *Socijalna povijest knjige*, 64–7).

[7] Konzul, *Katehismus*; Dalmatin and Konzul, *Parvi del posztile evanyeliov*; cf. Jembrih, *Postilla*.

graphetic system that was acceptable to a growing readership thus grew in importance. In addition to reading out loud, silent reading was becoming more common – a process which broke ties with the mediaeval reading culture, with its incomparably smaller audience and significantly different ratio of voiced to silent reading – and brought different requirements in text layout.[8] Until the sixteenth century, the Glagolitic was the most common alphabet for the Croatian language. Glagolitic had the longest tradition, it was the most developed among the three alphabets, with the broadest spectrum of use, and so its development has so far received the most attention in academia. Later, it became apparent that books printed in the Latin and Cyrillic alphabets were the future of the region (in east Slovenia), which was of interest to the Protestants. Soon, however, the region also became of interest to the Counter-Reformation, which, from the seventeenth century, would, to a great extent, define the Croatian literary language (based on the Štokavian dialect), as well as its graphemic system.

The traditional palaeographic approach insisted almost exclusively on the description of some of the developments described above with reference to letter forms throughout time and in different locations. In particular, it described changes in orthographic tradition separately from holistic descriptions of writing (foremost through descriptions of varieties of letter forms).[9] Traditional approaches to nineteenth-century Glagolitic and Cyrillic orthographies were centred around changes to letter forms through time and space, in order to date and locate newly discovered written documents. With this approach, the dynamics of the relationship between letters and phonemes, which lie at the core of orthography, remained almost entirely at the margins in palaeographic literature.[10] Furthermore, orthographic phenomena were not given the space that they deserved in the overall understanding of the linguistic development of writing texts as dynamic wholes, created as an act of communication between the author (scribe) and the reader (listener) in a given community, at a particular moment in time, and under particular material conditions. Modern palaeographic descriptions, inspired by grapholinguistic views, rather, place orthography within a holistic perception of texts as dynamic wholes that come about through the writing process, bearing in mind their assumed reader, the optimal conditions under which they are intended to be read, and the material conditions surrounding their composition

---

[8] Cf. Saenger, 'Silent reading'. For a comparison of the processes of fixing of orthographic features in order to address these different requirements in mediaeval Glagolitic printed texts, cf. Tomić, *Hrvatskoglagoljski brevijari.*

[9] E.g. Geitler, *Albanesischen und Slavischen Schriften*; ÍAgić, 'Glagolicheskoe pis'mo'; Vajs, *Rukovět' hlaholské paleografie.*

[10] For Glagolitic palaeography, cf. Eckhardt, *Azbuka*; ÍAgich, 'Glagolicheskoe pis'mo'; Kul'bakin, *Slavīanskaīa paleografīīa*; Vajs, *Rukovět' hlaholské paleografie*; Žagar, *Uvod u glagoljsku paleografiju 1.*

(writing materials, spatial conditions during transcription, and so on), all in light of the traditions of the particular place and time in which they are written. In accordance with recent trends in philology and Croatian studies, the study of orthography in modern texts written in the Latin alphabet has moved beyond the borders of traditional palaeography, primarily because palaeographic methodology cannot be fully tailored to the study of fixed, printed texts. With the introduction of modern, primarily structuralist, grapholinguistics, scholars can now work on a solid framework within which phenomena representing the direct written realisation of a linguistic unit are placed, together with the visual surroundings that optimise the transmission of a textual linguistic message (e.g. from the placement of a text field on a page to the use of abbreviations and ligatures).[11]

When using a grapholinguistic approach, the focus of analysis is implicitly placed on the differences between *idea* and *expression* (i.e. through the difference between phonology and phonetics), which results in an ideal division into two spheres, *graphemics* and *graphetics*.[12] Thus, the linguistic element of writing becomes of foremost importance, and undergoes analysis on a number of different levels (from graphemes to syntactically conceived punctuation). At the same time, the grapholinguistic approach regards anything that does not have a strict graphemic–graphetic relationship as background information, considered more as an aid for reading a textual message. Examples range from margin size, text fields, lines and letters, and the selection of line organisation, to kerning, abbreviations, ligatures, and finally to characteristic changes in letter forms in manuscripts (which are of greater interest to palaeographers). Although the term *orthography* primarily implies the description of the relationship between the visual and the auditory basis of linguistic units (spelling variations) in printed texts, this is only one level of written expression, although undoubtedly the most important in enabling an appropriate, unified reading, whether silent or out loud. Variations in the use of different combinations of letters for one grapheme (phoneme) and consistency in the solutions selected reflects how aware each author (and scribe) may have been of the stylistic level of the written text, while also reflecting their exposure to neighbouring prestigious written cultures (e.g. Italian, German and Hungarian in this case). The aforementioned grapholinguistic framework for orthographic

---

[11] For the most thorough overview of the structure of grapholinguistics and orthography as part of this framework, see Dürscheid, *Einführung in die Schriftlinguistik*. On some of the existing dilemmas regarding the linguistic definition of 'graphic elements' in written texts, cf. Gallmann, *Graphische Elemente*. On the relationship between graphemics and orthography, cf. Augst, *Graphematik und Orthographie*. Another collection worth mentioning here is Günther, *Geschriebene Sprache*. For more contemporary contributions, cf. Domahs and Primus, *Handbuch*.

[12] For a more thorough description of the difference between these two categories, see Žagar, *Grafolingvistika*.

analysis is especially appealing as it allows for clear insights into the connect-
edness and even the interdependence of all levels of written expression in the
texts studied, as well as providing a better stratification of all levels of orthographic design and making it easier to recognise the diverse 'rhythms' of their
design.

The Glagolitic editions published by the Protestant printing house provide a
good introduction to grapholinguistic methodology. On the one hand, these
editions show a high level of graphemic systematisation founded upon centuries of tradition in handwritten and early printed manuscripts in the Glagolitic
alphabet (as well as in the Cyrillic, to some extent), based on the Greek
orthographic standard. On the other hand, the editions display an unusually
high level of influence of the dominant and prestigious use of the Latin
alphabet. These two contrastive features are important in view of the
Protestants' printing policy, within which the complete, precise readability of
the Bible was of key importance. The Protestants' Glagolitic project thus set the
highest graphemic standards at a great watershed of eras in European history,
just before the accelerated development of written and linguistic standardisation processes which were, however, to unfold in the opposing direction – that
of the Counter-Reformation. In the sense of modern literary culture in Croatia,
the Counter-Reformation certainly did not have to begin *ab nihilo* in its Latin-
script editions (and its rare Glagolitic and Cyrillic ones), although it certainly
did have to invest great efforts to be able to meet the standards of the competition. With the present contribution, I therefore hope to showcase the analytical
potential of the grapholinguistic method and to set an example for a more
systematic method to approach the multilayered empirical analysis of diachronic orthography of the material introduced above.

9.2   The Graphemic and Graphetic Structures of the Glagolitic *New Testament* (1562/3): Between Mediaeval Templates and Modern Aspirations

The Glagolitic *New Testament* (1562/3) is a book of superb quality evincing the
high standards of the Protestant printing house's textual design at the turn of a
new epoch, as demonstrated by the frontispiece of the Glagolitic edition of the
New Testament and the first page of the Gospel of Saint Luke from the same
edition (Figures 9.1a and 9.1b). The Glagolitic *New Testament* documents
strong advances towards the establishment of a streamlined writing system,
although not in equal measure on all levels. This is chiefly apparent in the
refinement of the relationship between phonemes and graphemes towards the
ideal ratio of 1:1. Thanks to improved accessibility to the transliterated edition
of the Glagolitic *New Testament* with funding from the Croatian Science
Foundation, I am able to present results from my analysis of a digital version

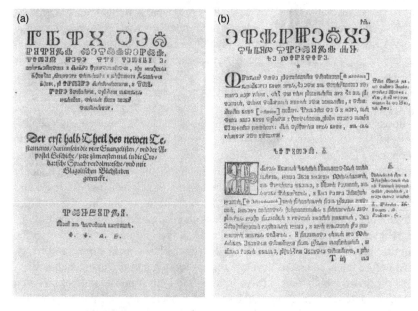

Figure 9.1   *New Testament* (1562/3), Glagolitic edition: (a) frontispiece; (b) first page of the Gospel according to Saint Luke

Source: Bayerische Staatsbibliothek München, call no. ESlg/4 B.rel. 15 c-1: (a) p. 5, http://daten.digitale-sammlungen.de/bsb00078762/image_5; (b) p. 205, http://daten.di gitale-sammlungen.de/bsb00078762/image_205.

of the Latin transcriptions.[13] I examined a corpus of approximately fifty pages from different places at regular intervals in Parts 1 and 2 of the Glagolitic *New Testament*. Innovations in the selected material which distinguish it from mediaeval practice are described below.

(1) The letters *iže* and *ot* vanished from usage in their graphemic function; their use continued only as numbers (10 and 700, respectively), like the letter *ʒêlo* (Ⰵ, *ʒ*), which was retained only as the symbol for the number 8. This practice was already dominant in late mediaeval Glagolitic texts.

(2) Use of the letter *šta* became more specialised as regards the representation of two different phonemes: in order to indicate /tʃ/, the typical letter was written Ⱋ, *ĉ*, while, to pronounce /ʃtʃ/, three dots were added (ⱋ̈). The same applied to the Cyrillic edition (ⱋ : ⱋ̈). However, this manner of writing with diacritics

[13]   Jembrih, *Novi testament* (1562/3), a facsimile edition of the Glagolitic original; Matak, *Prvi del Novoga testamenta 1562*; *Drugi del Novoga testamenta 1563* provide Latin transcriptions, which have been digitised for this research project.

(in which one letter represents two phonemes) was significantly less common than the use of two letters (ШѰ for the two phonemes /ʃtʃ/, e.g. in the word *iŝču* 'I seek'), which represented the most consistent adherence to the phonographic principle. For example, at the beginning of Part 1 of the Glagolitic *New Testament* (1562), in the Gospel of Saint Matthew (ninety pages), a single graph with diacritics (ѱ̈) appears only eight times for the phoneme /ʃtʃ/, while the two-letter form (*šč*) is used the remaining fifty-two times. The situation appears to be the opposite in the parallel corpus of the Cyrillic edition: the diacritic model is dominant, while deviations (most often in the combination *š* + *č*) are rare, with only twelve appearances in comparison to roughly fifty single graphs with diacritics.[14] Cyrillic texts were traditionally more prone to the inclusion of diacritics.

(3) The letter *đerv* (ꙉ, *ĵ*) in the oldest Glagolitic texts was used to represent the softened sound /ʝ/, imported from Ancient Greek; through the Middle Ages, it was increasingly used in Croatian Glagolitic texts to represent the sound /j/, mainly as a reflex of the common Slavic *dj (*meĵa* 'border', and so on). In the Protestant printing house's publications, beginning with the *New Testament*, the letter was used more frequently in word-initial and intervocalic positions, for example in *ĵere* 'because', *ĵesik* 'language, people' and *tvoĵe* 'you'. The letter *đerv* (*ĵ*) was also used increasingly more frequently in the *n* + *ĵe* endings of some neuter nouns (e.g. *spasenĵe* 'salvation', *poželenĵe* 'knowledge'). The reason for spelling the endings of this class of neuter nouns this way was probably functional, i.e. in order to differentiate the pronunciation of this form from the nominative and accusative plural form of the passive perfect participle. The grapheme <ĵ> was often used for the phoneme /j/ in place of the letter *i* in adjective forms, e.g. in *božĵi* 'divine',[15] *dažĵi* 'rainy'. In place of the inherited *yat* (ѣ) at the beginning of the word and following vowels for the phoneme group /ja/, the combination *đerv* + *a* was often used (*ĵa* 'I', *ĵaviti* 'appear'), just as the combination *đerv* + *u* was used in place of the letter ю for /ju/ (*ĵudeii* 'Jews'). More precise data for the marking of word-initial /je/ (in speech) are as follows: the first 50 pages of the *New Testament* feature 260 examples in which *đerv* appears before initial <e>, 45 examples in

---

[14] Jembrih, *Novi testament* (1563). The fact that the tendency towards monographic expression is significantly less noticeable in the Cyrillic edition than in the Glagolitic is apparent in the former's frequent use of multiple versions of letters, *o* (о) and *ô* (ѡ), *i* (и) and *ï* (і), and the inclusion of *yers* in word-final position, following consonants, and so on. (*Yers* are signs which had a semivowel phonological function in pre-twelfth-century Slavic texts. In Croatian texts, they had lost this function entirely by the sixteenth century and were retained only in their graphetic function.) On the basis of this comparison, the orderliness of the Glagolitic edition becomes rather apparent.

[15] The ratio is as follows in the observed samples: the form *božĵ-* appears twenty-four times, while the typical mediaeval form *boži-* appears only eight times. This represents a new tendency in which the relationship between graphemes and phonemes appears to be closer, although the relationship with tradition (of which Konzul and Dalmatin were constantly reminded by the mediaeval Croatian Glagolitic templates that they were using) had not yet been broken.

which the present form *'est* 'it is' is written as *e* with a 'tittle' (a small stroke/raised bar or dot indicating one or more omitted letters in a word, ꝝ),[16] 21 examples in which the same word is written with the letter *e* topped with an inclined line (ꝓ),[17] and 24 remaining examples (or 7% out of a total of 350 examples) in which iotation is unmarked. These examples suggest an obvious tendency towards a more fixed phonographic practice in which each phoneme is represented by a single letter.

(4) The phonemes /ʎ/ and /ɲ/ in mediaeval Glagolitic texts were initially represented with the help of letters for front vowels (*e*, *i*, *ê*, e.g. *tlmačene*, /tl̥matʃeɲe/ 'interpretation', *knige*, /kɲige/ 'books', *pole*, /poʎa/ 'field') or for iotated phonemes (ⱓ, *û*, e.g. *lûdi*, /ʎudi/ 'people', *bogolûbni*, /bogoʎubni/ 'God-loving'; Ⱔ, *ê*, e.g. *polê*, /poʎa/ 'fields').[18] The material analysed appears only partially to maintain this graphemic practice; readings could not be left up to the reader's interpretation, and so efforts were taken to clearly mark soft consonants. The writing system thus became increasingly more transparent: the phoneme /ɲ/, in addition to being represented by a digraph – a combination of the letter *n* with the letter *đerv*, *nĵ* – was often indicated with a superscripted diacritic above the *n* (p̄ /ɲ/: ⱂⰵⰳⰰⰹⱆ /ɲega/ 'him').[19] Examples of diacritic marks appearing above the letter *l* to indicate the phoneme /ʎ/ are much rarer (ꬺ: ⰽⰱⰰⰾⱡⰵⱄⱅⰲⱁ, /kraʎestvo/ 'kingdom', as opposed to the usual ⰽⰱⰰⰾⰴⰱⰹⰵⱄⱅⰲⱁ).[20] Even these inscribed lines, as in the example of ꝓ, undoubtedly hailed back to the apostrophe, one of the marks for *yer*, which served this function quite frequently in mediaeval texts, especially between consonants (e.g. *nič'tože* 'nothing', *prav'da* 'justice, truth'). The task of representing the

---

[16] The difference between ꝝ and ꝓ can be reduced to the specialisation of the two forms: the first is actually of ideographic (lexemic) character, as it presents the full form of the word *jest*. The inclined line in the latter example is of apostrophic origin and signifies the phonetic group /je/.

[17] The use of an inclined line as a diacritical mark is the result of a modification of the tittle, which was used to abbreviate the form *jest* in mediaeval texts (ꝝ).

[18] This text was written using the ZRCola input system (http://zrcola.zrc-sazu.si), developed at the Slovenian Academy of Sciences and Arts (SAZU) Research Centre in Ljubljana (http://www .zrc-sazu.si) by Peter Weiss (URLs last accessed 27 March 2020).

[19] In the fifty pages of material used here, there was only one example in the /ɲe/ group where the letter *e* with a superscripted inclined line expressed softening: *pregrišené* 'sinning' (Jembrih, *Novi testament* (1562/3), 10), while it is always marked with a tittle above the *n* in the group /ɲi/. There are a few more examples (nine, as opposed to multiple hundreds of examples of ꝝ) expressing the group /ɲe/ using the letter group *nie*, in accordance with mediaeval tradition. This example displays the most obvious bias towards early modern practice.

[20] The material investigated yields only five examples of *l* with a tittle for the phoneme /lj/. The writing of an inclined line above the following letter *é* prevails (thirty-three times). Examples of the group *lie* in this position are rare, while the group *lj* does not appear at all (as opposed to *nĵ*). It is important to note that softening is not signified in the majority of examples (thirty-five), which may point to phonological idiosyncrasies due to the influence of the Slovenian language or the Kajkavian dialect.

phoneme /j/ and the softened /ɲ/ and /ʎ/ was certainly difficult, however. Although still far from a final solution, a significant step forward seemed to have been taken towards a more transparent, consistent representation of these phonemes.

(5) The almost entirely regular signalling of the vocality of the syllabic phonemes /l̥/ and /r̥/ through the addition of a line above the prior letter (like a tittle, but also derived from the apostrophe) resulted in graphemic specialisation. This pattern appears to have led to a differentiation between these phonemes, even though they were only positionally determined variants of phonemes derived from consonants (ⰀⰆⰍⰒⰓⰟⰄ – *usk'rsnulъ* 'resurrected', ⰆⰐⰓⰎⰄ – *t'rpel* 'suffered', ⰐⰐⰝⰐⰓⰋ – *vêra* 'faith'; ⰟⰅⰓⰝⰗ – *s'lnce* 'sun', ⰐⰐⰄⰟⰇⰊⰞ – *vlize* 'enter', 3rd sg., present). This graphemic structure, where the line belongs to the prior letter and not to the letter that stands for the phoneme itself, is a graphemic specialisation also clearly derived from the mediaeval apostrophe (which in turn was taken from Greek writing of the ninth century). In the Middle Ages, the apostrophe was used to represent formerly neighbouring semivowels adjacent to these voiced phonemes. Although the key reason for the survival of marks like those above was traditional (graphetic) syllabism, the use of the graphemic indicator is also highly functional, in line with the previous trends noted so far.

(6) The conservative representation of *yat* (Ⱇ, *ê*) seems to have been reduced significantly: for example, in the Passion according to Saint Matthew (Mt. 26, covering six pages), *yat* is written only four times (*bê* 'was', *têlo* 'body', *vsêm* 'all', masc./neut. sg. dat., *ondê* 'there'),[21] a pattern remarkably different from the 1483 edition of the Glagolitic incunabulum *Misal po zakonu rimskoga Dvora* (the *Missale Romanum Glagolitice*), for instance, where *yat* appears hundreds of times.[22] The question of which phoneme the *yats* refer to in the selected material (i.e. whether /e/ or /i/) is an intriguing one which relates to

---

[21] *Yat* was much more consistently used to signify the pronunciation /ja/ at the beginning of words and after vowels or *yers*; in this case, it was often marked with a superscripted line (in just under 50% of cases in the observed material). The same phonemic group is occasionally marked with the combination *ja*.

[22] It is interesting to note that *yats* are rather more frequent in the Foreword (*New Testament* Part 1, 1–9), which was written by Konzul and Dalmatin. The significantly lower frequency of *yat* in the biblical text could be interpreted as due to the influence of the Latin-script original, especially as it may have been used in Latin-script lectionaries. In the entire Gospel of Saint Matthew, only 64 examples are noted (on 90 pages); the Gospel of Saint Mark is similar (62 examples on 55 pages); however, the number increases later on (the Gospel of Saint John has roughly 600 on 95 pages, while the Gospel of Saint Luke has around 700 on 70 pages). In *New Testament* Part 2, for example in Romans and 1 Corinthians (69 pages altogether), there are roughly 700 *yats* serving the same function. If one considers the ratio of their appearance to the number of pages, the influence of mediaeval Glagolitic originals becomes quite noticeable. The changed relationship in the use of *yat* also corresponds to other graphic indicators, which return to more traditional positions in Part 2 of the *New Testament*.

the marking of phonemic reflexes in the text. An answer to the question may be found in connection to issues like the place of origin of the mediaeval Glagolitic text template, as well as that of its editors, Konzul and Dalmatin (issues which deserve a whole separate chapter to allow for any meaningful discussion).[23] In any case, *yat* was no longer part of the phonological system of the sixteenth-century Croatian language; it was used for exclusively graphetic purposes in the Protestant Glagolitic editions, as a sign of continuity with the mediaeval tradition. As soon as this letter began to be replaced with letters representing its various reflexes in the living language of the Middle Ages (*e* or *i*), its orthographic use also gradually normalised.

(7) Both parts of the *New Testament* (1562 and 1563) show a relatively consistent separation of individual grammatical entities, including the division of the conjunction *i* 'and', the prepositions *od* 'from', *do* 'to', *po* 'on', the subordinating conjunction *da*, the negation *ne*, the reflexive personal pronoun *se*, and the aorist *bi* (from the conditional) if they occur next to a verb (*do danas* 'until today', *se isplni* 'be fulfilled', *da prose* 'let them beg'). The prepositions *v/va/u* 'in', *k/ka* 'towards', *s/sa/z* 'with', on the other hand, are the only ones that appear to remain connected to the words following them (*vonoi* 'in that', *knam* 'towards us', *sazali* 'with evils'), or to the words preceding them in the case of pronouns and verbal enclitics (*pokajase* 'he repented', *stavitih* 'to put them') and the causal conjunction *bo* (*znašebo* 'because s/he knew').[24] In other words, only short forms with a strong accentual relationship with their hosts still appear as written together. Another indication of a conscious, intentional choice to separate words is to be found in the marking of 'broken' words at the end of a line with an inclined double line (*⸗*), as introduced by Šimun Kožičić Benja in early 1530 in his Glagolitic publications under the influence of Latin orthographic practice.[25] These trends reflect a general pattern in Croatian Glagolitic texts of all registers, whereby writing words in continuity, i.e. without any spaces, was abandoned systematically from the thirteenth century.[26] By the time of the appearance of the printing press, the visual

---

[23] In fact, the textual representations are entirely out of balance with the dialectological and geographic relationships. In general, the Ikavian (/i/) reflex of *yat* prevails in root morphemes; however the *e* reflex is more apparent in some places than in others. There is a significant likelihood that the *e* reflex is frequently secondary and 'original', just like *yat*, added after the fact into a text already dominated by the Ikavian reflex of *yat* (**ê > i*) (Damjanović, *Novi filološki prinosi*, 119). This aspect certainly warrants further research.

[24] A radical example of the marking of broken words is that of an enclitic that does not belong to the preceding word, but is often still written together with it (e.g. *upita=ga* 'he/she asked him').

[25] Žagar, *Misal hruacki, faksimilno izdanje*; Ceković et al., *Misal hruacki: Latinička transliteracija*.

[26] Latin orthographic practice likely played a part here, as seen in the fact that separation first appeared in the western branch of Croatian Glagolitic writing (Žagar, 'Neke grafetičke osebuj-nosti'), just as in older Glagolitic texts in closer contact with Latin culture (e.g. the tenth-century *Kiev Missal*); cf. Žagar, *Uvod u glagoljsku paleografiju 1*, 227–30.

principle of separating words had been stabilised, while short (single-letter, two-letter, and often three-letter) forms stood in groups with the preceding or following word. The auditory principle of accentual wholes was a vital factor in forging this pattern.

(8) Abbreviations, typical of mediaeval texts (in accordance with Greek and Latin writing), appear quite rarely. Among the items affected by contractions in the main body of the text, the category of *nomina sacra* (i.e. sacred names, which deserve utmost respect) also appears to be affected, with a few exceptions: *I(su)s*, *Is(u)k('rs)t, Is(u)h('rs)tom, s(ve)ti* 'holy', *B(og)a* 'God' (gen. sg.), *h('rs)t'êne* 'Christians'. These words are more frequently abbreviated in the margins, where there was a greater need to save space, while they are used regularly as truncated (or 'suspended') forms without tittles only in the headers, e.g. *KAP(ITUL)*, *S(VETOGA)* 'holy' (gen. sg.), *MAT(EI) EVANGE(LIST)*, undoubtedly for reasons of space, time and effort. Only occasionally, and somewhat more often in Part 2 of the *New Testament*, words like *n(a)s* 'us' (gen.), *prav(a)dne* 'just', *svedet(e)lstvo* 'testimony', are also abbreviated – a practice which is likely as a reflex of Glagolitic texts. Aside from the traditional example of *ot* 'of' (ꙩ), where *t* is written above *o* (derived from Greek mediaeval writing), no suspensions related to superscripting were found – a procedure that was common in Croatian Church Slavonic Glagolitic texts.[27] It appears that anything that did not serve the function of transparent reading was avoided here as well.

(9) Ligatures (i.e. joined letters as special typographical units) appear quite frequently, which suggests that these elements were generally not considered a complication to the reading process, but rather an aid to the eye in finding letters in the text among the series of vertical lines that are a feature of sixteenth-century Glagolitic script.[28] In a twelve-page extract from the beginning of the Gospel of Saint Mark (Mk 1, 1–23), the following 'true' ligature types (i.e. ligatures which occupy an entire shared letter field, whether rectangular or circular) were identified: vertical (i.e. sharing a vertical extension: *bo, br, ko, mo, no, pl, po, pr, to, tr, vo, vr, zo*), horizontal (*go, gr, ho, lû, tv, za, zr*), and combined, three-letter (*ili, tvo*).[29] Much as in the *Artikuli* (another significant, and extensive, product of the Protestant printing house at Urach,

---

[27] Suspensions are a traditional type of abbreviation in old Glagolitic and Cyrillic texts, in which the right half of the word is removed, leaving only the first letters. In the first 100 pages of *New Testament* Part 1, *t* was superscripted above *o* only in the preposition *ot* 'of' (Cro. *od*) and in prefixes with the same source (rarely in examples of *o'ca* 'father' (gen.) and the like), which makes for less than 50% of cases. Only the group *ot*, and not the Croatian form *od*, is a mediaeval graphetic reflex.

[28] Eckhard pointed to this function of ligatures in *Azbuka*, 83, beginning with the standardisation of the squared Glagolitic alphabet in the thirteenth century.

[29] This list of ligatures in the Glagolitic *New Testament* is not complete, as it displays only the most common ligatures. Horizontal ligatures are significantly rarer, especially those connected to the letter *a*.

Table 9.1 *Most frequent ligatures in the Glagolitic* New Testament *(1562/3)*

bo	br	ko	mo	no	pl	po	pr	to	tr	vo
ଘ	ଘ	⅄	⅍	Ꝑ	ᵽᵹ	ꝑ	ᚠ	ഐ	ᴆ	ᴆ
vr	zo	go	gr	ho	lû	tv	za	zr	ili	tvo
ᴆ	ꝋ	ᵹᴤ	⅍	ᴌ	ᶁᵽ	ꟽ	ꝭᴌ	ꝋᴌ	Ꝋᴌ	ꟽᴌ

dating from 1562),[30] printers of the material under analysis appear not to have made full use of all thirty-four potential ligatures foreseen in their *pokusni list* ('test page') of 1560.[31] The 'true' ligatures were, however, used very consistently (the following examples represent proportions of 'used ligatures:unused ligatures'): *bo* (13:4), *br* (25:4), *ko* (89:13), *mo* (27:7), *no* (55:8), *pl* (16:4), *po* (86:5), *pr* (91:2), *to* (37:2), *tr* (10:6), *vo* (92:10), *vr* (25:16), *zo* (8:3), *go* (78:4), *gr* (10:0), *ho* (32:3), *lû* (20:2), *tv* (6:2), *za* (63:10),[32] *zr* (6:4), *ili* (5:2), *tvo* (28:7).[33] Broken ligatures (wherein the broken letter *a* was attached to a preceding or a following letter) were not counted among the items above, as their use is far rarer and almost random, and they do not contribute much to readability. Table 9.1 summarises the ligatures that are used most frequently and consistently. The frequent use of ligatures was probably aimed at improving readability and, importantly, to express a close relationship with the Croatian Glagolitic tradition.

(10) The material displays capitalisation at the beginning of sentences (for functional reasons), as well as a few scattered capitalised nouns, which likely indicate a sense of respect and importance (e.g. *Bog* 'God', *Sin Božji* 'Son of God', *K'rstianin* 'Christian', *Predikač* 'preacher', *Voivoda* 'duke', *Gospodin* 'Lord', *Cesar*, *Bratja* 'brothers', *Biblija*, *Stari Testament*, *Novi Testament*, *Artikuli*), personal names (e.g. *Adam*, *Noa*), as well as ethnonyms and their derived adjectives (e.g. *Hrvat* 'Croat', *Dalmatin*, *Srblan* 'Serb', *Kranjac*

---

[30] Facsimile edition and transliteration into Latin from original Glagolitic edition in Žagar, *Artikuli ili deli: faksimilno izdanje* and Ceković et al., *Artikuli ili deli: Glagoljski izvornik*.

[31] The Glagolitic letters from the *pokusni list* of the printing house in Urach, printed in Nuremberg in 1560, are included in Jembrih, 'Pogovor uz pretisak glagoljičkoga *Novoga testamenta*'. On the composition of ligatures in the Glagolitic *Artikuli* (1562), cf. Žagar 'Grafetički postav'.

[32] The ligature *za* is the only group to contain *a* in a typographic, cast unit. Other ligatures with *a* are broken ligatures (e.g. *va* ꟽꟸ).

[33] The ligatures *go* and *tr* are not listed in the *pokusni list*, and there are also opposing examples of ligatures in the *pokusni list* that are not found in the text of the *New Testament* (e.g. *aû*, *vt*). It appears that while most ligatures were cast before printing began, some were cast during the printing of the book.

'Slovene', *Hrvacki jezik* 'Croatian language', *Latinski, Nemški* 'German'). Overall, the level of consistency of capitalisation appears to be fairly high, although not absolute. The use of capital letters was one of the greatest novelties in the graphetic system of the Protestants' Glagolitic editions compared to the mediaeval Glagolitic tradition, and their use was certainly influenced by the German and Latin books available in Urach. The most striking difference with texts of the Croatian Church Slavonic tradition (both manuscripts and incunabula) is that this latter group featured a gradual increase in the use of capital letters at the beginning of syntactic wholes, with the exception of names, which were rarely marked with capital letters.

9.3   Concluding Remarks

Some of the elements discussed so far should be contextualised in a broader overview of the Glagolitic edition of the *New Testament*. In general, the graphemic structure of the Protestant printing house's Glagolitic edition mostly follows the late mediaeval textual traditions that were present in the first Glagolitic books, printed in Venice in 1483, several decades prior to the first editions from Urach.[34] Harmonisation of the graphemic structure appears to be in line with the corresponding phonemic structure through the matrix of the dominant monographic principle (wherein one grapheme is represented by only one letter). This structure had been well established in Glagolitic texts since the creation of the Glagolitic alphabet in the ninth century. The Latin alphabet had no significant influence on Glagolitic graphemics during the Middle Ages, as its functional unsuitability to the Slavic languages would only have made the orthography clumsier.[35]

However, some changes from the tradition are quite apparent in the Glagolitic edition as a whole. There were never any difficulties in the marking of the phonemes /a/, /b/, /v/, /g/, /d/, /e/, /ʒ/, /z/, /k/, /l/, /m/, /n/, /p/, /r/, /s/, /t/, /u/, /f/, /x/, /ts/, /tʃ/, /ʃ/, and their respective graphemes were simply represented by a single letter. Departures from the 1:1 concept in mediaeval Croatian texts included the writing of the graphemes <i> (which was marked with the letters *iže*, also in the forms ⱓ and ⱛ or with the letter *i*, Ⰸ, *ižica*, ⱑ) and <o> (with the letters *on*, Ⰸ, or *ot*, ⱁ), while phoneme compounds were written monographically, e.g. *šta*, ⱅ, for the phoneme /ʃtɕ/ or *ju*, Ⱓ, for the phoneme /ju/. The letter *šta*, which is indicated in transliteration as *ĉ*, could also be read as the phoneme /tɕ/, depending on its position in the word, but without any scribal marks (*oĉe*,

---

[34] Of all of the works produced by the printing house in Urach, the graphemic system is most thoroughly described for the 1562 *Artikuli* (Ceković, 'Grafematičke').

[35] Latin letters were occasionally written in Glagolitic texts, for the most part unintentionally. With the invention of the printing press, Latin initials began to be included more frequently (cf. Žagar, 'Die glagolitische Schriftreform', 170).

/oʃtɛe/ and *noĉ* /notɛ/). Some of the letters originated from ligatures (e.g. the letter *uk*, Ⱆ, for the phoneme /u/, as a compound of the letters *on*, Ⱁ, and *ižica*, Ⱏ, according to the Greek alphabet tradition, *oy*). Their digraphic origins were quickly forgotten, however, and they functioned as single graphs throughout the Middle Ages. The writing of the *yer*s in the form of the apostrophe ʼ or the short stick *ı* no longer served any graphemic function; they did not represent any phoneme, and thus they were not graphemes as such, but rather graphic elements that contributed to a certain extent to the visual optimisation of reading. The marks above indicated the final part of words ending in consonants; when words were not fully divided, they also frequently pointed to the softening of prior phonemes, most frequently /ʎ/ and /ɲ/, as well as to the vowel function of the voiced /r/ and /l/). The phoneme /j/ was also often not written, especially at the beginning of words before <e> (e.g. *erusolimʼ*, /jerusolim/), and in inter-vowel positions where its pronunciation was required (e.g. *moe*, /moje/ 'my'). The phoneme began to be written more frequently with the letter *đerv*, ⰼ, which was used in the oldest Glagolitic texts to write the soft Greek *g* (e.g. in the word εὐαγγέλιον), while its representation with the letter *i* remained common (*roistvo*, /rojstvo/ 'birth', and *moi*, /moj/ 'my').[36]

Regardless of the slight changes described above, however, the trends identified in my analysis in Section 9.2 above validate the truthfulness of the statement in the Foreword to the Glagolitic edition itself, where the editors (Konzul and Dalmatin) established their attempt to hold to tradition insofar as this approach presented no challenges to readability.[37] They appear to have improved on several orthographic and meta-orthographic processes which had begun to develop prior to their involvement in the Glagolitic edition, and also introduced new solutions in order to provide as transparent a reading experience as possible. It has become apparent, especially on the graphetic level of the language, that the editors drew inspiration from Latin-script practices. This hypothesis is further validated by the likelihood that they used Latin-script templates (lectionaries), subsequently accommodated to the Glagolitic alphabet. Their focus on readability in Glagolitic texts resulted in significantly more functional solutions than those commonly found in older Glagolitic texts or in concurrent Cyrillic and Latin-script editions of the *New Testament*. By uniting the rich tradition of Glagolitic literacy and valuable features of well-developed Latin literacy, Konzul and Dalmatin attained an optimal selection of orthographic solutions and a reasonably high level of overall standardisation. The structured grapholinguistic analysis conducted in this chapter has, I believe, proven this point.

---

[36] For a thorough overview of the graphemic system in Croatian Church Slavonic texts, cf. Gadžieva et al., *Hrvatski crkvenoslavenski jezik*.

[37] Matak, *Prvi del novoga testamenta*, 8–9.

10 Women's Spelling in Early Modern English
Perspectives from New Media

Mel Evans and Caroline Tagg

This chapter argues for a sociolinguistic approach to individual variation in Early Modern English spelling that draws on frameworks developed for twenty-first-century new media texts. Studies of Early Modern English spelling have tended to focus on the regularisation of the system; that is, research has sought to document, characterise and understand the process through which the localised and variable spelling systems found in Middle English transform into the regularised (and standardised) present-day English system. In this chapter, we show how micro-level individual spelling variation provides an important complement to the macro-level examination of regularisation of spelling in the period, arguing that, as with other sociolinguistic phenomena, local practices of early modern writers underpin the broader trajectories of change.[1] The motivations behind, and the interpersonal significance of, these local spelling practices can, we argue, be illuminated by drawing on research into new media practices, however disparate the writing systems in these two periods may initially appear. Sociolinguistic research has highlighted the potential of spelling as a resource for social meaning for individual language users. Whilst flexibility in spelling practice can be evidenced in informal, vernacular writing throughout the Modern English period, it can be argued that new media has 'diffused and magnified' such practices, deregulating what counts as English spelling and opening up the orthographic choices available in a broader range of writing contexts.[2] Within the medium of text-messaging, for example, writers can draw on standard and non-standard spelling forms to signal group membership, or to add a multi-modal dimension to the linguistic channel of communication. As Tim Shortis points out: 'Spelling is now a more flexible friend used for functional economy and identity performance.'[3] The increased scholarly interest that accompanied this shift has led to the development of

---

[1] Milroy, *Linguistic Variation and Change*.   [2] Shortis, 'Revoicing txt', 2.
[3] Shortis, 'Gr8 txtpectations', 21.

sociolinguistic frameworks which can inform our understanding of Early Modern English spelling practices.

Our focus is on the epistolary spelling of four high-ranking sixteenth-century women, Queen Elizabeth I, Elizabeth Bacon, Bess of Hardwick and Joan Thynne. Their correspondence, selected to represent two sub-periods of each woman's life, provides a rich dataset through which to explore the practices and potential social meanings of early modern spelling, and from which to better understand how writers in the period negotiated the various factors operating in a pre-standardised context. In the chapter, we outline some key theoretical and empirical studies relating to Early Modern English spelling, as well as socio-linguistic and digital media spelling variation, and introduce our corpus and our analytic framework. We then discuss our main findings, quantitatively and qualitatively exploring the preferences of the letter-writers, looking at intra- and inter-speaker variation, and assessing their practices in light of the macro-level norms in contemporary epistles – using the Parsed Corpus of Early English Correspondence (PCEEC) – and in print – using the Early English Books Online Text Creation Project (EEBO-TCP) N-Gram Browser.[4] Throughout, we appraise our findings and their potential significance using theoretical concepts and frameworks developed for the analysis of spelling variation in digital media, to establish points of continuity as well as points of difference, and to ascertain whether the 'flexible friend' of the twenty-first century has a comparable acquaintance in the early modern era.

10.1   Spelling Regularity and Ideologies

The forms and functions of spelling in the digital age may initially appear at something of a distant remove from Early Modern English. The meaning potential of spelling in recent periods of English (c. 1700 onwards) is achieved in part through the manner of deviation from the contemporary normative spelling system. The regularised English spelling system tends towards con-sistent, predictable forms and, moreover, is imbued with standard language ideological values; that is, specific forms are prescribed as 'correct' and 'accepted', and their counterparts are quashed and devalued in an attempt to curtail and control variation.[5] These ideological values, prescribed through institutional channels and public discourses, are subsequently internalised by language users, and inform their language choices. The degree and nature of deviation from the spelling 'standard' in present-day English is thus sensitive to the context of use. Personal texts such as letters and text-messages offer a more

---

[4] The N-Gram Browser enables one to examine the changing frequencies of words and word forms over time. Parsed Corpus of Early English Correspondence (PCEEC); Basu and Pentecost, 'EEBO N-Gram Browser'. See also Chapter 11, note 2.

[5] Milroy, 'Language ideologies'.

flexible space for spelling creativity than formal text-types such as public news; the latter are more constricted by pressures privileging homogeneity and conformity to the prescribed standard.[6]

The degree or extent of flexibility available to language users writing within a standardised system has been subject to debate. Mark Sebba uses the concept of the *zone of social meaning* to explain how such spellings are generally constrained to a set of options reliant on (the appreciable deviation from) the accepted graphic/phonemic conventions.[7] These restrictions mean that effective spelling variation entails knowledge of standard forms. As Shortis points out, spelling variation in the post-standardisation era can often be seen not as a sign of ignorance of spelling conventions, but as an indication of a 'credible mastery of standard conventions'.[8] However, Ana Deumert has contested whether deviant spellings are genuinely curtailed through their affinity to the spelling norms of a language system, positing that, in fact, all and any forms have the potential to become meaningful, despite, or because of, their higher degree of spelling 'deviancy'.[9] Deumert also speculates on how the creativity of new media spellers is acquired and developed; in twenty-first-century contexts, users have to relearn 'a way of writing that is not rule-governed but open', with peer networks and public media, rather than institutional forces, carrying the greatest influence. She notes that such spelling choices carry risk, such as the threat of ambiguity, but that users can adjust to such impediments.[10]

At first glance, Early Modern English spelling presents a challenge to the sociolinguistic models of variation developed expressly for new media writing, as it lacks the reference point of a standardised system. However, on closer reflection, the properties and potential meanings of spelling over time share many of the same elements; a point reflecting that made by Shortis, who observes the continuities between digital and pre-digital spelling practices 'at least to the nineteenth century'.[11] Early modern individuals' understanding of spelling variation and variant forms seems likely to have tended towards the 'open' comprehension envisaged by Deumert, with rule-governed forces only just starting to come into play. For such writers, the 'norm' would be an open system, one potentially shaped through peer networks and exposure to different media (e.g. manuscripts and print), with prescriptive institutional forces at a nascent stage. The contexts therefore involve the same factors, but with potentially different weightings and influence. Thus, whilst the linguistic, social and ideological landscapes are appreciably very different for spellers in the early modern period and those of the twenty-first century, we argue that there are consistencies in the formal and functional dimensions of spelling variation, and that historical spelling can be understood as a system of

---

[6] Sebba, 'Orthography as social action', 4–5.   [7] Ibid., 5.   [8] Shortis, 'Gr8 txtpectations', 21.
[9] Deumert, *Sociolinguistics*, 142–3.   [10] Ibid., 143.   [11] Shortis, 'Revoicing txt', 9.

(potential) local meaning, and not a chaotic or inconsistent system whose significance lies *only* in its regularised 'end-point' (itself a fallacy) in the early eighteenth century.

10.2   Early Modern Spelling

The history of English spelling can be understood as a series of developments moving towards, and retreating from, focused supralocal varieties. In the Anglo-Saxon period, Classical Late West Saxon, as the language of the educated elite, is the nominal 'standard', found in manuscripts produced outside of its geographical region.[12] Following the Norman Conquest and the supplanting of English within institutional and administrative contexts by French and Latin, written English is more localised and community-bound. The spelling system follows suit, diversifying into various diatopic systems linked to geographical and social practices, with writers adjusting the written system to accommodate regionally specific changes in their spoken language, as well as potentially capturing idiolectal practices.[13] As illustrated in the *Linguistic Atlas of Late Mediaeval English* (*ELALME*), the rich landscape of 'linguistic variation is fully reflected in the written mode'.[14] This can be seen, for instance, in the tens of variant spellings of 'though'. Towards the end of the Middle English period, the dialectal spelling systems begin to regularise. The functional ascendency of English into text-types with a national reach necessitated that the spelling system was streamlined and stripped of its local diversification, to ensure that these neutral forms were intelligible to a wider populace.[15] These changes did not go unnoticed; Chaucer's spelling choices, for example, show an awareness of the changing practices and tensions between spoken and written forms.[16] The forces can be divided into top-down (conscious) and bottom-up (unconscious) contributors to spelling change.[17] Printing, which was introduced in England in 1476, is a potential top-down factor; in part, because the spelling of printed texts becomes regular and consistent fairly swiftly, particularly when compared with contemporary manuscripts.[18] For instance, Hanna Rutkowska charts the decline of dialectal spellings in multiple editions of the fifteenth–sixteenth-century almanac, the *Kalender of Shepherdes*, as nascent regularisation (and the use of future standard forms) emerges over time.[19] It is generally agreed that print-based spelling in the early modern period was not regularised

---

[12] Horobin and Smith, *An Introduction*, 45.   [13] Nevalainen, 'Variable focusing'.
[14] Benskin et al., *Electronic Version of a Linguistic Atlas of Late Mediaeval English*; quotation from Horobin and Smith, *An Introduction*, 33.
[15] Ibid., 35–6; Nevalainen, 'Variable focusing'.
[16] Barootes, 'In fourme of speche is chaunge'.   [17] Labov, *Principles*, vol. 1, 78.
[18] Blake, 'English versions'; Howard-Hill, 'Early modern printers'.
[19] Rutkowska, 'Late medieval dialectal and obsolescent spellings'.

'by design' but was instead shaped by technical affordances of production, such as type-setting requirements.[20] In comparison to the apparent speed of change engendered by new media, the impact of print on individuals' manuscript spelling appears more subtle and gradual. Moreover, the stratification of literacies and access to printed texts suggests that printing can be only part of the story, particularly in the earlier stages of regularisation in the fifteenth and sixteenth centuries.

Spelling reformers also constitute a top-down force for regularisation. These men had an explicit ideological agenda, which equated orderly spelling with orderly society. Reformers such as John Hart despaired of the 'darke' spelling, which suffered from 'particular vices and abuse'.[21] They desired a better system of spelling; one, in Richard Mulcaster's words, both 'trew' and 'right'.[22] Frederick Brengelman sees the reformists' contribution as being largely ideological, rather than practical, promoting discourses that conceptualise spelling as fixed and regular.[23] Edward Coote's 1596 schoolbook, for example, which appeared in over forty editions, endorses spelling of limited variation: in the word *people*, <o> has 'no sound [...] yet we must write it, because it is one of the words we learned'.[24] As Kristian Berg and Mark Aronoff have recently commented, however, 'no single group seems to have played a notable role in the movement of English spelling toward greater consistency'.[25] Instead, bottom-up forces seem to have a greater explanatory value, 'presumably through the simple interaction of the members of the community of spellers, a sort of self-organizing social network'.[26] In their analysis of the Helsinki Corpus,[27] Berg and Aronoff observe the diachronic organisation of four derivational suffixes, the spelling of which regularises to differentiate homophonous forms from other phonologically similar morphemes (e.g. suffix <ous> and nouns *office*, *tennis*). Diachronically, their macro-level examination shows 'a clear trend toward consistency', and they speculate that 'this is an instance of a system organizing itself' – a statement that they qualify as 'shorthand' for 'the central role of users of the system'.[28]

The role of bottom-up processes in the regularisation of English spelling is both plausible and widespread. Samuli Kaislaniemi et al. find evidence of generational change in epistolary spellings in the Corpus of Early English Correspondence, although this sits alongside considerable noise and idiosyncratic variation.[29] Terttu Nevalainen suggests that the invariant spellings of

---

[20] Brengelman, 'Orthoepists'; McLeod, 'Spellbound'.   [21] Hart, *An Orthographie*, 2.

[22] Mulcaster, *The Elementarie*, 56, 153.   [23] Brengelman, 'Orthoepists'.

[24] Coote, *The English Schoole-Maister*, 32.   [25] Berg and Aronoff, 'Self-organization', 37.

[26] Ibid., 38, citing Mark Granovetter.

[27] The Helsinki Corpus is a collection of extracts from continuous texts that date from between 750 and 1700.

[28] Berg and Aronoff, 'Self-organization', 47 and fn. 11.

[29] Kaislaniemi et al., 'A graphic system'.

some words, particularly native vocabulary, indicate that writing communities agreed on a particular spelling at a fairly early date, achieved through a process of lexical diffusion. This 'relative consensus', or convergence, around a particular graphemic form impedes later top-down reformist attempts to reconfigure English spelling on wholly phonemic principles.[30] Thus, in the fifteenth and sixteenth centuries, institutional, top-down factors played only a partial role in the regularisation of the spelling system, and should be appreciated alongside the local behaviours of language users, who were negotiating the graphemic system and emergent discourses of acceptability in pursuit of particular communicative objectives. In this light, spelling regularisation is as much an individual, micro-level issue as it is a multi-generational, institutionalised, macro-level phenomenon.

10.3   Individual Spelling Practices

If spelling regularisation is an individual issue, then it is important to consider how socio-biographical context may inform the spelling choices of a language user. Nevalainen notes that '[a]s spelling is something that must be taught, variation is bound to occur as long as educational opportunities are unequally distributed'.[31] Gender therefore shapes manuscript-based spelling practices, with early modern women typically using less regularised spelling than men, reflecting their narrower educational opportunities.[32] In early corpus-based analyses of abbreviations practices, the greater use of abbreviations in male-authored letters is linked to their professional mercantile roles.[33] Margaret Sönmez explores the spelling practices of two seventeenth-century individuals: William Cavendish (Duke of Newcastle) and Lady Brilliana Harley, and finds that Harley uses more 'phonetically obscure spellings' that interfere with the 'visual aspects of reading' e.g. *beeg* for 'beg'.[34] Sönmez speculates that these spellings create cognitive delay for present-day English readers, contributing to a disproportionately negative characterisation of female spelling; Cavendish's spelling is no more regular, and he uses fewer present-day-English spellings than Harley. Metalinguistic comments of the period, even if circulating as stock epistolary phrases, suggest 'an increasing unacceptability and intolerance of poor writing skills and illiteracy among upper-class women'.[35] Women were a target audience for spelling manuals; Coote singles out gentlewomen who lack 'true orthography [and] are ashamed to write unto their best friends', signalling that gendered practices were part of an emerging appraisal of

---

[30] Nevalainen, 'Variable focusing.'   [31] Ibid., 146.
[32] Daybell, *Women Letter-Writers*, 99; Sönmez, 'Perceived and real differences'.
[33] Markus, 'Abbreviations'.   [34] Sönmez, 'Perceived and real differences', 420, 429.
[35] Daybell, *Women Letter-Writers*, 100.

spelling.[36] Present-day parallels, if not continuities, include the derogatory reactions to spelling creativity associated with feminine identities in new media. The historical trajectory of spelling practice as a gendered issue warrants further research.[37]

Generational change has also been identified as significant for the regularisation of early modern spelling.[38] By comparison, lifespan change has received less attention: Rutkowska and Paul Rössler propose that lifespan change will be most pronounced 'during the phase of writing acquisition', with minimal change in later life.[39] In relation to new media writing, Shortis shows how respelling choices in text-messaging change as adolescents take on adult roles and peer-group conformity becomes less important.[40] However, pre-standardised systems plausibly offer greater opportunity for change throughout the lifespan. In Middle English, shifts in spelling practice within the fifteenth-century Paston letters coincide with other linguistic changes, traceable at intra- and inter-speaker levels, correlating with changing social experiences.[41] To give one specific example studied by J. Camilo Conde-Silvestre and Juan Hernández-Campoy, the replacement of the runic thorn <þ> with the digraph <th> shows a 'positive linear pattern' when four generations of male Paston writers are compared, but intra-generational differences suggest that network membership, arising from geographical mobility among other biographical factors, shape an individual's uptake of the new spelling variant.[42] Mel Evans identifies later-life changes in the sixteenth-century spelling of Queen Elizabeth I, including the adoption of plural and genitive <z> (replacing <s>), which appears to have been an idiosyncratic development.[43] Evans hypothesises that these later-life spelling choices may have contributed to the construction of a distinctive written identity for the monarch, indexing her unique status and helping to authenticate her holograph writing. Anni Sairio identifies a lifespan shift in eighteenth-century Elizabeth Montagu's spelling. Over two decades, Montagu moves away from the emergent standard in the past inflection -ed, and increases her use of a local variant, <d>, potentially to signal her membership of the Bluestocking epistolary network.[44]

Stability across the lifespan is also significant. Graham Williams posits that persistent idiosyncratic spellings in the correspondence of Maria and Joan Thynne index their 'learning, their relationship with the written language,

---

[36] Coote, *The English Schoole-Maister*, as cited in Daybell, *Women Letter-Writers*, p. 99.
[37] Ling et al., 'Girls text really weird'.
[38] Bergs, *Social Networks*; Kaislaniemi et al., 'A graphic system'.
[39] Rutkowska and Rössler, 'Orthographic variables', 218.
[40] Shortis, 'Orthographic practices'.
[41] Bergs, *Social Networks*; Davis, 'The language of the Pastons'.
[42] Conde-Silvestre and Hernández-Campoy, 'Tracing the generational progress', 290.
[43] Evans, *The Language of Queen Elizabeth I*.   [44] Sairio, *Language and Letters*.

and possibly even their epistolary "voice"': '[I]t is hard to imagine that familiar correspondents would have completely missed an individual's personal habits of orthography'.[45] Such interpretations fit with the early modern Erasmian theorisation of the letter as intimate conversation, in which one's handwriting creates the illusion that the recipient is 'listening to their [authors'] voices and looking at them face to face'.[46] In essence, one's epistolary language undertakes identity work. Collectively, these examples suggest that spelling variation and change is motivated by local, as well as supralocal, factors. The concept of a community of practice provides a theoretical frame that can explain how particular forms were settled on, or rejected, within a local community of writers.[47] Whilst there is insufficient space to engage with this concept thoroughly here, it is hoped that the following discussion will provide a foundation for the future investigation of this dimension of spelling variation and change. Historical spelling variation is therefore as complex as other linguistic variables. In the sixteenth century, its potential social resonance may have been particularly acute for women from the upper ranks, situated at the pinch-point of gendered discourse and practice. This analysis provides new perspectives on the potential social meanings of early modern spelling, reading them against theoretical frameworks developed for present-day identity practices and spelling in new media.

10.4   New Media Spelling and Identity

The role of spelling in new media in present-day English (and other languages) has proven a rich area of study, involving both corpus-based studies which identify broad formal patterns of spelling variation and micro-level qualitative research into the motivations and social processes behind individuals' orthographic choices.[48] Given the substantial differences between present-day new media contexts and those in which our sixteenth-century women were writing, our intention is not to make empirical comparisons, but rather to explore what the theoretical concepts developed in relation to new media spelling might reveal about spelling practices and perceptions in the earlier period. Studies of new media spelling take an ideological perspective which has the potential to shed new light on earlier spelling practices. New media researchers see spelling as a social practice embedded in, and shaped by, a particular time and place and thereby reflecting a particular set of values, stances and identities.[49] In approaching spelling variation – or respelling – in text-messaging and other relatively unregulated digital modes of communication, researchers generally assume that spelling choices are socially meaningful. These studies identify

---

[45] Williams, *Women's Epistolary Utterance*, 50, 52.   [46] Eden, *Renaissance Rediscovery*, 76.
[47] Kopaczyk and Jucker, *Communities of Practice*.   [48] Eisenstein, 'Systematic patterning'.
[49] Sebba, *Spelling and Society*.

functional categories that focus on the social achievements of respelling rather than, or alongside with, its formal properties and the departure from conventional norms. Three main principles behind respelling practices in text-messaging emerge from the literature:

(1) performing brevity and speed;
(2) recreating orality;
(3) signalling difference from conventional norms.

These categories are not mutually exclusive and researchers recognise that any one respelling is likely to be driven simultaneously by all three principles, albeit to differing degrees. In a seminal study of British text-messaging, Crispin Thurlow found that, regardless of the underlying principle, respellings were driven primarily by the demands of social interaction. As Shortis argues, respellings emerge during interaction in response to immediate functional demands (and thus differ between texting communities).[50] In relation to the first category above, this means that the abbreviation of lexical items and omission of punctuation are motivated not so much by attempts to cut costs or reduce effort but to meet the communicative requirement for quick replies. Caroline Tagg suggests that abbreviations in her corpus of text-messaging are performative; they constitute part of individuals' identity performances rather than actual attempts to be quick.[51] In Shortis's words, '[a] styling of "brevity" and suggestion of implicit, context-dependent communication may function as a rhetorical orthographic deixis which implies shared context, shared values and more active modes of reading, so intimating the social closeness of its interlocutors'.[52] Abbreviations in early modern letters might be seen to share, in part, a similar intimation, in that these practices are thought to have signalled the social literacies of the mercantile and professional scribal communities.[53]

Functional strategies in the second category centre round 'conceptual orality', a term used by historical linguists and new media scholars to describe the way written texts can be experienced as 'speech-like'.[54] New media strategies to achieve this include 'paralinguistic restitution' (e.g. letter repetition to suggest emphasis) and 'phonological approximation'.[55] The latter is broken down by Jannis Androutsopoulos into 'colloquial spellings' (recreating conversational features) and 'regiolectal spellings' (reflecting regional pronunciation).[56] Importantly, attempts to reflect spoken language through writing are seen as indexical (that is, the sign carries broader, associated meanings) in that writers seek to recreate the informality and intimacy associated with spoken

---

[50] Thurlow, 'Generation txt?'; Shortis, 'Revoicing txt'.
[51] Tagg, *The Discourse of Text Messaging*.   [52] Shortis, 'Orthographic practices', 89.
[53] Markus, 'Abbreviations'.
[54] Koch and Oesterreicher, 'Language of immediacy', 441; Shortis, 'Texting and other messaging'.
[55] Thurlow, 'Generation txt?'   [56] Androutsopoulos, 'Non-standard spellings'.

conversation. In Thurlow's words, the performance of orality 'engenders the kind of playful, informal register appropriate to the relational orientation of text-messaging'.[57] This theorisation links to early modern ideas regarding the role that handwriting played in recreating spoken conversation, and may extend to explain orthographic practices of the period.[58] Strategies in the third category tend not to rely on spoken forms, but on exploiting graphemic properties of a word. According to Androutsopoulos, these include 'phonetic spellings' (known elsewhere as 'eye dialect'), 'homophone spellings' (lexical and graph-ical substitutions such as *u* for 'you' and *fone* for 'phone', respectively) and 'interlingual spellings' (where a word from one language is spelt using the orthographic norms of another).[59] Importantly, although these respellings often achieve social meaning through their departure from a recognised 'standard' norm, they are also constrained by the conventional sound–symbol relationships allowed for a particular language; they work only in a relatively narrow *zone of social meaning*.[60] Eye dialect, for example, is socially meaningful usually because it exploits the default, phonetic spelling of particular sounds in cases where the standard spelling does not (e.g. *luv* for 'love'). Sebba gives the example of respellings of 'school', suggesting that while *skool* appears unedu-cated or rebellious, *zgüül* generally fails to convey meaning because it departs too far from recognised orthographic principles.[61] Of course, as Deumert argues, the *zone of social meaning* is itself socially constructed; what is seen as meaningful shifts over time and varies between communities, and respelling often pushes at the boundaries of this.[62] The question this raises for the study of early modern spelling is whether adherence to, or departure from, the norms of a local writing community might signal social meaning in the immediate context, explaining the likely social significance of a writer's idiosyncratic choices.

Another important element of a new media framework of respelling is Androutsopoulos's distinction between regular and exceptional non-standard spellings: those that occur regularly throughout a text, and those that stand out and indicate a more localised meaning.[63] For example, Tagg shows how one (female) texter uses 'wot' as a *regular* respelling of 'what' throughout many of her text-messages to index an informal tone, but elsewhere in otherwise standard language text-messages she uses the non-standard form as an *excep-tional* form to key a switch in footing, such as when she approximates a locally relevant expression *Wot can i get in for ya?* in offering to buy a friend a drink.[64] As this example shows, exceptional spelling choices can serve to contextualise a text, or part of a text; they act as 'graphemic contextualisation cues' to key the

[57] Thurlow, 'Generation txt?'   [58] Eden, *Renaissance Rediscovery.*
[59] Androutsopoulos, 'Non-standard spellings'.   [60] Sebba, 'Orthography as social action', 6–7.
[61] Sebba, *Spelling and Society*, 30–1.   [62] Deumert, *Sociolinguistics*, 142.
[63] Androutsopoulos, 'Non-standard spellings'.   [64] Tagg, 'Heteroglossia in text-messaging'.

frame within which a text should be interpreted, signalling a contrast either with the regular spelling style of a text or with the word's default spelling.[65] As Alexandra Georgakopoulou argued in an early study of email, code-centred resources such as orthography likely take on a greater pragmatic load in the absence of other paralinguistic contextualisation cues.[66] Whilst it seems likely that early modern readers recognised correspondents' general orthographic profiles as indexical, the distinction between regularised and exceptional spellings may help to identify more localised ways in which a particular spelling conveyed meaning. Appreciably, the sites of new media and historical correspondence are undoubtedly very different; nevertheless, our interest lies in exploring the extent to which historical spelling can be (re-)conceptualised through the application of theoretical frameworks developed to understand new media spelling. As Nevalainen and Helena Raumolin-Brunberg observe, the remit of historical sociolinguistics is to apply, test and develop theories, concepts and methodologies developed for present-day language use, following the Uniformitarian Principle.[67] The core concepts relevant to new media spelling practices therefore offer potential insights for how we think about micro-level spelling practices in earlier eras. That is not to say that typologies of spelling and identity should be imported wholesale from the twenty-first century and applied without scrutiny to early modern texts. However, we suggest that new media research can provide a useful framework that helps us to make sense of historical spelling at the micro-level.

10.5   Methodology

10.5.1   The Corpus

The investigation focuses on the holograph epistolary spellings of four upper-ranking sixteenth-century women: Queen Elizabeth I, Elizabeth Bacon, Bess of Hardwick and Joan Thynne (hereafter, Elizabeth, Bacon, Hardwick, Thynne). By focusing on four women, the results can offer only a snippet view on the macro-level process of regularisation. However, the fine-grained information provided by the micro-level analyses enables an appraisal of how spelling practices may have been shaped by the top-down and bottom-up pressures operating in the period, and thus contributes new evidence of how different individuals may have conceptualised the flexibility of early modern spelling within personal writing. The selection of these particular women was determined by the availability of their correspondence in a suitable electronic

---

[65] Androutsopoulos, 'Non-standard spellings'; Gumperz, *Discourse Strategies*.
[66] Georgakopoulou, *Narrative Performances*.
[67] Nevalainen and Raumolin-Brunberg, *Historical Sociolinguistics*.

Table 10.1 *Details of SWES*

Writer	Time period	Dataset name	Word count
Queen Elizabeth I	1550–63	QE1 A	2,844
(b.1533, d.1603)	1590–5	QE1 B	7,501
Elizabeth Bacon	1576–85	BACON A	2,747
(b.?1541, d.1621)	1594–8	BACON B	1,054
Bess of Hardwick	1550–60	HARDWICK A	1,640
(b.?1521/2, d.1608)	1569–78	HARDWICK B	3,813
Joan Thynne	1575–90	THYNNE A	2,102
(b.1558, d.1612)	1595–1603	THYNNE B	1,363

format, the duration of their extant correspondence, and access to information about their background.

For the present study we compiled the Sixteenth-Century Women's Epistolary Spelling (SWES) corpus from select letter collections found in existing corpora and editions.[68] The corpus spans the mid to late sixteenth century: the period when English spelling shows evidence of focusing (that is, moving towards a regularised system), and ideologies appertaining to regular spelling begin to emerge.

Each writer's correspondence is split into two parts to investigate lifespan change (Table 10.1). These sub-periods were selected by sub-dividing the available correspondence for each writer. A semi-arbitrary period of five years was chosen as the dividing point, although the gap is longer when material permits. Roughly speaking, each writer's subset comprises between at least 1,000 and 2,000 words. Whilst these sample sizes are small for corpus-based studies, the graphemic units provide a useable quantity of data, balanced with the efforts of manual data processing.

The women's social backgrounds are important due to the hypothesised connections with education, literacy and peer networks. Whilst all four are from the upper ranks, there are significant differences. The highest-ranking woman in SWES is Queen Elizabeth I, who received a humanist education. Her knowledge of classical languages may have informed her English spelling. Writing was also a central activity in her role as monarch. The time periods span the years around her accession to the throne (A, 1550–63) and the twilight

---

[68] The datasets were taken from the following sources: Evans, *The Language of Queen Elizabeth I*; PCEEC; Wiggins et al., *Bess of Hardwick's Letters: The Complete Correspondence*; Williams, *The Letters of Joan and Maria Thynne*.

years of her reign (B, 1590–5). Elizabeth Bacon was the daughter of Sir Nicholas Bacon, the Lord Keeper of the Great Seal to Elizabeth I. Bacon's three marriages left her with ample wealth and means. She was responsible for the day-to-day management of her households, and her correspondence output also indicates her literacy skills in the vernacular. [69] Bacon's correspondence spans the period of her first and second marriages (A, 1576–85) and her third marriage (B, 1594–8). Bess of Hardwick was born c. 1521/2 in Derbyshire, of modest gentry status. Her ascendancy to become the second wealthiest, and perhaps most influential, woman in England after Queen Elizabeth I was the result of four marriages to increasingly high-ranking and wealthy men. [70] Although there is little evidence of her educational curriculum, her correspondence indicates her vernacular literacy met her needs as a head of household. The sub-periods cover her first (A, 1550–60) and fourth marriages (B, 1569–78). Finally, Joan Thynne's parents were aspirational gentry. Evidence of Joan's education is indirect: her marriage broker describes her as 'wyll brvght vp bothe in larnyng & in all thyngs that do a parten to a gentyllwoman'. [71] Joan was responsible for the running of her household, alongside advancing the political career of her husband. The correspondence sub-periods span the early (A, 1575–90) and later (B, 1595–1603) years of her marriage.

10.5.2 Exploring SWES

Using the AntConc corpus analysis toolkit to generate a word-list for each subset, we categorised every word by its present-day English form (headword), variant spellings (types) and their frequency (tokens) (Figure 10.1). [72] Similar quantitative methods have been used profitably in various macro- and micro-level studies of historical spelling. [73] To contextualise the SWES data, SWES variant forms are compared in the EEBO-TCP database using EEBO N-Gram Browser, and in the PCEEC. [74] This comparison enabled us to identify potentially idiosyncratic or unconventional forms in the SWES data.

The analysis explores the data from three perspectives (explored through various analytical steps in the following five sections):

(1) *Regularity* considers the number of variant forms per headword, producing a profile of spelling variation. For example, *cat, catt* and *kat* are variant spellings of the headword 'cat'. One writer may have all three variant forms

---

[69] Harley, '"My Ladye Nevell" revealed', 5–7.
[70] See Wiggins, *Bess of Hardwick's Letters: Language, Materiality.*
[71] Williams, *Women's Epistolary Utterance*, 19–20.   [72] Anthony, AntConc.
[73] See, for example, Berg and Aronoff, 'Self-organization'; Kaislaniemi et al., 'A graphic system'; Sönmez, 'Perceived and real differences'.
[74] Early English Books Online: Text Creation Partnership (EEBO-TCP); Basu and Pentecost, 'EEBO N-Gram Browser'; PCEEC.

HEADWORD	TOKENS	TYPES	VARIANT 1	FREQUENCY	VARIANT 2	FREQUENCY	VARIANT 3	FREQUENCY
to	98	1	to	98				
you	87	1	you	87				
I	72	1	i	72				
and	56	1	and	56				
my	55	1	my	55				
your	54	3	your	35	youre	17	yore	2
it	32	2	it	24	yt	8		
as	31	1	as	31				
for	31	1	for	31				
the	30	2	the	27	ye	3		

Figure 10.1 Example of spelling record – Thynne A

for 'cat', whereas another writer may have only one. The latter writer is considered more regular. This information provides a baseline from which intra- and inter-speaker practices can be compared, and to investigate more specific properties. For reasons of space, the analysis focuses on the range of variant types used by the writers, rather than on the proportions of tokens for each variant form. It looks at the regularity of writers' individual preferences, and the extent to which the women converge around the same variant forms.

(2) Standardness establishes the extent to which regularisation in print documents impacted private practices, as well as possible associations of 'correct' etymological spellings, by considering the frequency and distribution of present-day English standard variants in the data.

(3) Salience considers spellings that may have had (inter)personal significance, such as highly idiosyncratic spelling variants and personal names. This sub-group may foreground evaluative ideologies relating to regularity and 'correctness', due to the pragmatic salience of the headwords.

Throughout, we consider concepts and evidence derived from frameworks for new media spelling.

10.6   Results and Discussion

10.6.1   Regularity

The results from SWES suggest that the epistolary spelling of the four women was, overall, rather regular. All four women tend towards a one-variant spelling for the majority of words, with one- and two-variant spellings comprising over 80% of spellings (Table 10.2). Whilst the significance of the distribution of the number of variants used by the writers is difficult to assess for Early Modern English, due to the lack of baseline comparison data, it seems that Berg and Aronoff's argument for a tendency towards regularity (see Section 10.2 above) finds support in the micro-level practice of the four women. However, it is important to verify the reliability of the results drawn from the whole SWES

Table 10.2 *Consistency values (%) in SWES by writer*

Writer	*n*	per 1000 words	Variants					
			6	5	4	3	2	1
Elizabeth	953	92	0	0.1	0.4	2.0	24.3	73.1
Bacon	396	104	0	0.0	0.5	2.0	26.3	71.1
Hardwick	502	92	0	0.2	1.2	6.0	30.9	61.8
Thynne	792	238	0.4	1.0	2.3	8.8	39.1	48.4

Table 10.3 *Consistency values (%) for top 20% most frequent items in SWES by writer*

Writer	Total (*n*)	Variants					
		6	5	4	3	2	1
Elizabeth	144	0	0	0.7	4.2	19.5	75.7
Bacon	65	0	0	1.5	0	13.8	84.7
Hardwick	76	0	0	2.7	13.2	25	59.2
Thynne	148	1.3	3.4	3.4	10.8	33.1	47.9

corpus, as less common words, by definition, will offer a narrower picture of potential variation. Sampling offers a compromise, and consistency values were re-calculated using the 20% most frequent words in each woman's correspondence. The trends of the top 20% headwords are (reassuringly) similar to those for the whole dataset (Table 10.3).

Viewed individually, Bacon and Elizabeth show a greater preference for one- or two-variant spellings than Hardwick and Thynne. For Thynne, twelve words (8.1%) have four or more variant forms, including 'think', *thinke, thenke, thynke, thenk,* 'there', *there, thear, there, thar, theare, theyr, theyre* and 'which', *which, whiche, wich, wiche.* None of Thynne's spellings are particularly eccentric – the majority occur in the letters of the other authors in SWES – but it is striking that the variation persists for native, high-frequency lexical items in her writing. The results suggest that regularity in some aspects of an individual's practice may have little influence on other areas of their spelling repertoire. Seen as a social practice, it is possible that the patterns of spelling variation and regularity would index the women's educational status and learning. The regularity results correlate with each woman's social rank (at birth), and thus their inferred educational background. This correlation supports previous general observations of early modern spelling that connect higher

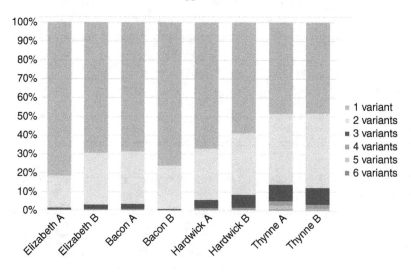

Figure 10.2 Spelling consistency in SWES – writer subsets compared

literacies with more consistent spelling.[75] However, it is unclear which top-down and bottom-up facets of literacy may promote regularity. It may be a quality emphasised when learning to write, as indicated by Coote's educational manual. The potential for ideological judgements privileging regularity would entail that the examples of less regular spelling are also significant; although the meanings of these would presumably be oriented around a necessarily fuzzy, or locally specific, *zone of social meaning*. Alternatively, or in addition, the cognitive impact of repetition – i.e. greater exposure to, and use of, writing – may also be a factor for the sixteenth-century women's practice, helping to consolidate their preferences towards particular spelling forms and graph conventions.

Perhaps surprisingly, given these hypotheses, the analysis of the lifespan subsets in SWES provides limited evidence of the consolidation of preferences (Figure 10.2). Bacon's letters show a decrease in the quantity of two or more variant spellings, indicating an increase in regularity. The letters of Elizabeth and Hardwick show a slight increase in variant forms, and thus a decrease in the regularity of their spelling. Thynne's results are relatively static. This suggests that the accruement of writing experience and/or exposure to spelling did not necessarily lead to an increase in an individual's spelling regularity; perhaps, as with other sociolinguistic phenomena, individuals respond differently to the

---

[75] See, for example, Salmon, 'Orthography and punctuation'.

same experience of language.[76] From the perspective of emergent standard ideologies, the lifespan results suggest that variable spelling was not stigmatised to the degree that the women felt it necessary to completely overhaul their practice. From a social practice standpoint, it is possible that, within the contemporary framework of expectations and practices, each individual's spelling choices may have indexed more than their learning and reading. This is explored further below.

10.6.2   Convergence

The analysis now explores the extent to which the women converge on the same variant forms for the headwords in SWES. Evidence of convergence may exemplify the process of regularisation at the micro-level. Comparative searches of EEBO-TCP and PCEEC provide an indication of whether the convergence may arise from supralocal or more local forces. Headwords occurring in at least two of the SWES subsets were selected, providing 443 words for analysis. In the dataset, function words show the greatest inter-speaker consistency. Conjunctions, definite and indefinite articles and prepositions occur in the same (typically present-day English standard) form in the letters of the four women (see the function words in Examples 10.1 and 10.2). These high-frequency words are prime examples for lexical diffusion and linguistic focusing, and thus inter-speaker consistency is expected.[77] Yet there are some exceptions. The conjunction *though* has seven variant spellings across the correspondence samples (there are no examples in Bacon's letters), and whilst the present-day English standard form occurs in Elizabeth's and Thynne's letters, it is not their preferred form:

(10.1)   thoth the Lade adely haue youseid all the polesy and coneinge to make it
          (Thynne B, to John Thynne)

(10.2)   Though at the first your carire was not the best (Elizabeth B, to James VI of
          Scotland)

The SWES results mirror the long-standing uncertainty over the spelling of *though* since Late Middle English, as seen in the 100+ forms documented in *ELALME*.[78] It is interesting to note that 'though' is frequently respelled in new media texts as *tho*, suggesting the continued flexibility of spellings with a weak phonetic correspondence.[79] In EEBO-TCP, *though* is the dominant variant by 1600. Elizabeth's and Thynne's preferred spellings – *thogth* and *thoth* respectively – are not found, and *tho* post-dates Hardwick's letters by over fifty years. This suggests that, whilst the present-day English standard form was circulating

---

[76] Labov, *Principles*, vol. 2, 409.   [77] Nevalainen, 'Variable focusing'.
[78] Benskin et al., *Electronic Version of A Linguistic Atlas of Late Mediaeval English*.
[79] Tagg, 'A corpus linguistic analysis of SMS text messaging'.

Table 10.4 *'Loving' spelling variants in SWES*

Writer	Variants
Elizabeth	*louinge, louing, loving*
Bacon	*Loving*
Thynne	*loueng, louing, louinge, loving*

in print, no writer in SWES adjusts her spelling to converge exclusively towards this form. As in new media texts, literate writers may draw on less conventional forms despite being aware of the conventional (regularised) alternatives. Following a new media framework, Hardwick's preferred spelling *tho* could, for example, be interpreted as a more economical spelling form. The variants used by Elizabeth and Thynne are less convincingly explained by this motivation. Another interpretation, also derived from those observed in new media practices, is that the preferred or regular spelling choices could be understood as part of an identity performance that involves the writer's adherence to idiosyncratic, or perhaps local, forms, despite exposure to more widespread forms. The strength of this interpretation is assessed in the subsequent sections.

The convergence analysis highlights particular graphemes, such as <u/v>, <i/y/e> and word-final <e>, as contributors to a large proportion of spelling variation in SWES. These conventionalised graphemic substitutions entail that some words have a greater opportunity for variance than others. Interchangeability is particularly prominent in content words that represent core vocabulary items. For example, 'loving' occurs in five variant forms that are attributable to conventional substitutions (Table 10.4). All these 'loving' variants are present in EEBO-TCP. (There are no examples of the word 'loving' in Hardwick's letters.)

Although examples such as 'loving' find formal parallels in new media respellings, there is little to indicate that the choice of one or the other carries social meaning for the writers in SWES; there is no obvious connection to addressee or topic, for example. Less consistent writers, such as Thynne, oscillate between the graph variables more frequently and extensively than the more consistent writers, such as Bacon. For example, all the women use *selfe* for 'self' (this is furthermore the most frequent variant in EEBO-TCP), but Thynne also uses idiosyncratic variants with doubled consonants, with or without a final <e>: e.g. 'I shall thenke my sellfe bownd vnto you' (Thynne A, to John Thynne). Thynne's practice can be compared to those of the female texter explored in Tagg's study who used certain respellings more frequently than her interlocutors, including *wot* for 'what' and *tho* for 'though'.[80] The

---

[80] Tagg, 'Heteroglossia in text-messaging'.

question is whether Thynne's idiosyncratic spelling choices – her particular choices and her general penchant for variability – can be seen as carrying out the kind of identity work described of the texter by Tagg, who used different respellings to convey emotions associated with distinct social roles (e.g. indignant friend).

Other words show what could be described as exceptional variation.[81] For instance, *good* occurs 201 times in SWES, of which 199 examples use the present-day English standard spelling; the *hapax legomena* variants *goode* and *goodde* are used by Hardwick and Thynne, respectively. There is no clear reason for the deviation from their usual practice, and the spellings do not appear to act as contextualisation cues, as is often the case for new media spellings. Instead, these might be attributed to the practice of spelling within a more open system, in which the ideological pressures of normative, rule-governed variants are weaker than in a post-regularised system, as well as to the potential for mechanical 'slips' arising from the technology of pen and paper. Overall, the inter-speaker spelling data suggests that there are tensions in the women's (epistolary) spelling systems. Spelling is more fluid and changeable than would be accepted today, perhaps even in new media contexts, and includes idiosyncratic spelling variants (see further below) which may have carried some of the social meanings now conveyed in new media texts. Yet, the women are also regularising towards a single variant in many cases, not necessarily the nascent present-day English standard form and presumably the result of various sociolinguistic pressures (local writing network norms, lexical diffusion, prescriptivism). The following section examines the potential impact of the emerging standard and associated (prescriptivist) ideologies in more detail.

10.6.3   Standard and Etymological Spelling

The proportion of present-day English standard spellings in SWES indicates how the private spelling of our sixteenth-century women fits with the trajectory of regularisation in the period. Whilst present-day English standard forms account for around 60% headwords in SWES, with all writers using some of the forms in their letters, they are not persistently their preferred variant. Nevalainen's suggestion that high-frequency core words were subject to focusing more extensively than less-frequent (and more etymologically diverse) words finds support in SWES: in the 20% most-frequent headwords, the proportion of forms using present-day English spellings increases to over 70%, compared to the 60% frequency identified in the corpus as a whole.[82] Regional differences in pronunciation, and local writing norms, may explain

---

[81] Androutsopoulos, 'Non-standard spellings'.   [82] Nevalainen, 'Variable focusing'.

inter-speaker differences. Elizabeth and Bacon, who lived in central and south-east regions of England, from where the standard forms typically originated, use more present-day English standard variants than Hardwick and Thynne. Hardwick, who uses the fewest present-day English standard spellings (around 40%), lived in Derbyshire, and her spelling may therefore contain early modern equivalents of what Androutsopoulos calls 'regiolectal spellings' in new media texts. In the light of this new media concept, it is interesting to speculate as to how such spellings may have been understood, and interpreted, by her correspondents further south.[83] Etymological (re-)spellings, e.g. *doubt*, are also relevant. Classical languages had more fixed spelling systems, and many loanwords underwent 'assimilation of English spelling to the Latin equivalent', at least for writers with the requisite education.[84] The regularity of spelling conventions for classical languages has been proposed as a primary factor in the regularisation of English spelling more broadly in the period.[85] Socially, etymological spellings were a contentious issue, part of the larger 'Inkhorn Controversy': they signalled learning, and adhered to the greater prestige of the source language, yet also impeded the regularisation of English spelling.[86]

Based on the evidence of the nine headwords (sorted by lemma) with a potential etymological (re)spelling (Table 10.5), Elizabeth uses the greatest proportion of etymological spellings. These occur only in her later writing. The evidence for *doubt* suggests that she may have shifted her practice over time, although it is not clear whether this was a conscious shift in practice. Interestingly, Thynne also uses etymological spellings, which would seem to conflict with other attributes of her spelling, and what we know of her education. Contrastingly, the evidence for Bacon suggests that she did not adjust her spelling towards etymological conventions, despite her posited education and general spelling regularity. The results illustrate further how aspects of spelling in one area are not necessarily coherent with an individual's practices elsewhere. Overall, Latinate spellings appear to have had limited significance for the women in their epistolary writing, despite the ongoing debates among reformers and educators.

10.6.4   Idiosyncratic Spellings

This section considers the potential significance of the most unique spellings found in SWES. These variants are the exceptions to the convergence noted above. Instead, the following idiosyncratic spellings represent the preferred spellings unique to individual writers in SWES, which appear immune to the influence of the most widely used conventional spellings circulating in private and public texts. The idiosyncratic variants include modal verbs (*might, shall*),

---

[83] Androutsopoulos, 'Non-standard spellings'.
[84] Salmon, 'Orthography and Punctuation', 28.   [85] Sampson, 'The redundancy'.
[86] Nevalainen, 'Lexis and semantics', 358–60.

Table 10.5 *Etymological spellings in SWES*

Lemma	Etymological spelling(s)	Writer(s)	Alternative spellings	Writer(s)
'account'	*accompt*	Bacon A		
'advice'	*aduis* *aduise*	Elizabeth B, Thynne B		
'advise' (v.)	*aduysed* *aduises*	Hardwick B, Elizabeth B		
'attempt'	*attempt* *attemps* *attemptz*	Elizabeth B		
'avow'	*aduowe* *advowe*	Elizabeth B		
'doubt'	*dowbt* *doubt*	Thynne B, Elizabeth B	*dowte* *dout* *doute* *douittinge*	Hardwick B Thynne B Elizabeth A & B
'fault'	*falte* *faulte* *fault*	Thynne B, Elizabeth B	*faut* *fawte*	Bacon A
'honest'	*honest*	Elizabeth A & B	*onnest* *onest*	Thynne B
'traffic'	*trafique*	Elizabeth B		

All names listed under 'Writer(s)' for each lemma use all forms given.

pronouns (*her, your*) and verbs (*trust, receive* and *assure*). Fourteen idiosyncratic variants in SWES occur at least once in EEBO-TCP texts, but the remaining seven spellings have no record in the database (Table 10.6).

Elizabeth's idiosyncratic spellings in SWES are fairly well attested in the reference corpora. *Receaue* and *hit* occur in over 1,000 documents, including mid-century publications of the Coverdale Bible and Erasmus. It is tempting to suggest that these humanist works may have influenced Elizabeth's spelling practices. If so, Elizabeth's spelling stabilised, despite the continuing regularisation in subsequent printed works, supporting observations that generational change is a relevant factor for manuscript spelling in the period.[87] Elizabeth's preferences also hint at inter-personal influence. Although fairly common in print (EEBO-TCP), the only other user of *receaue* in correspondence (PCEEC) is

---

[87] Kaislaniemi et al., 'A graphic system'.

Table 10.6 *Idiosyncratic spelling variants in SWES and EEBO-TCP (1510–1610)*

Headword	Variant	Writer	EEBO-TCP: number of texts
'receive'	*receaue*	Elizabeth	1,331
'it'	*hit*	Elizabeth	1,128
'which'	*whyche*	Hardwick	974
'thought'	*thoght*	Elizabeth	395
'been'	*byn*	Thynne	291
'shillings'	*shyllynges*	Hardwick	79
'receive'	*reseue*	Thynne	17
'your'	*yower*	Bacon	16
'might'	*migth*	Elizabeth	6
'consider'	*consither*	Thynne	5
'assured'	*ashured*	Thynne	3
'daughter'	*dowter*	Hardwick	2
'trust'	*trouste*	Hardwick	1
'trust'	*troste*	Thynne	1
'though'	*thoth*	Thynne	0
'shilling'	*sheleinges*	Thynne	0
'pleasure'	*plesher*	Thynne	0
'might'	*myghit(e)*	Thynne	0
'majesty'	*magystye*	Hardwick	0
'far'	*fur*	Elizabeth	0
'her'	*har*	Hardwick	0

Robert Dudley, Earl of Leicester, a life-long friend and counsellor. Dudley too uses *hit*. The other idiosyncratic spellings in Elizabeth's correspondence, *thoght*, *migth* and *fur*, are not present in Dudley's (PCEEC) letters. Nevertheless, the presence of the less conventional forms of two high-use lexical items could suggest that their epistolary exchanges helped to sustain the variants within their repertoires. Local influence may also inform Bacon's sole idiosyncratic spelling: *yower*, 'your'. The variant occurs in only sixteen works in EEBO-TCP, whereas *your* occurs in over 5,000. In PCEEC, *yower* is used by Elizabeth Bacon's brother, Nicholas Bacon, alongside his preferred spelling *your*. It also occurs in the letters of other Norfolk-based writers, including Thomas Calthorpe, a member of a local family associated with Bacon. Conversely, *yower* is not found in the letters of Elizabeth Bacon's other brother, Nathaniel, or those of her father, Nicholas Bacon, Lord Keeper. Evidence from *ELALME* indicates that *your* and *yower* are the preferred spellings in Norfolk manuscripts in the preceding century.[88] The idiosyncratic variant thus has a regional tradition, as well as a familial salience within Bacon's epistolary networks. However, Bacon is the

---

[88] Benskin et al., *Electronic Version of A Linguistic Atlas of Late Mediaeval English*.

only writer to use *yower* exclusively, in preference to the regularising form *your*. Curiously, what might be considered a related, or even contingent, spelling, *yow*, 'you', is not used by Bacon, although this form does occur in the letters of her father and brothers. Thus *yower* is a largely individualistic spelling practice, with some currency in the private spellings of Bacon's (epistolary) social circle.

Hardwick's idiosyncratic spellings include *dowter*, 'daughter' and *har*, 'her'. In EEBO-TCP, *dowter* occurs only in publications by Suffolk-born John Bale, with no examples in PCEEC sixteenth-century correspondence (although it does occur in the Norfolk-based Paston letters). The spelling *har* is not found in EEBO-TCP, but it does occur sporadically in early-sixteenth-century correspondence, including the letters of Henry VIII and Lady Whethill. There is no evidence of epistolary or face-to-face network associations here, unlike the examples of Elizabeth and Bacon, above. Instead, the graphemic representation of the vocalic elements in *dowter* and *har* could suggest differences between conventional spellings and Hardwick's pronunciation, which she attempts to remedy in these 'regiolectal' forms. Thynne's idiosyncratic spellings (e.g. *ashured*, *consither* and *plesher*) may also arise from an attempt to represent specific qualities of her pronunciation. In new media contexts, the adoption of phonetic (re)spellings has been linked to the construction of intimacy and informality between writer and addressee, in part because non-standard forms contrast with the standard variety, and partly due to their greater (iconic) proximity to the writer's spoken idiolect. In the historical setting, it is unclear how strongly these semiotic links would operate. As in present-day new media settings, we could suppose that a contrast with more conventional spellings might be appreciable, although it seems likely that this had little evaluative significance. The representation of the writer's voice seems a more tangible quality within a non-standardised system.

If upper-ranking women were the group most vulnerable to criticism (see Section 10.3 above), then unusual and atypical spellings (particularly for words in common usage) would be a site for potential conflict. However, whilst comprising a small proportion of each woman's spelling repertoire, the persistent use of these forms suggests that the social penalties were minimal. Moreover, the EEBO-TCP comparisons indicate that the emergence of print was insufficient, on its own, to influence spelling practice. Instead, the evidence suggests that some individual practices were linked to spoken language and/or connected to local network norms. For a present-day parallel, studies of respelling in text-messaging highlight the emergence of local forms in different contexts and among different communities, likening the language of text-messaging to a 'supervernacular' with different local realisations, usually shaped in part by the attempt to recreate local spoken forms.[89] In new media

---

[89] Blommaert, *Supervernaculars*.

texts, the extent to which individuals orientate towards these local orthographic dialects are seen to signal (dis)affiliation and (un)belonging to particular groups. Similar concerns surrounding local norms and inter-personal meaning could help to explain the sustained use of these idiosyncratic spellings in sixteenth-century correspondence, despite the shift towards supralocalisation. These idiosyncratic forms might also be conceived as individuation strategies for the written voice, part of the aesthetics of the Erasmian handwritten letter, distinct from the spoken identity of the writer, yet similarly indexical. Further work into the networks of epistolary writers and the potential impact on spelling practice is desirable.

10.6.5   Personal Names

Brengelman notes that the irregular spelling of personal names in Early Modern English contrasts with the regularisation of the system as a whole, although he does not explore this observation in any detail.[90] Shakespeare's variant eponymous spelling is perhaps the best-known exemplar of this irregular practice, and it has recently been used as evidence to discount the Bard of Avon's authorial legitimacy.[91] In present-day literacy research, 'learning to write one's name has both personal and social significance [and represents the] first opportunity to connect oral and written language'.[92] Personal names thus provide a linguistic area in which emergent ideologies surrounding spelling regularity may have been particularly salient. The SWES results suggest that the significance of personal names may be different for the four women. The headword 'Elizabeth' best illustrates these differences. The name has personal significance for (at least) three of the writers in SWES. Yet only Elizabeth I has a single variant spelling, *Elizabeth*. Her consistency can be explained by the authenticating function of her signature, which was designed to showcase her calligraphic skills (indexing her learning and intellect) and impede forgery. The consistency extends back to her adolescent letters, which may indicate that Elizabeth valued the fixedness of her name to a degree not typical of her contemporaries. The regularity of the spelling, bound up with the palaeographic form, can be seen as part of her identity performance as, firstly, a learned princess and, later, a queen. By contrast, Bacon uses four variant forms, attributable to <i/y/e> and <s/z> substitutions. The preferred spelling *Elizabeth* is used over three decades, exclusively so in the 1590s letters. In earlier letters, *Elezabeth* is the second most frequent form (six tokens), with *Elisabeth* and *Elyzabeth* used once each. Bacon thus regularises her spelling practice over time, bringing the spelling of her name in line with the consistency typical of her overall practice. The three examples (10.3–10.5) show some of these developments over time within her changing signature.

---

[90] Brengelman, 'Orthoepists', 348.   [91] Shahan, 'Introduction to Part I', 3.
[92] Puranik and Lonigan, 'Name-writing proficiency', 284.

(10.3)   Yowr lovinge Sister Elisabeth Doyly

(10.4)   Yower lovinge sister Elezabeth Nevell

(10.5)   Yowr lovinge sister Elizabeth Periam

Bess of Hardwick uses two variant forms, *Elyzabeth* and *Elyzabethe*, in her early correspondence subset. Unfortunately, her later letters see her switch to her initial, <E>, preventing a diachronic comparison. In EEBO-TCP, *Elizabeth* is the preferred spelling, found in 1,351 documents. *Elezabeth* occurs only in three texts, and *Elyzabeth* is recorded in eighty documents (the majority published before 1550). The <y/i> variable is thought to have regularised towards <i> in the latter half of the century, which may partly explain this shift.[93] However, the dominance of *Elizabeth* in printed works could also be attributed to the preferred spelling of the monarch herself. Personal names attest to the individualised nature of spelling in SWES and, moreover, offer no persuasive reason to believe that these women felt their epistolary identity was negatively impacted through the use of variable forms. Only Elizabeth I appears to have had a more fixed and regularised approach to personal names, which could reflect the greater significance of these items in written language, connected to her role as a monarch.

10.7   Conclusion

This analysis of SWES illustrates the complexity of spelling variation in private writing in sixteenth-century English, and provides a new perspective on the historical development of English spelling from a sociolinguistic perspective, which draws in part on frameworks established in studies of new media spelling. Firstly, the quantitative analysis suggests that spelling regularity showed a possible correlation with education (and may have indexed an individual's educational status), although there is no clear evidence of the most probable causes. Conversely, the results also confirm that spelling variation could be extensive even among highly educated women. SWES contains headwords with up to four or five different spellings within the same woman's writing, although comparison with other epistolary spelling is necessary to confirm whether this level of variation is particularly exceptional and potentially connected to gendered literacy. Secondly, the comparative analysis of each woman's subset suggests that regularisation is not a uni-directional or pan-community process. The lifespan trends reveal a mixed picture. Elizabeth, who received the most extensive education, becomes marginally less consistent over time. Thynne, who was an extensive user of correspondence throughout her

---

[93] Salmon, 'Orthography and punctuation', 42.

life, shows minimal changes to her practice in terms of consistency. The comparison between SWES and EEBO-TCP attests to the divergence between print and private spelling (an issue further discussed in Chapter 8). More significantly, it also suggests that print norms did not have an incontrovertible impact on private practices; whilst many forms show convergence, others show a persistent difference between the print majority and the women's personal preferences. Their education and social status suggests this finding may be representative of the literate community more broadly, although further research is necessary. Thirdly, based on the spelling variants of high-frequency and socially salient headwords which deviate from the conventional print forms, the results offer little evidence that the women were concerned with negative associations arising from their idiosyncratic spellings. Similarly, the absence of a shift towards a more regular system over time also indicates that irregularity was not necessarily stigmatised within the social circles of each woman; at least, not to the degree intimated by reformers' contemporaneous debates (see Section 10.2 above). All of this raises the question as to whether, and to what degree, irregularity in spelling practice may have signalled an attempt to index social meaning or would have been perceived as such by correspondents.

The SWES evidence suggests that spelling was a flexible and local practice, subject to bottom-up and top-down pressures. Hence, the spelling systems of the four women converge for many high-frequency functional and core head-words, and these spellings are also shared with the spelling systems deployed by their contemporaries in print (e.g. EEBO-TCP) and private writing (e.g. PCEEC). The distribution of such forms might be seen as part of the regularis-ing process, through the intersection of local and supralocal practices. The exceptions to the emergent regularity, such as idiosyncratic spellings, indicate that spelling remained an open system, which could therefore be shaped by idiosyncratic and local network practices. The evidence from PCEEC indicates that spellings may have been shared within epistolary networks, such as Bacon's *yower* and Elizabeth's *hit*, and this area requires further investigation. Whilst studies of Modern English spelling and twenty-first-century new media practices alike have observed the potential for localised practices to emerge in specific correspondent networks, these occur against the backdrop of a (near-) regularised system.[94] For earlier periods, local networks of spelling forms contribute to the subsequent supralocalisation of variants, but the process through which different networks come to converge around particular forms, and thus regularise, and the possible causes and motivations of those writers for converging, remain unclear.[95] It seems likely that both bottom-up and top-

---

[94] E.g. Osselton, 'Informal spelling systems'; Sairio, *Language and Letters.*
[95] Cf. Berg and Aronoff, 'Self-organization'.

down factors contribute to such processes at the micro-level. Relatedly, the possible impact of socio-pragmatic factors, such as recipient and register, and interactive phenomena, such as accommodation, also warrant consideration, having been pinpointed in new media studies as crucial determinants of present-day spelling choices (chiefly between standard and non-standard forms).[96] The sequentiality of correspondence provides a rich dataset through which to investigate these hypothetical influences.

Another outstanding question is whether the aforementioned properties of each woman's spelling system had social meaning relevant to their identity performance, and it is here that the new media concepts become particularly useful. The SWES data provides no strong evidence that the women were reacting to a proto-standard ideology: there is no coherent shift towards a more consistent or shared system of variants. Instead, the data reveals areas of variation within their practice, linked to accepted conventions of graph substitution (e.g. 'loving'), local forms shared within their epistolary network, idiosyncratic forms that constitute an individualised norm, and one-off examples of 'exceptional variation'. Sebba's *zone of social meaning* was developed to explain the extent of socially significant deviation from a prescribed orthographic norm. For the sixteenth-century data, it might be more effective to talk of 'localised zones of social meaning'. Rather than an overarching top-down normative system from which writers deviate, the women's spelling systems suggest that variants are connected to inter-linked localised systems, which are personalised, habitual and (at times) shared with (some of) their interlocutors. The supralocal dimension of some of their spelling choices (e.g. convergence for many function words and core vocabulary items) may have had minimal resonance when local-level associations took precedence. The divergence between SWES and EEBO-TCP indicates that exposure to prestigious public, printed writing was not a guarantee of influence on an individual's personal practice. The evidence of localised forms, such as *yower*, however, does not necessarily imply that all variants were used because they indexed membership of a particular social network. Rather, the patterns in the data suggest a habitual usage that was sensitive, to a degree, to the usage of other writers, as well as one's own personal preferences. In terms of the social meaning of the use or non-use of a particular variant spelling, only Elizabeth may have paid any sustained attention to the particular forms (e.g. personal name, etymological spellings). Her anticipation of the hegemonic standard spelling ideology could reflect the special significance of the written language for the construction of her social identity as a monarch.

For the other writers, spelling may have had more flexible *zones of social meaning*. It may be that the patterning of variation, rather than specific variant

---

[96] Grace et al., 'Undergraduates' attitudes'.

forms, carried more significance as an epistolary identity marker. Thynne, for example, has a variable spelling system that makes extensive use of (accepted) interchangeable graph forms, alongside less conventional spelling practices of the period. The overall result is an epistolary spelling system with a distinctive texture. Unlike present-day English, in which readers accustomed to a standardised system home in on deviant forms, it seems plausible that readers of Thynne's letters, and those of the other women considered here, would have engaged with the spellings more holistically; that is, they would have recognised patterns and preferences across the writing system as a whole, as well as responding to particular variants of particular words. If so, we might point to possible parallels between the regular patterns of respelling seen to characterise 'unregulated' new media texts and the potentially indexical nature of individuals' distinctive spelling profiles in the sixteenth century. Analysis of spelling practice in the epistolary writings of individuals of other genders and social ranks, as well as in other private text-types, is necessary to confirm these hypotheses. Overall, the new media framework helps to articulate and interpret the complex patterns in the SWES data, offering a critical platform through which to evaluate the sociolinguistic dimensions of historical spelling.

11   Towards a Relativity of Spelling Change

Marco Condorelli

Empirical research in orthography has recently seen a rapid increase in the use of digital corpora. The main reason behind the growth of corpus-based work is the rising interest in the compilation of structured collections of historical texts, afforded by digitisation and the internet. With respect to English orthography and Early Modern English spelling in particular, researchers are in an excellent position, thanks to the dynamic and continuous production of transcribed corpora like the Corpus of English Dialogues (CED),[1] Early English Books Online: Text Creation Partnership (EEBO-TCP),[2] Early Modern English Medical Texts (EMEMT),[3] the Lampeter Corpus,[4] the Lancaster Newsbooks Corpus[5] and the Shakespeare First Folio.[6] Over the last decade or so, a number of scholars have undertaken exploratory, quantitative investigations of spelling variation in some of the corpora above using normalisation tools, which generally transform texts into a single canonical form in order to allow for further comparative research.[7] Linear models of spelling analysis have offered some of the most interesting preliminary outlooks on Early Modern English spelling. Such linear models – which compare two values, and the consistent

---

[1] Culpeper and Kytö, *A Corpus of English Dialogues*.
[2] Early English Books Online: Text Creation Partnership (EEBO-TCP). EEBO contains facsimiles of all printed books in English from c. 1473 to 1700. The EEBO-TCP project is an ongoing initiative to create searchable marked-up full-text transcriptions for all the works in EEBO; its Phase 1 (2001–9) encompassed more than 25,000 works, which have been available since January 2015 on the websites of the University of Michigan Library and of the Bodleian Libraries at the University of Oxford. The transcription work is continuing under Phase 2 while this chapter is being written. Although access to texts made available as part of EEBO-TCP Phase 2 is still restricted to institutions that subscribe to its licence agreement, a relatively large number of researchers are authorised to use Phase 2 by way of the Joint Information Systems Committee (JISC) Historical Texts Collection licence.
[3] Taavitsainen et al., *Early Modern English Medical Texts*.
[4] Schmied et al., *The Lampeter Corpus*.
[5] McEnery and Hardie, *The Lancaster Newsbooks Corpus*.
[6] Shakespeare First Folio, Oxford Text Archive.
[7] E.g. Archer et al., 'Guidelines'; Auer and Fairman, 'Letters'; Baron et al., 'Automatic standardization of spelling'; 'Innovators'; 'Quantifying Early Modern English spelling variation'; Craig and Whipp, 'Old spellings, new methods'; Evans, *The Language of Queen Elizabeth I*; Hendrickx and Marquilhas, 'From old texts to modern spellings'; Kopaczyk, *The Legal Language*.

change between these values – have pioneered the analysis of full corpora and have sometimes featured a complex structure of tagging and text-encoding schemes. The NUPOS tag set and TEI, for example, have provided an excellent level of deep tagging and mark-up of texts using finely grained part-of-speech tagging.[8] DICER, on the other hand, is a tool that uses word/variant pairs in order to learn the 'cost' or 'weight' assigned to individual spelling changes in combination with the variant detector tool VARD.[9] Preliminary, quantitative insights into spelling variation in Early Modern English corpora using DICER and VARD have generated clear and linear patterns of standardisation. If these patterns are to be used purely for studying historical spelling, however, they need to be revised entirely, as further elaborated below.[10]

11.1   Models of Quantitative Analysis

The patterns of spelling standardisation in English described using normalisation tools are relatively straightforward, and indicate a reasonably consistent process of standardisation, which appears to have begun at the onset of the Early Modern English era and continued gradually and relatively slowly throughout this era. With this understanding of standardisation, English spelling is seen as increasingly haphazard and irregular the further back in history one goes, and vice versa.[11] Unfortunately, however, there are some issues in earlier investigations and the standardisation trends which they detect.[12] One of the problems entails the use of heavily edited corpora such as A Representative Corpus of Historical English Registers (ARCHER)[13] and the Innsbruck Texts.[14] Another problem consists in the use of Shakespeare's First Folio to plot alleged diachronic patterns even though the collection was printed entirely in 1623. Most importantly, however, the patterns drawn using normalisation tools are the result of a fundamental methodological and conceptual shortcoming. Spelling variation rarely morphed consistently and linearly from one historical stage to a final, 'standardised' form; rather, spelling variants most likely followed a complex framework of internal regularities which shaped words through different forms, before taking the forms that we would expect by the end of the Early Modern English period.

The process of regularisation by internal regularities has been entirely overlooked in normalisation-based approaches, as these methods address spelling as an element to correct before other levels of analysis are explored. Normalisation tools have privileged modern spelling forms and marked any spellings that differ from

---

[8] Mueller, 'NUPOS'; the Text Encoding Initiative (TEI) is a consortium which collectively develops and maintains a standard for the representation of texts in digital form.
[9] Baron et al., 'Innovators'.
[10] My chapter takes the remarks made in Basu, 'Ill shapen sounds', as its point of departure.
[11] Archer et al., 'Guidelines', 9.   [12] Ibid.   [13] Denison and Yáñez-Bouza, ARCHER.
[14] Markus, *Innsbruck Texts*.

present-day English as a variant, essentially overlooking any internal consistencies. Thus, tools like VARD and DICER have generally provided a prescriptive view of spelling developments in Early Modern English. For most of the corpora analysed in previous normalisation-based investigations,[15] the degree of spelling variation appears quite high over most of the sixteenth century, more likely because there is an obvious difference between older spellings and present-day English forms, rather than because of a real process of standardisation of spelling forms as a system. These remarks are on the same lines as Anupam Basu's statement[16] about the degree of spelling variation from a diachronic perspective, namely the fact that spelling variation may be overestimated if *modernisation* and *regularisation* are used as synonyms for *standardisation*.

Aside from the conceptual problems described above, there are also some lexical issues in normalisation approaches, which likely skew diachronic projections of spelling change. Early Modern English vocabulary is rife with words which, to a present-day reader, look like obsolete and archaic lexical items. These words do not have immediate present-day English etymological equivalents and are therefore untreatable in a normalisation-based approach: *anon, belike, betimes, betwixt, bourn, bruit, cozen, didst, doeth, fain, haply, nonce, palter, prithee, quoth, sayst, swain, thou, verily, whence, wherefore, withal* and *wonted* are only some of the many examples which fall into this category. Traditional computational approaches have also made compromises which sacrifice morphological reliability in order to address some of the differences between the Early Modern English language and present-day English vocabulary.[17] Early Modern English vocabulary is populated with items which follow different morphological forms over a diachronic perspective (e.g. *to night, your self, a bout, shalbe* and *wilbe*), which may not necessarily follow the same spelling developments as their correspondent present-day English forms. The number of words and spelling forms which may fall within and across the categories above appear to be higher in frequency in the first half of the Early Modern English period than in the second half,[18] thus inevitably affecting our perception of spelling trends from a continuous, overarching point of view. An additional factor illustrating the fragility of results based on a comparison between Early Modern English and present-day English forms is the fact that English continued to undergo processes of spelling codification and regularisation beyond 1700. Epistolary, handwritten material, for example, exhibits a much larger range of spelling variation than printed texts, some of which appears to continue to the early eighteenth century and makes comparisons with present-day English conceptually difficult.[19] Some of the computational tools most recently developed for

---

[15] Archer et al., 'Guidelines'; Tyrkkö, 'Printing houses'.   [16] Basu, 'Ill shapen sounds', 174.
[17] Cf. Archer et al., 'Guidelines'.   [18] Cf. Tyrkkö, 'Printing houses', 161–2.
[19] Cf. Görlach, *Introduction to Early Modern English*, 75–85; Sairio, *Language and Letters*; Schneider, 'Computer assisted spelling normalization'; Tieken-Boon van Ostade, 'English at the onset'; 'Lowth's language'.

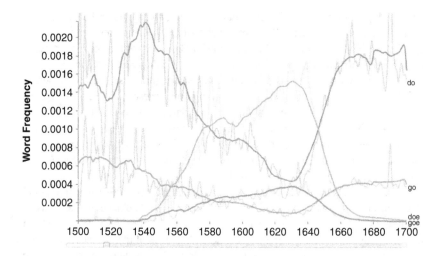

Figure 11.1 *do*, *doe*, *go* and *goe* in EEBO-TCP Phase 1

Note: 'Word frequency' refers to the relative proportions of the numbers of each word out of the overall number of words for each year.
Source: Basu and Pentecost, 'EEBO N-Gram Browser'

exploring large databases like EEBO-TCP validate these statements, revealing more objectively the complexity of spelling variation over the Early Modern English period and pointing to a more composite internal structure among different word forms in Early Modern English vocabulary. The EEBO N-Gram Browser (also used in Chapter 10),[20] for example, shows diachronic trends in EEBO-TCP Phase 1 for individual words, thus enabling users to glean insights into frequencies and proportions of different variant word forms. The words *do/doe* and *go/goe* (Figure 11.1) are excellent illustrative examples of two variant groups where those featuring a word-final <e> actually become more popular and take over the role of 'standard' forms between the mid-sixteenth and early seventeenth centuries, before disappearing during the following seventy years.

Another example where a cluster of variant forms shows interesting diachronic patterns of internal regularisation is represented by *enough*, *inough* and *ynough* (Figure 11.2). The trends generated for these word forms suggest that variant words like *inough* and *ynough* co-existed in parallel with *enough* for roughly a century (c. 1540–1640) and that, to the eyes of a writer from the end of the sixteenth century, all three variant words may have been viable variant forms, potentially

[20] Cf. Basu, 'Ill Shapen Sounds'; Basu and Pentecost, 'EEBO N-Gram Browser'. The N-Gram Browser enables one to examine the changing frequencies of words and word forms over time.

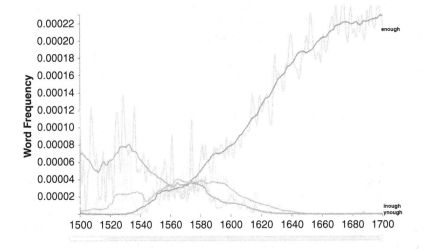

Figure 11.2 *enough, inough* and *ynough* in EEBO-TCP Phase 1

Note: 'Word frequency' refers to the relative proportions of the numbers of each word out of the overall number of words for each year.

Source: Basu and Pentecost, 'EEBO N-Gram Browser'

competing on equal terms as a dominant form for at least a couple of decades. For an early-sixteenth-century writer, the present-day English form *enough* may have not existed at all, so interpreting <i> and <y> consistently as variants of <e> in the *nough environment according to the policy used in normalisation tools does not hold up to the reality of historical, diachronic developments. In view of the patterns shown in Figure 11.2, discarding high-frequency forms like *inough* and *ynough* from a systematic analysis of the alternation between <i> and <y> would provide an incomplete overview of diachronic patterns for the two alternant characters over the Early Modern English period, as *inough* and *ynough* are indeed legitimate variants in the complex scenario of Early Modern English changes, and could be part of an incipient and evolving standard.

Likewise, the variation between *Munday, Mvnday* and *Monday*[21] should be accounted for in analyses of <u>/<v>, <v>/<o> and <u>/<o> (the latter two variant pairs admittedly being less typical in Early Modern English). In other words, a historically reliable quantitative analysis of spelling changes should

---

[21] For single examples out of many: *Munday,* in a religious document published in 1626 (A00260); *Mvnday,* in a translation of a popular collection of sermons, published in 1629 (A01020); *Monday,* in an early-sixteenth-century translation of a late-fourteenth-century 'universal history' (A00005). References of the form Axxxxx (where 'x' represents a digit) are to the filenames provided in EEBO-TCP; of the form Dx$$$$$$ (where 'x' represents a digit and '$' a letter) are to the filenames in CED.

not just assume that *Munday* simply becomes *Monday* consistently and at a given time within Early Modern English, but should account for both *Mvnday* and *Monday*, as both are attested within the Early Modern English period. In light of these data, the process of standardisation should be seen not as a process whereby one variety gradually spreads through Early Modern English spelling structures, but rather as a complex interaction among individual spelling developments which stem from a number of competing variant forms. The shaping of each spelling feature should thus be seen as determined by historical processes of selection, repetition and circulation, rather than as the 'prescription' of a single dominant Early Modern English form.[22] A revised approach to understanding and counting spelling variants over the course of Early Modern English promises to challenge radically the rather simplistic orthographic patterns detected with normalisation tools. Patterns of regularisation may show unexpected trends, which do not necessarily follow a linear trajectory from 1500 right to the end of the Early Modern English era. This could encourage us to reassess the idea of 'standard' spelling as chiefly relative to the historical and systemic context in which the spellings are used, which means that the concept of 'standard' may not always necessarily correspond with our contemporary interpretation of 'standard'. Although it is difficult to quantify the extent to which patterns from the examples given above are found in other words from Early Modern English vocabulary, general complexity and variability of spelling clearly affect the majority of it, including very to moderately high-frequency words (e.g. *bicause*/*bycause*, *betwyxt*/*betwixt* for <i>/<y> as above). These categories of words will have a crucial weight in the overall trends of spelling developments from a wholesale and overarching perspective. If radical changes to analysing historical spelling are implemented to address the remarks made above, a more faithful analysis of spelling developments could challenge our current understanding of Early Modern English spelling as a monolithic whole.

11.2 A New Approach to Studying Spelling Change

The digitisation of large Early Modern English databases, and especially the publication of the transcribed version of EEBO-TCP in 2015,[23] now affords scholars the ability to analyse spelling changes from new perspectives, and to trace developments in spelling variation from a descriptive point of view. The existing large databases of Early Modern English vocabulary can be used to validate variants in combination with new technologies for a systematic, quantitative analysis of Early Modern English spelling. In particular, a brand new

---

[22] Cf. Hope, 'Rats, bats, sparrows, and dogs', 51–2; Milroy, 'Historical description', 20–2.
[23] See note 2.

search mechanism was created with the aim of detecting quantitative spelling variation in a conceptually more accurate manner than do normalisation-based tools.[24] The new tool focuses on detecting variation in spelling purely within and across historical texts, and aims to compare word forms in a given text or corpus with word forms existing in Early Modern English vocabulary (based on the sources from the time which have survived and have been transcribed to date), in order to identify and count character (grapheme) variants. Thus, given the word *vvouldde*, for example, the software will look for *wouldde* in Early Modern English vocabulary, in order to validate the word as a variant if instructed to search for vv/w,[25] and will include *vvouldde* in the validated counts for the corpus and relative year of publication under analysis if at least one instance of *wouldde* exists in Early Modern English. The variation between vv/w in word variants like *vvouldde*, *vvolde*, *vvoueld*, *vvould*, *wouldde*, *wolde*, *woueld* and *would* will be identified when looking at vv/w if each of the forms above has at least one variant with each of <vv> and <w> in Early Modern English. Tracking one position per variation across the whole of Early Modern English vocabulary ensures that real grapheme variants in full word contexts are identified and that gradual changes are followed diachronically to include internal regularities.

A more granular identification of spelling changes has the potential to initiate a reassessment of diachronic spelling developments in Early Modern English. The new model of analysis could bring to light diachronic patterns of regularisation that were overlooked in previous approaches to studying Early Modern English spelling and respond more effectively to an increasing demand for overarching investigations of Early Modern English spelling developments across time.[26] In order to take a first step forward in this direction, the rest of this chapter will offer an overview of the work conducted to develop the methodology necessary for a new, systematic analysis of spelling change, in light of the comments offered so far. The preliminary results presented in the remaining part of this chapter will also aim to demonstrate what appears to be a postulate of spelling in Early Modern English from a grand-scale perspective: spelling largely changes independently of meaning. These insights potentially afford some encouraging implications for the feasibility of the methodology described in this chapter, which lead to the possibility of conducting large-scale, systematic analyses without implementing a complex semantic tagging system.

---

[24] Special thanks are owed to Patrick Schultz and Elizabeth Esswein (Python programmers), for their technical assistance with the coding of the scripts discussed in this chapter. Patrick Schultz developed a first version of the basic search mechanism and rationale, and I am therefore very grateful to him in particular for his valuable technical insights.

[25] The lack of angle brackets here indicates that these are rules used for automatic searching, though there is a direct correlation with their correspondent variant characters.

[26] As mentioned for example by Archer et al., 'Guidelines', 17; Evans, 'Early modern spelling', 166; Grund, 'Scribes and scribal practices', 159.

11.3   The Early Modern English Vocabulary (EMEV) Database

EEBO-TCP Phases 1 and 2 are two outstandingly large datasets encompassing a total of 60,326 files to date, each of which often contains a book-length text. All of the texts available in EEBO-TCP Phases 1 and 2 are faithfully transcribed from facsimile copies of texts in EEBO (printed between c. 1473 and 1700).[27] The transcribers have been most careful to make sure that no reprints or later editions were included in the corpus and the transcriptions present the originals in as neutral and unaltered a way as possible, without prejudice to the type of use for which the texts were destined. While transcription always entails compromising on linguistic faithfulness, the EEBO-TCP transcribers appear to have made some very sensible decisions to limit subjective influences on the transcriptions. Potential weaknesses in EEBO-TCP's transcription policy relate to the normalisation of both tall and round 's' to <s>; the normalisation of some illegible superscript characters (y^e or y^t, which are sometimes difficult to distinguish) to the correct value; the usual disambiguation of homoglyphs like 1/l and 0/O into the correct character; and occasional character substitutions with glyphic value (e.g. <lr> for <k>). All of the elements above are minor, infrequently arising issues in the context of a research focus on spelling changes rather than on more fine-grained glyphic developments; in fact, EEBO-TCP's transcription policy makes the texts suitable for a historical study of spelling, and the transcribed corpus can be confidently used as a core vocabulary dataset for quantitative investigations of Early Modern English spelling developments.[28] The language available in EEBO-TCP Phases 1 and 2 thus constitutes the foundation of the EMEV database, a vocabulary tool in a CSV file[29] containing Early Modern English vocabulary from these texts.

The process of extraction of the vocabulary material from EEBO-TCP for the creation of the EMEV database entailed a series of decisions aimed at eliminating the influence of mark-up material (i.e. elements introduced by the transcribers to signpost page breaks and similar information), in order to enable word identification and to preserve original, historical spellings. In addition, any texts written entirely in foreign languages were hidden in order to limit any unwanted influences on results for the Early Modern English language. Foreign language sections were identifiable using the <TEXT LANG> tags available in the transcribed files. The discrimination between Early Modern English and 'foreign' language texts was not always clear cut in the original EEBO-TCP,

---

[27] See note 2.

[28] Some of the insights into the transcription policies in EEBO-TCP were gained following conversations with Paul Schaffner, Manager of the Text Creation Partnership, University of Michigan.

[29] This is a comma-separated values file, which allows data to be saved in a tabular format.

due to occasional errors made by the transcribers (which are inevitable, given the large size of the corpus). As a result, it is possible that even in texts broadly marked as 'foreign', there are occasional Early Modern English sections (cf. for example file A40902 in EEBO-TCP Phase 1, a mid-seventeenth-century anthology of Greek and Latin epigrams); or indeed vice versa. While smaller errors are inevitable, I conducted systematic (sample) searches in order to minimise and almost completely erase the impact of any major oversights, especially in texts marked as anything other than <LANGUSAGE ID= "eng">. Thus, the chance of finding a real Early Modern English language match is a great deal higher than a foreign text match, not least because the EEBO-TCP corpus collects almost exclusively English language texts anyway. Following the steps described above, the EEBO-TCP texts were processed to extract individual word types and tokens[30] to form a CSV file containing the EMEV database. The formatted EEBO-TCP material was then merged with vocabulary from CED, the Shakespeare First Folio, the Lampeter Corpus, the Lancaster Newsbooks Corpus and EMEMT; these include the vast majority of the corpora available to date with reliable Early Modern English spelling and encompassing printed texts from c. 1450 to c. 1750.[31]

In order to enhance comparability and to support word identification in a linguistically meaningful way, minimal tokenisation options were implemented in the new tool's variant search system (i.e. search scope options to overcome differences in capitalisation and hyphenation, as these are not the focus of the present analysis), while still of course retaining all original spellings from the transcribed material. All of the parameters were implemented with the sole aim of affording a systematic identification of individual word material internally, and to overcome orthographic layers of information which would hinder a comprehensive process of word identification if they are not of immediate interest to the analysis.[32] For all corpora, metadata information from the corpus compilers was also included in the search mechanism and formatted into a uniform tagging system, to allow for a degree of comparison across corpora and for a more consistent, automatic search. When using different corpora to form one database, multiple individual vocabulary sets can be

---

[30] Here, the term 'type' refers to the number of distinct words, and 'token' refers to the total number of words.

[31] Texts from the latter part of the fifteenth century were included in the EMEV database to better account for and represent the complexity of spelling patterns in Early Modern English, especially at its onset. Due to space constraints, a full discussion of the steps followed to extract historical vocabulary from EEBO-TCP and all of the other smaller corpora will have to be provided in a future paper entirely devoted to the topic.

[32] The parameters can be switched off to add additional layers of analysis. In this chapter, spelling is of course intended as indicating the basic character units of Early Modern English words, and orthography as indicating the character units as well as any additional layers of information, including accents, diacritics, punctuation, capitalisation, fonts and so on. Cf. Rutkowska, 'Linguistic levels'; Rutkowska and Rössler, 'Orthographic variables'.

assigned to the same database name to form one dataset, and more than one vocabulary dataset can thus be used jointly for validation when conducting a variant pair search. As a result of the merging of datasets, any word that appears in any of the existing parts of the EMEV database is used for validation during a given variant search. The final version of the EMEV database contains more than 4.6 million types and more than 1.4 billion tokens in total, with all entries appearing in one column and word token counts appearing in another adjacent column. While no other specific organisation format in the database is required for performance, items can be ordered alphabetically and by word count using any piece of software that works as a database platform (e.g. Microsoft Access). The EMEV database represents an ideal basis for a quantitative approach to analysing spelling variation in and across smaller, individual corpora, as it covers the entire Early Modern English period and represents the entirety of the reliably transcribed material available to date.

The purpose of the EMEV database is to inform the variant analysis search mechanism about whether a word in any given corpus (following any variant search) can be included in the search results as a valid variant form. The EMEV database largely replaces manual judgement about whether a given variant word exists within the Early Modern English period: it informs the search script about whether each word in any given analysed corpus is attested in the Early Modern English period as having a pair of word types which differ by any two variants ('variant 1' and 'variant 2') in any given search for variants 1 or 2; analyses of larger clusters of variants can be undertaken by combining and comparing binary sets. In the framework of the search rationale described here, the EMEV database represents a constant against which each individual, smaller corpus and variant pair (set of variables) can be analysed in order to detect patterns of regularisation, similarities and differences. With the search rationale afforded by the EMEV database, variant graphemes (whether single-letter variants or variant letter clusters) are understood as integral elements of real-word items. If a word is never attested in the EMEV database to show spelling alternation for a specific variant pair, but rather a different combination of graphemes alternate jointly, the large datasets used for validation suggest the likely possibilities that (1) the variation affecting a specific non-variant word involves a more complex grapheme alternation than originally envisaged, with different characters varying either adjacently or at different positions, or that (2) the word spelling in question may be idiosyncratic.[33] While variant valid-ation may be somewhat regulated by word frequency, any invalidated matches can be considered statistically irrelevant to the main trends which characterise

---

[33] Here, 'idiosyncratic' refers to word spellings which do not have at least one alternant variant 2 form for a search undertaken for given variants 1 or 2. Idiosyncrasies can however be identified at different frequencies of occurrence, by means of a higher threshold level.

the Early Modern English period, given the size and coverage of the EMEV database.

As part of the set-up illustrated so far, a workflow mechanism was created with a view to producing precise and granular variant searches that are also flexible and reusable in the event that the EMEV database is extended at a later stage. The search will find any word containing a given variant pair in a corpus and will store all base forms and their possible candidate variants, regardless of whether they occur as variants in the EMEV database. Subsequently, all potential variant 1 or variant 2 candidates in a given corpus can be checked for corresponding variant forms appearing in the same word and in the same character position in the material available in the EMEV database (the alternative variants 1 and 2 can of course flexibly represent any number of characters, without skewing detection of string matches). For simplicity in the internal system of analysis and to avoid errors in the automatic counts, any matches for variants 1 or 2 during this first stage happen simultaneously; word variants are found during any given search without an initial focus on the token counts (i.e. frequencies are calculated as a second step). By default, a threshold of 0 (indicating a one-item minimum frequency threshold) is applied for validation, which means that one variant 1 or 2 pair in the EMEV database will be sufficient to validate a word as a variant for that variant 1 or 2 pair.[34]

The simplest case to illustrate the validation principle based on a 0 threshold would be a pair like *but/bvt*, where each of the tokens must actually occur at least once in the EMEV database for them to be counted as a validated result of a u/v search in a given corpus where *but* or *bvt* (or indeed both) are found. When there are multiple relevant variant characters in a word, any character position within the word will be counted independently, in order to allow for a flexible focus on individual graphemes rather than entire word variants. In the word *turbulent*, for example, there are four potential combinations of <u>/<v> variation, and both places of alternation would be considered valid if just two of the four potential variations are seen individually (e.g. *tvrbulent* and *turbvlent* or *turbulent* and *tvrbvlent*), which greatly improves flexibility in searches for less frequent words. Thus, if one or more of *turbulent*, *turbvlent*, *tvrbulent* and *tvrbvlent* are found in a corpus, base forms will be generated for each of the two positions where variant 1 could alternate with variant 2, and counts for each of the word forms will be stored as individual entries. Results would therefore

---

[34] As briefly mentioned in the previous note, validation can also occur at different frequencies of occurrence, by means of the threshold tool implemented in the search system, which can be used for validation within the EMEV database. In addition to frequency, dialectal variation plays a role in complicating patterns of regularisation, even though most of the books in EEBO-TCP were printed in and around London. In any case, the system does account for variables like dialects and authorship; these issues will be addressed fully in future discussions, as the main focus of this chapter is large-scale mainstream trends.

be stored as *turbulent/tvrbulent*_1 and *turbulent/turbvlent*_4 (indexing starting at 0): the <u> in *turbulent* will be counted once under _1 and once under _4 and the same would apply to <v> in *tvrbvlent*, while <u> and <v> would be counted once each in *turbvlent* and *tvrbulent*.

While the methodology described so far promises new, exciting insights into the diachronic distribution of spelling developments, however, there may also be potential difficulties resulting from a system of analysis that matches variant words according to their form, independently of their meaning. The following section will explore these potential issues and will illustrate a case study for a preliminary insight into the relationship between semantic ambiguity and spelling variation, with some rather encouraging results.

11.4   Semantic Disambiguation

In this section, 'semantic ambiguity' indicates the overlapping of meaning occurring across identical spellings or variant 1 or 2 forms which etymologic-ally belong to different words and/or carry unrelated meanings. Within the context of a typical variant pair search in the mechanism described above, potential cases of semantic ambiguity generally fall within the categories of minimal pairs, homophones and homographs.[35] The first category (minimal pairs) encompasses words that change in meaning upon the alternation of a single sound between them, which can be represented by one or a cluster of characters. For instance, the Early Modern English words *sin*, *tin* and *chin* alternate between <s>, <t> and <ch> (most often representing /s/, /t/ and /tʃ/) and, as a result, produce words with different meanings. The homophones category, in its turn, includes words which are pronounced the same but which have different meanings and may appear under different spellings, for example the Early Modern English words *two* and *too* whenever <wo> and <oo> represent the same vowel. The homographs category, finally, comprises words which are spelled the same way in Early Modern English but which can have different meanings, for instance the word *heer* may be only a variant of *her*, only a variant of *here* or a variant of both *her* and *here* at any moment in time within the Early Modern English period. The category of homographs may also include a subgroup of foreign cross-language homographs, which can be confused with Early Modern English words. Typical examples are the words *fit* and *die*, which can be both Early Modern English and Latin loanwords with consequential different meanings. The two words can display different patterns of diachronic spelling variation depending on the language that they belong to and their meaning in each language. Most of these potential shortcomings have

---

[35] Cf. Salmon, 'Orthography and punctuation', 14, especially with reference to the latter two categories of ambiguity.

already been encountered in previous software-based analytical approaches to studying spelling variation, including VARD,[36] which does not perform syntactic or semantic analysis when normalising historical texts.[37] Semantic ambiguities can be true for the Early Modern English language more broadly, and examples of words falling within the categories mentioned above may appear both in a given individual text and within the EMEV database as a whole. In the case of cross-language homographs like *fit* and *die*, for instance, the words may end up being counted as part of the main count datasets regardless of whether *fit* and *die* actually show any variation when they are used in their Latin meaning, thus potentially creating false matches.

While the ambiguities above are all cases to be wary of during a given analysis, the errors that researchers might encounter are in principle not likely to be significant in number (at least no more than when using traditional quantitative methods). Firstly, proportionally low numbers of homographs and homophones are expected in any language, as languages are naturally prone to communicative efficiency.[38] The search mechanism will also have a bottle-neck effect on the range of vocabulary falling within two variant groups, as, for all variant 1 and 2 items within a search, the only varying items will be variants 1 and 2 in the same position in every given word. Concurrently, potential errors will be greatly mitigated by the fact that foreign language texts have been largely eliminated from EEBO-TCP, thus drastically limiting the possibility of false matches with non-Early Modern English vocabulary.

These suppositions were confirmed by a first read-over of validated entries from a variant search of <u> and <w> between 1560 and 1750 in CED, conducted as a test case in order to evaluate the extent of potential ambiguity existing in a given dataset. The <u>/<w> variants represent an ideal case for a test, as they are likely to be found in a reasonably large amount of vocabulary.[39] In addition, the texts contained in CED are spread across the greater part of the Early Modern English period, and are representative of a variety of texts, which means that the patterns are less likely to be affected by peculiarities of a single register or style.

The number of word types generated as validated variants on a 0 threshold for u/w were 1,688 for variant 1 (<u>) and 1,245 for variant 2 (<w>). Among these word sets, 527 word types for <u> and 300 word types for <w> were

---

[36] Cf. Baron and Rayson, 'Automatic standardization of texts'; Baron et al., 'Automatic standardization of spelling'.

[37] Cf. Tyrkkö, 'Printing houses', 161–2.

[38] Cf. Comrie, *Language Universals*; Dixon, 'Ergativity'; Haspelmath, 'Creating economical morphosyntactic patterns'; Hawkins, *Cross-Linguistic Variation*; Newmeyer, *Possible and Probable Languages*.

[39] Blake, 'English versions'; Rutkowska, *Orthographic Systems*; Scragg, *A History of English Spelling*; Sönmez, 'English spelling'.

identified as potentially semantically ambiguous following a first read-over. These values roughly correspond to c. 31% and 24% (percentages rounded for simplicity) of the overall counts extracted for <u> and <w> respectively, which means that about a third of the result datasets were identified as potentially ambiguous at a first glance. For a more objective analysis of potential ambiguities, word types from each report were also processed in VARD, in order to produce automatic suggestions of possible present-day English equivalents for each word with a confidence score. Albeit normalisation systems are unsuitable for a reliable analysis of historical spelling, the translation system embedded in VARD provided a useful confidence score to discern the likelihood of possible ambiguous matches, and gave a somewhat more objective measure to pursue semantic disambiguation for this case study (potential suggestions with a score of more than 30% indicated that the word could be semantically ambiguous). Of course, any semantic mismatches between Early Modern English and present-day English in lexical items were also accounted for with individual searches of suspicious material in CED and EEBO-TCP. With these considerations in mind, a second step of analysis was conducted with a view to pursue a systematic, word-by-word contextual investigation on the subgroup identified for <u> variants. The chief reason behind the narrowing to a subset from one variant set rather than looking at the entire datasets for both variant sets is that the semantic disambiguation analysis involved some detailed, case-by-case contextual searches. The process of semantic disambiguation was carried out primarily by means of a context-finding tool, purposely created as an appendix to the main search mechanism. The tool generates contextual quotations from EEBO-TCP and all other individual corpora for each given validated word and its correspondent variant 2 form, and helps to verify validation both within the corpus under analysis and within the EMEV database more broadly. For the collection of contextual quotes, relevant searches were tokenised, in order to overcome identification issues due to the influence of capitalisation and punctuation.

In general, semantic patterns were investigated following two levels of analysis: a search within CED aimed to identify quotes where a given variant form might be used under different meanings in different quotations; and a search within the EMEV database in order to verify whether the corresponding alternate words appeared under the same meaning as the words in the search report at least once in the Early Modern English period (reflecting the 0 threshold validation policy). If different, unrelated meanings (minimal pairs, homophones and homographs) existed for a given word in CED, these were checked individually against the EMEV database. Cognate meanings broadly falling within the same semantic sphere and polysemic nuances of individual lexemes were excluded from semantic disambiguation, largely due to the lower proportions of transcribed material available for most of the early part of the

Figure 11.3 Semantic spectrum of selected <u> variants from u/w in CED
Note: This is a simplified version of the search report sheet, which was then subjected to colour coding.

Early Modern English period, as well as to physiological linguistic and cultural differences between the onset and the end of the Early Modern English era. An interesting example is that of the word *counsel*, which evolves from indicating a private figure serving a monarch *at* court to a more public, legal advisor *in* court between the two points in time, which means that some of the more archaic variants in the EMEV database may otherwise not be directly applicable to some of the strictly legal documents in CED.

With these caveats in mind, then, the proportions of semantically validated material resulting from a search of <u> variants from a <u>/<w> population in CED are represented in Figure 11.3. The spectrum represents word type results according to how word entries appear in a typical search report sheet. Entries are ordered by character length first and then alphabetically, with the longer word types appearing on the left-hand side of the spectrum. For illustrative purposes in this discussion, items were coded (black columns) to indicate word types with multiple meanings which were validated in CED against the EMEV database. The columns in white therefore indicate word types with non-validated meanings; their relative width gives a broader sense of the proportion of validated to non-validated material.

Among the results in the subset of <u> variants from the u/w search under discussion, there appears to be a high correspondence between the semantic values represented in the validated items and their alternates in the EMEV database, which in turn indicates a low frequency of false validations. Falsely validated word types are c. 21% of all items in the subgroup selected as the test case (113 types out of 527 entries), which is already a remarkably low percentage. Additionally, word types within the 21% are generally very low-frequency items, and 88 out of 113 types feature fewer than ten tokens in the whole corpus, often spread evenly across decades as one-item entries. A comparison between word types and tokens is even more meaningful as there is also a number of word items which are more difficult to validate only in a smaller subgroup of tokens (c. 5% of the subset material), and were not represented in the spectrum for the sake of simplicity. One of the most interesting examples is the word *but*, which is validated correctly in all cases in which the word is used as a conjunction, but not when it is used as an abbreviation for *butler* (D2CWILKI, c. 1% of the overall tokens).

From a wholesale perspective, word spellings in the selected subset largely appear to be spread across the EMEV database without many remarkable semantic-related boundaries. The spectrum drawn in Figure 11.3 possibly reflects the condition of chaos existing in the EMEV database from a grand-scale perspective, where virtually all variant spellings of a word can exist across all possible meanings (or indeed, the other way around).[40] While the semantic patterns discussed above as a whole may potentially be somewhat dependent on the variant pair under analysis, the trends appear to support Matti Rissanen's remarks on Early Modern English 'standardisation' more broadly. In particular, spelling, while being a part of the overall regularisation of Early Modern English, may be 'wholly a matter of written language; in addition, it is independent of meaning'[41] and hence develops with relative autonomy as a function of print. As an additional piece of evidence in support of these statements, my results suggest that ambiguous cases are largely proportional to the decrease in character length for each word item, with the final portion of bisyllabic and trisyllabic ambiguous items being more susceptible to ambiguity and false validation than longer word strings (these items alone make up c. 35% of all the false matches detected and also represent all bisyllabic and trisyllabic items in the full report). Conversely, words of six or more characters appear to be much less prone to ambiguity than shorter word strings (twenty-two false validations contain six or more characters, i.e. c. 19% of the false matching material detected). In general, words longer than six characters are infrequent in the subset containing words identified as potentially ambiguous and comprise c. 33% of the subset, the majority of which are words shorter than eight characters (e.g. *glaunce, faultes, espouse*, and so on).

The largely predictable distribution of ambiguity and potential false validations gives in turn some reassurance about the items that were left out at the first stage of analysis, which are most frequently longer words and were discarded as non-ambiguous from the very beginning. Among the items discarded at this early stage from semantic disambiguation in <u> variants, c. 55% word types (926 out of 1689) contain six or more characters, which further supports the remarks above about the correlation between word length and basic ambiguity, and most likely lowers considerably the proportions of false matches relative to the full report. While my findings indicate that ambiguity may also be possible in slightly longer word strings, these are very infrequent

---

[40] This of course does not mean that all candidate words in a corpus are expected to alternate at 0 threshold; this point can be demonstrated quite straightforwardly with non-variant proportions across different variant pairs.

[41] Rissanen, 'Standardisation', 118.

and decreasingly proportional in number to the length of word items. Among the longest words detected as false validations are idiosyncrasies like *shoule* for 'soul' (occurring only in D4CSHADW), and highly infrequent spellings like *droughts* for 'medicinal draughts' (D4FWARD, occurring once in the whole corpus). Other noteworthy idiosyncrasies include *pursuer* (D5CHOADL, also occurring once) which translates to 'pursue her', and some instances of cross-language homophony. The word *pour*, for instance, is attested in CED as a French preposition in D4HEMIEG and also as an Early Modern English verb in D4HOLUCI, but neither form is represented by *powr* in the EMEV database. Likewise, the word *virtu* (D5CHOADL) appears once as an Italian word but its variant *virtw* refers only to the Latin word 'virtus'; the Latin verb *suum* (D1MDANDO, also occurring once), however, is validated incorrectly by the form *swum*, which refers only to the meaning 'to swim'. The subset also contains some examples of minimal pairs which were found to be false valid-ations, for example *duel/dwel, groue/growe, louer/lower* and *sure/swre* (cor-responding variant 2 forms are given here for illustrative purposes only). Minimal pairs are possibly the most important category of false validations to look out for and correct during any given disambiguation analysis, as they can (albeit rarely) include high-frequency words, e.g. *sure* features 616 times in CED, but *swre* refers only to the verb 'to swear'.[42]

Turning to examples from semantically validated items (i.e. words repre-sented in the EMEV database as valid variant spellings for all meanings detected), the word *where* occurs 1487 times in CED, of which two instances appear to indicate the verb 'were' (e.g. in D5WBLAND), in alternation with the more frequent 'where'. The word *pounde* may refer to both a unit of measure (e.g. D1HFDESA) and a currency name in CED (e.g. D1HONICH), and the variant word *pownde* (for the <u>/<w> variant pair) is attested under both meanings in the Early Modern English period. Another example is the variant pair *poure/powre*; aside from the idiosyncratic Frenchism *pour* (above) for instance, it indicates 'pour' and 'power', and occasionally also 'poor' in CED. The three meanings are distributed between the two variant forms in Early Modern English vocabulary irrespective of the archaicity of the form. For instance, *powre* is attested in EEBO-TCP as 'pour' in 1588 (file no. A09123) and 1635 (A23279), as 'poor' in 1580 (A18760), and as 'power' in 1553 (A07873) and 1565 (A08567), among other dates of publication. Likewise, *poure* appears as 'pour' in 1569 (A02923) and 1643 (A39792), as 'poor' in 1528 (A21334) and 1567 (A03432) and as 'power' in 1548 (A02738). As yet another example, the word *draughts* exists in CED both under the meaning of

---

[42] Given the small number of minimal pairs and how easy they are to identify, it is definitely more straightforward and less time-consuming to address them at report analysis stage rather than by means of a semantic tagging system, which would have to be tailored to cover the complexity of the entire EMEV database.

'draughts' (i.e. quantity of liquid, cf. D4CKILLI) and 'drafts' (i.e. preliminary notes, cf. D5TREDDI), and both meanings are represented in Early Modern English by the word *drawghts* (cf. e.g. A02775 and A44721).

Among the semantically validated items, there are also some peculiar cases which provide more evidence for the conceptual validity of the new approach proposed here, including the form *youl* (D4HOKATE), which stands for present-day English 'you'll' and has a legitimate variant 2 version in the EMEV database (i.e. *yowl*, which is attested five times under the meaning of 'you'll' in the EEBO-TCP Phase 1 texts, for example). Another interesting example is the word *thorough*, which indicates two different, equally frequent word items in CED, i.e. 'thorough' and 'through'. The two semantic values of *thorough* in Early Modern English vocabulary appear to behave the opposite way to the protocol expected from a present-day English perspective, with the more 'archaic' variant (i.e. *thorowgh*) actually showing a relative state of semantic consistency and the 'newer' variant displaying semantic fluctuation. Thus, *thorowgh* as 'through' is attested in EEBO-TCP in 1572 (A18004) and 1638 (A10652), while *thorough* appears as 'through' in 1569 (A02923) and 1688 (A52133), and as 'thorough' in 1658 (A46807) and 1684 (A56396). In general, the meaning of 'through' appears to be more frequent even towards the end of the Early Modern English period, against expected patterns of standardisation based on a comparison with the present-day English form.

Aside from the examples mentioned so far, there are also a few elements among the least frequent items in the subset under consideration (of <u> variants from a u/w population) where validations can be made with a level of compromise, if comparable options and proportions are retained consistently within and across searches. Among the items analysed in the subset, sixteen word types (e.g. *auant*) were found to be more difficult to identify as either true or false validations, because of the very small number of quotes available in the corpora for disambiguation. Difficult entries were processed permissively[43] using the same policy across the full spectrum, and, for simplicity, they are amongst those represented as semantically validated in Figure 11.3. Much like the uncertain validations, proper names across all corpora (e.g. last names like *Faulkner*) were also treated permissively, regardless of whether they indicated a personal name or a common noun. Another interesting case, besides the example of *but* for *butler* mentioned above, is represented by abbreviations (e.g. *bour* for *boutcher*, D2CBARRE, and *leut* for *leutenant*, D3TLILBU). In this case character variants were validated by comparing the full variant 2 version of the correspondent words, when the items could not be validated directly by means of their correspondent short-form variants. Rarely occurring phrasal verbs were also treated in a permissive way where necessary, if their

---

[43] I.e. matching results even if the validating material happens to fall under a different word class.

phrasal forms did not vary considerably from the main verb or a similar phrasal combination. The verb, *hauling off*, for example refers to the act of 'pulling away' (a ship, in D5TAMBRO) and was validated by the sentence *that you are hawling her away from her Parents and Kindred* in EEBO-TCP Phase 2 (B18863). Multiple meanings were occasionally validated semantically regardless of word class, where there was an insufficient number of quotations available. As an example, the word *queenes* refers both to the plural form and to the possessive singular form of 'queen' in CED, though it is attested in the possessive singular form only as *qwenes* in EEBO-TCP Phase 2 (A86107). Likewise, the verb *paunched* (D5WTOFT, meaning 'disembowelled') was semantically validated with *pawnche*, which is a noun indicating 'entrails'.

Overall, the number of validations where compromises were made is proportionally very low (i.e. only fifty-one very low-frequency cases in the whole subset, corresponding to c. 10% of the material in the subset, spread evenly across the full diachronic scope of the search report), which guarantees that the vast majority of all trends detected in a validated dataset are still highly reliable and comparable. The types of compromises discussed above are also largely comparable with those of normalisation tools, and, more broadly, are the inevitable results of large-scale quantitative approaches to studying linguistic areas as unpredictable as spelling.[44]

11.5   Looking Ahead

Without a doubt, future analyses could become increasingly complex as technology develops, especially when further advances in transcription enterprises are made to afford finer layers of analysis. At the same time, however, the patterns discussed in this chapter provide a glimpse into trends in Early Modern English vocabulary, which are pivotal for large-scale quantitative investigations of spelling patterns across Early Modern English corpora. Spelling changes and developments from a grand-scale perspective appear to largely occur regardless of meaning, which is rather reassuring within the remits of the methodology discussed here. A careful analysis aimed to identify occasional high-frequency false validations across searches, therefore, will ensure that the proportions detected are comparable and reliable, and will overcome any issues resulting from semantic ambiguity. That said, a rigorous, precise, large-scale investigation of spelling variants and their diffusion in Early Modern English vocabulary can certainly be conducted already.

---

[44] While compromises can be accepted for the sake of simplicity consistently across searches, most ambiguities can also be addressed by raising the validation threshold to as low a number as five (c. 74% of material where compromises were made are represented by fewer than five alternate word quotations in the EMEV database). A higher threshold is more likely to generate fewer ambiguous items, but thresholds should remain reasonably low to retain a wide scope of analysis and also to account for the fact that validation matches are usually made with a low number of quotations in the first place, especially among more archaic variants.

12   Synergic Dialogue in Historical Orthography
National Philologies, Comparability and Questions for the Future

Marco Condorelli and Anja Voeste

Historical orthography is among the most underrated subfields in linguistics and has been explored mainly from a language-specific perspective. Over the last few decades, however, a number of publications have begun to cover interesting aspects of orthography from more generalised perspectives, building something of a foundation for the field of enquiry as a whole. The *Handbook of Orthography and Literacy*[1] and *Writing Systems*,[2] for example, have given useful insights into aspects of orthography from a present-day perspective that are also relevant for historical linguists, while volumes like *The Oxford Handbook of Historical Phonology*[3] and *The Handbook of Historical Sociolinguistics*[4] have explored issues related to orthography from a historical perspective in close connection with specific areas of investigation (i.e. phonological and sociolin-guistic matters). There are also a number of research contributions which provide evidence for an overall attempt towards reaching a bolder, more comprehensive outlook on historical orthography. Today, work in historical orthography is published widely in international, world-leading journals like *Diachronica*, *Folia Linguistica Historica*, *Language Variation and Change* and *Historische Sprachforschung/Historical Linguistics*. Research work somewhat related to orthography is also published in major generalist journals like the *Journal of Linguistics* and *Language*, as well as in more specialised journals, as mentioned in the introduction to this volume.

The achievements attained above are testimony to the highly promising situation in which the field of enquiry currently sits, and to the relevance of orthography in the historical linguistics realm. The importance of orthography within the context of historical linguistics is obvious: orthography constitutes the first-order witness to the linguistic past and, as such, both the diachronic and

---

[1] Joshi and Aaron, *Handbook of Orthography and Literacy.*
[2] Coulmas, *Writing Systems: An Introduction.*
[3] Honeybone and Salmons, *Oxford Handbook of Historical Phonology.*
[4] Hernández-Campoy and Conde-Silvestre, *Handbook of Historical Sociolinguistics.*

the synchronic dimensions of orthography are of fundamental importance to anyone with an interest in historical linguistics. Spelling evidence can be and has been widely employed by historical phonologists and dialectologists as a primary source for uncovering distinctive features of phonological and morphological systems of languages and dialects from the past, viewed both from a synchronic perspective, at a given point in time, and also diachronically, spanning different time periods. For a few decades, orthographic evidence has furthermore been used by historical sociolinguists in their search for correlations between socio-historical and socio-cultural factors and linguistic features. Nevertheless, a combined approach, i.e. including both a historical and an international perspective on issues related to orthography, has so far been almost completely shunned by generations of scholars. Here, we advocate the need for more work in establishing patterns of comparability in the field as a first step towards working as a self-contained, yet at the same time ever-growing and open, community of scholars interested in orthography. In order to identify orthographic patterns across languages, it would be advisable to work towards a shared apparatus, including common protocols (i.e. official procedures of academic practice), to be generally accepted by researchers in the field. This can be achieved only by improving communication between individual scholars, and overcoming some of the conceptual boundaries which stem directly from scholarly disunity and professional individualism. Unless some common ground is built, it can be difficult, if not impossible, to ensure comparability of our approach to understanding orthographic systems. At the same time, we must remain wary of any superficial generalisations that may result from comparative overviews, because some of the differences existing in the approaches and policies used to study individual orthographies are largely due to the very history of each individual European language.[5] In the following sections, we develop this point in greater detail, and then attempt to reflect on possible routes of comparability across languages.

12.1   Beyond National Philologies?

In Europe, philologies generally had and still have a strong national orientation. Consequently, language histories are histories of national languages to a considerable extent – one might say primarily, if not exclusively, so. This holds true with respect to the research structures, as well as to the nationally limited thematic content. From a historical perspective, these patterns could be explained by the fact that philologies are the product of the national age, i.e. the formative period of the European nation states. The nationalistic orientation of

---

[5] In this concluding chapter, we make reference mainly to European languages, in line with the focus of this volume.

some of these philologies was so intense that their scholars even tried to integrate their prenational prehistories into an unbroken line of continuity. In this way, national continuities are also claimed for those phases in which the nations in question did not yet exist as political entities, i.e. when the respective linguistic areas were territorially fragmented and, from today's point of view, one can at best speak of cultural nations (e.g. Italy and Germany); or when the nations themselves did not yet even exist as social or imagined units or had only just begun to establish themselves as such (e.g. the Czechs in Bohemia and Moravia).

Since the age of cultural nationalism in the late eighteenth and nineteenth centuries, language history has thus become a nationally constructed object, and supra-regionally unified orthography turned into a 'national monument'. This development entailed consequences, especially for orthographic research, which continue to have an effect to this day. In the course of the nineteenth century, the modern age initiated a general trend towards the formation of expert cultures. This often led to the emergence of specialised disciplines and corresponding academic institutions, which were financed by the state as 'national projects'. While, on the one hand, academic experts in their ivory towers were busy studying language (sound laws, wave models, or later on *langue* and *parole*), on the other, new educational tasks were assigned to them. Universities became a place of teacher training in modern mass society. The academic experts were thus no longer just knowledgeable people, but became potential 'know-it-alls'. They could and they did instruct and correct laypersons. The interplay between academic research and teacher training led to tensions between those who wanted to study language with scientific methods and those who wanted to teach the national language to 'the people' or even impose language norms on them. Against this background it is no wonder that historical orthography as an academic discipline is sometimes closely associated or even completely identified with this national educational project. Its scholars were and still are often perceived as both conservative and conscious of tradition.

However, we do not want to insinuate that the 'national path' of our disciplines was an aberration – as long as this national perspective is not made historically absolute in retrospect. The formation of nations was a key driving force for change, especially in matters related to orthography. National societies and nation states have their own identity and individuality, they have grown historically as cultural phenomena or have been legally constructed. But if we are to adopt a cross-linguistic perspective in future discussions beyond this volume, then we must strive to think more often that they are not unique specimens, but rather examples of *European* national societies and *European* nation states, that is to say, entities with family resemblance.

Apart from these partially problematic national prehistories, there are also practical difficulties that arise in the comparative study of (even just only European) orthographies. Each individual language history is in itself an enormously complex cosmos of facts and figures, sometimes extremely difficult to fully understand within the remits of a given language; a comparative approach is thus only going to multiply the required effort to investigate patterns and trends. In addition, there are language barriers, as well as poor accessibility to both resources and literature to consider – problems which are not necessarily easily solved. This perhaps provides the clearest difference between synergic endeavours in historical orthography and international collaborations in the field of natural sciences; when it comes to chemistry or physics, for example, all national scientific systems are based on the same periodic table of the elements, or the same understanding of gravity and the speed of light. With this in mind, we now proceed to discussing the question of how to approach comparison and comparability of orthographies across languages, drawing on the examples available in the present volume.

12.2   Comparability across Languages

Comparability across languages requires in the first place that the field of comparison be defined precisely. First of all, we need to agree on a historical period of focus, which, in this book, is the early modern era. In principle, orthographic phenomena can be analysed without considering time-related aspects. However, language historians tend not to focus on a given point in time only, and they do not only ask about static cause-and-effect relationships, but rather they concentrate on dynamic interrelationships. Language historians thus systematically broaden their perspective to include the processual dimension; they are interested in looking into longer paths of development. These development paths can be linear or cyclic, or form other patterns altogether. They can also be disruptive, incremental, jolting forward in small steps, or continuously accelerating; or they can proceed in a stop-and-go manner, with relatively stable intermediate phases in between. In any attempt to compare languages, however, there is also a more pragmatic need to tailor our considerations and discussions to shorter periods of time in a more linear way, of which the present book represents an excellent example. Focusing on case studies over shorter time periods allows us to make more reliable claims based on the specific categories of scholarship, expertise, languages and areas of research that are most familiar to us. This, in turn, enables us to make more confident suggestions regarding possible solutions for comparability, because we have a clearer idea about how fellow researchers approach the subject and where their interests lie.

   In addition to time, a geographical limit may work well for practical reasons, as with the discussions in this volume. Nevertheless, it is not always easy to make a selection here; not because Europe's borders have changed, but rather because shared historical–cultural experiences have to be included. The type of comparison that we are interested in can be broadly defined by the histories of languages *in Europe*, although some of these languages (e.g. English, French, Spanish, or Portuguese) have gained global importance during the course of colonisation. If we imagine 'Europe' as our radius of comparison, it is not so much the geographical area but rather 'Europe' as a historical and cultural entity that interests us. Its parts are, as this perception suggests, more closely connected with each other than with the world 'outside'. The various Christian denominations and shared Latin–Greek roots, which have led to the joint use of the Latin, Greek or Cyrillic alphabets, are of course a major historical cornerstone that is common to all orthographies in 'cultural Europe' in the above-mentioned sense. Furthermore, the multitude of ties and shared networks within Europe adds to this foundation. From the late Middle Ages onwards, the considerable mobility of people and ideas and the resulting multitude of interchanges have established a transnational European public sphere, and have also made orthographic transfers possible. One need only think of the spread of printing and typesetting knowledge and of the 'European' individuals involved in the transmission of this art, including Demetrius Damilas, Nicolas Jenson, Johann of Speyer, Colard Mansion, Francysk Skaryna, Johann Snell, Florian Ungler, or Wynkyn de Worde, all of whom left their mark far from their homelands. Or consider the interspatial transfers from one language to another, brought about by the famous printer Ivan Fyodorov (1525–83), who originated in Russian Muscovy but exerted his influence in several places, e.g. in Polish–Lithuanian Lviv (nowadays in Ukraine).

As regards the methodology of comparison, the basic technique consists in specifying and formulating a *tertium comparationis* ('the third component of a comparison')[6] as a way to establish comparability across languages. This is a traditional, long-established method, that many readers will be familiar with. According to this principle, any comparison presupposes that two elements to be compared have at least one characteristic in common, namely the *tertium comparationis*. If one wishes to compare apples and oranges, one does not consider their *differentia specifica*, but their common fruity nature. It is, of course, possible to make comparisons not only on the macro-level (e.g. on the level of national languages), but also on the micro-level of very specific orthographic features. Furthermore, unusual experimental pairs are admissible, even if the objects seem to stem from very different worlds. At an abstract level of comparison, one could, for instance, compare the phenomena of Lithuanian phonotactics in the nineteenth century with those of Spanish graphotactics in the sixteenth century, either by acknowledging a phonemic definition of graphemes as a *tertium comparationis*,[7] or by investigating possible shared constraints on the combination of elements (phonemes/graphemes). In the present collection, empirical advances have been used somewhat like a *tertium comparationis*, and we suggest that a similar approach could also

---

[6] Cf. *Aristotle's Metaphysics*, Book 10, Ch. 1.   [7] Rogers, *Writing Systems*, 272–3.

be fruitful in future attempts to establish bridges across individual orthographies, for a number of reasons.

The most immediate advantage of methods of orthographic enquiry as a *tertium comparationis* lies in their potential to establish a valuable dialogue between the past and the present. The analytical approaches explored in the case studies in this volume generally build upon existing theoretical frameworks, and the authors find ways to expand or modify them, applying them to a wide range of data. The researchers also combine various approaches in order to acquire in-depth insights into various parts of orthographic systems in specific historical and linguistic contexts, and offer their own contributions to the development of models of analysis. Chapter 3, for example, offers a new model of biscriptal isomorphism, applied to different levels of orthographic systems in specific sixteenth-century Church Slavonic texts. The contribution also reconsiders several basic units commonly used as foci of enquiry in the vast majority of research in orthography, including, for example, graph, grapheme and allograph. Likewise, Chapter 5 builds upon general premises of earlier studies and offers a new, comprehensive theoretical model, taking a cross-linguistic stance in order to gain insights into orthographic patterns from a diachronic and comparative graphematic perspective. Chapter 2 uses the traditional phonological–graphemic approach to investigate the functionality of Early Modern Polish spelling systems, but also combines it with socio-historical insights which explain the extralinguistic motivation behind the creation of new spelling systems, in particular the role of printers' practices as well as Czech influences in this process. In Chapter 4, the authors also contribute to the dialogue of past and present approaches, combining the factors considered in previous studies on capitalisation (especially reverence and animacy) with new or at least under-researched factors (word frequency, syntactic function, socio-pragmatic functions), moving the focus from printed to handwritten texts. Chapter 6, in turn, reconsiders the traditional views on the relation between variation and standardisation in Lithuanian orthography, in order to move on to the hitherto neglected aesthetic motivations behind spelling variation. A dynamic interaction between the past and the present can also be found in Chapter 7's aim to investigate methods: the approaches employed in previous research (separately and under various names) are brought together, their scopes and typical applications are compared and delimited, and necessary methodological conditions for each approach are specified.

One more inherent value of focusing on empirical models and methods as a basis for building scholarly dialogue in the future consists in the possibility of applying them across languages, which could result in interesting instances of cross-fertilisation. The model of quantitative analysis presented in Chapter 11 is applicable to virtually any other language, and promises to provide direct large-scale access to the complexity of longitudinal patterning of spelling and to open a broader perspective on the spelling regularisation process. Obviously, the necessary condition for the application of the model developed in Chapter 11 is the availability of sufficiently large and representative transcribed corpora, which, unfortunately, is not always the case for all languages. However, considering the ever increasing interest in corpus linguistics and, specifically, in the compilation of corpora in various languages, more advances in this field may soon become feasible. Chapter 10 shows that micro-level findings can provide useful insights into the nature of macro-level phenomena within the framework of diachronic orthography. This approach could well be extended to the investigation of similar phenomena in other languages in the early modern era, with focus on, for example, how the orthographic choices of individuals (including influential ones) relate to the selection of the variants which eventually become standardised. Chapter 7 draws on examples from printed documents in German, but, as a more linguistically informed approach to defining and comparing methods of analysis, it serves as a set of guidelines for orthographies more broadly. Likewise, the combination of philological and sociolinguistic approaches developed in Chapter 8 can be used to further our understanding of the motivations behind the formation of the 'dual standard' in orthographic conventions on a much broader scale, not least because the phenomenon of different standards for handwritten and printed texts seems to have been widespread across most of early modern Europe.

Another inherent value of empirical approaches to research in historical orthography lies in their potential to open interdisciplinary dialogue, which can be an invaluable source of innovation. Research in historical orthography as a scholarly discipline is not only defined in the constraints of a community of those who are interested in the discipline per se, but also encompasses a much larger audience of scholars, not least those interested in phonology, etymology, semantics, syntax, lexicography, sociolinguistics, socio-pragmatics, stylistics, corpus linguistics, philology, literature, history, art history, palaeography, bibliology and the history of the book. Empirical methods of analysis from each and every one of these fields of enquiry may potentially be relevant for researching in historical orthography, and shed new light on various aspects of the subject. The most obvious and basic example seems to be the link between orthography and phonology, which in the present volume is explored more explicitly in Chapters 2, 6, 8 and 9. In these chapters, the authors refer to correspondences between graphemes and phonemes in order to assess the functionality of the spelling conventions, compare the features of the orthographic system depending on the medium (handwritten and printed), and relate these correspondences to the distinction between the graphemic and graphetic levels. The models of analysis proposed in Chapters 4 and 5 incorporate semantic and syntactic components, which attempt to determine patterns of punctuation and capitalisation within the orthographic sub-systems of their language specialisms. Chapters 2, 8 and 10 also touch upon the interrelation between orthography and etymology, in order to explain patterns of change. Connections with philology are present in Chapters 5, 8 and 9, which demonstrates that this traditional discipline is still useful for investigations of orthography. Among the interdisciplinary approaches followed in the volume, the ones considering sociolinguistic, socio-pragmatic and stylistic factors have a particularly high explanatory value with regard to orthographic variation. These aspects are to a greater or lesser extent explored or touched upon in Chapters 2 to 6, 8 and 10, amongst others. The factors and pressures which could have interfered with orthography, as discussed in these chapters, comprise, for instance, local network norms, as well as the educational background and the gender of the writers. The list is definitely not exhaustive and could be easily expanded with additional examples; some of the areas of enquiry discussed here are less widely known and developed than others.

One young area towards which researchers interested in comparing methods of orthographic analysis could work together is that of materiality, understood as the medium in which orthographic elements, both handwritten and printed, are documented. Empirical insights into the medium work particularly well as a *tertium comparationis* in orthography, due to their links with areas like palaeography, bibliology and the history of the book. The chapters in this anthology show a tendency towards the analysis of printed documents, which should hardly surprise a scholar of early modern languages, given that the centuries under investigation in this collection are typically characterised by the rise of printing as a revolutionary technology. The volume, however, also contains chapters which focus on analytical approaches for handwritten texts, like Chapters 4, 6 and 10. Chapter 8 also makes use of handwritten texts, but in a dynamic way, as it compares orthographic systems in printed documents with those of manuscripts. Among the examples above, Chapter 6 provides a particularly interesting reference to the understanding of materiality and of its potential for influencing linguistic phenomena, emphasising the ideological and identity-boosting implications of the overall impression made by grandiose volumes, and resulting in the enhancement to the perceived prestige and importance of Lithuanian. It would be interesting to explore with new empirical methods whether such aesthetic motivations are merely idiosyncratic or can be identified in writers of different languages, and, if the latter is true, to what extent such preferences translated across to the selection of variants which eventually became standardised. More generally, these examples could encourage us to re-evaluate the centrality of handwritten material in the early modern era, and to focus our energies on finding a better balance between handwriting and printed orthography in any future dialogue on methods of orthographic enquiry across languages.

12.3   Considerations and Questions for the Future

In the previous section, we have attempted to demonstrate that the rationale followed in the present volume for collecting case studies, namely the focus on empirical approaches to researching orthographies, could work as an efficient tool to establish future lines of synergic dialogue and cross-fertilisation in historical orthography. Among the topics explored in the case studies, there seem to emerge some promising pathways for future empirical research that have a high potential for bringing new insights into orthographic variation not only for languages in the early modern era, but also within a broader historical spectrum. Some of the most remarkable pathways include the combination of traditional (e.g. philological) methods with a variety of sociolinguistic and socio-pragmatic approaches. Another element of interest relates to the progress made in the use of digitised material, and the approach to large corpora of texts in a more philological way, as well as the application of new empirical methods across languages. The consistent use of corpora witnesses to the researchers' growing reliance on corpus linguistics methods and also suggests that any potential future developments in corpus linguistics are likely to be relevant to research in orthography.

The analytical approaches presented in this book were geared to serving specific lines of research interests – which poses the question of whether future ecumenical dialogue in historical orthography (whether focused on empirical methods or not) should be guided by more theoretical planning. Abstract, theory-driven thinking would of course be a difficult task, given the number and the intricacy of the issues to be considered, for example, the relations between orthographies and other levels of language (phonology, morphology, syntax, semantics and others), including language-specific differences in orthographic systems. These concern, for instance, orthographic depth, the type of phonography and the amount of morphography.[8] It could be the case, therefore, that we need to look at historical orthography from a more pragmatic point of view. The co-existence of qualitative and quantitative approaches in the volume as a whole are evidence for the fact that both aspects are in fact important and will likely continue to be so in the future of the field. The advantages of a combined use of qualitative and quantitative approaches in historical orthography are potentially endless: qualitative analysis can provide great richness and precision, whereas quantitative analysis can provide statistically reliable and generalisable data. The mixed nature of the perspectives adopted in the present collection reflects a more general move in social science research towards a combined methodology, which favours the breadth of information that arises from the use of more than one approach.[9]

---

[8] Ibid., 273–5.   [9] McEnery and Wilson, *Corpus Linguistics*, 77.

There are clearly many other routes that one could take for the purposes described above, but there still remains an important question to be answered. Why do we expect so much from a comparative perspective? In the field of national languages and their histories, comparisons of selected orthographic features, of their development and their metalinguistic discourses are more or less obvious and self-evident. We believe that many interesting phenomena surface only during a second step, when we focus comparatively on entities of smaller order, on dialects, on other domains of exogenous variables or on certain endogenous features. There is much more than that, however. The distance that a scholar of a comparative study keeps from his or her objects of investigation is relatively greater. This has a direct impact on empirical work. The expansion of the scope of languages leads to the point where differences in detail between the objects of comparison lose their importance, and it is only at this stage that fundamental similarities become apparent. In other words, we suggest that comparability fosters new horizons of investigation and exploration, which may not necessarily be apparent to any scholar solely interested in individual philologies. Thus, the comparative historical approach is not merely about *l'art pour l'art* ('art for art's sake'); it carries a specific epistemological value. Since a comparison often determines differences between the compared objects, their possible causes are also brought into view. Starting from the description of differences between the objects of comparison, one has, almost automatically, arrived at the first attempts to explain linguistic change. For if the same conditions have led to different orthographic features, *differentia specifica* must exist and be responsible for this difference. The specific epistemological value of the comparative approach thus lies in its inherent explanatory potential, in the way it detects causes – or, more cautiously put, in the way it finds correlations that could be *interpreted* as causes. It is the comparative approach that actually makes causal analyses possible in the grand scheme of things.

Another advantage of a comparative perspective lies in the potential to resolve the old question of whether endogenous (internal systemic) or exogenous (external socio-cultural, political or economic) determinants were more responsible for the development and standardisation of individual orthographies. If taken individually, these determinants can act either as impulses or as limiting factors. Endogenous factors can hinder, weaken, slow down, or, on the contrary, reinforce, accelerate, or even help uncover the effects of exogenous factors. In order to explain complicated cases, comparisons across language families can be instructive. If systemically similar languages, e.g. from the Romance language family, develop differently in the period under study, regardless of their endogenous similarity, then different exogenous influences are likely to be the primary cause. If, on the other hand, systemically different languages – e.g. a Slavic and a Germanic one – develop in a similar way, then similar exogenous influences may have been the decisive factor. The comparison of languages with regard to their language families, therefore, does facilitate the identification of relevant exogenous determinants.

   That said, the advantages of a comparative, synergic approach to historical orthography as established above may appear insufficient to the most cynical readers in the face of all potential difficulties resulting from it. Anyone seeking to embark on a comparative pathway will have by now been made aware (if they were not already) of inevitable clashes and contradictions that stem from cultural, nationalistic, chronological and geographical limitations, and a potentially endless number of questions that are likely to remain unresolved for a long time. To give an example immediately relevant to the discussion developed in this chapter, it is not yet clear to us whether focusing on spelling can work as a feasible way to establish a commonly understood ground of dialogue on methods of orthographic research. Most of the authors in the present collection have focused on spelling, and rightly so as this is indeed the core unit where central changes and developments in historical orthography are attested to have taken place across languages. However, would continuing in this direction mean neglecting other areas of discussion, like punctuation and capitalisation? Or should more work be conducted in these other, hitherto often neglected, aspects of orthographic systems? And does a harmonious, well-balanced coverage of all aspects of orthography as a system necessarily mean progress in establishing a more universal approach to studying orthography across languages? Would it cause some languages to be discriminated against, or some areas of discussion to be neglected? Aside from these subject-specific questions, then, we also wonder how scholars of historical orthography can interact with cognate families of researchers. Should we gear our theoretical practices and protocols to work in synchrony with other fields which have been very much in vogue in recent times, for example historical sociolinguistics? What would such practices and protocols entail in pragmatic factors, and what would be the effects of comparing our practices with cognate communities of research? More visibility? More empirical rigour? More relevance in the family of historical linguistics? Should we even have to draw a line at all between scholars interested in orthography and those who explore other branches of historical linguistics?

   There are no definitive answers to these questions, but these and other issues undoubtedly represent interesting elements for future consideration. Continuing our discussion in this direction can lead us, as researchers, to a deeper awareness of the role and relevance of our scholarly efforts. While comparative approaches have been explored widely in other subfields of historical linguistics like phonology and syntax, this has not been the case for orthography. We are not sure if this is simply because of the relative youth of the field as such, or because of the complications that result from a comparative perspective in orthography. Nevertheless, we should not be discouraged by the complexities presented here. On the contrary, comparative research in historical orthography is a large, tantalising experimental laboratory, and much of the data, often already digitised, is just waiting to be captured. Overall, the present collection demonstrates a very promising step forward towards the synergy which may stem from interdisciplinary perspectives. In the midst of the difficulties resulting from attempting to contribute to such a monumental task, there are definitely some milestone targets that we can already identify. To give an example, from a theoretical and methodological point of view, arriving at generally accepted terminology would definitely be an asset, particularly for comparative, cross-linguistic studies. Merja Stenroos is one of the few scholars to date to have explicitly made reference to this issue: 'the description of orthography is a field undergoing development, and so far there seems to be no one established system of terminology in use'.[10] We agree with Stenroos's suggestions that a more explicit agreement on technical aspects in the field is important, and we are fully aware that this can be achieved only by improving discussion between scholars of different academic environments. We hope that our thoughts will initiate efforts towards a solid, long-lasting, synergic dialogue in the field.

---

[10] Stenroos, 'Regional dialects', 263.

Bibliography

Abad Nebot, F. 'Juan de Valdés y la conciencia lingüística de los Erasmistas españoles' [Juan de Valdés and the linguistic consciousness of the Spanish Erasmians], in M. Revuelta Sañudo and C. Morón Arroyo (eds.), *El Erasmismo en España. Ponencias del coloquio celebrado en la Biblioteca de Menéndez Pelayo del 10 al 14 de junio de 1985* [Erasmism in Spain. Presentations from the colloquium held at the Biblioteca de Menéndez Pelayo, 10–14 June 1985] (Santander: Sociedad Menéndez Pelayo, 1986), pp. 479–89.

Ackroyd, P. *Shakespeare: The Biography* (London: Random House, 2005).

Agata, M. 'Improvements, corrections, and changes in the *Gutenberg Bible*', in Thaisen and Rutkowska (eds.), *Scribes*, pp. 135–55.

Almeida Cabrejas, B. 'Escuchar los textos. El análisis de los textos en el estudio de la fonética y fonología de épocas pasadas' [Listening to texts. Text analysis in the study of the phonetics and phonology of bygone ages], *Lingüística en la Red*, 11 (2013), https://dialnet.unirioja.es/servlet/articulo?codigo=4714106 [last accessed 3 June 2020].

Alphabetum Boëmicum in quo singularum litterarum proprietates novâ & facili methodo proponuntur [Czech alphabet, in which the singular properties of the letters are presented in a new and easy way ...] (Prague: Karel František Rosenmüller senior, 1718), KPS no. K00129.

Amirova, T. I. *K istorii i teorii grafemiki* [Towards a history and theory of graphemics] (Moscow: Nauka, 1977).

Andrieux-Reix, N. and S. Monsonégo (eds.), *Segments graphiques du français. Pratiques et normalisations dans l'histoire* [Graphical segments of French. Practices and standardisation in history], *Langue Française*, 119 (1998).

Androutsopoulos, J. K. 'Non-standard spellings in media texts: the case of German fanzines', *Journal of Sociolinguistics*, 4 (4, 2000), pp. 514–33.

Andry de Boisregard, N. *Réflexions, ou Remarques Critiques sur L'usage Present de la Langue Françoise* [Critical reflections and notes on the current use of the French language], 2nd ed. (Paris: Laurent d'Houry, 1692), in Colombat et al. (compilers), *Grand Corpus*.

Anis, J. 'Les Linguistes français et la ponctuation' [French linguists and punctuation], *L'Information Grammaticale*, 102 (2004), pp. 5–10.

Anis, J. 'Pour une graphématique autonome' [Towards autonomous graphematics], *Langue française: Le Signifiant graphique*, 53 (1983), pp. 31–44.

Anis, J., J.-L. Chiss and Ch. Puech, *L'Écriture: théories et descriptions* [Writing: theories and descriptions] (Brussels: De Boeck University, 1988).

Anónimo de Lovaina, *Gramatica de la lengua vulgar de España* [Grammar of the Common Language of Spain] (Louvain: Bartolomé Gravio, 1559), facsimile edition in Gómez Asencio (ed.), *Antiguas gramáticas*.

Anthony, L. AntConc (version 3.5.6), www.laurenceanthony.net/software/antconc [last accessed 5 May 2020].

Aquino-Weber, D., S. Cotelli and A. Kristol, *Sociolinguistique historique du domaine gallo-roman: Enjeux et méthodologies* [Historical sociolinguistics of the Gallo-Roman domain: Issues and methodologies] (Bern: Peter Lang, 2009).

Arabyan, M. 'Histoire et emplois de l'alinéa ouvrant en diachronie (XIIIe–XVIIe siècles)' [History and diachronic uses of the opening paragraph (C13–C17)], *Signata. Annales des Sémiotiques*, 9 (2018), pp. 427–58.

Arabyan, M. 'La Notion de paragraphe en rédaction: Narration vs dissertation' [The notion of the paragraph in writing: story-telling versus commentary], *Le Français Aujourd'hui*, 187 (4, 2014), pp. 19–29.

Arabyan, M. *Le Paragraphe narratif. Étude typographique et linguistique de la ponctuation textuelle dans les récits classiques et modernes* [The narrative paragraph. Typographical and linguistic study of textual punctuation in classical and modern narratives] (Paris: L'Harmattan, 1994).

Archer, D., M. Kytö, A. Baron and P. Rayson, 'Guidelines for normalising Early Modern English corpora: Decisions and justifications', *ICAME Journal*, 39 (2015), pp. 7–42.

Arellano, I. 'La puntuación en los textos del Siglo de Oro y en el Quijote' [Punctuation in Golden Age Spanish texts and in the *Quijote*], *Anales Cervantinos*, 42 (2010), pp. 15–32.

Arias Álvarez, B. 'Problemas en el análisis gráfico de documentos novohispanos' [Problems in the graphical analysis of American-Spanish documents], in Girón Alconchel and de Bustos Tovar (eds.), *Actas del VI Congreso*, pp. 261–70.

Aristotle's Metaphysics, transl. J. Sachs, 2nd ed. (Santa Fe: Green Lion Press, 2002).

Aronoff, M. 'The orthographic system of an early English printer: Wynkyn de Worde', *Folia Linguistica Historica*, 8 (1–2, 1989), pp. 65–97.

Audisio, G. and I. Bonnot-Rambaud, *Lire le français d'hier. Manuel de paléographie moderne* [Reading yesterday's French. A manual of modern paleography] (Paris: Armand Colin, 2003).

Auer, A. and T. Fairman, 'Letters of artisans and the labouring poor (England, c. 1750–1835)', in P. Bennett, M. Durrell, S. Scheible and R. J. Whitt (eds.), *New Methods in Historical Corpus Linguistics* (Tübingen: Narr, 2013), pp. 77–91.

Auer, A. and A. Voeste, 'Grammatical variables', in Hernández-Campoy and Conde-Silvestre (eds.), *Handbook of Historical Sociolinguistics*, pp. 253–70.

Auer, P. 'Europe's sociolinguistic unity, or: A typology of European dialect-standard constellations', in N. Delbecque, J. van der Auwera and D. Geeraerts (eds.), *Perspectives on Variation* (Berlin: de Gruyter, 2005), pp. 7–42.

Augst, G. (ed.), *Graphematik und Orthographie* [Graphematics and orthography] (Frankfurt am Main; Bern; New York: Peter Lang, 1985).

Ayres-Bennett, W. *A History of the French Language through Texts* (London; New York: Routledge, 1996).

Azorín Fernández, D. and H. Provencio Garrigós, 'La puntuación en las obras editadas en los siglos XVI y XVII' [Punctuation in texts published during C16 and C17], in Sánchez Méndez et al. (eds.), *Temas, problemas y métodos*, pp. 437–68.

Baayen, R. H. *Analysing Linguistic Data: A Practical Introduction to Statistics Using R* (Cambridge: Cambridge University Press, 2008).

Baddeley, S. 'Accents, signes auxiliaires et signes de ponctuation: Leurs appellations chez les imprimeurs (XVIe–XVIIe siècles)' [Accents, special symbols and punctuation marks: The names given to them by printers in C16 and C17], *Le Français Préclassique 1550–1650*, 17 (2015), pp. 21–60.

Baddeley, S. 'French orthography in the 16th century', in Baddeley and Voeste (eds.), *Orthographies*, pp. 97–125.

Baddeley, S. *L'Orthographe française au temps de la réforme* [French orthography at the time of the Reformation] (Geneva: Droz, 1993).

Baddeley, S. 'Sources pour l'étude de la ponctuation française du XVIe siècle' [Sources for the study of C16 French punctuation], in N. Dubois and J. Dürrenmatt (eds.), *La Ponctuation à la Renaissance* [Punctuation in the Renaissance], (Paris: Garnier, 2011), pp. 191–227.

Baddeley, S. and A. Voeste, 'Introduction: Orthographies in early modern Europe: A comparative view', in Baddeley and Voeste (eds.), *Orthographies*, pp. 1–13.

Baddeley, S. and A. Voeste (eds.), *Orthographies in Early Modern Europe* (Berlin; Boston: de Gruyter, 2012).

Badiou-Monferran, C. '"Ponctuation noire", "ponctuation blanche" et "contes bleus": L'Évolution du codage des discours directs dans *La Barbe bleue* de Perrault (1695–1905)' ['Black punctuation', 'white punctuation' and '*contes bleus*': The evolution of the coding of direct speech in Perrault's *La Barbe bleue* (1695–1905)], in Parussa et al. (eds.), *Enregistrer la parole*, pp. 143–77.

Badiou-Monferran, C. (ed.), *La 'Rémanence': un concept opératoire pour la linguistique diachronique? Le cas du français* ['Persistence': a useful concept for diachronic linguistics? The case of French], special issue of *Le Français Moderne*, no. 2 (2020).

Bajerowa, I. *Kształtowanie się systemu polskiego języka literackiego w XVIII wieku* [The emergence of the Polish literary language system in C18] (Wrocław: ZNIO, 1964).

Bajerowa, I. 'Zanik samogłosek pochylonych w języku polskim jako wynik działania ogólniejszych tendencji językowych' [The disappearance of narrow vowels in the Polish language as the result of general linguistic tendencies], *Sprawozdania z Posiedzeń Komisji Polskiej Akademii Nauk. Oddział w Krakowie*, 7 (1963), pp. 103–21.

Baranda, N. 'Mujeres y escritura en el Siglo de Oro: Una relación inestable' [Women and writing in the Spanish Golden Age: An unstable relationship], *Litterae, Cuadernos de Cultura Escrita* (3–4, 2003–4), pp. 61–83.

Bargieł, M. *Cechy dialektalne polskich zabytków rękopiśmiennych pierwszej połowy XVI wieku* [Dialectal features of Polish manuscripts from the first half of C16] (Wrocław: ZNIO, 1969).

Baron, A. and P. Rayson, 'Automatic standardization of texts containing spelling variation: How much training data do you need?', in M. Mahlberg, V. González-Díaz and C. Smith (eds.), *Proceedings of the Corpus Linguistics Conference, CL2009*, 20–23 July 2009 (Liverpool: University of Liverpool, 2009), http://ucrel.lancs.ac.uk/publications/cl2009/314_FullPaper.pdf [last accessed 3 June 2020].

Baron, A., P. Rayson and D. Archer, 'Automatic standardization of spelling for historical text mining', Digital Humanities 2009 (University of Maryland, 22–25 June 2009).

Baron, A., P. Rayson and D. Archer, 'Innovators of Early Modern English Spelling Change: Using DICER to Investigate Spelling Variation Trends', Helsinki Corpus Festival (Helsinki, 28 September–2 October 2011), https://www.slideshare.net/VARIE NG/innovators-of-the-early-modern-english-spelling-change-using-dicer-to-investigate -spelling-variation-trends [last accessed 9 May 2020].

Baron, A., P. Rayson and D. Archer, 'Quantifying Early Modern English spelling variation: change over time and genre', Conference on New Methods in Historical Corpora (University of Manchester 29–30 April 2011).

Baron, A., P. Rayson and D. Archer, 'Word frequency and key word statistics in historical corpus linguistics', *Anglistik: International Journal of English Studies*, 20 (1, 2009), pp. 41–67.

Barootes, B. S. W. '"In fourme of speche is chaunge": Final -e in Troilus and Criseyde, book II, lines 22–28'. *The Chaucer Review*, 53 (1, 2018), pp. 102–11.

Barteld, F., R. Szczepaniak and H. Zinsmeister, 'The definition of tokens in relation to words and annotation tasks', in V. Henrich, E. Hinrichs, D. de Kok, P. Osenova and A. Przepiórkowski (eds.), *Proceedings of the Thirteenth International Workshop on Treebanks and Linguistic Theories, TLT13* (Tübingen: University of Tübingen, 2014), pp. 250–7, http://tlt13.sfs.uni-tuebingen.de/tlt13-proceedings.pdf [last accessed 3 June 2020].

Barteld, F., S. Hartmann and R. Szczepaniak, 'The usage and spread of sentence-internal capitalisation in Early New High German: A multifactorial approach', *Folia Linguistica*, 50 (2, 2016), pp. 385–412.

Bartoš, F. M. *Soupis rukopisů Národního musea v Praze* I, II [Catalogue of manuscripts of the National Museum of Prague I, II] (Prague: Melantrich, 1926–7).

Bartoszewicz, A. *Piśmienność mieszczańska w późnośredniowiecznej Polsce* (Warsaw: WUW, 2012). [English edition: A. Bartoszewicz, *Urban Literacy in Late Medieval Poland* (Turnhout: Brepols, 2017).]

Barzizza, G. *Gasparini Pergamensis orthographia liber* [Gasparino Pergamensis's book of orthography] (Paris: U. Gering, M. Crantz, M. Friburger, 1470), https:// gallica.bnf.fr/ark:/12148/bpt6k131477g/f474.image [last accessed 11 June 2020].

Barzizza, G. *Liber de arte punctandi* [The book on the art of punctuation], MS, Bibliothèque nationale de France, MS lat. 8731, https://gallica.bnf.fr/ark:/12148/btv 1b10035384j/ [last accessed 18 April 2020], fols. 35–40.

Basu, A. '"Ill shapen sounds, and false orthography": A computational approach to Early English orthographic variation', in L. Estill, D. Jackaki and M. Ullyot (eds.), *Early Modern Studies after the Digital Turn* (Tempe: Iter and Arizona Center for Medieval and Renaissance Studies, 2016), pp. 167–200.

Basu, A. and S. Pentecost, 'EEBO N-Gram Browser' (Saint Louis: Humanities Digital Workshop at Washington University in Saint Louis, 2014), https://earlyprint .wustl.edu [last accessed 5 May 2020].

Bataillon, M. 'Diego de Enzinas en Amberes: Ortografía castellana de un libro prohibido' [Diego de Enzinas in Antwerp: Castilian spelling of a forbidden book], in M. Bataillon, D. Devoto and C. Amiel (eds.), *Erasme et l'Espagne* [Erasmus and Spain], vol. 3 (Geneva: Droz, 1991), pp. 249–75.

Bates, D., M. Mächler, B. Bolker and S. Walker, 'Fitting linear mixed-effects models using lme4', *Journal of Statistical Software*, 67 (1, 2015), pp. 1–48.

Baugh, A. C. and T. H. Cable, *A History of the English Language*, 6th ed. (London: Routledge, 2012 [1951]).

Bédmar Sancristóbal, M. E. 'Problemas de edición de textos manuscritos modernos: la puntuación' [Problems on editing modern manuscript texts: punctuation], in L. Pons (ed.), *Historia de la lengua y crítica textual* [Language history and textual criticism] (Madrid, Frankfurt am Main: Iberoamericana-Vervuert, 2006), pp. 127–80.

Behr, M. *Buchdruck und Sprachwandel. Schreibsprachliche und textstrukturelle Varianz in der 'Melusine' des Thüring von Ringoltingen (1473/74–1692/93)* [Book printing and language change. Graphic and textual variance in Thüring von Ringoltingen's 'Melusina' (1473/74–1692/93)] (Berlin; Boston: de Gruyter, 2014).

Bellosta von Colbe, V. 'Is role and reference grammar an adequate grammatical theory for punctuation?', in R. D. Van Valin, Jr (ed.), *Investigations of the Syntax–Semantics–Pragmatics Interface* (Amsterdam and Philadelphia: John Benjamins, 2008), pp. 245–62.

Beltrán, E. 'Un traité inconnu de Guillaume Fichet sur la ponctuation' [An unknown treatise on punctuation, by Guillaume Fichet], *Scriptorium*, 39 (1985), pp. 284–91.

Benskin, M., M. Laing, V. Karaiskos and K. Williamson, *An Electronic Version of a Linguistic Atlas of Late Mediaeval English*, http://www.lel.ed.ac.uk/ihd/elalme/elalme.html [last accessed 4 May 2020].

Berg, K. and M. Aronoff, 'Self-organization in the spelling of English suffixes: the emergence of culture out of anarchy', *Language*, 93 (1, 2017), pp. 37–64.

Berger, T. 'Religion and diacritics: The case of Czech orthography', in Baddeley and Voeste (eds.), *Orthographies*, pp. 255–68.

Berger, T. 'Užívání češtiny jako úředního jazyka v druhé polovině 18. století na příkladě města Chrudimě' [Using Czech as a language of administration in the second half of C18: the example of the town of Chrudim], in V. Petrbok, R. Lunga and J. Tydlität (eds.), *Východočeská duchovní a slovesná kultura v 18. století. Sborník příspěvků ze sympozia konaného 27.–29. 5. 1999 v Rychnově nad Kněžnou* [East Bohemian spiritual and literary culture in C18. Collection of papers from the symposium held at 27 to 29 May 1999 in Rychnov nad Kněžnou] (Boskovice: Albert, 1999), pp. 43–78.

Bergmann, R. 'Zur Herausbildung der deutschen Substantivgroßschreibung. Ergebnisse des Bamberg-Rostocker Projekt' [On the evolution of German noun capitalisation. Results of the Bamberg–Rostock project], in Hoffmann et al. (eds.), *Das Frühneuhochdeutsche*, pp. 59–79.

Bergmann, R. and D. Nerius, *Die Entwicklung der Großschreibung im Deutschen von 1500–1700* [The evolution of capitalisation in German from 1500 to 1700], 2 vols. (Heidelberg: Winter, 1998).

Bergs, A. *Social Networks and Historical Sociolinguistics: Studies in Morphosyntactic Variation in the Paston Letters (1421–1503)* (Berlin: de Gruyter, 2005).

Besch, W. 'Entstehung und Ausformung der neuhochdeutschen Schriftsprache/Standardsprache' [Origin and formation of the New High German written/standard language], in Besch et al. (eds.), *Sprachgeschichte*, vol. 3, pp. 2252–96.

Besch, W. 'Sprachliche Änderungen in Lutherbibel-Drucken des 16.–18. Jahrhunderts' [Linguistic changes in printed edition of the Luther Bible C16–C18], in J. Schildt (ed.), *Luthers Sprachschaffen. Gesellschaftliche Grundlagen, geschichtliche Wirkungen* [Luther's (influence on German) language formation. Societal foundations, historical effects] (Berlin: Akademie der Wissenschaften, 1984), pp. 108–33.

Besch, W., A. Betten, O. Reichmann and St. Sonderegger (eds.), *Sprachgeschichte. Ein Handbuch zur Geschichte der deutschen Sprache und ihrer Erforschung* [History of language. A handbook on the history of the German language and research on it], 2nd ed., vols. 1 and 3 (Berlin; New York: de Gruyter, 2003).

Biblioteca Digital Hispánica [Spanish digital library]. Biblioteca Nacional de España, http://www.bne.es/es/Catalogos/BibliotecaDigitalHispanica/Inicio/index.html [last accessed 16 April 2020].

Bičan, A. 'Fonématika' [Phonemics], in Karlík et al. (eds.), *CzechEncy*, https://www.czechency.org/slovnik/FONÉMATIKA [last accessed 3 June 2020].

Biedermann-Pasques, L. *Les Grands Courants orthographiques au XVIe siècle et la formation de l'orthographe moderne* [Major orthographical trends in the C16 and the formation of modern spelling] (Tübingen: Niemeyer, 1992).

Bikialo, S. and J. Rault (eds.), *Imaginaires de la ponctuation. Ordre et inquiétude du discours* [Imaginary punctuation. Order and chaos in discourse], *Linx*, 75 (2017).

Blahoslav, J. *Grammatica čefká, od Knĕza Benefſe Optáta, a od Knĕze Wáclawa Filomátefa predeſſlých let wydaná . . .* [Czech grammar published several years ago by priests Beneš Optát and Václav Filomátes], manuscript, 1571 (copy c. 1670), Moravian Provincial Library, Brno, Rkp 114 (RKP2-0047.982).

Blake, N. F. 'Manuscript to print', in J. Griffiths and D. Pearsall (eds.), *Book Production and Publishing in Britain 1375–1475* (Cambridge: Cambridge University Press, 1989), pp. 403–33.

Blake, N. F. 'Early Modern English', in C. Nocera Avila, N. Pantaleo and D. Pezzini (eds.), *Early Modern English: Trends, Forms and Texts* (Fasano: Schena editore, 1992), pp. 13–37.

Blake, N. F. 'English versions of "Reynard the Fox" in the fifteenth and sixteenth centuries', *Studies in Philology*, 62 (1965), pp. 63–77.

Blas Arroyo, J. L. 'Tras las huellas de la variación y el cambio lingüístico a través de textos de inmediatez comunicativa: Fundamentos de un proyecto de sociolingüística histórica' [Following the traces of variation and linguistic change through texts of communicative immediacy: Foundations of a historical sociolinguistics project], in García Martín (ed.), *Actas*, vol. 2, pp. 1737–56.

Blažević Krezić, V. *Književnimi radnjami za crkvu i domovinu. O novocrkvenoslavenskome jeziku* Parčićeva misala *iz 1893*. [Literary works for church and homeland. On the New Church Slavonic language of Parčić's *Missal* of 1893] (Zagreb: Matica hrvatska, 2020).

Blecua, J. M. 'Notas sobre la puntuación española hasta el Renacimiento' [Notes on Spanish punctuation up to the Renaissance], in M. R. Alonso and J. del Agua (eds.), *Homenaje a Julián Marías* [Studies in honour of Julián Marías] (Madrid: Espasa-Calpe, 1984), pp. 121–30.

Blommaert, J. *Supervernaculars and their Dialects*, King's College London Working Papers in Urban Languages and Literacies, 81 (2011), https://www.kcl.ac.uk/ecs/research/research-centres/ldc/publications/workingpapers/the-papers/wp81.pdf [last accessed 4 June 2020].

Bock, M. 'Lesen in Abhängigkeit von der Groß- und Kleinschreibung' [Reading as a function of upper- and lowercase spelling], *Sprache und Kognition*, 8 (3, 1989), pp. 191–209.

Bock, M., K. Hagenschneider and A. Schweer, 'Zur Funktion der Groß- und Kleinschreibung beim Lesen deutscher, englischer und niederländischer Texte' [On the function of upper- and lowercase spelling in the reading of German, English and Dutch texts], in Eisenberg and Günther (eds.), *Schriftsystem und Orthographie*, pp. 23–55.

Bončkutė, R. 'Alberto Vijūko-Kojalavičiaus veikalo *Historia Lituana* recepcija Simono Daukanto darbe "Istorija Žemaitiška"' [Reception of Albertas Vijūkas Kojelavičius's opus *Historia Lituana* in Simonas Daukantas's work 'History of the Lithuanian Lowlands'], *Senoji Lietuvos literatūra* 27 (2009), pp. 353–76.

Borecki, M. *Kształtowanie się normy językowej w drukach polskich xvi wieku (na przykładzie oboczności typu* pirwszy ‖ pierwszy) [The formation of a linguistic norm in C16 Polish printed texts (with special reference to *pirwszy ‖ pierwszy* type alternations)] (Warsaw; Cracow: ZNIO and Polish Academy of Sciences, 1974).

Boscán, J. *Las obras de Boscán y algunas de Garcilasso de la Vega: Repartidas en quatro libros* [The works of Boscán and some of Garcilasso de la Vega, distributed in four books] (Barcelona, Carles Amorós, 1543).

Bosquet, J. *Elemens ou Institutions de la langue françoise* [Elements or institutions of the French language] (Mons: Charles Michel, 1586), in Colombat et al. (compilers), *Grand Corpus*.

Boucheron-Pétillon, S. *Les Détours de la langue. Étude sur la parenthèse et le tiret double* [Detours of language. A study of brackets and the double hyphen] (Louvain; Paris: Peeters, 2003).

Brajerski, T. *O języku polskim dawnym i dzisiejszym* [On the historical and modern Polish language] (Lublin: KUL, 1995).

Branca-Rosoff, S. 'Deux points, ouvrez les guillemets: notes sur la ponctuation du discours rapporté au XVIIIe siècle' [Colon, begin quotation: notes on the punctuation of C18 discourse], *Le Gré des Langues*, 5 (1993), pp. 178–202.

Branca-Rosoff, S. 'Sociolinguistique historique et analyse du discours du côté de l'histoire: Un chantier commun?' [Historical sociolinguistics and discourse analysis on a historical period: A common project?], *Langage et Société*, 121–2 (2007), pp. 163–76, https://www.cairn.info/revue-langage-et-societe-2007-3-page-163.htm [last accessed 4 June 2020].

Branca-Rosoff, S. and N. Schneider, *L'Écriture des citoyens: Une analyse linguistique de l'écriture des peu-lettrés pendant la période révolutionnaire* [The writing of citizens: A linguistic analysis of the writing of the semi-literate during the revolutionary period] (Paris: Klincksieck, 1994).

Bravo García, E. M. 'Indicadores sociolingüísticos en la documentación indiana (Cartas e informes de particulares)' [Sociolinguistic indicators in Indian documentation (Letters and reports by individuals)], in W. Oesterreicher, E. Stoll and A. Wesch (eds.), *Competencia escrita, tradición discursiva y variedades lingüísticas. El español en los siglos XVI y XVII* [Written competence, discursive tradition and linguistic varieties. Spanish in C16 and C17] (Tübingen: Narr, 1998), pp. 125–42.

Brengelman, F. H. 'Orthoepists, printers, and the rationalization of English spelling', *The Journal of English and Germanic Philology*, 79 (3, 1980), pp. 332–54.

Bruthiaux, P. 'Knowing when to stop: Investigating the nature of punctuation', *Language and Communication*, 13 (1, 1993), pp. 27–43.

Bučar, F. and F. Fancev, 'Bibliografija hrvatske protestantske književnosti za reformacije' [Bibliography of Croatian Protestant literature during the Reformation], *Starine JAZU*, 39 (1938), pp. 49–125.

Bunčić, D. 'In-group spelling in Novgorod birch-bark letters', in K. Juffermans and C. Weth (eds.), *The Tyranny of Writing: Ideologies of the Written Word* (London: Bloomsbury, 2018).

Bunčić, D. 'Introduction', in Bunčić et al. (eds.), *Biscriptality*, pp. 15–26.

Bunčić, D. 'The standardization of Polish orthography in the 16th century', in Baddeley and Voeste (eds.), *Orthographies*, pp. 219–54.

Bunčić, D., S. L. Lippert and A. Rabus (eds.), *Biscriptality: A Sociolinguistic Typology* (Heidelberg: Winter, 2016).

Bünting, K. D. *Einführung in die Linguistik* [Introduction to linguistics] (Königstein: Athenäum, 1981).

Buridant, C. *Grammaire du français médiéval* [Grammar of medieval French] [1st ed., 2000] (Strasbourg: Société de Linguistique Romane, 2019).

Buridant, C. '*Varietas delectat*. Prolégomènes à une grammaire de l'ancien français' [*Varietas delectat*. Prolegomena to a grammar of Old French], *Vox Romanica*, 55 (1996), pp. 87–125.

Burke, W. E. 'Let's get physical: Bibliography, codicology, and seventeenth-century women's manuscripts', *Literature Compass*, 4/6 (2007), pp. 1667–82.

Burkhard, C. 'Zur Ungleichzeitigkeit in der Weltgesellschaft. Erkenntnistheoretische Kommentare zur Kriegsursachenforschung, Arbeitspapier 1/2002' [Non-simultaneity in global society. Comments on the study of the causes of wars from the perspective of theory of knowledge] (Working Paper, University of Hamburg) https://core.ac.uk/download/pdf/71735506.pdf [last accessed 4 June 2020].

Bustos Tovar, J. J. 'Las propuestas ortográficas de Gonzalo Correas' [Spelling proposals by Gonzalo Correas], *DICENDA, Cuadernos de Filología Hispánica*, 16 (1998), pp. 41–62.

Capdevilla, L., S. Cassagnes, M. Cocaud, D. Godineau, F. Rouquet and J. Sainclivier, *Le Genre face aux mutations: masculin et féminin, du moyen âge à nos jours* [Gender in the face of change: male and female, from the Middle Ages to the present] (Rennes: PUR, 2003).

Carrasco Santos, I. and P. Carrasco Santos, 'Las ordenanzas sevillanas de 1492: grafemática y fonética de sus versiones manuscritas' [The Sevillian ordinances of 1492: graphematics and phonetics of their handwritten versions], in E. M. Cartelle and C. M. Rovira (eds.), *Actas del VIII Congreso Internacional de Historia de la Lengua Española (Santiago de Compostela 14–18 de Septiembre 2009)* [Proceedings of the VIII International Congress of History of the Spanish Language (Santiago de Compostela, 14–18 September 2009)] (Madrid: Meubook/AHLE, 2011), pp. 641–52.

Carrasco Santos, P. 'Análisis fonético fonológico y gráfico de los documentos malagueños (s. XVI)' [Phonetic, phonological and graphical analysis of documents from Malaga (C16)], in I. Carrasco (ed.), *Textos para la historia del español* [Texts for the history of Spanish], vol. 7 (Alcalá de Henares: Universidad de Alcalá de Henares, 2012).

Castillo Gómez, A. 'Del tratado a la práctica. La escritura epistolar en los siglos XVI y XVII' [From treatise to practice. Epistolary writing in C16 and C17], in C. Sáez Sánchez and A. Castillo Gómez (eds.), *Congreso Internacional de Historia de la Cultura Escrita* [International Congress on the History of Literacy], vol. 1 (Alcalá de Henares: Calambur, 2002), pp. 79–107.

Catach, N. 'La Ponctuation' [Punctuation], *Langue Française*, 45 (1980), pp. 16–27.

Catach, N. *La Ponctuation: histoire et système* [Punctuation: history and system] (Paris: PUF, 1994).

Catach, N. *L'Orthographe française à l'époque de la renaissance* [French orthography in the Renaissance] (Geneva: Droz, 1968).

Cattan, M. 'Cuestiones de género y autoría: La retórica clásica en la *Instrucción* de Titu Cusi Yupanqui' [Gender and authorship: classical rhetoric in Titu Cusi Yupanqui's *Instrucción*], *Revue Romane*, 49 (1, 2014), pp. 120–46.

Cazal, Y. and G. Parussa, *Introduction à l'histoire de l'orthographe* [Introduction to the history of orthography] (Paris: Armand Colin, 2015).

Čejka, M. 'Srovnání Devotyho opisu Loutny české Adama Michny z Otradovic s původním tiskem' [A comparison of Devoty's transcription of 'Czech Lute' by Adam Michna z Otradovic with the original printed version], in G. Zand and J. Holý (eds.), *Tschechisches Barock: Sprache, Literatur, Kultur = České baroko: Jazyk, literatura, kultura* [Czech Baroque: language, literature, culture] (Frankfurt am Main: Peter Lang, 1999), pp. 34–42.

Ceković, B. 'Grafematičke osobitosti glagoljičnog izdanja *Artikula* (1562)', in Kuštović and Žagar (eds.), *Meandrima hrvatskoga glagoljaštva*, pp. 41–56.

Ceković, B., I. Eterović, T. Kuštović and M. Žagar, *Misal hruacki Šimuna Kožičića Benje: Latinička transliteracija glagoljskog izvornika . . .* [The Croatian Missal of Šimun Kožičić Benja: transliteration into Latin script of the Glagolitic edition . . .] (Zagreb: NSK, 2016).

Ceković, B., I. Eterović, T. Kuštović and M. Žagar (eds.), *Artikuli ili deli stare krstjanske vere, Urach 1562: Glagoljski izvornik prepisali latinicom i usporedili s ćiriličkim izdanjem* [Articles or parts of the old Christian faith: Glagolitic edition transliterated into Latin script and compared with the Cyrillic edition] (Zagreb: NSK, 2017).

Černá, A. M. 'Specifika pravopisného úzu rukopisných textů 16. století' [Specifics of the orthography of the manuscript texts from C16], in Čornejová et al. (eds.), *Dějiny českého pravopisu*, pp. 224–34.

Cerquiglini, B. *L'Accent du souvenir* [The accent of remembrance] (Paris: Minuit, 1995).

Cerquiglini, B. *Le Roman de l'orthographe. Au paradis des mots, avant la faute (1150–1694)* [The story of spelling. In the paradise of words, before the fall (1150–1694)] (Paris: Hatier, 1996).

Cerquiglini, B. 'L'Orthographe des *Précieuses*' [The orthography of the *Précieuses*], in *La Genèse de l'orthographe française (XIIe–XVIIe siècles)* [The genesis of French orthography (C12–C17)] (Paris: Champion, 2004), pp. 133–9.

Cervantes, M. de, *El ingenioso hidalgo don Quixote de la Mancha* [The ingenious Gentleman Don Quixote of La Mancha] (Madrid: Juan de la Cuesta, 1605), http://www.cervantesvirtual.com/obra/el-ingenioso-hidalgo-don-quixote-de-la-mancha–9/ [last accessed 23 May 2020].

Chanson de Roland [The song of Roland], MS, University of Oxford, Bodleian Libraries, MS Digby 23.

Chanson de Saint Alexis [The song of Saint Alexis], MS, Hildesheim, Dombibliothek, Saint Godehard, No. 1, fols. 57–68.

CHARTA: Corpus hispánico y americano en la red [Spanish and American corpus on the web], www.redcharta.es/ [last accessed 30 March 2020].

Chartier, R. *La Main de l'auteur et l'esprit de l'imprimeur* [The author's hand and the printer's mind] (Paris: Gallimard, 2015).

Chrisomalis, S. *Numerical Notation: A Comparative History* (Cambridge: Cambridge University Press, 2010).

CICA: *Corpus Informatizat del Català Antic* [Computerised corpus of Old Catalan], www.cica.cat [last accessed 30 March 2020].

CODEA+ 2015: *Corpus de documentos españoles anteriores a 1800* [Corpus of Spanish documents from before 1800], Universidad de Alcalá de Henares, http://corpuscodea.es/ [last accessed 30 March 2020].

Codex Aemilianensis 60, *Sermones et Homiliae* [Codex from the monastery of San Millán de la Cogolla 60: Sermons and Homilies], MS, Real Academia de la Historia, Madrid.

Colombat, B., J.-M. Fournier and W. Ayres-Bennett (compilers), *Grand corpus des grammaires françaises, des remarques et des traités sur la langue (XIVe–XVIIe s.)* [Great corpus of French language grammars, commentaries and treatises on language (C14–C17)] (Paris: Classiques Garnier, 2011), classiques-garnier.com/numerique/ [last accessed 3 June 2020].

Colombo Timelli, M. 'Les Dialogues dans les *Cent nouvelles nouvelles*. Marques linguistiques et (typo)graphiques, entre manuscrit et imprimé' [Dialogues in *Les Cent nouvelles nouvelles*. Linguistic and typographical marks, between manuscript and printed texts], in Parussa et al. (eds.), *Enregistrer la parole*, pp. 123–41.

Comrie, B. *Language Universals and Linguistic Typology* (Chicago: University of Chicago Press, 1981).

Conde-Silvestre, J. C. and J. M. Hernández-Campoy, 'A sociolinguistic approach to the diffusion of Chancery written practices in late fifteenth century private correspondence', *Neuphilologische Mitteilungen*, 105 (2004), pp. 133–52.

Conde-Silvestre, J. C. and J. M. Hernández-Campoy, 'Tracing the generational progress of language change in fifteenth-century English: the digraph in the "Paston letters"', *Neuphilologische Mitteilungen*, 114 (3, 2013), pp. 279–99.

Coote, E. *The English Schoole-Maister Teaching all his Scholers, the Order of Distinct Reading, and True Writing our English Tongue* (London: Printed by the widow Orwin, for Ralph Iackson, and Robert Dextar, 1596), https://search.proquest.com/eebo [last accessed 28 Dec. 2018].

CORDE – Corpus diacrónico del español [Diachronic corpus of Spanish], https://www.rae.es/recursos/banco-de-datos/corde [last accessed 11 May 2020].

Čornejová, M., L. Rychnovská and J. Zemanová (eds.), *Dějiny českého pravopisu (do r. 1902). Sborník příspěvků z mezinárodní konference Dějiny českého pravopisu (do r. 1902). 23.–25. září 2010, Brno, Česká Republika* [History of Czech orthography (up to 1902). Proceedings of the International Conference History of Czech Orthography (up to 1902). 23–25 September 2010, Brno] (Brno: Masaryk University, 2010).

Corpus del español [Spanish language corpus], www.corpusdelespanol.org [last accessed 30 March 2020].

Corpus of Early English Correspondence, http://www.helsinki.fi/varieng/CoRD/corpora/CEEC/pceec.html [last accessed 5 May 2020].

Coseriu, E. *Principios de semántica estructural* [Principles of structural semantics], 2nd ed. (Madrid: Gredos, 1981).

Coseriu, E. 'Structure lexicale et enseignement du vocabulaire' [Lexical structure and vocabulary teaching], in S. M. Lamb, B. L. Pottier and G. Bourquin (eds.), *Actes du Premier Colloque International de Linguistique Appliquée. Organisé par la Faculté des Lettres et Sciences Humaines de l'Université de Nancy (26–31 octobre 1964)* [Proceedings of the First International Colloquium on Applied Linguistics. Organised by the Faculty of Arts and Humanities of the University of Nancy (26–31 October 1964)] (Nancy: Mémoires des Annales de l'Est, 1966), pp. 175–252.

Coulmas, F. *The Writing Systems of the World* (Oxford; Cambridge: Basil Blackwell, 1991).

Coulmas, F. *Writing Systems: An Introduction to their Linguistic Analysis* (Cambridge: Cambridge University Press, 2012).

Craig, H. and R. Whipp, 'Old spellings, new methods: automated procedures for indeterminate linguistic data', *Literary and Linguistic Computing*, 25 (1, 2010), pp. 37–52.

Crick, J. C. and A. Walsham, *The Uses of Script and Print, 1300–1700* (Cambridge: Cambridge University Press, 2004).

Crystal, D. *Making a Point: The Pernickety Story of English Punctuation* (London: Profile Books, 2015).

Culpeper, J. and M. Kytö (compilers), *A Corpus of English Dialogues: 1560–1760*, CD-ROM (Uppsala: Uppsala University, 2006).

Cybulski, M. *Język piętnastowiecznej części Psałterza floriańskiego. Ortografia, fonetyka, fleksja* [The language of C15 part of the Saint Florian Psalter. Orthography, phonetics, inflection] (Łódź: Łódź University, 1988).

Cybulski, M. 'Na obrzeżach głównego nurtu. O grafii urzędowych rękopisów średniopolskich' [On the fringes of the main tendencies. On the spelling of Middle-Polish official manuscripts], in Kuźmicki and Osiewicz (eds.), *Dokument pisany*, pp. 167–88.

Cyran, W. 'Ślady iloczasu w głównych zabytkach języka polskiego XIV i XV wieku' [Traces of vowel length in the most prominent historical texts in Polish form of C14 and C15], *Biuletyn Polskiego Towarzystwa Językoznawczego*, 11 (1952), pp. 1–21.

Dahlet, V. *Ponctuation et énonciation* [Punctuation and enunciation] (Guadeloupe: Ibis Rouge Éditions, 2003).

Dalmatin, A. and S. Konzul [Istrianin], *Parvi del posztile evanyeliov, koi sze vszaku nedillu po obitsayu otsito u czrikvi tstu . . .* [The first part of the homilies that are read every Sunday in church . . .] (Regensburg, 1568).

Damjanović, S. 'Kakav je jezik za knjige prikladan (Neke napomene uz jezikoslovne dvojbe hrvatskih protestanata)' [What kind of language is suitable for books (Remarks on the linguistic dilemma of the Croatian Protestants)], in Damjanović, *Novi filološki prinosi*, pp. 130–9.

Damjanović, S. *Novi filološki prinosi* [New philological contributions] (Zagreb: Matica hrvatska, 2014).

Daukantas, S. *Budą Senowęs-Lëtuwiû Kalnienû ir Żámajtiû* [The character of the ancient Lithuanians, Highlanders and Samogitians] (Saint Petersburg: C. Hintze, 1845).

Daukantas, S. 'Didysis lenkų–lietuvių kalbų žodynas' [Great Polish–Lithuanian dictionary], manuscript, 1852–6 and 1858, Library of the Institute of Literature and Folklore in Vilnius, Lithuania, call no. f. 1 – SD 12; ed. by Giedrius Subačius and published as *Didysis lenkų–lietuvių kalbų žodynas*, 3 vols. (Vilnius: MELC, 1993–6).

Daukantas, S. 'Istoryje Zemaytyszka' [History of the Lithuanian Lowlands], manuscript, 1831–4, Institute of Lithuanian Literature and Folklore in Vilnius, call no. f. 1 – SD 2.

Daukantas, S. *Prasmą Łotinû Kałbôs, Paraszę K. W. Myle* (pseudonym of Daukantas) [Understanding of the Latin language, written by K. W. Myle] (Saint Petersburg: K. Hintze, 1837).

Daukantas, S. (ed.), *Ch. F. Lhomond, Epitome historiae sacrae* [Lhomond, an abridgement of the holy history] (Saint Petersburg: Hintze, 1838).

Dauvois, N. and J. Dürrenmatt (eds.), *La Ponctuation à la renaissance* [Punctuation in the Renaissance] (Paris: Garnier, 2011).

Davis, N. 'The language of the Pastons', in J. Burrow (ed.), *Middle English Literature: British Academy Gollancz Lectures* (Oxford: Oxford University Press, 1954), pp. 45–70.

Daybell, J. *Women Letter-Writers in Tudor England* (Oxford: Oxford University Press, 2006).

Decyk-Zięba, W. 'Ortografia Stanisława Zaborowskiego' [The orthography of Stanisław Zaborowski], *Poradnik Językowy*, 5 (2014), pp. 101–9.

Demaizière, C. *L'Écriture des femmes à la renaissance française* [The writing of women in the French Renaissance] (Montreal: McGill University, 1998).

Demonet, M.-L. 'Ponctuation et narration chez Rabelais et ses contemporains' [Punctuation and narration in Rabelais and his contemporaries], in J. Dürrenmatt (ed.), *La ponctuation* [Punctuation] (Poitiers: Université de Poitiers, 2000), pp. 37–62.

Demonet, M.-L. 'Rhétorique de l'écrit imprimé à la Renaissance' [Rhetoric of printed texts from the Renaissance], *Dossiers d'HEL, SHESL, Écriture(s) et Représentations du Langage et des Langues*, 9 (2016), pp. 146–61.

Demonet, M.-L. 'Tentatives de modernisation de la langue et des graphies à la Renaissance' [Attempts to modernise language and writing in the Renaissance], *Revue de l'Académie de l'Orléanais* (2016), pp. 77–98.

Denison, D. and N. Yáñez-Bouza (compilers), ARCHER: A Representative Corpus of Historical English Registers, https://www.projects.alc.manchester.ac.uk/archer/ [last accessed 10 May 2020].

Deumert, A. *Sociolinguistics and Mobile Communication* (Edinburgh: Edinburgh University Press, 2014).

Diccionario de abreviaturas novohispanas [Dictionary of American-Spanish abbreviations], Universidad Nacional Autónoma de México (2013), http://www .iifilologicas.unam.mx/dicabenovo/ [last accessed 2 April 2020].

Díez del Corral Areta, E. 'Encrucijada de ediciones: La accesibilidad a los textos documentales' [A melting pot of textual editions: accessibility to documentary texts], *Versants*, 59 (3, 2012), pp. 35–44.

Díez del Corral Areta, E. 'La problemática de las tradiciones textuales en el estudio lingüístico del documento indiano' [The problem of textual traditions in the linguistic study of the Indian documentation], in Torrens Álvarez and Sánchez Prieto Borja (eds.), *Nuevas perspectivas*, pp. 323–34.

Díez del Corral Areta, E. 'Utilidad y límites de la diplomática en el estudio lingüístico del *documento indiano*' [Usefulness and limits of diplomacy in the linguistic study of the 'Indian document'], in M. Salamanca (ed.), *La materialidad escrita: nuevos enfoques para su interpretación* [Written materiality: new approaches to its interpretation] (Oviedo: IEPC, 2011), pp. 11–48.

Díez del Corral Areta, E. and L. Martín Aizpuru, 'Sin corpus no hay historia: La Red CHARTA como un proyecto de edición común' [Without a corpus there is no history: The CHARTA Network as a co-editing project], *Cuadernos de Lingüística de El Colegio de México*, 2 (2014), pp. 287–314.

Dik, S. C. *The Theory of Functional Grammar*, part 1: *The Structure of the Clause* (Dordrecht; Providence: Foris, 1989).

Dixon, R. M. W. 'Ergativity', *Language*, 55 (1, 1979), pp. 59–138.

Dobson, E. J. *English Pronunciation 1500–1700*, vols. 1–2 (Oxford: Clarendon Press, 1968).

Dolet, E. 'De la pvnctuation de la langue francoyse' [French language punctuation], in *La Maniere de bien traduire d'vne langve en avtre . . .* [How to translate well from one language to another] (Lyon: E. Dolet, 1540), pp. 21–9, https://gallica.bnf.fr/ark:/12148/bpt6k106073c.image [last accessed 4 June 2020].

Dollinger, S. 'What the capitalisation of early nouns in Canadian English may tell us about "colonial lag" theory: methods and problems', *Views*, 12 (1, 2003), pp. 24–44.

Domahs, U. and B. Primus (eds.), *Handbuch Laut, Gebärde, Buchstabe* [Handbook of sounds, signs and letters] (Berlin: de Gruyter, 2016).

Đorđić, P. *Istorija srpske ćirilice* [History of Serbian Cyrillic] (Belgrade: Institute for Textbook Publishing of the Socialist Republic of Serbia, 1971).

Dowty, D. 'Thematic proto-roles and argument selection', *Language*, 67 (3, 1991), pp. 547–619.

Dücker, L. 'Die Getrennt- und Zusammenschreibung von Komposita in frnhd. Hexenverhörprotokollen' [Separate and compound spelling of compounds in Early New High German protocols of witch trials], *Zeitschrift für Wortbildung*, 2 (1, 2018), pp. 33–60.

Dumville, D. *English Caroline Script and Monastic History: Studies in Benedictinism A.D. 950–1030* (Woodbridge: The Boydell Press, 1993).

Dürscheid, Ch. *Einführung in die Schriftlinguistik* [Introduction to grapholinguistics] (Wiesbaden: Springer, 2002).

Early English Books Online: Text Creation Partnership (EEBO-TCP), https://textcreation partnership.org/tcp-texts/eebo-tcp-early-english-books-online/ [last accessed 4 May 2020].

Early European Books, https://www.proquest.com/products-services/databases/eeb .html [last accessed 30 March 2020].

Eckhardt, T. *Azbuka. Versuch einer Einführung in das Studium der slavischen Paläographie* [Azbuka. A primer on the study of Slavic palaeography] (Vienna; Cologne: Böhlau, 1989).

Eden, K. *The Renaissance Rediscovery of Intimacy* (Chicago; London: The University of Chicago Press, 2012).

Egido, A. 'Los manuales de escribientes desde el Siglo de Oro. Apuntes para la teoría de la escritura' [The scribes' manuals since the 'Spanish Golden Century'. Notes on the theory of writing], *Bulletin Hispanique*, 97 (1995), pp. 67–94.

Ehmer, H. 'Hans Ungnad von Sonnegg und die Uracher Druckerei 1560–1564' [Hans Ungnad von Sonnegg and the Urach printing house, 1560–1564], in S. Lorenz,

A. Schindling and W. Setzler (eds.), *Primus Truber 1508–1586: Der slowenische Reformator und Württemberg* [Primus Truber 1508–1586: the Slovenian reformer and Württemberg] (Stuttgart: Kohlhammer, 2011), pp. 201–16.

Ein gebet aus heiliger Göttlicher geschrifft gezogen [A prayer drawn from the sacred divine scriptures] (Regensburg: Hans Kohl, 1555) (VD 16 G 574).

Eisenberg, P. and H. Günther (eds.), *Schriftsystem und Orthographie* [Writing system and orthography] (Tübingen: Niemeyer/Berlin: de Gruyter, 1989).

Eisenstein, E. *The Printing Press as an Agent of Change. Communications and Cultural Transformations in Early Modern Europe.* 2 vols. (Cambridge: Cambridge University Press, 1979).

Eisenstein, J. 'Systematic patterning in phonologically-motivated orthographic variation', *Journal of Sociolinguistics*, 19 (2, 2015), pp. 161–88.

Elmentaler, M. 'Der Erkenntniswert der schreibsprachlichen Variation für die Sprachgeschichte. Überlegungen zu den Ergebnissen eines Duisburger Graphematikprojektes' [The epistemological value of written language variation for language history. Considerations of the results of a Duisburg graphics project], *Rheinische Vierteljahrsblätter*, 65 (2001), pp. 290–314.

Elmentaler, M. *Struktur und Wandel vormoderner Schreibsprachen* [Structure and changes of premodern regional written languages] (Berlin; New York: de Gruyter, 2003).

Encyclopédie d'Yverdon = Felice, F. B. *L'Encyclopédie ou Dictionnaire universal raisonné des connaissances humaines* [The encyclopaedia or universal dictionary of human knowledge] (Yverdon, 1770–1780), digital edition by C. Blum (ed.) in *Dictionnaires, grammaires, encyclopédies* [Dictionaries, grammars, encyclopedias] (Paris: Classiques Garnier, 2011), https://classiques-garnier.com/encyclopedie-d-yverdon.html [last accessed 11 June 2020].

Esteve Serrano, A. *Estudios de teoría ortográfica del español* [Studies on Spanish orthographical theory] (Murcia: Universidad de Murcia, 1982).

Estienne, R. *Traicté de la Grãmaire Francoise* [A treatise on French Grammar] (Paris: Iaques du Puis, 1559), in Colombat et al. (compilers), *Grand Corpus*.

Evans, M. 'A sociolinguistics of early modern spelling? An account of Queen Elizabeth I's correspondence', *Studies in Variation, Contacts and Change in English*, vol. 10: *Outposts of Historical Corpus Linguistics: From the Helsinki Corpus to a Proliferation of Resources* (University of Helsinki, 2012), http://www.helsinki.fi/varieng/series/volumes/10/evans/#daybell_2001 [last accessed 9 May 2020].

Evans, M. *The Language of Queen Elizabeth I: A Sociolinguistic Perspective on Royal Style and Identity* (Chichester: Wiley Blackwell, 2013).

Evans, V. and M. Green, *Cognitive Linguistics: An Introduction* (Edinburgh: Edinburgh University Press, 2006).

Evertz, M. *Visual Prosody. The Graphematic Foot in English and German* (Berlin: de Gruyter, 2018).

Ewald, P. and D. Nerius, 'Die Alternative: gemäßigte Kleinschreibung' [The alternative: minimum capitalisation], in G. Augst, K. Blüml, D. Nerius and H. Sitta (eds.), *Zur Neuregelung der deutschen Orthographie. Begründung und Kritik* [On the revision of German orthography. Rationale and critique] (Tübingen: Niemeyer, 1997), pp. 419–34.

Ezell, M. J. *Social Authorship and the Advent of Print* (Baltimore; London: The Johns Hopkins University Press, 1999).

Fancev, F. 'Jezik hrvatskih protestantskih pisaca XVI. vijeka [1]' [The language of the Croatian Protestant writers of C16], *Rad JAZU*, 212/92 (1916), pp. 147–225.

Fancev, F. 'Jezik hrvatskih protestantskih pisaca XVI. vijeka [2]' [The language of the Croatian Protestant writers of C16], *Rad JAZU*, 214/93 (1916), pp. 1–112.

Farnaby, T. *Florilegium epigrammatum græcorum, eorumque latino versu à varijs redditorum* [Anthology of Greek epigrams, translated into Latin by various hands] (London: Christopher Meredith, 1650), EEBO-TCP Phase 1 file A40902.

Favriaud, M. 'Ponctuation(s) et architecturation du discours à l'écrit' [Punctuation(s) and architecturing of written discourse], *Langue Française*, 172 (Paris: Colin, 2011).

Ferdinand II, ... *Obnowené Práwo a Zřjzenj Zemſké Dědjčného Králowſtwj Cžeſkého* ... [... Reformed law and constitution of the hereditary Kingdom of Bohemia ...] (Prague: Jan Schumann, 1627), KPS no. K02447.

Ferdinand II, ... *Obnowene Prawo a Zržizenj Zemſke Dědiczneho Kraloſtwj Cžeſkeho* ... [... Reformed law and constitution of the hereditary Kingdom of Bohemia ...] (second half of C17). East Bohemian Museum, Pardubice, Rkp 393, *Repertorium* 5046.

Ferdinand II, ... *Obnowene Prawo a Zřizeni Zemſke. Diedicžneho Kralowſtwj Cžeſkeho...* [... Reformed law and constitution of the hereditary Kingdom of Bohemia ...] (Solnice, 1672). Library of the National Museum, Prague, IV C 2, Bartoš *Soupis* 981.

Fernández, M. *Olla podrida a la española* [Spanish miscellany] (Antwerp; Amsterdam: Felipe van Eyck, 1655).

Fidlerová, A. A. 'Ke vztahům mezi písařským a tiskařským pravopisným územ v raněnovověkých rukopisech' [On the relations between scribal and printers' orthographies in early modern manuscripts], *Bohemica Olomucensia 3 – Linguistica Juvenilia* (2009), pp. 40–7.

Fidlerová, A. A. 'Rukopisná kultura Čech 17. a 18. století v zrcadle muzejních sbírek' [Manuscript culture of Bohemia in C17 and C18 in the mirror of museum collections], *Folia Historica Bohemica*, 28 (2013), pp. 181–224.

Fidlerová, A. A., J. Andrle, T. Bernhardt, R. Těšínská Lomičková, D. Timofeev et al. (eds.), *Repertorium rukopisů 17. a 18. století z muzejních sbírek v Čechách* III/1–2, P–Š [Inventory of C17 and C18 manuscripts from the museum collections in Bohemia, part 3, vols. 1 and 2 (P–Š)] (Prague: Karolinum, in press).

Fidlerová, A. A., M. Bekešová et al. (eds.), *Repertorium rukopisů 17. a 18. století z muzejních sbírek v Čechách* II/1–2, K–O [Inventory of C17 and C18 manuscripts from the museum collections in Bohemia, part 2, vols. 1 and 2 (K–O)] (Prague: Karolinum, 2007).

Fidlerová, A. A., R. Dittmann and V. S. Vladimírová, 'Užívání velkých písmen v českých tištěných Biblích raného novověku' [Capitalisation in Early Modern Czech printed Bibles], in Čornejová et al. (eds.), *Dějiny českého pravopisu*, pp. 285–308.

Fournier, J.-M. 'La Généralité dans la théorie des sons à l'âge classique' [Generality in the theory of sounds in the classical age], in J.-M. Fournier and S. Verleyen (eds.), *Histoire des théories du son* [History of sound theories], *Histoire, Epistémologie, Langage*, 29 (1, 2007), pp. 85–105.

Fournier, J.-M. 'La Notion d'unité sonore dans les grammaires françaises des 17e et 18e siècles' [The notion of sound unity in C17 and C18 French grammars], in D. A. Kibbee (ed.), *History of Linguistics 2005* (Amsterdam; Philadelphia: John Benjamins, 2007), pp. 120–30.

Frantext, ATILF-CNRS, Université de Nancy 2, www.frantext.fr/ [last accessed 30 March 2020].

Fuhrhop, N. and F. Buchmann, 'Die Längenhierarchie: Zum Bau der graphematischen Silbe' [The length hierarchy: on the structure of the graphematic syllable], *Linguistische Berichte*, 218 (2009), pp. 127–55.

Fujii, A. 'Zur Methode der Exzerption älterer Drucke. Ein Beitrag zum Problem des Setzerwechsels in Frühdrucken' [Excerpting from early printed texts. A contribution to the problem of multiple typesetters in early printing], *Zeitschrift für deutsche Philologie*, 115 (1996), pp. 393–432.

Gadet, F. *La Variation sociale en français* [Social variation in French] (Paris: Ophrys, 2007).

Gadžieva, S., A. Kovačević, M. Mihaljević, S. Požar, J. Reinhart, M. Šimić and J. Vince, *Hrvatski crkvenoslavenski jezik* [The Croatian redaction of the Church Slavonic language] (Zagreb: Croatian University Press, Old Church Slavonic Institute, 2014).

Gallica, the digital library of the Bibliothèque Nationale de France, gallica.bnf.fr [last accessed 16 April 2020].

Gallmann, P. *Graphische Elemente der geschriebenen Sprache* [Graphic elements of the written language] (Tübingen: Niemeyer, 1985).

García Macho, M. L. and J. A. Pascual, 'Sobre la lengua de Santa Teresa y el valor de sus elecciones gráficas evitadas por Fray Luis' [The language of Saint Teresa and the graphical choices she made that were avoided by Fray Luis], *Mélanges de la Casa de Velázquez*, 26–2 (1990), pp. 129–40.

García Martín, J. M. (ed.), *Actas del IX Congreso Internacional de Historia de la Lengua Española, Cádiz, Setiembre 2012* [Proceedings of the IX International Congress of the History of the Spanish Language] (Madrid; Frankfurt: Iberoamericana Vervuert, 2015), 2 vols.

García Santos, J. F. 'La ortografía nebrisense' [Nebrija's orthography], in Gómez Asencio (ed.), *El castellano y su codificación gramatical*, vol. 1, pp. 335–64.

Gautier, A., S. Pétillon and F. Rinck (eds.), *La Ponctuation à l'aube du XXIe siècle. Perspectives historiques et usages contemporains* [Punctuation at the beginning of C21. Historical perspectives and contemporary uses] (Limoges: Lambert-Lucas, 2016).

Geitler, L. *Die Albanesischen und Slavischen Schriften* (Vienna: A. Hölder, 1883).

Georgakopoulou, A. *Narrative Performances: A Study of Modern Greek Storytelling* (Amsterdam; Philadelphia: John Benjamins, 1997).

Gfroerer, S., H. Günther and M. Bock, 'Augenbewegungen und Substantivgroßschreibung – Eine Pilotstudie' [Eye movements and noun capitalisation: a pilot study], in Eisenberg and Günther (eds.), *Schriftsystem und Orthographie*, pp. 111–35.

Giesecke, M. 'Orthotypographia. Der Anteil des Buchdrucks an der Normierung der Standardsprache' [Orthotypography. The contribution of printing to the standardisation of the standard language], in C. Stetter (ed.), *Zur Theorie der Orthographie. Interdisziplinäre Aspekte gegenwärtiger Schrift- und Orthographieforschung* [On the theory of spelling. Interdisciplinary aspects of recent research on writing and spelling] (Tübingen: Niemeyer, 1990), pp. 65–89.

Girón Alconchel, J. L. 'Las gramáticas del español y el español de las gramáticas en el Siglo de oro' [Spanish grammars and the Spanish language in grammars from the Golden Age], *Boletín de la Real Academia Española*, 76 (269, 1996), pp. 285–308.

Girón Alconchel, J. L. and J. J. de Bustos Tovar (eds.), *Actas del VI Congreso Internacional de Historia de la Lengua Española: Madrid, 29 de septiembre–3 octubre 2003* [Proceedings of the 6th International Congress of the History of the Spanish Language, Madrid, 29 September–3 October 2003] (Madrid: Arco Libros, 2006), vol. 1.

Glaser, E. 'Zu Entstehung und Charakter der neuhochdeutschen Schriftsprache: Theorie und Empirie' [On the origin and character of the New High German written language: Theory and practice], in R. Berthele, H. Christen, S. Germann and I. Hove (eds.), *Die deutsche Schriftsprache und die Regionen* [German written language and the regions] (Berlin: de Gruyter, 2003), pp. 57–78.

Golubović, B. 'Nauka o pismu u srpskoj lingvistici – o dosadašnjim istraživanjima i mogućnostima razvoja' [The science of writing in Serbian linguistics – the latest research and perspectives], in C. Voß and B. Golubović (eds.), *Srpska lingvistika / Serbische Linguistik: Eine Bestandsaufnahme* [Serbian linguistics: A survey] (Munich; Berlin: Sagner, 2010), pp. 33–54.

Gómez Asencio, J. J. (ed.), *Antiguas gramáticas del castellano* [Old grammars of Castilian language] [CD-ROM] (Madrid: Fundación Histórica Tavera, 2001).

Gómez Asencio, J. J. (ed.), *El castellano y su codificación gramatical*, vol. 1: *De 1492 (A. de Nebrija) a 1611 (John Sanford)*; vol. 2: *De 1614 (B. Jiménez Patón) a 1697 (F. Sobrino)* [The Castilian language and its grammatical rules: vol. 1: From 1492 (A. de Nebrija) to 1611 (John Sanford); vol. 2: from 1614 (B. Jiménez Patón to 1697 (F. Sobrino)] (Salamanca: Instituto Castellano y Leonés de la Lengua, 2006).

Görlach, M. *Eighteenth-Century English* (Heidelberg: Winter, 2001).

Görlach, M. *Introduction to Early Modern English*, revised ed. (Cambridge: Cambridge University Press, 1991).

Graband, G. *Die Entwicklung der frühneuenglischen Nominalflexion* [The development of Early Modern English nominal inflection] (Tübingen: Niemeyer, 1965).

Grace, A., N. Kemp, F. H. Martin and R. Parrila, 'Undergraduates' attitudes to text messaging language use and intrusions of textisms into formal writing', *New Media & Society*, 17 (5, 2015), pp. 792–809.

Gries, S. Th. *Statistics for Linguistics with R: A Practical Introduction* (Berlin; New York: de Gruyter, 2009).

Grimalauskaitė, D. and E. Remecas, *Pinigai Lietuvoje* [Money in Lithuania] (Vilnius: National Museum of Lithuania, 2016).

Grund, P. J. 'Scribes and scribal practices', in M. Kytö, P. J. Grund and T. Walker (eds.), *Testifying to Language and Life in Early Modern England* (Amsterdam; Philadelphia: John Benjamins, 2011), pp. 147–80.

Guarino Veronese, *In presenti libro continentur, item ars dipthongandi Guarini Veronensis. Item compendiosus dialogus de arte punctandi. Item tractatus utilis de accentu* [This book contains the art of diphthongisation by Guarino Veronese, the instructional dialogue about the art of punctuation, and a useful treatise on accents]

(Lyon: P. Ungarum/P. Hongre, 1482), gallica.bnf.fr/ark:/12148/bpt6k535510/ f5.item [last accessed 4 June 2020].

Gumperz, J. J. *Discourse Strategies* (Cambridge; New York: Cambridge University Press, 1982).

Günther, H. 'Eine Etüde zur Entwicklung der deutschen Interpunktion 1522–1961' [A study on the development of German punctuation 1522–1961], in R. Thieroff, M. Tamrat, N. Fuhrhop and O. Teuber (eds.), *Deutsche Grammatik in Theorie und Praxis* [German grammar in theory and practice] (Tubingen: Niemeyer, 2000), pp. 275–86.

Günther, H. (ed.), *Geschriebene Sprache – Funktion und Gebrauch, Struktur und Geschichte* [Written language – function and use, structure and history] (Munich: FIPKM, 1981).

Güthert, K. *Herausbildung von Norm und Usus Scribendi im Bereich der Worttrennung am Zeilenende (1500–1800)* [Formation of norm and *usus scribendi* in the field of word separation (1500–1800)] (Heidelberg: Winter, 2005).

Gutiérrez Cabero, A. M. 'La enseñanza de la caligrafía en España a través de los Artes de Escribir de los siglos XVI al XX: La construcción de un estilo de escritura' [The teaching of calligraphy in Spain through Arts of Writing from C16 to C20: The construction of a style of writing], unpublished PhD thesis (Universidad Complutense, Madrid, 2014), http://eprints.ucm.es/29371/1/T35921.pdf [last accessed 14 May 2020].

Hall, D. D. *Ways of Writing. The Practice and Politics of Text-Making in Seventeenth-Century New England* (Philadelphia: University of Pennsylvania Press, 2008).

Hamesse, J. 'Reportations, graphies et ponctuation' [Note taking, spelling and punctuation], in Maierù (ed.), *Grafia e interpunzione del latino*, pp. 135–51.

Han (Gallus), N. *Catechismvs, Predigsweise gestelt, für die kirche zu Regenspurg* [Catechism as preached for the church in Regensburg] (Regensburg: Hans Kohl, 1554) (VD 16 G 277).

Harley, J. '"My ladye Nevell" revealed', *Music and Letters*, 86 (1, 2005), pp. 1–15.

Hart, J. *An Orthographie Conteyning the due Order and Reason, Howe to Write or Paint Thimage of Mannes Voice, Most Like to the Life or Nature* (London: Henry Denham for William Seres, 1569), https://search.proquest.com/eebo [last accessed 28 Dec. 2018].

Hartweg, F. and K.-P. Wegera, *Frühneuhochdeutsch. Eine Einführung in die deutsche Sprache des Spätmittelalters und der frühen Neuzeit*, 2nd ed. [Early New High German. An introduction to the German language of the late Middle Ages and the early modern period] (Tübingen: Niemeyer, 2005).

Haspelmath, M. 'Creating economical morphosyntactic patterns in language change', in J. Good (ed.), *Language Universals and Language Change* (Oxford: Oxford University Press, 2008), pp. 185–214.

Hatz, E. R. R. 'Die Durchführung des "etymologischen Prinzips" bei der Graphie der Umlaute von "a" und "au" untersucht an Drucken der Lutherbibel des 16. bis 18. Jahrhunderts' [The implementation of the 'Etymological Principle' in the graphemes of the umlauts of 'a' and 'au', investigated in printed editions of the Luther Bible of C16–C18], unpublished PhD thesis (Heidelberg University, 1986).

Hawkins, J. A. *Cross-Linguistic Variation and Efficiency* (Oxford: Oxford University Press, 2014).

Hellinga, L. *Texts in Transit: Manuscript to Proof and Print in the Fifteenth Century* (Leiden: Brill, 2014).

Hellinga-Querido, L. 'Methode en praktijk bij het Zetten van Boeken in den vijftiende eeuw' [Method and practice of setting books in C15], unpublished PhD thesis (University of Amsterdam, 1974).

Hendrickx, I. and R. Marquilhas, 'From old texts to modern spellings: an experiment in automatic normalisation', *Journal for Language Technology and Computational Linguistics*, 26 (2, 2011), pp. 65–76.

Hercigonja, E. *Tropismena i trojezična kultura hrvatskoga srednjovjekovlja* [The tri-alphabetic and tri-lingual culture of the Croatian Middle Ages] (Zagreb: Matica hrvatska, 2014).

Hernández-Campoy, J. M. 'Authorship and gender in English historical sociolinguistic research: samples from the Paston Letters', in Russi (ed.), *Current Trends*, pp. 108–42.

Hernández-Campoy, J. M. and J. C. Conde-Silvestre, 'Sociolinguistic and geolinguistic approaches to the historical diffusion of linguistic innovations: incipient standardisation in Late Middle English', *International Journal of English Studies*, 5 (1, 2005), pp. 101–34.

Hernández-Campoy, J. M. and J. C. Conde-Silvestre, 'The social diffusion of linguistic innovations in fifteenth century England: Chancery spellings in private correspondence', *Cuadernos de Filología Inglesa*, 8 (1999), pp. 251–74.

Hernández-Campoy, J. M. and J. C. Conde-Silvestre (eds.), *The Handbook of Historical Sociolinguistics* (Oxford: Wiley Blackwell, 2014).

Hie kompt ein Beüerlein zu einem reichen Burger [Here is a peasant coming to a rich burgher] (Speyer: Johann Eckhart, 1522) (VD 16 H 3466).

HIe yn diesem büchlin vindet man die grossen wunder werck der heyligen stat Rome [Here in this booklet you will find the great marvels of the holy city of Rome] (Strasbourg: Matthias Hupfuff, 1500) (ISTC im00613100).

Hill, P. and V. Lehmann (eds.), *Standard Language in the Slavic World. Papers on Sociolinguistics by Hamburg Slavists* (Munich: Otto Sagner, 1988).

Hilpert, M. *Constructional Change in English: Developments in Allomorphy, Word Formation, and Syntax* (Cambridge: Cambridge University Press, 2013).

Hinrichs, L. and J. White-Sustaíta, 'Global Englishes and the sociolinguistics of spelling: a study of Jamaican blog and email writing', *English World-Wide*, 32 (1, 2011), pp. 46–73.

Hintze, C. 'Signed receipt for the print of two books by Simonas Daukantas', a manuscript with no title in Russian at the Institute of the Lithuanian Literature and Folklore (Vilnius, call no. f. 1 – SD 32, 1838).

'*Historia* und Geschicht von Melusina/ der Edlen und Hochgebornen Königin auß Franckreich' [*Historia* and tale of Melusina, the noble and high-born queen from France], in *Das Buch der Liebe* [The book of love] (Frankfurt am Main: Feyerabend, 1587) (VD 16 B 8959), fols. 262v–284v.

Hockett, Ch. *A Course in Modern Linguistics* (New York: Macmillan, 1967).

Hoffmann, T. *Preposition Placement in English: A Usage-Based Approach* (Cambridge: Cambridge University Press, 2011).

Hoffmann, W., J. Macha, K. J. Mattheier, H.-J. Solms and K.-P. Wegera (eds.), *Das Frühneuhochdeutsche als sprachgeschichtliche Epoche* [Early New High German as a period of language history] (Frankfurt am Main: Peter Lang, 1999).

Holtus, G., M. Metzeltin and C. Schmitt (eds.), *Lexicon der Romanistischen Linguistik: les différentes langues romanes et leurs régions d'implantation du Moyen Âge à la Renaissance* [Lexicon of Romance linguistics: The various Romance languages and their areas of establishment from the Middle Ages to the Renaissance], vol. 2, part 2 (Tübingen: Niemeyer, 1996).

Honeybone, P. and J. Salmons (eds.), *The Oxford Handbook of Historical Phonology* (Oxford: Oxford University Press, 2015).

Hope, J. 'Rats, bats, sparrows, and dogs: biology, linguistics, and the nature of standard English', in Wright (ed.), *Development of Standard English*, pp. 49–56.

Horobin, S. 'The language of the fifteenth-century printed editions of *The Canterbury Tales*', *Anglia*, 119 (2, 2001), pp. 249–58.

Horobin, S. and J. J. Smith, *An Introduction to Middle English* (Edinburgh: Edinburgh University Press, 2009).

Hosmer, D. W. and S. Lemeshow, *Applied Logistic Regression*, 2nd ed. (New York: Wiley, 2000).

Houston, K. *Shady Characters: Ampersands, Interrobangs and other Typographical Curiosities* (London: Penguin, 2013).

Howard-Hill, T. 'Early modern printers and the standardization of English spelling', *The Modern Language Review*, 101 (2006), pp. 16–29.

Hubert, Ph.-M. 'Corpvs stigmatologicvm minvs' [Compendium of texts on punctuation], *Archivvm Latinitatis Medii Aevi*, 37 (1970), pp. 5–171.

Hubert, Ph.-M. 'Notes de lexicographie thomiste. V. Présentation, ponctuation et mots-outils' [Notes on Thomist lexicography. V. Presentation, punctuation and terminology] *Archivvm Latinitatis Medii Aevi*, 36 (1969), pp. 59–108.

Huchon, M. 'Pour une histoire de la ponctuation 1532–1553: les variations des éditions des premiers livres de Rabelais' [A history of punctuation 1532–1553: variations in the editions of Rabelais's early books], *Nouvelle Revue du XVIe Siècle*, 6 (1988), pp. 15–28.

Hus, J. *Magistri Iohannis Hus Opera omnia*, vols. 1–4 (Prague: Academia, 1975–95).

Ĩagich, I. V. 'Glagolicheskoe pis'mo' [The Glagolitic script], *Enciklopediĩa slaviãnskoĩ filologii*, 3 (1911), pp. 51–262.

In dem buechlein steet geschriben wie Rom gepauet wart [In this guide it is told how Rome was built] (Rome: Stephan Plannck) (ISTC im00612000).

Isasi, C. 'Peculiaridades lingüísticas geográficas: interpretación filológica y marcación' [Peculiarities in geographical linguistics: philological interpretation and marking], in Sánchez Méndez et al. (eds.), *Temas, problemas y métodos*, pp. 197–212.

Item in dem püchlein stet geschriben wie Rome gepauet wart [In this guide it is told how Rome was built] (Nuremberg: Peter Wagner, 1491) (ISTC im00608500).

Item in dem püchlin stet geschriben wie Rom gepauet ward [In this guide it is told how Rome was built] (Munich: Johann Schaur, 1482) (ISTC im00607300).

Jaffe, A. M. 'Introduction: Non-standard orthography and non-standard speech', *Journal of Sociolinguistics*, 4 (2000), pp. 497–513.

Jaffe, A. M., J. Androutsopoulos, M. Sebba and S. Johnson (eds.), *Orthography as Social Action: Scripts, Spelling, Identity and Power* (Berlin; Boston: de Gruyter, 2012).

Janečková, M. *K jazyku českého baroka. Hláskosloví, pravopis a tisk, označování kvantity* [Towards the language of the Czech baroque. Phonology, orthography and letter printing, quantity distinction] (Prague: Arsci, 2009).

Janów, J. *Jan Sandecki (Malecki), Ewangeliarz z początku XVI wieku i dwa późniejsze druki polskie tegoż autora* [Jan Sandecki (Malecki), Gospel from the beginning of C16 and two later Polish printed texts by the same author] (Cracow: PAU, 1949).

Janów, J. 'O stosunku dwu wydań *Żywota Pana Jezu Krysta* z r. 1522 i wynikających stąd wnioskach o redaktorze druku Ossolińskiego nr 60862 oraz o zaginionem wydaniu *Historii o św. Annie* ok. 1522 r.' [On the relationship between the two 1522 editions of *Żywot Pana Jezu Krysta* and the resulting conclusions on the editor of the Ossoliński print no. 60862 and the lost edition of the *History of Saint Anna* around the year 1522], *Sprawozdania Towarzystwa Naukowego we Lwowie*, 8 (1928), pp. 43–51.

Jembrih, A. 'Pogovor uz pretisak ćiriličkoga *Novoga testamenta* [1563]' [Afterword to the facsimile reprint of the Cyrillic *New Testament* (1563)] (Zagreb: MVI, 2008).

Jembrih, A. 'Pogovor uz pretisak glagoljičkoga *Novoga testamenta* [1562/3]' [Afterword to the facsimile reprint of the Glagolitic *New Testament* (1562/3)], 2nd ed. (Zagreb: MVI, 2016).

Jembrih, A. (ed.), *Antun Dalmatin, Stipan Konzul. Postilla, Ratisbona 1568*, facsimile (Pazin: Juraj Dobrila, 1993).

Jembrih, A. (ed.), *Novi testament* (1562/3), facsimile edition of the Glagolitic original printed in Urach/Tübingen (Zagreb, 2007).

Jembrih, A. (ed.), *Novi testament* (1563), facsimile edition of the Cyrillic original printed in Urach/Tübingen (Zagreb, 2008).

Jiménez Patón, B. *Epitome de la ortografia latina, y castellana* [The handbook of Latin and Castilian orthography] (Baeza: P. de la Cuesta, 1614).

Jodłowski, S. *Losy polskiej ortografii* [Vicissitudes of Polish spelling] (Warsaw: National Scientific Publishing House, 1979).

Johnston, M. D. 'Mateo Alemán's problem with spelling', *PMLA*, 103/5 (1988), pp. 759–69.

Joshi, R. M. and P. G. Aaron (eds.), *Handbook of Orthography and Literacy* (London; New York: Routledge, 2014).

Juda, M. *Pismo drukowane w Polsce XV–XVIII wieku* [Printed fonts in C15–C18 Poland] (Lublin: Maria Curie-Skłodowska University, 2001).

Kaempfert, M. 'Motive der Substantivgroßschreibung. Beobachtungen an Drucken des 16. Jahrhunderts' [Reasons for noun capitalisation. Observations on the basis of C16 printed texts], *Zeitschrift für deutsche Philologie*, 99 (1980), pp. 72–98.

Kaislaniemi, S., M. Evans, T. Juvonen and A. Sairio, '"A graphic system which leads its own linguistic life?" Epistolary spelling in English, 1400–1800', in T. Säily, A. Nurmi, M. Palander-Collin and A. Auer (eds.), *Exploring Future Paths for Historical Sociolinguistics* (Amsterdam: John Benjamins, 2017), pp. 187–213.

Kamińska, K. 'Pisownia druków polskich XVI wieku' [Spelling in C16 Polish printed texts], *Prace Polonistyczne*, 11 (1953), pp. 5–28.

Kamińska, M. *Psałterz floriański. Monografia językowa*, vol. 1: *Ortografia, fonetyka, fleksja imion* [Saint Florian Psalter. A linguistic monograph, vol. 1: Spelling, phonetics, inflection] (Wrocław: ZNIO, 1981).

Kapatsinski, V. 'What is it I am writing? Lexical frequency effects in spelling Russian prefixes: Uncertainty and competition in an apparently regular system', *Corpus Linguistics and Linguistic Theory*, 6 (2, 2010), pp. 157–215.

Karaś, M. and Z. Perzanowski, *Statuty kapituły norbertańskiej z r. 1541* [Statutes of the Premonstratensian Order chapter from the year 1541] (Cracow: Jagiellonian University, 1970).

Karlík, P., M. Nekula and J. Pleskalová (eds.), *CzechEncy – Nový encyklopedický slovník češtiny* [CzechEncy – New encyclopaedic dictionary of Czech] (2017), https://www.czechency.org/ [last accessed 3 June 2020].

Karskiĭ, E. F. *Slavi͡anskai͡a kirillovskai͡a paleografii͡a* [Slavic Cyrillic palaeography] (Leningrad: USSR Academy of Sciences, 1928 [reprint: Moscow: Nauka, 1979]).

Kaverina, V. V. *Stanovlenie russkoĭ orfografii XVII–XIX vv.: Pravopisnyĭ uzus i kodifikacii͡a* [The establishment of Russian orthography in C17–C19: orthographical use and codification], Dissertation summary (Moscow State University, 2010).

Kaverina, V. V. 'Ustranenie omofonii v istorii russkogo pis'ma' [Homophony neutralisation in the history of Russian writing], *Vestnik Moskovskogo Universiteta*, 9 (5, 2008), pp. 40–65.

Kawecka-Gryczowa, A. *Drukarze dawnej Polski od XV do XVIII wieku*, vol. 1: *Małopolska*, part 1: *Wiek XV–XVI* [Printers of old Poland from C15 to C18, vol. 1: Lesser Poland, part 1: C15–C16] (Wrocław: ZNIO, 1983).

Kawecka-Gryczowa, A. 'Miejsce książki w kulturze polskiej XVI wieku' [The role of the book in the Polish culture in C16], in A. Wyczański (ed.), *Polska w epoce Odrodzenia. Państwo, społeczeństwo, kultura* [Poland in the age of the Renaissance. State, society, culture] (Warsaw: PWN, 1986), pp. 411–54.

Keller, R. E. *Die deutsche Sprache* [The German language] (Hamburg: Buske, 1995).

Keszler, B. 'A magyar írásjelhasználat és Európa' [Hungarian punctuation and Europe], *Magyar Nyelvőr*, 127 (2003), pp. 24–36.

Keszler, B. *Írásjeltan. Az írásjelhasználat szabályai, problémái és történet* [The study of punctuation. The use of punctuation, its rules, problems and history] (Budapest: National Textbook Publisher, 2004).

Kirchhoff, F. and B. Primus, 'The architecture of punctuation systems: a historical case study of the comma in German', *Written Language and Literacy*, 17 (2, 2014), pp. 195–224.

Klemensiewicz, Z. *Historia języka polskiego* [The history of the Polish language], 2nd ed. (Warsaw: PWN, 1985).

Klemensiewicz, Z., T. Lehr-Spławiński and S. Urbańczyk, *Gramatyka historyczna języka polskiego* [Historical grammar of the Polish language] (Warsaw: PWN, 1965).

Klimaŭ, I. P. *Rėfarmatsyi͡a ŭ historyi litaraturnykh moŭ slavi͡an: Ŭklad pol'ska-belaruskaha i slavenska-kharvatskaha pratėstantyzmu 16 st.* [Reformation in the history of the Slavic standard languages: Contribution of Polish–Belorussian and Slovene–Croatian Protestantism in C16] (Minsk: Belarusian State University of Culture, 2004).

Klimek, Z. *Język polski w rozmówkach polsko-niemieckich Książeczek polskich z r. 1539* [The Polish language in Polish–German phrasebooks in Polish publications from the year 1539] (Wrocław: ZNIO, 1978).

Koch, P. and W. Oesterreicher, 'Gesprochene Sprache und geschriebene Sprache' / 'Langage parlé et langage écrit' ['Spoken language and written language'], in Holtus et al. (eds.), *Lexikon der Romanistischen Linguistik*, pp. 584–627.

Koch, P. and W. Oesterreicher, 'Language of immediacy – language of distance: orality and literacy from the perspective of language theory and linguistic history', in C. Lange, B. Weber and G. Wolf (eds.), *Communicative Spaces. Variation, Contact, and Change. Papers in Honour of Ursula Schaefer* (Frankfurt am Main: Peter Lang, 2012), pp. 441–73.

Kohrt, M. *Problemgeschichte des Graphembegriffs und des frühen Phonembegriffs* [A problematic history of the concepts of the grapheme and of the early phoneme] (Tübingen: Niemeyer, 1985).

Koialowicz, A. W. *Historiae Litvanae pars prior* [History of Lithuania, part 1]) (Danzig: Svmptibus Georgii Försteri, 1650).

Konstanc, J. *Lima lingvae Bohemicae. To geſt: BRUS Gazyka Czeſkého ...* [Whetstone of the Czech language ...] (Prague: Impressí akademická, 1667), KPS no. K04307.

Konzul, S. *Katehismus, edna malahna kniga v koi yeszu vele potribni i korisni nauci* [The catechism, one small book with very useful lessons] (Tübingen, 1564) in A. Jembrih (ed.), *Katekizam, jedna malahna knjiga v hrvatski jazik istumačena* [Catechism, a small book translated into the Croatian language] (Pazin: Juraj Dobrila, 1991), pp. 1–141.

Kopaczyk, J. *The Legal Language of Scottish Burghs* (Cambridge: Cambridge University Press, 2013).

Kopaczyk, J. and A. H. Jucker (eds.), *Communities of Practice in the History of English* (Amsterdam; Philadelphia: John Benjamins, 2013).

Korompay, K. '16th-century Hungarian orthography', in Baddeley and Voeste (eds.), *Orthographies*, pp. 321–49.

Kosek, P. 'Bratrský pravopis' [Brethren's orthography], in Karlík et al. (eds.), *CzechEncy*, https://www.czechency.org/slovnik/BRATRSKÝ PRAVOPIS [last accessed 3 June 2020].

Kosek, P. 'Interpunkce českých tištěných kancionálů 17. a 18. století a její transkripce' [Punctuation of the Czech printed hymn-books of C17 and C18 and the methods of its transcription], in Čornejová et al. (eds.), *Dějiny českého pravopisu*, pp. 250–84.

Koselleck, R. *Vergangene Zukunft. Zur Semantik geschichtlicher Zeiten* [Future past. On the semantics of historical times] (Frankfurt am Main: Suhrkamp, 1979).

Koupil, O. '*Alphabetum Boëmicum* (1718): slabikář pro učené' [*Alphabetum Boëmicum* (1718): a primer for scholars], *Listy filologické*, 136 (2013), pp. 365–82.

Koupil, O. 'Druhé vydání náměšťské mluvnice (1543) znovu nalezeno' [The second edition of the grammar of Náměšť (1543) lost and found], *Česká literatura*, 64 (2016), pp. 243–66.

Koupil, O. 'Psáti neb tisknouti? (Nám4, ŠtVýb1 a písaři)' [To write or to print? (Nám4, ŠtVýb1 and the scribes)], in Čornejová et al. (eds.), *Dějiny českého pravopisu*, pp. 235–49.

Kovačević, A. 'Neki novi glagololjupci [Some new Glagolitic-lovers], *Bašćina: Glasilo Društva Prijatelja Glagoljice*, 18 (2017), pp. 37–9.

Kowalska, A. 'Końcówka *-ej* w odmianie rzeczowników rodzaju żeńskiego w języku polskim' [The *-ej* ending in the feminine gender noun inflectional paradigm], *Prace Naukowe Uniwersytetu Śląskiego. Prace Językoznawcze*, 1 (1976), pp. 58–81.

Kozhinova, A. 'Rannie vostochnoslaviãnskie kriptograficheskie sistemy v kontekste iãzykovykh kontaktov' [Early Eastern Slavic cryptographic systems in the context of language contacts], in Tomelleri and Kempgen (eds.), *Slavic Alphabets in Contact*, pp. 291–305.

KPS – Knihopis Database of Czech and Slovak printed texts, http://www.knihopis.cz/knihopis-eng.html [last accessed 25 April 2020].

Kraus, K. *Ausgewählte Schriften*, vol. 4: *Pro Domo et Mundo* [Selected writings, vol. 4: To use at home and elsewhere] (Munich: Langen, 1912).

Kresa, M. 'Gramatyka dla szkół narodowych Onufrego Kopczyńskiego' [Onufry Kopczyński's Grammar for the national schools], *Poradnik Językowy* (1, 2016), pp. 86–93.

Kress, G. *Early Spelling. Between Convention and Creativity* (London; New York: Routledge, 2000).

Kristián z Koldína, P. *Artykulowe Praw Meſtſkých* (1619). [Articles of the municipal law], National Library of the Czech Republic, Prague, XVII G 18, Truhlář, *Katalog 307*.

Kristián z Koldína, P. *Práwa Měſtſká Králowſtwij Czieſkého* ... [Municipal law of the Kingdom of Bohemia ...] (Prague: Daniel Adam z Veleslavína, Jiří Melantrich z Aventýna senior, 1579), KPS no. K04564.

Kristián z Koldína, P. *Prawa Měſtſka Kralowſtwj Czieſkého* [Municipal law of the Kingdom of Bohemia] (Hřešihlavy, 1661). Library of the National Museum, Prague, V C 45, *Prozatímní katalog*.

Kristián z Koldína, P. *Práwa Měſtſká Králowſtwij Czieſkého. Práwa a Zřijzenij zemſká Králowſtwj Czeſkého* [Municipal law of the Kingdom of Bohemia. Law and constitution of the Kingdom of Bohemia] (Nový Bydžov, 1624). Library of the National Museum, Prague, IV C 15, Bartoš *Soupis 994*.

Kristián z Koldína, P. *Práwa Měſtſká Králowſtwij Czeſkého / w krátkau Summu vwedená* ... [Short summary of the municipal law of the Kingdom of Bohemia ...] (Prague: Jiří Černý z Černého Mostu, 1582), KPS no. K04567.

Kristián z Koldína, P. *Práwa a Zřijzenij Zemſká Králowſtwij Czeſkého w krátkau Summu vwedená* ... [Short summary of the law and constitution of the Kingdom of Bohemia ...] (Prague: Jiří Černý z Černého Mostu, 1583), KPS no. K04574.

Kristián z Koldína, P. *Prawa Mieſtſka Kralowſtwi Czeſkeho, wkratkau Summu Vwedena* ... [Short summary of the Municipal law of the Kingdom of Bohemia ...] (before 1685). National Library of the Czech Republic, Prague, XVII C 39, Truhlář, *Katalog 117*.

Kristián z Koldína, P. *Prawa Mieſtſka Kralowſtwj Czeſkeho w Kratkau Summu Vwedena* ... [Short summary of the municipal law of the Kingdom of Bohemia ...] (early C18). Museum and Gallery of the Orlické Mountains, Rychnov nad Kněžnou, 562/74, *Repertorium 3477*.

Kristián z Koldína, P. *Prawa Mieſtſka Kralowſtwy Czeſkeho. Wnowie Přzepſana Letha Panie 1682, Dne 28. Magij* [Municipal law of the Kingdom of Bohemia ...] (1682). Library of the National Museum, Prague, IV C 22, Bartoš *Soupis 1001*.

Kristol, A. 'Sociolinguistique historique et analyse de la conversation: Une nouvelle approche du *Journal d'Hygiène* de Jean Héroard' [Historical sociolinguistics and conversational analysis: A new approach to the *Journal d'Hygiène* by Jean Héroard], *Vox Romanica*, 68 (2009), pp. 169–86.

Kruming, A. A. *Svodnyĭ katalog staropechatnyx izdanij glagolicheskogo shrifta 1483–1812 gg.* [Union catalogue of early Glagolitic printed books, 1483–1812] (Moscow: Russian State Library, 1995).

Książek-Bryłowa, W. 'Uwarunkowania społeczne normy językowej w XVI wieku' [Social aspects of linguistic norms in C16], *Rozprawy Komisji Językowej Łódzkiego Towarzystwa Naukowego*, 32 (1986), pp. 139–46.

Kucała, M. *Jakuba Parkosza Traktat o ortografii polskiej* [Jakub Parkosz's treatise on Polish orthography] (Warsaw: PWN, 1985).

Kučera, K. 'Dodatek ke kvantitativním charakteristikám vývoje českého pravopisu od 13. do 20. století' [An addition to the quantitative characterisation of the development of Czech orthography from C13 to C20], *Slovo a Slovesnost*, 60 (1999), pp. 301–3.

Kučera, K. 'Vývoj účinnosti a složitosti českého pravopisu od konce 13. do konce 20. Století' [Development of orthographical efficiency and complexity in Czech texts from the end of C13 to the end of C20], *Slovo a Slovesnost*, 59 (1998), pp. 178–99.

Kudirka, V. 'Statrašos ramsčiai' [Buttresses of orthography], MS (Vilnius University Library, call no. f. 1 – E 333, 1890).

Kul'bakin, S. M. *Slaviānskaiā paleografiiā* [Slavic palaeography] (Belgrade: SANU, 2008).

Künast, H.-J. *'Getruckt zu Augspurg'. Buchdruck und Buchhandel in Augsburg zwischen 1468 und 1555* ['Printed in Augspurg'. Book printing and the book trade in Augsburg between 1468 and 1555] (Tubingen: Niemeyer, 1997).

Kuraszkiewicz, W. *Polski język literacki. Studia nad historią i strukturą* [Polish literary language. Studies on history and structure] (Warsaw: PWN, 1986).

Kuštović, T. 'Jezik hrvatskog protestantskog ćiriličkog Novog Zavjeta (1563.) prema hrvatskoglagoljskoj tradiciji' [The language of the Croatian Protestant Cyrillic *New Testament* (1563) in the Croatian Glagolitic tradition], *Filologija*, 62 (2014), pp. 115–29.

Kuštović, T. and M. Žagar (eds.), *Meandrima hrvatskoga glagoljaštva. Zbornik posvećen akademiku Stjepanu Damjanoviću o 70. rođendanu* [Through the meanders of the Croatian Glagolitic tradition. An anthology dedicated to Stjepan Damjanović] (Zagreb: Croatian University Press, 2016).

Kuźmicki, M. and M. Osiewicz (eds.), *Dokument pisany w badaniach historyka języka polskiego. Z badań nad grafią i fonetyką historycznej polszczyzny* [A written document as a source of diachronic investigations of Polish. Remarks on the spelling system and on the phonetics of historical Polish] (Zielona Góra; Poznań: University of Zielona Góra, 2010).

Labov, W. *Principles of Linguistic Change*, vol. 1: *Internal Factors* (Oxford: Blackwell, 1992).

Labov, W. *Principles of Linguistic Change*, vol. 2: *Social Factors* (Malden: Blackwell, 2002).

Labs-Ehlert, B. *Versalschreibung in althochdeutschen Sprachdenkmälern. Ein Beitrag über die Anfänge der Großschreibung im Deutschen unter Berücksichtigung der Schriftgeschichte* [Uppercase spelling in Old High German texts. A contribution on the beginnings of capitalisation in German in the context of the history of writing] (Göppingen: Kümmerle, 1993).

Lamprecht, A. *Vývoj fonologického systému českého jazyka* [Development of the Czech language phonological system] (Brno: J. E. Purkyně University, 1966).

Langacker, R. W. *Cognitive Grammar: A Basic Introduction* (Oxford: Oxford University Press, 2008).

Lass, R. (ed.), *The Cambridge History of the English Language*, vol. 3: *1476–1776* (Cambridge: Cambridge University Press, 2000).

Lavrentiev, A. 'Linguistique de corpus: Idéologie, méthodologies, technologies' [Corpus linguistics: ideology, methodologies, technologies], *Sibirskiĭ Filologicheskiĭ Zhurnal*, 3–4 (2004), pp. 121–34.

Lavrentiev, A. 'Ponctuation française du Moyen Âge au XVIe siècle: théories et pratiques' [French punctuation from the Middle Ages to C16: theory and practice], in S. Pétillon, F. Rinck and A. Gautier (eds.), *La Ponctuation à l'Aube du XXIe Siècle. Perspectives Historiques et Usages Contemporains* [Punctuation at the dawn of C21: historical perspectives and contemporary practices], (Limoges: Lambert-Lucas, 2016), pp. 39–62.

Lavrentiev, A. 'Tendances de la ponctuation dans les manuscrits et incunables français en prose, du XIIIe au XVe siècle' [Trends in punctuation in French manuscripts and incunabula in prose, from C13 to C15], unpublished PhD thesis, 2 vols. (ENS Lyon, 2009), tel.archives-ouvertes.fr/tel-00494914 [last accessed 5 June 2020].

Lazar, M. 'Transfer des Rechts und Transfer der Rechtssprache. Sächsisch-magdeburgisches Recht und seine Verbreitung im Ostmitteleuropa nach den Hussitenkriegen' [Transfer of the law and transfer of the legal language. Saxon-Magdeburg law and its spread in East-Central Europe after the Hussite Wars], in H. Kuße and H. Kosourová (eds.), *Persönlichkeiten in der tschechischen Sprach- und Kulturgeschichte.* [Personalities in Czech language and cultural history] (Bern: Peter Lang, 2016), pp. 177–202.

Lehmann, V. 'An essay on crosslinguistic phenomena in the development of Slavic standard languages', in Hill and Lehmann (eds.), *Standard Language in the Slavic World*, pp. 129–46.

Leith, D. *A Social History of English* (London: Routledge, 1983).

Levshina, N. *How to do Linguistics with R. Data Exploration and Statistical Analysis* (Amsterdam; Philadelphia: John Benjamins, 2015).

Lewaszkiewicz, T. 'O potrzebie nowego spojrzenia na genezę polskiego języka literackiego (z uwzględnieniem tła ogólnoeuropejskiego)' [The need for a new look at the origin of the Polish literary language (including the European background)], in M. Kucała and Z. Krążyńska (eds.), *Studia historycznojęzykowe* [Studies in historical linguistics] (Cracow: IJP PAN, 1994), pp. 213–20.

Lewaszkiewicz, T. 'Rola kontaktów językowych we wstępnym okresie formowania się słowiańskich języków literackich (na tle ogólniejszym)' [Role of language contacts in the preliminary period of the formation of the Slavic literary languages (on the more general background)], in B. Galster (ed.), *Z polskich studiów slawistycznych* [From Polish Slavonic studies] (Warsaw: Energeia, 1992), pp. 133–8.

Lewaszkiewicz, T. 'Rola przekładów Biblii w formowaniu języków literackich europejskiego kręgu kulturowego' [The role of Bible translations in forming the literary languages of the European *Kulturkreis*], in M. Kamińska and E. Małek (eds.), *Biblia a kultura Europy* [The Bible and European culture] (Łódź: Łódź University, 1992), pp. 232–48.

Lillis, T. M. *The Sociolinguistics of Writing* (Edinburgh: Edinburgh University Press, 2013).

Linda, J., A. Stich, A. Fidlerová, M. Šulcková et al. (eds.), *Repertorium rukopisů 17. a 18. století z muzejních sbírek v Čechách* I/1–2, A–J [Inventory of C17 and C18 manuscripts from the museum collections in Bohemia, Part 1, vols. 1 and 2 (A–J)] (Prague: Karolinum, 2003).

Ling, R., N. S. Baron, A. Lenhart and S. W. Campbell, '"Girls text really weird": gender, texting and identity among teens', *Journal of Children and Media*, 8 (4, 2014), pp. 423–39.

Lisowski, T. 'Economic calculation and Polish alphabetic writing', in T. Sekiguchi (ed.), *Spotkania polonistyk trzech krajów – Chiny, Korea, Japonia* [Meetings of Polish studies scholars from three countries – China, Korea, Japan] (Tokyo: Tokyo University of Foreign Studies, 2009), pp. 195–204.

Lisowski, T. 'Geneza imiesłowu *reca* w Kazaniach świętokrzyskich. Trzy modele interpretacji historycznojęzykowej' [Origin of the participle *reca* in the Holy Cross Sermons. Three models of historical–linguistic interpretation], in R. Laskowski and R. Mazurkiewicz (eds.), *Amoenitates vel lepores philologiae* [Pleasance and charm of philology] (Cracow: Lexis, 2007), pp. 175–84.

Lisowski, T. *Grafia druków polskich z 1521 i 1522 roku. Problemy wariantywności i normalizacji* [Spelling of Polish printed books from 1521 and 1522. Problems with variation and standardisation] (Poznań: UAM, 2001).

Lisowski, T. 'Ideographization of the Polish writing system and the historical linguistic interpretation, i.e. what we know about the old Polish spelling system', *Journal of Central & East European Studies*, 5 (2, 2003), pp. 89–112.

Lisowski, T. 'Jan Sandecki, redaktor *Żywota Pana Jezu Krysta* wobec ortografii druków czeskich' [Jan Sandecki, the editor of *Żywot Pana Jezu Krysta* from 1522, and his approach to the spelling of Bohemian printed texts], *Slavia Occidentalis*, 50 (1993), pp. 93–104.

Lisowski, T. *Polszczyzna początku XVI wieku. Problemy wariantywności i normalizacji fonetyki i fleksji* [The Polish language at the beginning of C16. Problems with the variation and standardisation of phonetics and inflection] (Poznań: WiS, 1999).

Lisowski, T. 'Ślady graficznej tradycji rękopisów w dwu edycjach *Żywota Pana Jezu Krysta* Baltazara Opeca z 1522 roku' [Traces of manuscript spelling traditions in the two 1522 editions of *Żywot Pana Jezu Krysta* by Baltazar Opec], *Slavia Occidentalis*, 51 (1994), pp. 66–73.

Lisowski, T. 'The beginning of the typographical era in Poland', *Journal of Central & East European Studies*, 6 (2, 2004), pp. 139–65.

Lisowski, T. 'The Polish printed book and development of the Polish spelling system', *East European Studies*, 12 (1, 2003), pp. 111–35.

Lisowski, T. and M. Osiewicz, 'Leksykalizacja pisowni polskiej w dobie staroi średniopolskiej jako problem badawczy. Uwagi na marginesie prac Władysława Kuraszkiewicza' [Lexicalization of Polish spelling in the Old Polish and Middle Polish periods as a research problem. Notes in the margins of Władysław Kuraszkiewicz's studies], in Kuźmicki and Osiewicz (eds.), *Dokument pisany*, pp. 149–66.

Llamas-Pombo, E. 'Administración, cultura escrita y puntuación. Documentación castellana y anglonormanda (siglos XII–XIII)' [Administration, literacy and punctuation. Castilian and Anglo-Norman documents (C12 and C13)], in

A. Arizaleta and F. Bautista (eds.), *Los modelos anglo-normandos en la cultura letrada en Castilla (siglos XII–XIV)* [Anglo-Norman models in Castilian literacy (C12 and C13)] (Toulouse: PUM, 2019), pp. 119–34.

Llamas-Pombo, E. 'Graphie et ponctuation du français médiéval. Système et variation' [Spelling and punctuation in mediaeval French. System and variation], in Parussa et al. (eds.), *Enregistrer la parole*, pp. 39–87.

Llamas-Pombo, E. '*Gratiam varietatis*. Paramètres de variation stylistique de la lettre au Moyen Âge' [The pleasure of variation. Parameters of the stylistic variation of the letter in the Middle Ages], *Scrinium Friburgense*, 44 (2019), pp. 193–214.

Llamas-Pombo, E. 'Marques graphiques du discours rapporté. Manuscrits du *Roman de la Rose*, XVe siècle' [Quotation marks in reported speech. The manuscripts of the *Roman de la Rose*, C15], in B. Combettes, C. Guillot, É. Oppermann-Marsaux, S. Prévost and A. Rodríguez Somolinos (eds.), *Le Changement en français. Études de linguistique diachronique* [Linguistic change in French. Studies on diachronic linguistics] (Bern: Peter Lang, 2010), pp. 249–69.

Llamas-Pombo, E. 'Metro, ritmo y puntuación en los repertorios hispánicos de refranes (siglos XVI–XVII)' [Meter, rhythm and punctuation in Hispanic collections of proverbs (C16 and C17)], *Rilce*, 34 (2, 2018), pp. 456–82.

Llamas-Pombo, E. 'Ponctuation médiévale, pragmatique et énonciation. Lire l'*Ovide moralisé* au XIVe siècle' [Mediaeval punctuation, pragmatics and enunciation. Reading the *Ovide moralisé* in C14], *Linx*, 73 (2016), pp. 113–45.

Llamas-Pombo, E. 'Ponctuer, éditer, dire. Notes sur la ponctuation du discours dans l'écriture médiévale' [Punctuating, editing and speaking. Notes on punctuation of speech in mediaeval writing], in J. M. López Muñoz (ed.), *Aux marges du discours (personnes, temps, lieux, objets)* [On the margins of discourse. People, times, places, objects] (Limoges: Lambert-Lucas, 2015), pp. 212–23.

Llamas-Pombo, E. 'Ponctuer, éditer, lire. État des études sur la ponctuation dans le livre manuscrit' [Punctuating, editing and reading. The state of the art of punctuation in mediaeval manuscript books], *Syntagma*, 2 (2008), pp. 131–73.

Llamas-Pombo, E. 'Pour une étude de la ponctuation du *Halotti beszéd és könyörgés* dans un contexte européen' [Towards a study of the punctuation of the *Halotti beszéd és könyörgés* in a European context], in Z. S. Bartók and B. Horváth (eds.), *Írások a Pray-Kódexről* [Writings on the Pray Codex] (Budapest: Argumentum Kiadó, 2019), pp. 111–28.

Llamas-Pombo, E. 'Réflexions méthodologiques pour l'étude de la ponctuation médiévale' [Methodological reflections for the study of mediaeval punctuation], in A. Lavrentiev (ed.), *Systèmes graphiques de manuscrits médiévaux et incunables français. Ponctuation, segmentation, graphies* [The graphic systems of mediaeval manuscripts and French incunables. Punctuation, segmentation, spelling] (Chambéry: Université de Savoie, 2007), pp. 11–48.

Llamas-Pombo, E. 'Variación gráfica y secuenciación de la palabra en manuscritos medievales hispánicos' [Graphic variation and word sequencing in mediaeval Spanish manuscripts], in P. M. Cátedra (ed.), *Los códices literarios de la Edad Media. Interpretación, historia, técnicas y catalogación* [Literary codices from the Middle Ages. Interpretation, history, techniques and cataloging] (San Millán de la Cogolla: Cilengua, 2009), pp. 225–57, gredos.usal.es/jspui/handle/10366/122006 [last accessed 5 June 2020].

Llamas-Pombo, E. 'Variation and standardization in the history of Spanish spelling', in Baddeley and Voeste (eds.), *Orthographies*, pp. 15–62.

López de Velasco, J. *Orthographia y pronunciacion castellana* [Castilian pronunciation and orthography] (Burgos: n.p., 1582), http://www.proyectos.cchs.csic.es/humanismo yhumanistas/juan-lopez-de-velasco/ortograf%C3%ADa-y-pronunciaci%C3%B3n-castellana [last accessed 23 May 2020].

Love, H. *Scribal Publication in Seventeenth-Century England* (Oxford: Clarendon Press, 1993).

Lunt, H. 'Ligatures in Old Church Slavonic Glagolitic manuscripts', *Slavistična Revija*, 10 (1957), pp. 253–67.

Maas, U. 'Einige Grundannahmen zur Analyse der Groß- und Kleinschreibung im Deutschen, insbesondere zu ihrer Grammatikalisierung in der Frühen Neuzeit' [Some basic assumptions regarding the analysis of upper- and lowercase spelling in German, especially its grammaticalisation in the early modern age], in G. Lerchner, M. Schröder and U. Fix (eds.), *Chronologische, areale und situative Varietäten des Deutschen in der Sprachhistoriographie* [Chronological, areal and situative varieties of German in language historiography] (Frankfurt am Main: Peter Lang, 1995), pp. 85–100.

Maas, U. 'Geschriebene Sprache' [Written language], in U. Ammon, N. Dittmar, K. J. Mattheier, and P. Trudgill (eds.), *Sociolinguistics. An International Handbook of the Science of Language and Society*, vol. 1, 2nd ed. (Berlin; New York: de Gruyter, 2004), pp. 633–45.

Macha, J. *Der konfessionelle Faktor in der deutschen Sprachgeschichte der Frühen Neuzeit* [The denominational factor in the German language history of the early modern period] (Würzburg: Ergon, 2014).

Macha, J., E. Topalović, I. Hille, U. Nolting and A. Wilke (eds.), *Deutsche Kanzleisprache in Hexenverhören der Frühen Neuzeit*, vol. 1: *Auswahledition* [German chancellery language in witch trials of the early modern age, vol. 1: Anthology] (Berlin; Boston: de Gruyter, 2005).

Maierù, A. (ed.), *Grafia e interpunzione del latino nel medioevo (Seminario Internazionale, Roma, 27–29 Septembre 1984)* [Spelling and punctuation of the Latin language in the Middle Ages. International seminar, Rome, 27–29 September 1984] (Rome: Ateneo, 1987).

Maître, M. *Les Précieuses. Naissance des femmes de lettres en France au XVIIe siècle* [The *Précieuses*. The birth of letter-writing women in C17 France] (Paris: Honoré Champion, 1999).

Malicki, J. 'Język czeski na Śląsku w kontekście śląskich dziejów języka polskiego i niemieckiego. Pytanie o granice historii języka' [The Czech language in Silesia in the context of the history of Polish and German languages in Silesia. A question about border in historical linguistics], in J. Lipowski and D. Żygadło-Czopnik (eds.), *Podzwonne dla granic: Polsko-czeskie linie podziałów i miejsca kontaktów w języku, literaturze i kulturze* [A knell for borders: Polish–Bohemian lines of division and points of contact in language, literature and culture] (Wrocław: University of Wrocław, 2009), pp. 375–87.

Malicki, J. 'Slezské jazykové spektrum a kategorie okraje a středu ve vývoji komunikace společnosti zemí Koruny české ve 14. až 18. století' [The Silesian language spectrum and the periphery and centre categories in the development of

Czech Crown communications from C14 to C18], in M. Hałub and A. Mańko-Matysiak (eds.), *Śląska republika uczonych* – *Schlesische Gelehrtenrepublik* – *Slezská vědecká obec* [Silesian Republic of scholars], vol. 2 (Wrocław: ATUT, 2006), pp. 15–27.

Mancho Duque, M. J. *Teresa de Jesús. La Oralidad de una Santa Escritora* [Saint Teresa of Jesus. The spoken language of a writer saint] (Salamanca: CES, 2015).

Maquieira, M. 'Teoría y práctica ortográficas en las gramáticas del español del siglo XVI'; 'Teoría ... siglo XVII' [Theory and practice of spelling in C16/C17 Spanish grammars], in Gómez Asencio (ed.), *El castellano y su codificación gramatical*, vol. 1: pp. 365–95 and vol. 2, pp. 491–545.

Marchello-Nizia, C. 'Écrire une nouvelle grammaire historique du français à la lumière de l'histoire des descriptions de la langue' [Writing a new historical grammar of French in light of the history of language descriptions], in B. Colombat, J.-M. Fournier and V. Raby (eds.), *Vers une histoire générale de la grammaire française. Matériaux et perspectives* [Towards a general history of French grammar. Materials and perspectives] (Paris: Champion, 2012), www.unice.fr/bcl/rubrique137?lang=es [last accessed 5 June 2020].

Marchello-Nizia, C. 'L'Oral représenté en français médiéval: un accès construit à une face cachée des "langues mortes"' [Representing oral discourse in mediaeval French: building an approach to a hidden facet of dead languages], in C. Guillot, B. Combettes, A. Lavrentiev and E. Oppermann-Marsaux (eds.), *Le Changement en français. Études de linguistique diachronique* [Language change in French. Studies on diachronic linguistics] (Bern: Peter Lang, 2012), pp. 247–64.

Marchello-Nizia, C. 'Ponctuation et "unités de lecture" dans les manuscrits médiévaux ou: je ponctue, tu lis, il théorise' [Punctuation and reading features in mediaeval manuscripts: I punctuate, you read, he theorises], *Langue Française*, 40 (1978), pp. 32–44.

Marcos Marín, F. *Reforma y modernización del español. Ensayo de sociolingüística histórica* [Reform and modernisation of Spanish. An essay in historical sociolinguistics] (Madrid: Cátedra, 1979).

Mareš, F. V. 'Die kyrillo-methodianischen Wurzeln der tschechischen diakritischen Orthographie' [The Cyrillo-Methodian roots of Czech diacritic orthography], *Anzeiger der phil.-hist. Klasse der Österreichischen Akademie der Wissenschaften*, 110 (3, 1973), pp. 81–99.

Maretić, T. *Istorija hrvatskoga pravopisa latinskijem slovima* [The history of Croatian orthography in the Roman alphabet] (Zagreb: Yugoslav Academy of Arts, 1889).

Markov, I., V. Nastase and C. Strapparava, 'Punctuation as native language interference', in E. M. Bender, L. Derczynski and P. Isabelle (eds.), *Proceedings of the 27th International Conference on Computational Linguistics* (Santa Fe: Association for Computational Linguistics, 2018), pp. 3456–66.

Markus, M. 'Abbreviations in Early Modern English correspondence', in M. Dossena and S. M. Fitzmaurice (eds.), *Business and Official Correspondence: Historical Investigations* (Bern: Peter Lang, 2006), pp. 107–29.

Markus, M. (compiler), *Innsbruck Computer Archive of Machine-Readable English Texts (ICAMET)* (Innsbruck: University of Innsbruck, 1999).

Marti, R. 'Ein "Kulturkampf" in der *Slavia romana*: "Deutsch" vs. "Slavisch" in Schrift und Schreibung' [The 'cultural struggle' in the *Slavia romana*: 'German' versus

'Slavic' in script and orthography], in Tomelleri and Kempgen (eds.), *Slavic Alphabets in Contact*, pp. 159–88.

Marti, R. 'On the creation of Croatian: The development of Croatian Latin orthography in the 16th century', in Baddeley and Voeste (eds.), *Orthographies*, pp. 269–319.

Martineau, F. 'Pratiques d'écriture des peu-lettrés en Québéquois ancien: Morphologie verbale' [Writing practices of the semi-literate in ancient Quebec French: Verbal morphology], in P. Larrivée (ed.), *Variation et stabilité du français. Des notions aux opérations. Mélanges de linguistique française offerts à J.-M. Léard* [Variation and stability in French. From notions to operations. French linguistic studies in honour of J.-M. Léard] (Louvain; Paris; Dudley: Peeters, 2007), pp. 201–20.

Martinez, C. (ed.), *La Variation graphique: Champs, facteurs* [Graphic variation: Fields, factors] (Paris: Klincksieck, 2010).

Martínez Alcalde, M. J. (ed.), *Textos clásicos sobre historia de la ortografía castellana* [Classical texts on the history of Spanish spelling] [CD-ROM] (Madrid: Digibis-Fundación Histórica Tavera, 1999).

Martínez de Sousa, J. *Reforma de la ortografía española. Estudio y pautas* [Reform of the Spanish spelling. Analysis and guidelines] (Madrid: Visor, 1991).

Martínez Marín, J. 'La estandarización de la puntuación en español: Siglos XV–XVII' [The standardisation of punctuation in Spanish from C15 to C17], in R. Escavy, M. Hernández and A. Roldán (eds.), *Actas del Congreso Internacional de Historiografía Lingüística. Nebrija V Centenario* [Proceedings of the International Congress of Linguistic Historiography. Nebrija's fifth centenary] (Murcia: Universidad de Murcia, 1994), pp. 437–50.

Martínez Marín, J. 'La ortografía española: perspectiva historiográfica' [Spanish spelling: a historiographical perspective], *Cauce*, 14–15 (1991–2), pp. 125–34.

Matak, D. (ed.), *Drugi del Novoga testamenta 1563, latinički prijepis glagoljskog izdanja* [Second part of the New Testament 1563, Latin transcription of the Glagolitic edition] (Zagreb: University of Zagreb, 2015).

Matak, D. (ed.), *Prvi del Novoga testamenta 1562, latinički prijepis glagoljskog izdanja* [First part of the New Testament 1562, Latin transcription of the Glagolitic edition] (Zagreb: University of Zagreb, 2013).

Mathesius, V. *Jazyk, kultura a slovesnost* [Language, culture and literacy], ed. J. Vachek (Prague: Odeon, 1982).

Mazziotta, N. *Ponctuation et syntaxe dans la langue française médiévale. Étude d'un corpus de chartes originales écrites à Liège entre 1236 et 1291* [Punctuation and syntax in mediaeval French. Study of a corpus of original charters written in Liège between 1236 and 1291] (Tübingen: Niemeyer, 2009).

McConchie, R. 'Compounds and code-switching: Compositorial practice in William Turner's *Libellus de re Herbaria Novvs*, 1538', in Thaisen and Rutkowska (eds.), *Scribes*, pp. 177–90.

McEnery, T. and A. Hardie (compilers), *The Lancaster Newsbooks Corpus* (Lancaster: University of Lancaster, 2007).

McEnery, T. and A. Wilson, *Corpus Linguistics: An Introduction* (Edinburgh: Edinburgh University Press, 2001).

McLeod, R. 'Spellbound: typography and the concept of old-spelling editions', *Renaissance and Reformation*, n.s. (3, 1979), pp. 50–65.

McLuhan, H. M. 'Address at Vision 65', *The American Scholar*, 35 (2, 1966), pp. 196–205.

McLuhan, M. M. *The Gutenberg Galaxy: The Making of Typographical Man* (Toronto: University of Toronto Press, 1962).

Meckhart, J. *Catechismus. Ain kurtze Christliche Leer vnd vnderweysung für die Jugent* [Catechism. A brief Christian lesson and instruction for young people] (Augsburg: Hans Zimmerman) (VD 16 M 1803).

Mediavilla, C. *Histoire de la calligraphie française* [History of French calligraphy] (Paris: Albin Michel, 2006).

Medina Morales, F. 'Problemas metodológicos de la sociolingüística histórica' [Methodological problems in historical sociolinguistics], *Forma y Función*, 18 (2005), pp. 115–37.

Medina-Sánchez, B. 'Punctuation in eighteenth-century English grammars', unpublished PhD thesis (Universidad de Las Palmas de Gran Canaria, 2015), https://accedacris .ulpgc.es/handle/10553/17011 [last accessed 5 June 2020].

Medina-Sánchez, B. and A. Rodríguez-Álvarez, 'Estudio comparativo de los primeros tratados de puntuación en lengua inglesa (1672–1704): terminología y función de la puntuación' [A comparative study of the first treatises on punctuation written in English (1672–1704): terminology and function of punctuation], *Onomázein*, 31 (2015), pp. 99–112.

Meigret, L. *Le Traité de la grammaire française* [The treatise of French grammar], ed. F.-J. Hausmann (Tübingen: Narr, 1980), in Colombat et al. (compilers), *Grand Corpus*.

Meigret, L. *Le Trętté de la grammęre françoęse* [The treatise of French grammar] (Paris: Chrétien Wechel, 1550), https://gallica.bnf.fr/ark:/12148/btv1b8624665r/ [last accessed 23 May 2020].

Melusina. Von Lieb und Leyd/ Ein schöne und lustige Histori. Ausz Frantzösischer Spraach in Teutsch verwandelt [Melusina. Of love and sorrow. A beautiful and merry history. Translated from French into German] (Frankfurt am Main: Egenolff heirs, c. 1580) (VD 16 ZV 28676).

Mentrup, W. *Die Groß- und Kleinschreibung im Deutschen und ihre Regeln. Historische Entwicklung und Vorschlag zur Neuregelung* [Upper- and lowercase spelling in German and its rules. Historical development and a proposal for revision] (Tübingen: Narr, 1979).

Merkys, V. *Simonas Daukantas* (Vilnius: Vyturys, 1991).

Messerli, A. 'Das Lesen von Gedrucktem und das Lesen von Handschriften – zwei verschiedene Kulturtechniken?' [Reading printed texts and reading hand-written texts – two different cultural techniques?], in A. Messerli and R. Chartier (eds.), *Lesen und Schreiben in Europa 1500–1900* [Reading and writing in Europe 1500–1900] (Basel: Schwabe, 2000), pp. 235–46.

Mey, F. *De ortografía libelus* [Handbook of orthography], in B. Bravo, *Thesaurus verborum, ac frasivm, ad orationem latine efficiendam, et locvpletandam* (Palma de Mallorca: Gabriel Guasp, 1607).

Michel, A. 'Italian orthography in early modern times', in Baddeley and Voeste (eds.), *Orthographies*, pp. 63–96.

Miguel Franco, R. and P. Sánchez-Prieto Borja, 'CODEA: A primary corpus of Spanish documents', *Variants. The Journal of the European Society for Textual Scholarship*, 12–13 (2016), pp. 211–28.

Mihm, A. 'Druckersprachen und gesprochene Varietäten. Der Zeugniswert von Bämlers Melusinendruck (1474) für eine bedeutende Frage der Sprachgeschichte' [The language of print and spoken varieties. Evidence from Bämler's printed *Melusine* (1474) for an important question in language history], in Rautenberg et al. (eds.), *Zeichensprachen*, pp. 163–203.

Mihm, A. 'Graphematische Systemanalyse als Grundlage der historischen Prosodieforschung', in P. Auer, P. Gilles and H. Spiekermann (eds.), *Silbenschnitt und Tonakzente* [Syllable cut and tonal accents] (Tübingen: Niemeyer, 2002), pp. 235–64.

Mihm, A. 'Regionalsprachen in vorreformatorischer Zeit. Die Überlieferung des Buschmann-Mirakels als Zeugnis polyzentrischer Sprachorganisation' [Regional languages in the pre-Reformation period. The tradition of the Buschmann miracle as a testimony of polycentric language organization], in L. Horstkötter (ed.), *Arnt Buschmanns Mirakel. Eine Jenseitsvision des 15. Jahrhunderts. Untersuchungen zu Textentstehung und Verbreitung mit einer Edition der Hamborner Handschrift* [Arnt Buschmann's miracle. A C15 vision of the afterworld. Studies on formation and spread, with an edition of the Hamborn manuscript] (Münster: MV Wissenschaft), pp. 209–49.

Mihm, A. 'Zur Deutung der graphematischen Variation in historischen Texten', in A. Häcki Buhofer (ed.), *Vom Umgang mit sprachlicher Variation: Soziolinguistik, Dialektologie, Methoden und Wissenschaftsgeschichte* [How to deal with linguistic variation: sociolinguistics, dialectology, methods and history of science] (Tübingen; Basel: Francke, 2000), pp. 367–90.

Miklas, H. 'Zur Struktur des kyrillisch-altkirchenslavischen (altbulgarischen) Schriftsystems' [On the structure of the Cyrillic Old Church Slavonic (Old Bulgarian) script], *Palaeobulgarica*, 12 (3, 1988), pp. 52–65.

Miller, D. 'Why it's safer to build on concrete than epistemology. A comment on "On Materiality" by Gosewijn van Beek', *Etnofoor*, 9 (1, 1996), pp. 25–7.

Milroy, J. 'Historical description and the ideology of the standard language', in Wright (ed.), *Development of Standard English*, pp. 11–28.

Milroy, J. 'Language ideologies and the consequences of standardisation', *Journal of Sociolinguistics*, 5 (4, 2001), pp. 530–55.

Milroy, J. *Linguistic Variation and Change: On the Historical Sociolinguistics of English* (Oxford: Blackwell, 1992).

Misal po zakonu rimskoga dvora [Missale Romanum Glagolitice], 1st ed. (Venice 1483), in I. Frangeš (ed.), *Misal po zakonu rimskoga dvora* (Zagreb: Liber, 1971).

Morales, J. B. de, *Pronvnciaciones generales de lengvas, ortografia, escvela de leer, escriuir, y contar, sinificación de letras en la mano* [The pronunciation of languages, orthography, learning of reading, writing and counting, the meaning of the letters in the hand] (Montilla: Juan Batista de Morales, 1623).

Morin, Y.-C. 'The phonological status of nasal vowels in XVI century French', in R. Sampson and W. Ayres-Bennet (eds.), *Interpreting the History of French. Festschrift for Peter Rickard* (Amsterdam: Rodopi, 2002), pp. 95–129.

Mortara Garavelli, B. *Storia della punteggiatura in Europa* [History of punctuation in Europe] (Rome: Laterza, 2008).

Moulin, C. *Der Majuskelgebrauch in Luthers Deutschen Briefen (1517–1546)* [The use of capital letters in Luther's German letters (1517–1546)] (Heidelberg: Winter, 1990).

Moyna, M. I. *Compound Words in Spanish: Theory and History* (Amsterdam: John Benjamins, 2012).

Mueller, M. 'NUPOS: A part of speech tag set for written English from Chaucer to the present', *WordHoard* (2009), http://wordhoard.northwestern.edu/userman/nupos.pdf [last accessed 9 May 2020].

Mulcaster, R. *The First Part of the Elementarie VVhich Entreateth Chefelie of the Right Writing of our English Tung, Set Furth by Richard Mulcaster* (London: Tomas Vautroullier, 1582), https://search.proquest.com/eebo [last accessed 28 Dec. 2018].

Nebrija, E. A. de, *Grammatica de la lengua castellana* [Grammar of the Castilian language] (Salamanca, 1492), facsimile (Valencia: Librerías París-Valencia, 1992).

Nebrija, E. A. de, *Introductiones in latinam grammaticem* [Introduction to Latin grammar], 3rd ed. (Seville: Johannes Pegnitzer and Magnus Herbst, 1502) [1st ed. 1481].

Nebrija, E. A. de, *Reglas de orthographia en la lengua castellana* [Spelling rules in the Castilian language] (Alcalá de Henares: A. G. de Brocar, 1517).

Neef, M. *Die Graphematik des Deutschen* [Graphematics of German] (Tubingen: Niemeyer, 2005).

Nejedlý, P. 'Humanistický a barokní pravopis z pohledu lexikologického' [Humanistic and baroque orthography from lexicological viewpoint], in Čornejová et al. (eds.), *Dějiny českého pravopisu*, pp. 209–17.

Nemirovskiĭ, E. L. *Slavi͡anskie izdani͡a kirillovskogo (t͡serkovnoslavi͡anskogo) shrifta: 1491–2000. Inventar' sokhranivshikhsi͡a ekzempli͡arov i ukazatel' literatury* [Slavic editions in the Cyrillic (Church Slavonic) script: 1491–2000. Inventory of extant copies and references to the literature], vol. 1: *1491–1550* (Moscow: Znak, 2009); vol. 2, Part 1: *1551–1590* (Moscow: Znak, 2011).

Nevalainen, T. *An Introduction to Early Modern English* (Edinburgh: Edinburgh University Press, 2006).

Nevalainen, T. 'Early Modern English lexis and semantics', in Lass (ed.), *The Cambridge History of the English Language*, pp. 332–458.

Nevalainen, T. 'Variable focusing in English spelling between 1400 and 1600', in Baddeley and Voeste (eds.), *Orthographies*, pp. 127–65.

Nevalainen, T. and H. Raumolin-Brunberg, *Historical Sociolinguistics: Language Change in Tudor and Stuart England* (London: Pearson Education, 2003).

Newmeyer, F. J. *Possible and Probable Languages: A Generative Perspective on Linguistic Typology* (Oxford: Oxford University Press, 2005).

Nichols, J. 'Diversity and stability in language', in B. D. Joseph and R. D. Janda (eds.), *The Handbook of Historical Linguistics* (Malden; Oxford: Blackwell, 2003), pp. 283–310.

Nikitina, E. A. 'Istori͡a perenosa slov v russkoĭ orfograficheskoĭ tradit͡sii (XIV–XX vv.)' [History of the line break in Russian orthographical tradition (C14–C20)], unpublished PhD thesis (Omsk State University, 1997).

Nobels, J. and G. Rutten, 'Language norms and language use in seventeenth-century Dutch', in Rutten et al. (eds.), *Norms and Usage*, pp. 21–48.

Nordlund, T. 'Standardization of Finnish orthography: From reformists to national awakeners', in Baddeley and Voeste (eds.), *Orthographies*, pp. 351–72.

Nottbusch, G. and J. Jonischkait, 'Einzeluntersuchungen zur GKS, GZS und Interpunktion' [Case studies of upper- and lowercase spelling, compound and separate spelling, and punctuation], in U. Bredel (ed.), *Weiterführender*

Orthographieerwerb [Advanced acquisition of orthography] (Baltmannsweiler: Schneider, 2011), pp. 164–89.

Novi Testament (Urach, 1562 and 1562/3): *1: Prvi del Novoga testamenta (teštamenta)* ... */ Der erst halb Theil des newen Testaments, darinn sein die vier Evangelisten, und der Apostel Geschicht; / 2: Drugi del Novoga testamenta (teštamenta)* ... */ Der ander halb Theil des newen Testaments* [1: The first half of the New Testament, in which are the four Gospels, and the Acts of the Apostles; / 2: The second half of the New Testament], available at Bayerische Staatsbibliothek München, https://daten.digitale-sammlungen.de/0007/bsb00078762/images/index.html; Württembergische Landesbibliothek, Stuttgart: http://digital.wlb-stuttgart.de/purl/bsz362618305 [URLs accessed 7 Sept. 2020].

Nowak, J. 'A diachronic contrastive study of sentence-internal capitalisation in Dutch and German', in G. de Vogelaer (ed.), *German and Dutch in Contrast: Synchronic, Diachronic and Psycholinguistic Perspectives* (Berlin; Boston: de Gruyter, 2018).

Núñez de Toledo y Guzmán, H. *Refranes o proverbios en romance* [Proverbs in Spanish] (Salamanca: Juan de Cánova, 1555; Valencia University Library, ref. BH Z-03/081, http://roderic.uv.es/handle/10550/52803 [last accessed 20 April 2020]).

Núñez de Toledo y Guzmán, H. *Refranes o proverbios en romance* [Proverbs in Spanish] (Lérida: Luis Manescal Mercader de Libros, 1621).

Oesterreicher, W. 'Aproximación a una tipología de las fuentes escritas para la investigación de las variedades de la inmediatez' [Approximation to a typology of the written sources for the investigation of varieties of immediacy], in R. Cano (ed.), *Historia de la lengua española* [History of the Spanish language] (Madrid: Ariel, 2005), pp. 746–56.

Oldireva-Gustafsson, L. *Preterite and Past Participle Forms in English: 1680–1790* (Stockholm: Uppsala University, 2002).

Ong, W. J. *Orality and Literacy: The Technologizing of the Word* (New York: Routledge, 1982).

Opec, B. *Żywot Pana Jezu Krysta* [The life of Our Lord Jesus Christ] (Cracow: Florian Ungler, 1522).

Opec, B. *Żywot Wszechmocnego Syna Bożego, Pana Jezu Krysta* [The life of the Almighty Son of God, Our Lord Jesus Christ] (Cracow: Hieronim Wietor, 1522).

Optát, B. and P. Gzel, *Iſagogicon genž gt / prwnij vwedenij / každému počijnágijcýmu ſe včiti*...*[Isagogicon*, or primer for novices in learning...] (Náměšť nad Oslavou: Jan Pytlík z Dvořiště, 1535), KPS no. K06640.

Optát, B., P. Gzel and V. Philomathes, *Grāmatyka cžeſka w dwogij ſtránce* ... [Czech grammar in two parts ...] (Náměšť nad Oslavou: Kašpar Aorg, Matěj Pytlík z Dvořiště, 1533), KPS no. K06637.

Orobius, A. A. *Libellus de ratione punctorum* [Handbook of punctuation] (Bologna: Benedictum Hectoris, 1518).

Osiewicz, M. *Fonetyka listów polskich z pierwszej połowy XVI wieku* [The phonetics of Polish correspondence in the first half of C16] (Poznań: UAM, 2004).

Osiewicz, M. *Wariantywność graficzna* Ksiąg o Gospodarstwie *Piotra Krescentyna z 1549 roku. Studium przypadku* [Multiple graphic variants in *Księgi o Gospodarstwie* (Housekeeping Books, 1549) by Piotr Krescentyn. A case study] (Poznań: Rys, 2013).

Osiewicz, M. *Wariantywność leksemów w zakresie nieseryjnych zmian fonetycznych w listach polskich z pierwszej połowy XVI wieku* [Lexical variability under non-serial phonetic changes in Polish letters from the first half of C16] (Poznań: PTPN, 2007).

Osipov, B. I. *Istoriĩa russkoĭ orfografii i punktuat͡sii* [History of Russian orthography and punctuation] (Novosibirsk: University Publishing House, 1992).

Osipov, B. I. 'Istoriĩa slitnykh i razdel'nykh napisaniĭ v russkoĭ rukopisnoĭ knizhnosti kont͡sa XVII–XVIII vv.' [History of compound and separate spelling in Russian handwritten literacy of the late C17–C18], unpublished PhD thesis (Barnaul Polytechnic Institute, 1968).

Osipov, B. I. (ed.), *Fonetika i pis'mo na raznykh etapakh ikh istoricheskogo razvitiĩa* [Phonetics and graphemics at different stages of their development] (Omsk: State University, 1995).

Osipov, B. I. (ed.), *Fonetika i pis'mo v ikh razvitii* [Phonetics and graphemics in their development] (Omsk: State University, 1992).

Osselton, N. E. 'Informal spelling systems in Early Modern English, 1500–1800', in N. F. Blake and C. Jones (eds.), *English Historical Linguistics: Studies in Development* (Sheffield: CECTAL, University of Sheffield, 1984), pp. 123–37. Reprinted in M. Ryden, I. Tieken-Boon van Ostade and M. Kytö (eds.), *A Reader in Early Modern English* (Frankfurt am Main: Peter Lang, 1998), pp. 33–45.

Osselton, N. E. 'Spelling-book rules and the capitalisation of nouns in the seventeenth and eighteenth centuries', in M.-J. Arn, H. Wirtjes and H. Jansen (eds.), *Historical and Editorial Studies in Medieval and Early Modern English for Johan Gerritsen* (Groningen: Wolters-Noordhoff, 1985), pp. 49–61.

Ouy, G. 'La Ponctuation des premiers humanistes français' [The punctuation of the first French humanists], in N. Catach and J. Petit (eds.), *La Ponctuation. Recherches Historiques et Actuelles* [Punctuation. Historical and current research] (Paris, CNRS, 1979), vol. 2, pp. 56–89.

Ouy, G. 'Orthographe et ponctuation dans les manuscrits autographes des humanistes français des XIVe et XVe siècles' [Spelling and punctuation in autograph manuscripts of the French humanists of C14 and C15], in Maierù (ed.), *Grafia e interpunzione del latino*, pp. 169–205.

Ovide moralisé [Ovid moralised], MS, Bibliothèque nationale de France, fr. 24305.

Oxford Psalter, MS, University of Oxford, Bodleian Libraries, MS Douce, 320. fols. 37r–75v.

Pablo Núñez, L. 'El español de los *Emblemas cristianos* (1619) de Georgette de Montenay y otras obras religiosas y emblemáticas plurilingües de los siglos XVI y XVII' [The Spanish of the *Christian Emblems* (1619) by Georgette de Montenay and other religious and emblematic plurilingual works of C16 and C17], *Bulletin Hispanique*, 111 (1, 2009), pp. 219–43.

Pablo Núñez, L. 'Las *Machinæ Novæ* de Fausto Verancio: un ejemplo barroco de obra técnica políglota sobre ingenios y máquinas' [The *Machinæ Novæ* by Fausto Verancio: a Baroque example of a polyglot technical work on contraptions and machines], *Interlingüística*, 16 (2, 2005), pp. 859–71.

Pagani-Naudet, C. 'Ponctuer en 1550: l'exemple de Meigret' [Punctuating in 1550: the case of Meigret], in Bikialo and Rault (eds.), *Imaginaires de la ponctuation*, pp. 17–34.

Palafox y Mendoza, J. *Breve tratado de escribir bien, y de la perfecta ortographia* [Short treatise on writing well, and on perfect orthography] (Madrid: María de Quiñones, 1662).

Palumbo, A. *Skriftsystem i förändring. En grafematisk och paleografisk studie av de svenska medeltida runinskrifterna* [Script systems in development. A graphematic and palaeographic study of Swedish mediaeval Runic inscriptions] (Uppsala: Uppsala University, 2018).

Pangkofer, J. A. and J. R. Schnegraf, *Geschichte der Buchdruckerkunst in Regensburg* [History of the art of printing in Regensburg] (Regensburg: Manz, 1840).

Paredes, A. V. de, *Institución y origen del arte de la imprenta. Reglas generales para los componedores* (1680) [The institution and origin of printing. General rules for typographers], ed. J. Moll (Madrid: El Crotalón, 1984).

Parkes, M. B. *Pause and Effect: An Introduction to the History of Punctuation in the West* (Aldershot: Scolar Press, 1992).

Parkes, M. B. 'Punctuation, or pause and effect', in J. J. Murphy (ed.), *Medieval Eloquence. Studies in the Theory and Practice of Medieval Rhetoric* (Berkeley; Los Angeles; London: University of California Press, 1978), pp. 127–42.

Parsed Corpus of Early English Correspondence (PCEEC), text version, compiled by T. Nevalainen, H. Raumolin-Brunberg, J. Keränen, M. Nevala, A. Nurmi and M. Palander-Collin, with additional annotation by A. Taylor (Helsinki: University of Helsinki and York: University of York, 2006). Distributed through the Oxford Text Archive.

Partridge, A. C. *Tudor to Augustan English* (London: André Deutsch, 1969).

Parussa, G. 'La *Vertu* ou la *puissance* de la lettre. Enquête sur les fonctions attribuées à certaines lettres de l'alphabet latin dans les systèmes graphiques du français entre le 11e et le 16e siècle' [The *virtue* or *power* of the letter. A survey on the functions attributed to some letters of the Latin alphabet in the French graphic systems between C11 and C16], in Parussa et al. (eds.), *Enregistrer la parole*, pp. 89–109.

Parussa, G., M. Colombo Timelli and E. Llamas-Pombo (eds.), *Enregistrer la parole, écrire la langue dans la diachronie du français* [Recording speech and writing language in French diachronic linguistics] (Tübingen: Narr, 2017).

Parussa, G., M. Colombo Timelli and E. Llamas-Pombo, 'Introduction', in Parussa et al. (eds.), *Enregistrer la parole*, pp. 9–17.

Pauly, D. N. and G. Nottbusch, 'Die Groß- und Kleinschreibung (beim Lesen) – kognitive Prozesse und didaktische Implikationen' [Upper- and lowercase spelling in reading – cognitive processes and didactic implications], in B. Mesch and C. Noack (eds.), *System, Norm und Gebrauch – drei Seiten derselben Medaille? Orthographische Kompetenz und Performanz im Spannungsfeld zwischen System, Norm und Empirie* [System, norm and usage – three sides of the same coin? Orthographical competence and performance between system, norm and empirical research] (Baltmannsweiler: Schneider, 2016), pp. 122–45.

Polanco Martínez, F. 'Análisis grafemático de las sibilantes dentales en algunos documentos del País Vasco (ss. XV y XVI)' [Graphical analysis of dental sibilants in some documents from the Basque Country (C15 and C16)], in Girón Alconchel and de Bustos Tovar (eds.), *Actas del VI Congreso*, pp. 341–54.

Polański, E. (ed.), *Encyklopedia językoznawstwa ogólnego* [Encyclopaedia of general linguistics] (Wrocław: ZNIO, 1993).

Porák, J. *Humanistická čeština. Hláskosloví a pravopis* [Humanistic Czech. Phonology and orthography] (Prague: Charles University, 1983).

Práwa a Zřijzenij zemſká Králowſtwj Cžeſkého. Létha M. D. Lxiiij [Law and constitution of the Kingdom of Bohemia . . .] (Prague: Jiří Melantrich z Aventýna senior, 1564), KPS no. K14317.

Prozatímní katalog rukopisů Knihovny Národního muzea [Provisional catalogue of manuscripts of the National Museum Library], http://www.nm.cz/Katalogy-a-data baze/ [last accessed 5 June 2020].

Puranik, C. S. and C. J. Lonigan, 'Name-writing proficiency, not length of name, is associated with preschool children's emergent literacy skills', *Early Childhood Research Quarterly*, 27 (2, 2012), pp. 284–94.

R Core Team, *R: A Language and Environment for Statistical Computing*, https://www .R-project.org [last accessed 5 June 2020].

Ramat, P. *Linguistic Typology* (Berlin; New York; Amsterdam: de Gruyter, 1987).

Ramírez Santacruz, F. 'Ruptura y renovación en la *Ortografía castellana* (1609): Las 'novedades verdades' de Mateo Alemán' [Rupture and renewal in *Castilian Spelling* (1609): The 'new truths' by Mateo Alemán], *Criticón*, 120–1 (2014), pp. 103–16, criticon.revues.org/793 [last accessed 5 June 2020].

Ramus, P. *Grammaire* [Grammar] (Paris: A. Wechel, 1572), https://gallica.bnf.fr/ark:/ 12148/bpt6k50850r.image [last accessed 22 May 2020].

Rautenberg, U., H.-J. Künast, M. Habermann and H. Stein-Kecks (eds.), *Zeichensprachen des literarischen Buchs in der frühen Neuzeit. Die 'Melusine' des Thüring von Ringoltingen* [Languages of connotation in the literary book of the early modern age: the 'Melusina' by Thüring von Ringoltingen] (Berlin; Boston: de Gruyter, 2013).

Real Academia Española (RAE), 'La puntuación a través de la historia' [Punctuation through history], in *Ortografía de la Lengua Española* [Spanish orthography] (Madrid: Espasa, 2010), pp. 288–92.

Real Academia Española (RAE), *Orthographía española* [Spanish orthography] (Madrid: Imprenta de la Real Academia Española, 1741).

Repertorium, see Fidlerová, Andrle, et al. (eds.); Fidlerová, Bekešová, et al. (eds.); Linda et al. (eds.).

Reske, Ch. *Die Buchdrucker des 16. und 17. Jahrhunderts im deutschen Sprachgebiet* [The printers in the German-speaking area in C16 and C17], 2nd ed. (Wiesbaden: Harrassowitz, 2015).

Reutter, G. 'The language shift from Latin to Polish: Die Ablösung des Latein durch das Polnische in schriftlich geprägten Funktionsbereichen' [The replacement of Latin by Polish in functional areas characterised by writing], in Hill and Lehmann (eds.), *Standard Language in the Slavic World*, pp. 110–28.

Reynaud Oudot, N. 'Aspectos ortográficos de los documentos coloniales ecuatorianos de los siglos XVI a XVIII: ¿Cómo se escribía durante la época de la colonia?' [Orthographical aspects of Ecuadorian colonial documents from C16–C18: How did they write during the colonial age?], in García Martín (ed.), *Actas*, vol. 2, pp. 2013–24.

Rezetko, R. and I. Young, *Historical Linguistics and Biblical Hebrew: Steps Toward an Integrated Approach* (Atlanta: SBL Press, 2014).

Richardson, B. *Manuscript Culture in Renaissance Italy* (Cambridge: Cambridge University Press, 2009).

Richelet, C.-P. *Dictionnaire françois* (Geneva: Jean Herman Widerhold, 1680), http s://gallica.bnf.fr/ark:/12148/bpt6k509323/f1.image [last accessed 23 May 2020].

Rieke, U. *Studien zur Herausbildung der neuhochdeutschen Orthographie. Die Markierung der Vokalquantitäten in deutschsprachigen Bibeldrucken des 16.–18. Jahrhunderts* [Studies on the formation of New High German orthography. Marking vowel quantities in printed German Bibles, C16–C18] (Heidelberg: Winter, 1998).

Right Spelling Very Much Improved (London: n.p., 1704).

Rissanen, M. 'Standardisation and the language of early statutes', in Wright (ed.), *Development of Standard English*, pp. 117–30.

Risse, U. *Untersuchungen zum Gebrauch der Majuskel in deutschsprachigen Bibeln des 16. Jahrhunderts. Ein historischer Beitrag zur Diskussion um die Substantivgroßschreibung* [Investigations on the use of capital letters in C16 German Bibles. A historical contribution to the discussion on noun capitalisation] (Heidelberg: Winter, 1980).

Rivarola, J. L. 'Ortografía, imprenta y dialectalismo en el siglo XVI. El caso de Pedro Cieza de León', in A. Alonso González, L. Castro Ramos, B. Gutiérrez Rodilla and J. A. Pascual Rodríguez (eds.), *Actas del III Congreso Internacional de Historia de la Lengua Española (Salamanca, 22–27 de noviembre de 1993)* [Proceedings of the 3rd International Congress on the History of the Spanish Language (Salamanca, 22–27 November 1993], 2 vols., vol. 1, Madrid: Arco Libros, 1996), pp. 887–97.

Robles, Juan de, *Primera parte del culto sevillano* [Sevilla, 1631] (Seville: Sociedad de Bibliófilos Andaluces, 1883).

Roelcke, Th. 'Die Periodisierung der deutschen Sprachgeschichte', in Besch et al. (eds.), *Sprachgeschichte*, vol. 1, pp. 798–815.

Rogers, H. *Writing Systems: A Linguistic Approach* (Malden: Blackwell, 2005).

Ropelewski, S. *Słownik polsko-francuzki. Dictionaire polonais-français*, 3 vols. [Polish–French dictionary] (Berlin: B. Behr, 1847).

Rosa, V. J. *Czech Grammar (Čechořečnost) 1672*, trans. G. Betts and J. Marvan (Prague: Porta Prague, 1991).

Rosa, V. J. *Grammatica linguae Bohemicae Quatuor Partibus Orthographiâ, Ethymologiâ, Syntaxi, & Profodiâ conftans ...* [Czech grammar containing four parts, orthography, etymology, syntax and prosody ...] (Prague: Jan Arnolt z Dobroslavína, 1672), KPS no. K14884.

Rospond, S. *Dawność mazurzenia w świetle grafiki staropolskiej* [The age of Mazovianism in the light of Old Polish spelling] (Wrocław: ZNIO, 1957).

Rospond, S. 'Dyspalatalizacja spółgłosek funkcjonalnie miękkich' [Depalatalisation of functionally soft consonants], *Język Polski*, 33 (1953), pp. 368–75.

Rospond, S. 'Kultura językowa w Polsce XVI w.: I. Polemika poprawnościowa Jana Maleckiego z Janem Seklucjanem' [Language culture in C16 Poland. Part 1: Discussion on language rules between Jan Malecki and Jan Seklucjan], *Język Polski*, 23 (1938), pp. 45–52.

Rospond, S. 'Kultura językowa w Polsce XVI w.: II. Polemika poprawnościowa Jana Maleckiego ze Stanisławem Murzynowskim [Language culture in C16 Poland. Part

2: Discussion on language rules between Jan Malecki and Stanisław Murzynowski]',
Język Polski, 24 (1939), pp. 115–21.

Rospond, S. *Studia nad językiem polskim XVI wieku* [Studies on C16 Polish language]
(Wrocław: ZNIO, 1949).

Rospond, S. 'Z badań nad stosunkami językowymi polsko-czeskimi do końca XVI
wieku' [Research into the relationship between the Polish and Czech languages to the
end of C16], *Rozprawy Komisji Językowej Wrocławskiego Towarzystwa Naukowego*,
4 (1963), pp. 103–215.

Rössler, P. 'Die Großschreibung in Wiener Drucken des 17. und frühen 18.
Jahrhunderts' [Capitalisation in Viennese printed texts of C17 and early C18], in
W. Bauer and H. Scheuringer (eds.), *Beharrsamkeit und Wandel* [Continuity and
change] (Vienna: Praesens, 1998), pp. 205–38.

Rössler, P. *Schreibvariation, Sprachregion, Konfession. Graphematik und Morphologie
in österreichischen und bayerischen Drucken vom 16. bis ins 18. Jahrhundert* [Spelling
variation, linguistic region, denomination. Graphematics and morphology in Austrian
and Bavarian printed texts from C16 to C18] (Frankfurt am Main: Peter Lang, 2005).

Ruge, N. *Aufkommen und Durchsetzung morphembezogener Schreibungen im
Deutschen 1500–1770* [The emergence and implementation of morphematic
elements in German spelling 1500–1770] (Heidelberg: Winter, 2004).

Ruge, N. 'Die Graphematik-Morphologie-Schnittstelle in der Geschichte des
Deutschen' [The interface between graphematics and morphology in the history of
German], in M. Neef and C. Scherer (eds.), *Die Schnittstelle von Morphologie und
geschriebener Sprache* [The interface between morphology and written language]
(Berlin; Boston: de Gruyter, 2013), pp. 39–68.

Russi, C. (ed.), *Current Trends in Historical Sociolinguistics* (Berlin: de Gruyter Open,
2016).

Russkiĭ rubl'. Dva veka istorii. XIX–XX vv. [Russian rouble. Two centuries of history,
C19–C20] (Moscow: Progress, Akademiia, 1994).

Ruszkiewicz, P. *Modern Approaches to Graphophonemic Investigation in English*
(Katowice: University of Silesia, 1976).

Rutkowska, H. 'Late medieval dialectal and obsolescent spellings in the sixteenth-
century editions of the *Kalender of Shepherdes*', in J. C. Conde-Silvestre and J. Calle-
Martín (eds.), *Approaches to Middle English: Variation, Contact and Change*
(Frankfurt am Main: Peter Lang, 2015), pp. 129–47.

Rutkowska, H. 'Linguistic levels: Orthography', in A. Bergs and L. J. Brinton (eds.),
English Historical Linguistics: An International Handbook (Berlin: de Gruyter,
2012), pp. 224–37.

Rutkowska, H. 'Orthographic regularization in Early Modern English printed books:
Grapheme distribution and vowel length indication', in Russi (ed.), *Current Trends*,
pp. 165–93.

Rutkowska, H. *Orthographic Systems in Thirteen Editions of the* Kalender of
Shepherdes *(1506–1656)* (Frankfurt am Main: Peter Lang, 2013).

Rutkowska, H. 'Selected orthographic features in English editions of the *Book of Good
Maners* (1487–1507)', *SELIM: Journal of the Spanish Society for Medieval English
Language and Literature*, 12 (2005), pp. 127–42.

Rutkowska, H. 'Typographical and graphomorphemic features of five editions of the
Kalender of Shepherdes as elements of the early printers' community of practice', in
Kopaczyk and Jucker (eds.), *Communities of Practice*, pp. 123–49.

Rutkowska, H. and P. Rössler, 'Orthographic variables', in Hernández-Campoy and Conde-Silvestre (eds.), *Handbook of Historical Sociolinguistics*, pp. 213–36.

Rutten, G. J. and M. J. van der Wal, *Letters as Loot. A Sociolinguistic Approach to Seventeenth- and Eighteenth-Century Dutch* (Amsterdam; Philadelphia: John Benjamins, 2014).

Rutten, G. J. and M. J. van der Wal, 'Local dialects, supralocal writing systems. The degree of orality of Dutch private letters from the seventeenth century', *Written Language and Literacy*, 14 (2, 2011), pp. 251–74.

Rutten, G., R. Vosters and W. Vandenbussche (eds.), *Norms and Usage in Language History, 1600–1900: A Sociolinguistic and Comparative Perspective* (Amsterdam: John Benjamins, 2014).

Rütter, S. *Konstruktion von Bekenntnisidentität in Konversionsschriften der Frühen Neuzeit* [Constructing denominational identities in religious conversion in early modern times] (Berlin; Münster: LIT, 2014).

Saenger, P. 'Silent reading: Its impact on late medieval script and society', *Viator*, 13 (1982), pp. 367–414.

Saenger, P. 'The impact of the early printed page on the history of reading', in I. Gadd (ed.), *The History of the Book in the West: 1455–1700* (Farnham; Burlington: Ashgate, 2010), pp. 385–449.

Sáez Rivera, D. M. 'Discurso referido y puntuación en el Siglo de Oro: el caso de la *Olla podrida a la española* (1655) de Marcos Fernández' [Reported speech and punctuation in the Golden Age: the case of the *Olla podrida a la española* (1655) by Marcos Fernández], *Recherches*, 7 (2014), pp. 235–54.

Sáez Rivera, D. M. 'La lengua de las gramáticas y métodos de español como lengua extranjera en Europa (1640–1726)' [The language of grammars and textbooks of Spanish as a foreign language in Europe (1640–1726)], unpublished PhD thesis (Universidad Complutense, Madrid, 2007), eprints.ucm.es/7813/1/T30253.pdf [last accessed 6 June 2020].

Sáez Rivera, D. M. 'Marcos Fernández y su versión española de los diálogos latino-franceses de Philippe Garnier (Amsterdam, 1656; Estrasburgo, 1659)' [Marcos Fernández and his Spanish version of the Latin–French dialogues by Philippe Garnier], *Recherches*, 5 (2010), pp. 173–201.

Sairio, A. 'Elizabeth Montagu's *Shakespeare essay* (1769): The final draft and the first edition as evidence of two communities of practice', in Kopaczyk and Jucker (eds.), *Communities of Practice*, pp. 177–97.

Sairio, A. *Language and Letters of the Bluestocking Network: Sociolinguistic Issues in Eighteenth-Century Epistolary English* (Helsinki: Société Néophilologique, 2009).

Salmon, V. 'English punctuation theory, 1500–1800', *Anglia*, 106, 3–4 (1998), pp. 285–314.

Salmon, V. 'Orthography and punctuation', in Lass (ed.), *The Cambridge History of the English Language*, pp. 13–55.

Sampson, G. 'The redundancy of self-organisation as an explanation of English spelling', *Language*, 94 (1, 2018), pp. 43–7.

Sánchez-Martínez, F., I. Martínez-Sempere, X. Ivars-Ribes and R. C. Carrasco, 'An Open Diachronic Corpus of Historical Spanish: Annotation Criteria and Automatic Modernisation of Spelling', http://arxiv.org/abs/1306.3692 [last accessed 6 June 2020].

Sánchez Méndez, J. P., M. de la Torre and V. Codita (eds.), *Temas, problemas y métodos para la edición y el estudio de documentos hispánicos antiguos* [Subjects, problems and methods for editing and studying old Spanish texts] (Valencia: Tirant Lo Blanch, 2015).

Sánchez Prieto Borja, P. 'Para una historia de la escritura castellana' [A history of Castilian writing], in C. García Turza, F. González Bachiller and J. J. Mangado Martínez (eds.), *Actas del IV Congreso Internacional de Historia de la Lengua Española: La Rioja, 1–5 de abril de 1997* [Proceedings of the IV International Congress of the History of the Spanish Language: La Rioja, 1–5 April 1997], vol. 1 (Logroño: Universidad de La Rioja, 1998), pp. 289–302.

Santiago, R. 'Apuntes para la historia de la puntuación en los siglos XVI y XVII' [Notes on the history of punctuation in C16 and C17], in J. M. Blecua, J. Gutiérrez Cuadrado and L. Sala (eds.), *Estudios de Grafemática en el Dominio Hispano* [Studies on graphematics in the Spanish language] (Salamanca: Instituto Caro y Cuervo/ Universidad de Salamanca, 1998), pp. 243–80.

Santiago, R. 'La puntuación según Nebrija' [Punctuation according to Nebrija] *Dicenda*, 14 (1996), pp. 273–84.

Santillana, Marqués de (Í. López de Mendoza), *Los prouerbios vtilissimos del illustre cauallero don Íñigo Lopez de Mendoza Marques de Santillana con la glosa del dicho marques e con la glosa del Doctor Pero Diaz de Toledo* [Useful proverbs by the Illustrious Gentleman Íñigo López de Mendoza, Marqués de Santillana with a gloss by said marquis and with a gloss by Dr Pero Díaz of Toledo] (Salamanca, c. 1500), Bibliotecas Universidad de Salamanca, ref. BG/34600, https://gredos.usal.es/handle/ 10366/83363 [last accessed 20 April 2020].

Saussure, F. de, *Troisième cours de linguistique générale (1910–1911): D'après les cahiers d'Emile Constantin* [Third course of lectures on general linguistics (1910–1911): from the notebooks of Emile Constantin], ed. E. Komatsu and trans. R. Harris (Oxford: Pergamon Press, 1993).

Scherrer, Y. and T. Erjavec, 'Modernising historical Slovene words', *Natural Language Engineering*, 22 (6, 2016), pp. 881–905.

Schlögl, R. *Alter Glaube und moderne Welt* [Old faith and the modern world] (Frankfurt am Main: S. Fischer, 2013).

Schmied, J., C. Claridge and R. Siemund (compilers), *The Lampeter Corpus of Early Modern English Tracts* (Chemnitz: Chemnitz University of Technology, 1994).

Schnee, L. 'Gender und Großschreibung. Misogyner Einfluss in der Entwicklung der satzinternen Großschreibung im Frühneuhochdeutschen' [Gender and capitalisation: Misogynistic influence in the development of sentence-internal capitalisation in Early New High German], unpublished term paper (University of Hamburg, 2017).

Schneider, P. 'Computer assisted spelling normalization of 18th century English', in P. Peters, P. Collins and A. Smith (eds.), *New Frontiers of Corpus Research: Papers from the 21st International Conference on English Language Research on Computerized Corpora, Sydney, 2000* (Amsterdam: Rodopi, 2002), pp. 199–211.

Schøsler, L. 'The importance of diasystematic parameters in studying the history of French', in Y. Kawaguchi, M. Minegishi and W. Viereck (eds.), *Corpus-Based Analysis and Diachronic Linguistics* (Amsterdam: John Benjamins, 2011), pp. 91–109.

Schröder, B., K-P. Wegera, H-J. Solms, H-C. Schmitz and B. Fisseni (compilers), *Das Bonner Frühneuhochdeutschkorpus* [The Bonn Early New High German corpus], https://korpora.zim.uni-duisburg-essen.de/Fnhd/ [last accessed 30 March 2020].

Schröpfer, J. *Hussens Traktat 'Orthographia bohemica'* [Hus's treatise 'Orthographia bohemica'] (Wiesbaden: Otto Harrassowitz, 1968).

Schutzeichel, M. and R. Szczepaniak, 'Die Durchsetzung der satzinternen Großschreibung in Norddeutschland am Beispiel der Hexenverhörprotokolle' [The establishment of sentence-internal capitalisation in Northern Germany from the example of witch trial protocols], in M. Hundt and A. Lasch (eds.), *Deutsch im Norden. Varietäten des norddeutschen Raumes* [German in the North. Varieties of the northern German region] (Berlin; Boston: de Gruyter, 2015), pp. 151–67.

Scragg, D. G. *A History of English Spelling* (Manchester: Manchester University Press, 1974).

Sebastián, M. *Orthographia, y orthologia* [Orthography and orthology] (Zaragoza: Juan de Larumbe, 1619).

Sebastián Mediavilla, F. 'A propósito del *Persiles*, la ortografía (puntuación y acentuación) de los textos de Cervantes' [The *Persiles*: orthography (punctuation and accentuation) in Cervantes' texts], *eHumanista*, 36 (2017), pp. 353–85.

Sebastián Mediavilla, F. *Fray Luis y Santa Teresa, imprentas y editores (cuestiones de ortografía y puntuación)* [Fray Luis and Santa Teresa. Printers and editors (studies on spelling and punctuation)] (Vigo: Academia del Hispanismo, 2010).

Sebastián Mediavilla, F. *La puntuación del* Quijote *(1605–1615)* [Punctuation in the *Quixote* (1605 and 1615)] (Vigo: Academia del Hispanismo, 2008).

Sebastián Mediavilla, F. *La puntuación en el Siglo de Oro: Teoría y práctica* [Punctuation in the *Siglo de Oro*: theory and practice] (Barcelona: UAB, 2002).

Sebastián Mediavilla, F. *La puntuación en los siglos XVI y XVII* [Punctuation in C16 and C17] (Barcelona: UAB, 2002).

Sebastián Mediavilla, F. *Puntuación, humanismo e imprenta en el Siglo de Oro* [Punctuation, humanism and the printing press during the *Siglo de Oro*] (Vigo: Academia del Hispanismo, 2007).

Sebba, M. 'Orthography as social action: Scripts, spelling, identity and power', in Jaffe et al. (eds.), *Orthography as Social Action*, pp. 1–20.

Sebba, M. 'Sociolinguistic approaches to writing systems research', *Writing Systems Research*, 1 (1, 2009), pp. 35–49.

Sebba, M. 'Spelling as a social practice', in J. Maybin and J. Swann (eds.), *Routledge Companion to English Language Studies* (London: Routledge, 2009).

Sebba, M. *Spelling and Society: The Culture and Politics of Orthography around the World* (Cambridge: Cambridge University Press, 2007).

Šefčík, O. 'K základním pojmům grafémiky' [On fundamental concepts of graphemics], in Čornejová et al. (eds.), *Dějiny českého pravopisu*, pp. 30–41.

Serments de Strasbourg [Strasbourg oaths], MS, Bibliothèque nationale de France, lat. 9768.

Sgall, P. 'Towards a theory of phonemic orthography', in P. A. Luelsdorff (ed.), *Orthography and Phonology* (Amsterdam; Philadelphia: John Benjamins, 1987), pp. 1–30.

Shahan, J. M. 'Introduction to Part I: Overview of reasons to doubt', in P. Edmondson and S. Wells (eds.), *Shakespeare beyond Doubt: Evidence, Argument, Controversy* (Cambridge; New York: Cambridge University Press, 2013), pp. 2–12.

Shakespeare First Folio, Oxford Text Archive, http://ota.ox.ac.uk/desc/0119 [last accessed 10 May 2020].

Short, I. *The Oxford Psalter (Bodleian MS Douce 320)* (Oxford: The Anglo-Norman Text Society, 2015).

Shortis, T. 'Gr8 txtpectations: the creativity of text spelling', *English Drama Media* (8, 2007), pp. 21–6.

Shortis, T. 'Orthographic practices in SMS text messaging as a case signifying diachronic change in linguistic and semiotic resources', unpublished PhD thesis (UCL Institute of Education, London, 2016).

Shortis, T. 'Revoicing txt: Spelling, vernacular orthography and "unregimented writing"', in P. Santiago, M. J. Esteve and M. L. Gea-Valor (eds.), *The Texture of Internet: Netlinguistics in Progress* (Newcastle upon Tyne: Cambridge Scholars Publishing, 2007), pp. 2–23.

Shortis, T. 'Texting and other messaging', in V. Cook and D. Ryan (eds.), *The Routledge Handbook of the English Writing System* (London; New York: Routledge, 2016), pp. 487–516.

Shute, R. 'Pressed for space: The effects of justification and the printing process on fifteenth-century orthography', *English Studies*, 98 (3, 2017), pp. 262–82.

Siatkowski, J. *Bohemizmy fonetyczne w języku polskim* [Phonetic Bohemianisms in Polish], vols. 1–3 (Wrocław: ZNIO, 1965).

Siatkowski, J. 'Wpływ języka czeskiego jako arbitra na polską fleksję' [Influence of the Czech language as a pattern source on Polish inflection], in J. Zieniukowa (ed.), *Studia linguistica memoriae Zdzislai Stieber dedicata* [Linguistic studies dedicated to the memory of Zdzisław Stieber] (Wrocław: ZNIO, 1983), pp. 97–106.

Šlosar, D. 'Diakritický pravopis' [Diacritical spelling], in Čornejová et al. (eds.), *Dějiny českého pravopisu*, pp. 200–5.

Šlosar, D. 'Poznámky k vývoji české interpunkce v 16. století' [Notes on the development of Czech punctuation in C16], *Listy filologické*, 87 (1, 1964), pp. 126–35.

Šlosar, D. 'Průřez vývojem staročeské interpunkce' [Cross-section through the development of Old Czech punctuation], *Listy filologické*, 89 (2, 1966), pp. 164–9.

Šmahel, F. and O. Pavlíček (eds.), *A Companion to Jan Hus* (Leiden; Boston: Brill, 2015).

Smith, J. *An Historical Study of English. Function, Form and Change* (London: Routledge, 2005).

Solling, D. *Zur Getrennt-, Zusammen- und Bindestrichschreibung von Substantivkomposita im Deutschen (1550–1710)* [On separation, compound spelling and hyphenation of complex nouns in German (1550–1710)] (Uppsala: Uppsala University, 2012).

Sönmez, M. J.-M. 'English spelling in the seventeenth century: a study of the nature of standardisation as seen through the MS and printed versions of the Duke of Newcastle's "A New Method ... "', unpublished PhD thesis (University of Durham, 1993).

Sönmez, M. J.-M. 'Perceived and real differences between men's and women's spelling in the early to mid-seventeenth century', in D. Kastovsky and A. Mettinger (eds.), *The*

History of English in a Social Context: A Contribution to Historical Sociolinguistics (Berlin: de Gruyter, 2000), pp. 405–39.

Soukup, P. *Jan Hus. Prediger – Reformator – Märtyrer* [Jan Hus. Preacher – reformer – martyr] (Stuttgart: Kohlhammer, 2014).

Sourkova, E. '*Azbuka i/ili Abeceda*: Ob istorii graficheskikh sistem v Belarusi' [*Azbuka and/or Abeceda*: About the history of graphic systems in Belorussia], in Tomelleri and Kempgen (eds.), *Slavic Alphabets in Contact*, pp. 95–130.

Štajer, M. V. *Wýborně dobrý způſob Yak ſe má dobře po Čeſku pſáti* ... [Good and excellent way to write and print well in Czech ...] (Prague: Impressí Universitatis, 1668), KPS no. K15948.

Stenroos, M. 'Regional dialects and spelling conventions in Late Middle English: Searches for (th) in the LALME data', in M. Dossena and R. Lass (eds.), *Methods and Data in English Historical Dialectology* (Bern: Peter Lang, 2004), pp. 257–85.

Stęplewski, A. *Pismo i pisarze w średniowiecznej Polsce. Grafia wielkopolskich rot sądowych* [Writing and clerks in mediaeval Poland. Spelling of court oaths from the province of Greater Poland] (Poznań: Rys, 2013).

Stetson, R. H. 'The phoneme and the grapheme', in J. Renders (ed.) *Mélanges de linguistique et de philologie offerts à Jacq. van Ginneken* (Paris: Klincksieck, 1937), pp. 353–6, reprinted in P. Ruszkiewicz (ed.), *Graphophonemics. A Book of Readings* (Katowice: University of Silesia, 1981), pp. 35–44.

Stich, A. 'Všechno je jinak a většinou složitě: Jak to skutečně bylo s českým jazykem a literaturou v pobělohorském období' [Everything is different and usually complex: How it truly was with the Czech language and literature in the post-White Mountain period], *Britské Listy* (9, 1997), http://www.britskelisty.cz/9709/19970911a.html [last accessed 5 June 2020].

Stieber, Z. *Rozwój fonologiczny języka polskiego* [Phonological development of the Polish language] (Warsaw: PWN, 1958).

Stieber, Z. *Świat językowy Słowian* [The linguistic universe of the Slavs] (Warsaw: PWN, 1974).

Stipčević, A. *Socijalna povijest knjige u Hrvata* [A social history of the book in Croatia] (Zagreb: Školska knjiga, 2005).

Stockmann-Hovekamp, Ch. *Untersuchungen zur Straßburger Druckersprache in den Flugschriften Martin Bucers. Graphematische, morphologische und lexikologische Aspekte* [Investigations into Strasbourg printing practices in pamphlets by Martin Bucer. Graphematic, morphological and lexicological aspects] (Heidelberg: Winter, 1991).

Stutzmann, D. 'Variability as a key factor for understanding medieval scripts: the ORIFLAMMS project (ANR-12-CORP-0010)', in S. Brookes, M. Rehbein and P. Stokes (eds.), *Digital Palaeography* (Abingdon: Routledge, 2017), https:// halshs.archives-ouvertes.fr/halshs-01778620/document [last accessed 5 June 2020].

Subačius, G. 'Pirmasis Simono Daukanto rašybos lūžis (1827–1828): Raidė y, garsas ę, diakritikai ir geminatos' [The first turning point in Simonas Daukantas's orthography [1827–1828]: Letter y, sound ę, diacritics and geminates], *Archivum Lithuanicum*, 16 (2014), pp. 203–68.

Subačius, G. 'Simono Daukanto dvibalsio [ęi] ženklinimas Istorijoje Žemaitiškoje (1828–1834): <ei, ęi, ie, iei, iey, ij, yi>' [Orthographic variation of the diphthong [ẹi] in Simonas Daukantas's *History of the Lithuanian Lowlands* [1828–1834]: <ei, ẹi, ie, iei, iey, ij, yi>], *Darbai ir dienos*, 66 (2016), pp. 11–88.

Subačius, G. 'Two types of standard language history in Europe', *Res Balticae*, 8 (2002), pp. 131–50.

Szczepaniak, R. and F. Barteld, 'Hexenverhörprotokolle als sprachhistorisches Korpus' [Witch trial protocols as a diachronic corpus], in S. Kwekkeboom and S. Waldenberger (eds.), *PerspektivWechsel oder: Die Wiederentdeckung der Philologie*, vol. 1: *Sprachdaten und Grundlagenforschung in der Historischen Linguistik* [Change of perspective or: The rediscovery of philology, vol. 1: Linguistic data and fundamental research in historical linguistics] (Göttingen: Erich Schmidt, 2016), pp. 43–70.

Taavitsainen, I. 'Scientific language and spelling standardisation', in Wright (ed.), *Development of Standard English*, pp. 131–54.

Taavitsainen, I. 'Scriptorial "house-styles" and discourse communities', in I. Taavitsainen and P. Pahta (eds.), *Medical and Scientific Writing in Late Medieval English* (Cambridge: Cambridge University Press, 2004), pp. 209–40.

Taavitsainen, I., P. Pahta, T. Hiltunen, M. Mäkinen, V. Marttila, M. Ratia, C. Suhr and J. Tyrkkö (compilers), *Early Modern English Medical Texts*, CD-ROM (Amsterdam: John Benjamins, 2010).

Tagg, C. 'A corpus linguistic analysis of SMS text messaging', unpublished PhD thesis (University of Birmingham, 2009).

Tagg, C. 'Heteroglossia in text-messaging: performing identity and negotiating relationships in a digital space', *Journal of Sociolinguistics*, 20 (1, 2016), pp. 59–85.

Tagg, C. *The Discourse of Text Messaging: Analysis of SMS Communication* (London; New York: Continuum, 2012).

Tainturier, M. J. and B. C. Rapp, 'Complex graphemes as functional spelling units: Evidence from acquired dysgraphia', *Neurocase*, 10 (2, 2004), pp. 122–31.

Takada, H. *Grammatik und Sprachwirklichkeit von 1640–1700. Zur Rolle deutscher Grammatiker im schriftsprachlichen Ausgleichsprozeß* [Grammar and linguistic reality 1640–1700. On the role of German grammarians in the process of linguistic levelling] (Tübingen: Niemeyer, 1998).

Tarelka, M. 'Adaptacyĭa arabskaga pis'ma dlĭa peradachy slavianskikh (belaruskikh i pol'skikh) tekstaŭ' [Adaptation of the Arabic script for transmitting Slavic (Belorussian and Polish) texts], in Tomelleri and Kempgen (eds.), *Slavic Alphabets in Contact*, pp. 263–90.

Tejera, M. J and L. Silva Nones, 'El seseo en las actas del Cabildo de Caracas y la influencia de las escuelas de escribanos' [The *seseo* in the acts of the Cabildo of Caracas and the influence of the scribal schools], in García Martín (ed.), *Actas*, vol. 1, pp. 573–81.

Thaisen, J. and H. Rutkowska (eds.), *Scribes, Printers, and the Accidentals of their Texts* (Frankfurt am Main: Peter Lang, 2011).

Thurlow, C. 'Generation txt? The sociolinguistics of young people's text-messaging', *Discourse Analysis Online*, 1 (1, 2003).

Tieken-Boon van Ostade, I. '"Disrespectful and too familiar?" Abbreviations as an index of politeness in 18th-century letters', in C. Dalton-Puffer, D. Kastovsky, N. Ritt and H. Schendl (eds.), *Syntax, Style and Grammatical Norms: English from 1500–2000* (Bern: Peter Lang, 2006), pp. 229–47.

Tieken-Boon van Ostade, I. 'English at the onset of the normative tradition', in L. Mugglestone (ed.), *The Oxford History of English* (Oxford: Oxford University Press, 2003), pp. 240–73.

Tieken-Boon van Ostade, I. 'Lowth's language', in M. Dossena and C. Jones (eds.), *Insights into Late Modern English* (Bern: Peter Lang, 2003), pp. 241–64.

Tieken-Boon van Ostade, I. 'Social network theory and eighteenth-century English: The case of Boswell', in D. Britton (ed.), *English Historical Linguistics 1994: Papers from the 8th International Conference on English Historical Linguistics* (Amsterdam: John Benjamins, 1996), pp. 327–37.

Tomelleri, V. S. and S. Kempgen (eds.), *Slavic Alphabets in Contact* (Bamberg: University of Bamberg Press, 2015).

Tomić, M. *Hrvatskoglagoljski brevijari na razmeđu rukopisne i tiskane tradicije* [Croatian Glagolitic breviaries at the border between the handwritten and printed traditions] (Zagreb: Naklada Ljevak, 2014).

Torquemada, A. de, *Manual de escribientes. Coloquios satíricos. Jardín de flores curiosas* [The scribes' handbook. Satirical colloquia. The garden of curious flowers], ed. L. Rodríguez Cacho (Madrid: Biblioteca Castro/Turner, 1994).

Torrens Álvarez, M. J. and P. Sánchez Prieto Borja (eds.), *Nuevas perspectivas para la edición y el estudio de documentos hispánicos antiguos* [New perspectives into the editing and studying of ancient Hispanic documents] (Bern: Peter Lang, 2012).

Tory, G. *Champ Fleury. Au quel est contenu lart & science de la deue & vraye proportion des lettres attiques* [...] [*Champ Fleury*. Which contains the art and the science of the due and true proportion of old letters] (Paris: Geoffroy Tory and Giles Gourmont, 1529).

Tournier, C. 'Histoire des idées sur la ponctuation: des débuts de l'imprimerie à nos jours' [History of ideas on punctuation: from the invention of printing to the present day], *Langue Française*, 45 (1980), pp. 28–40.

Traxel, O. M. *Language Change, Writing and Textual Interference in post-Conquest Old English Manuscripts: The Evidence of Cambridge University Library, Ii. l. 33* (Frankfurt am Main: Peter Lang, 2004).

Truhlář, J. *Katalog českých rukopisů c. k. veřejné a universitní knihovny pražské* [Catalogue of Czech manuscripts of the royal imperial public and university library in Prague] (Prague: Emperor Franz Josef's Czech Academy for Science, Literature and Art, 1906), https://biblio.hiu.cas.cz/documents/260043?locale=cs [last accessed 5 June 2020].

Twardzik, W. *O uważniejszym aniżeli dotychmiast tekstu staropolskiego czytaniu i jakie z niego pożytki płyną rozprawa śliczna i podziwienia godna* [A straightforward and admirable treatise on a more attentive than usual reading of Old Polish texts and on the benefits of doing so] (Cracow: IJP PAN, 1997).

Tyne, H., M. Bilger, P. Cappeau and E. Guerin, *La Variation en question(s). Hommages à Françoise Gadet* [Variation in question(s). Homage to Françoise Gadet] (Bern: Peter Lang, 2017).

Tyrkkö, J. 'Printing houses as communities of practice: Orthography in early modern medical books', in Kopaczyk and Jucker (eds.), *Communities of Practice*, pp. 151–76.

Ulewicz, T. *Wśród impresorów krakowskich doby Renesansu* [Among the Cracow printers of the Renaissance] (Cracow: Literary Publishing House, 1977).

Urbańczyk, S. and R. Olesch (eds.), *Die altpolnischen Orthographien des 16. Jahrhunderts. Stanisław Zaborowski, Jan Seklucjan, Stanisław Murzynowski, Jan Januszowski* [Old Polish orthographies of C16. Stanisław Zaborowski, Jan Seklucjan, Stanisław Murzynowski, Jan Januszowski] (Cologne; Vienna: Böhlau, 1983).

Vachek, J. 'English orthography: A functional approach', in W. Haas (ed.), *Standard Languages: Spoken and Written* (Manchester: Manchester University Press, 1982), pp. 37–56.

Vachek, J. *Selected Writings in English and General Linguistics* (Prague: Academia, 1976).

Vachek, J. *Written Language: General Problems and Problems of English* (The Hague: Mouton, 1973).

Vajs, J. *Rukověť hlaholské paleografie* [Handbook of Glagolitic palaeography] (Prague: Orbis, 1932).

Valdés, J. de, *Diálogo de la lengua* [1535–6] [Discourse on the (Spanish) language], MS 8629, Biblioteca Nacional de España, http://www.bne.es/es/Micrositios/Guias/Lengua/Origen_lengua/Galeria/Obra2.html [last accessed 5 June 2020].

Vallins, G. H. and D. G. Scragg, *Spelling* (London: André Deutsch, 1965).

Van Beek, G. 'On materiality', *Etnofoor*, 9 (1, 1996), pp. 5–24.

Vaugelas, C. F. de, *Remarques sur la langue françoise utiles à ceux qui veulent bien parler et bien escrire* [Remarks on the French language, useful for those who want to speak and write correctly] (Paris: Veuve J. Camusat and P. Lepetit, 1647), in Colombat et al. (compilers), *Grand Corpus*.

Venegas, A. *Tractado de orthographia y accentos en las tres lenguas principales* [Treatise of orthography and accents in the main three languages] (Toledo: Lazaro Salvago Ginoues, 1531), bdh-rd.bne.es/viewer.vm?id=0000092102&page=1 [last accessed 5 June 2020].

Veyrin-Forrer, J. 'Aux origines de l'imprimerie française: l'atelier de la Sorbonne' [The origins of French printing: the printing workshop of the Sorbonne], *La Lettre et le texte* [The letter and the text] (Paris: Editions de l'ENS, 1987), pp. 161–87.

Villa, L. and R. Vosters (eds.), *The Historical Sociolinguistics of Spelling*: Special issue of *Written Language and Literacy*, 18 (2, 2015).

Vintr, J. *Das Tschechische. Hauptzüge seiner Sprachstruktur in Gegenwart und Geschichte* [Czech. Main features of its language structure in the present and the past] (Munich: Otto Sagner, 2005).

Voeste, A. 'Den Leser im Blick. Die Professionalisierung des Setzerhandwerks im 16. Jahrhundert und ihre Auswirkungen auf die Orthographie der Melusinedrucke' [With the reader in view. The professionalisation of typesetting during C16 and its impact on spelling in printed *Melusinas*], in Rautenberg et al. (eds.), *Zeichensprachen*, pp. 129–50.

Voeste, A. 'Die Norm neben der Norm. Zum Zusammenhang von Graphienwahl und Überlieferungsform' [Norm next to norm. On the connection between graph choice and form transmission], in T. Gloning, I. Bons and D. Kaltwasser (eds.), *Fest-Platte für Gerd Fritz* [Anniversary (hard) disk for Gerd Fritz] (Gießen, 2010), http://www.festschrift-gerd-fritz.de/files/voeste_2010_norm-neben-der-norm.pdf [last accessed 26 April 2020].

Voeste, A. 'Interpunktion und Textsegmentierung im frühen deutschsprachigen Prosaroman' [Punctuation and text segmentation in the Early German prose novels], *Beiträge zur Geschichte der deutschen Sprache und Literatur (PBB)*, 140 (2018), pp. 1–22.

Voeste, A. *Orthographie und Innovation. Die Segmentierung des Wortes im 16. Jahrhundert* [Orthography and innovation. Word segmentation in C16] (Hildesheim: Olms, 2008).

Voeste, A. 'Proficiency and efficiency: Why German spelling changed in early modern times', *Written Language and Literacy*, 18 (2, 2015), pp. 248–59.

Voeste, A. 'The emergence of suprasegmental spellings in German', in Baddeley and Voeste (eds.), *Orthographies*, pp. 167–91.

Voeste, A. 'Variability and professionalism as prerequisites of standardization', in S. Elspaß, N. Langer and J. Scharloth (eds.), *Germanic Language Histories 'from Below' (1700–2000)* (Berlin; Boston: de Gruyter, 2007), pp. 295–307.

Voeste, A. 'Variantenbildung und Zeilenausgleich im Inkunabeldruck' [Variant formation and line adjustments in incunabula], presented at the 'Disziplinäre Zugänge zur Typographie' [Disciplinary approaches to typography] workshop (Erlangen, February 2018), https://www.academia.edu/35920869/Workshop_Disziplinäre_Zur_Typographie [last accessed 10 Aug. 2020].

Voit, P. 'Netolický z Netolic, Bartoloměj', in *Encyklopedie knihy: starší knihtisk a příbuzné obory mezi polovinou 15. a počátkem 19. století* [Encyclopedia of the book: older letterpress printing and related fields between the mid-C15 and early C19] (Prague: Libri, 2006), pp. 623–4.

Vokabulář webový. Webové hnízdo pramenů k poznání historické češtiny [The web vocabulary. Web hub of resources for the study of historical Czech], http://vokabular.ujc.cas.cz/moduly/mluvnice [last accessed 26 April 2020].

Völker, H. 'La Linguistique variationnelle et la perspective intralinguistique' [Variational linguistics and the intra-linguistic perspective], *Revue de Linguistique Romane*, 73 (2009), pp. 289–90.

Völker, H. 'Linguistique variationnelle historique et traitement de textes: présentation d'une méthode d'analyse' [Variational and diachronic linguistics and text processing: presentation of a method of analysis], Séminaires de l'ATILF, Nancy, 2005, http://atilf.fr/IMG/pdf/seminaires/Seminaire_atilf_Volker_2002-11.pdf, [last accessed 5 June 2020].

Voltmer, R. 'Vom getrübten Blick auf die frühneuzeitlichen Hexenverfolgungen – Versuch einer Klärung' [On the impaired perspective on early modern witch persecutions – an attempt at a clarification], *Magister Botanicus – Magische Blätter*, 8 (2006), pp. 61–72.

von Eye, A. *Introduction to Configural Frequency Analysis: The Search for Types and Antitypes in Cross-Classification* (Cambridge: Cambridge University Press, 1990).

Vorndran, R. *Südslawische Reformationsdrucke in der Universitätsbibliothek Tübingen. Eine Beschreibung der vorhandenen glagolitischen, kyrillischen und anderen Drucke der 'Uracher Bibelanstalt'* [South Slavic Reformation printed texts in the Tübingen University Library. A description of the extant Glagolitic, Cyrillic, and other printed books of the 'Urach Bible Institute'] (Tübingen: Mohr, 1977).

Vosters, R. 'Dutch, Flemish or Hollandic? Social and ideological aspects of linguistic convergence and divergence during the United Kingdom of the Netherlands (1815–1830)', in E. Barát and P. Studer (eds.), *Ideological Conceptualisations of*

Language. Discourses of Linguistic Diversity (Frankfurt am Main: Peter Lang, 2013), pp. 35–54.

Vosters, R., E. Belsack, J. Puttaert and W. Vandenbussche, 'Norms and usage in 19th-century Southern Dutch', in Rutten et al. (eds.), *Norms and Usage*, pp. 73–100.

Vosters, R. and G. Rutten, 'Three Southern shibboleths. Spelling features as conflicting identity markers in the Low Countries', *Written Language and Literacy*, 18 (2, 2015), pp. 260–74.

Vosters R., G. J. Rutten, M. J. van der Wal and W. Vandenbussche, 'Spelling and identity in the southern Netherlands (1750–1830)', in Jaffe et al. (eds.), *Orthography as Social Action*, pp. 135–60.

Wal, van der, M., G. Rutten, J. Nobels and T. Simons (compilers), The *Letters as Loot/ Brieven als Buit Corpus* (Leiden University, 2015), http://brievenalsbuit.inl.nl [last accessed 30 March 2020].

Walczak, B. 'Komu zawdzięczamy polski język literacki?' [Who do we owe the Polish literary language to?], in I. Bajerowa, M. Karpluk and Z. Leszczyński (eds.), *Język a chrześcijaństwo* [Language and Christianity] (Lublin: KUL, 1993), pp. 23–42.

Walczak, B. *Zarys dziejów języka polskiego* [An outline history of the Polish language] (Poznań: SAAW, 1995).

Wandt, C. *Die Schreibsprache des Julius Pflug im Konfessionsstreit. Schreibsprachanalyse und ein edierter Dialog* [The writing of Julius Pflug during the denominational dispute. Investigation and an edited dialogue] (Berlin: Akademie, 2012).

Warmbrunn, P. *Zwei Konfessionen in einer Stadt. Das Zusammenleben von Katholiken und Protestanten in den paritätischen Reichsstädten Augsburg, Biberach, Ravensburg und Dinkelsbühl von 1548 bis 1648* [Two denominations in one city. The coexistence of Catholics and Protestants in the imperial cities of Augsburg, Biberach, Ravensburg and Dinkelsbühl from 1548 to 1648] (Wiesbaden: Steiner, 1983).

Watson, C. 'Points of contention: Rethinking the past, present, and future of punctuation', *Critical Inquiry*, 38 (2012), pp. 649–72, www.jstor.org/stable/10.1086 /664555 [last accessed 2 April 2020].

Weber, W.-R. *Das Aufkommen der Substantivgroßschreibung im Deutschen: Ein historisch-kritischer Versuch* [The emergence of noun capitalisation in German: A critical–historical investigation] (Munich: Uni-Druck, 1958).

Wegera, K.-P. 'Zur Geschichte der Adjektivgroßschreibung im Deutschen: Entwicklung und Motive' [On the history of capitalisation of adjectives in German: development and motives], *Zeitschrift für Deutsche Philologie*, 115 (1996), pp. 382–92.

Wegera, K.-P., S. Kwekkeboom, D. Pachurka, H. Cosson, I. Lemke and A. Müller (compilers), *Referenzkorpus Frühneuhochdeutsch (1350–1650)* [Reference corpus of Early New High German (1350–1650)], http://www.ruhr-uni-bochum.de/wegera/ref/ index.htm [last accessed 30 March 2020].

Weingarten, R. 'Comparative graphematics', in S. R. Borgwaldt and T. Joyce (eds.), *Typology of Writing Systems* (Amsterdam; Philadelphia: John Benjamins, 2013), pp. 13–40.

Wiesinger, P. 'Zur oberdeutschen Schriftsprache des 16. und frühen 17. Jahrhunderts in Österreich unter dem Einfluß von Reformation und Gegenreformation' [On the High German written language of C16 and early C17 in Austria under the influence of the

Reformation and Counter-Reformation], in Hoffmann et al. (eds.), *Das Frühneuhochdeutsche*, pp. 241–73.

Wiggins, A. *Bess of Hardwick's Letters: Language, Materiality and Early Modern Epistolary Culture* (London; New York: Routledge, 2017).

Wiggins, A., D. Starza Smith, A. Timmermann and G. Williams (eds.), *Bess of Hardwick's Letters: The Complete Correspondence c. 1550–1608* (University of Sheffield Humanities Research Institute, 2013), www.bessofhardwick.org [last accessed 5 June 2020].

Williams, G. T. *Women's Epistolary Utterance: A Study of the Letters of Joan and Maria Thynne, 1575–1611* (Amsterdam: John Benjamins, 2014).

Williams, G. T. (compiler), *The Letters of Joan and Maria Thynne, 1575–1611* (Oxford: Oxford Text Archive), http://purl.ox.ac.uk/ota/2545 [last accessed 5 May 2020].

Winiarska-Górska, I. 'Krótka a prosta nauka czytania i pisania języka polskiego Jana Seklucjana' [Jan Seklucjan's short and easy lesson on reading and writing the Polish language], *Poradnik Językowy*, 6 (2014), pp. 101–7.

Winiarska-Górska, I. 'Ortografia polska Stanisława Murzynowskiego' [Stanisław Murzynowski's Polish orthography], *Poradnik Językowy*, 7 (2014), pp. 102–9.

Woudhuysen, H. R. *Sir Philip Sidney and the Circulation of Manuscripts 1558–1640* (Oxford: Oxford University Press, 1996).

Wright, L. (ed.), *The Development of Standard English, 1300–1800: Theories, Descriptions, Conflicts* (Cambridge; New York: Cambridge University Press, 2000).

Wydra, W. 'Drukarstwo nasze nic podobnego później nie wydało' [Polish printing has not published anything like it since], in W. Wydra, R. Wójcik and K. Krzak-Weiss (eds.), *Baltazar Opec, Żywot Pana Jezu Krysta (1522)* [Baltazar Opec, *Life of the Lord Jesus Christ* (1522)] (Poznań: UAM, 2014), pp. xi–xxix.

Wydra, W. and W. R Rzepka, *Chrestomatia staropolska. Teksty do roku 1543* [Old Polish chrestomathy. Texts printed up to the year 1543] (Wrocław: ZNIO, 1984).

Wydra, W. and W. R. Rzepka, 'Niesamoistne drukowane teksty polskie sprzed 1521 i ich znaczenie dla historii drukarstwa i języka polskiego' [Supplementary printed texts in Polish before the year 1521 and their role in the history of printing and of the Polish language], in S. Grzeszczuk and A. Kawecka-Gryczowa (eds.), *Dawna książka i kultura. Materiały międzynarodowej sesji naukowej z okazji pięćsetlecia sztuki drukarskiej w Polsce* [The ancient book and culture. Contributions to the International Scientific Conference on the Occasion of the Five-Hundredth Anniversary of the Art of Printing in Poland] (Wrocław: ZNIO, 1975), pp. 263–88.

Ycíar, J. de, *Orthographia pratica* [Handbook of orthography] (Zaragoza: Bartholome de Nagera, 1548), Biblioteca Nacional de España, http://bdh-rd.bne.es/viewer.vm?id=0000047523 [last accessed 23 May 2020].

Zaenen, A., J. Carletta, G. Garretson, J. Bresnan, A. Koontz-Garboden, T. Nikitina, M. C. O'Connor and T. Wasow, 'Animacy encoding in English: Why and how', in B. Webber and D. Byron (eds.), *DiscAnnotation '04* (Stroudsburg: Association for Computational Linguistics, 2004), pp. 118–25.

Žagar, M. 'Contesto filologico delle edizioni in glagolitico e cirillico della stampa protestante ad Urach (1561–1564)' [The philological context of the Glagolitic and Cyrillic publications of the Protestant printing house in Urach (1561–1564], in

G. Brogi Bercoff and R. Marti (eds.), *La riforma protestante nei paesi Slavi* [The Protestant reform in Slavic countries] (Milan: Centro Ambrosiano, 2018), pp. 119–32.

Žagar, M. 'Die glagolitische Schriftreform des 13. Jahrhunderts im Kontext der lateinischen Schriftreform' [Glagolitic writing reform in C13 in the context of the Latin writing reform], in W. Potthoff (ed.), *Dalmatien als europäischer Kulturraum* [Dalmatia as a European cultural space] (Split: Faculty of Philosophy, 2010), pp. 163–80.

Žagar, M. *Grafetički postav glagoljičkog izdanja Artikula (Tübingen/Urach 1562)* [The graphetic layout of the Glagolitic edition of *Artikuli* (Tübingen/Urach 1562)], in Kuštović and Žagar (eds.), *Meandrima hrvatskoga glagoljaštva*, pp. 585–606.

Žagar, M. *Grafolingvistika srednjovjekovnih tekstova* [Grapholinguistics of mediaeval texts] (Zagreb: Matica hrvatska, 2007).

Žagar, M. 'Neke grafetičke osebujnosti u hrvatskoglagoljskim tekstovima' [Some graphetic particularities in Croatian Glagolitic texts], in H. Miklas (ed.), *Glagolitica. Zum Ursprung der slavischen Schriftkultur* [The Glagolitic alphabet. At the source of Slavic written culture] (Vienna: ÖAW, 2000), pp. 164–74.

Žagar, M. *Uvod u glagoljsku paleografiju 1 (X. i XI. st)* [Introduction to Glagolitic palaeography 1 (C10 and C11)] (Zagreb: Institute for Croatian Language and Linguistics, 2013).

Žagar, M. (ed.), *Artikuli ili deli stare krstjanske vere, Urach 1562: faksimilno izdanje glagoljskog izvornika* [Articles or parts of the old Christian faith: facsimile edition of the Glagolitic original] (Zagreb: NSK, 2017).

Žagar, M. (ed.), *Misal hruacki Šimuna Kožičića Benje, 1531, faksimilno izdanje* [The Croatian missal of Šimun Kožičić Benja, 1531, facsimile edition] (Zagreb: NSK, 2016).

Zalizniak, A. A. 'O poniatii grafemy' [On the notion of the grapheme], in T. V. Tsiv'ian (ed.), *Balcanica. Lingvisticheskie issledovaniia* [Balcanica. Linguistic investigations] (Moscow: Nauka, 1979), pp. 134–52.

Zheltukhin, A. 'Variable norms in 16th-century Swedish orthography', in Baddeley and Voeste (eds.), *Orthographies*, pp. 193–218.

Zheltukhin, A. *Orthographic Codes and Code-Switching: A Study in 16th-Century Swedish Orthography* (Stockholm: Almqvist & Wiksell, 1996).

Zhivov, V. M. 'Deadaptatsiia v orfografii' [Deadaptation in orthography], in Zhivov, *Istoriia iazyka russkoi pis'mennosti*, vol. 2, pp. 836–47.

Zhivov, V. M. *Istoriia iazyka russkoi pis'mennosti* [History of the Russian written language], vols. 1–2 (Moscow: Dmitry Pozharsky University, 2017).

Zhivov, V. M. 'Norma i variativnost' v pravopisanii. Orfograficheskie kharakteristiki registrov' [Norm and variation in orthography. Orthographical peculiarities of registers], in Zhivov, *Istoriia iazyka russkoi pis'mennosti*, vol. 1, pp. 658–730.

Zhivov, V. M. 'Sozdanie grazhdanskogo shrifta' [Introducing a civil font], in Zhivov, *Istoriia iazyka russkoi pis'mennosti*, vol. 2, pp. 936–44.

Index

Diacritics are ignored in alphabetisation. **Bold** page numbers indicate illustrations.

/ɔi/ in Daukantas's 'History', 125–32
❦ (*hedera*), 103
☞ (*manicule*), 103

abbreviation(s)
  to aid composition, in C16 German
    pamphlet, 145–6, 152
  in *New Testament* (1562/3), 49, 61–2, 64,
    65–6, 187
  in semantic disambiguation, 236
  to signal social literacy, in Early Modern and
    C21 English, 196, 199
  supragrapheme, 49, 56
absorption, in punctuation, 115
abstract concepts/nouns, 67, 70–1, 73, 75, 79,
  87–8, 90–2
accents of intensity, in Anglo-Norman
  manuscripts, 103
Ackroyd, Peter, 131
addressee, influence of, 142
aesthetic principle, 130–1, 171, 245
  in Daukantas, 128–32
  in Early Modern Czech scribal
    orthography, 166
  in Early New High German, 130–1
agentivity, as factor in capitalisation, 68, 71, 73,
  81–3
allographs, 48
  analysis of, in *New Testament* (1562/3), 51,
    53–5, 63–4, 66
  fossilisation of, 26
  variation, 53, 54, 60, 63–4, 66
alphabet(s), alphabetical
  in Croatia, 51, 176–81
  Cyrillic, 176–8
  Glagolitic, 176–8
  Latin: adapted for Polish, 16–17;
    influence, in Croatia, 176–8, 180–1, 189

order: effect on numerical notation systems
  in *New Testament* (1562/3), 54–6, 64;
  in quantitative analysis, 228, 233
  Slavic, 176
Alphabetum Boëmicum (1718), 157, 166, 168
Amorós, Carles, 103
Androutsopoulos, Jannis, 199, 200, 210
Andry de Boisregard, Nicolas, 118
Anglo-Norman manuscripts, 103
Anglo-Saxon period, 194
animacy, factor in capitalisation, 77–92
Anónimo de Lovaina (Castilian grammar,
  1559), 96, 114–15
AntConc (corpus analysis toolkit),
  203
apostrophe, 117, 185
  for /ł/, 31
  mediaeval, 185
  for *yer*, 184, 190
Arabic script, 46
ARCHER (A Representative Corpus of
  Historical English Registers), 220
Arellano, Ignacio, 101
Aronoff, Mark, 195, 204
articles, definite and indefinite, 207
articulus, articulo, 107–8
Artykulowe Praw Mejtſkých (*Articles of the
  Municipal Law*) (Bohemia, 1619), 161
audience
  collective, 103
  Protestant Croatian, 51
  women, target for spelling manuals,
    196
auditory principle (in Croatian Glagolitic
  texts), 187
Augsburg, 147–8
Aušra (newspaper, Lithuania), 124
Austro-Slavism, 177

CPSIA information can be obtained
at www.ICGtesting.com
Printed in the USA
LVHW022024030121
675578LV00006B/147